Canis Africanis

Human-Animal Studies

Editor
Kenneth Shapiro
Animals & Society Institute

Editorial Board
Ralph Acampora
Hofstra University

Clifton Flynn
University of South Carolina

Hilda Kean
Ruskin College, Oxford

Randy Malamud
Georgia State University

Gail Melson
Purdue University

VOLUME 5

Canis Africanis

A Dog History of Southern Africa

Edited by
Lance van Sittert and Sandra Swart

BRILL

LEIDEN • BOSTON
2008

Cover design: Wim Goedhart

Cover illustration:
Title of art work: Bitumen Dogs
Artist: Imke Rust (P.O. Box 86241, Windhoek, Namibia)
Triptych 97 × 76cm each. Acrylic and bitumen on cardboard
Permanent Collection of the Arts Association of Namibia
Copyright © Imke Rust

This book is printed on acid-free paper.

Library of Congress Cataloging-in-Publication Data

A C.I.P. record for this book is available from the Library of Congress.

ISSN 1573-4226
ISBN 978 90 04 15419 3

Copyright 2008 by Koninklijke Brill NV, Leiden, The Netherlands.
Koninklijke Brill NV incorporates the imprints Brill, Hotei Publishers,
IDC Publishers, Martinus Nijhoff Publishers and VSP.

All rights reserved. No part of this publication may be reproduced, translated,
stored in a retrieval system, or transmitted in any form or by any means, electronic,
mechanical, photocopying, recording or otherwise, without prior written permission
from the publisher.

Authorization to photocopy items for internal or personal use is granted by
Koninklijke Brill NV provided that the appropriate fees are paid directly to
The Copyright Clearance Center, 222 Rosewood Drive, Suite 910,
Danvers, MA 01923, USA.
Fees are subject to change.

PRINTED IN THE NETHERLANDS

For Shumba Swart, 1998–2007 and Davey van Sittert, 1991–2002

CONTENTS

List of Illustrations	ix
Notes on Contributors	xi
Canis Familiaris: A Dog History of Southern Africa Lance van Sittert and Sandra Swart	1
Africanis: The Pre-Colonial Dog of Africa Tim Maggs and Judith Sealy	35
A Short Paper about a Dog Susie Newton-King	53
What the Dogs Knew: Intelligence and Morality in the Cape Colony Elizabeth Green Musselman	77
Dogs and the Public Sphere: The Ordering of Social Space in Early Nineteenth-Century Cape Town Kirsten McKenzie	91
Class and Canicide in Little Bess: The 1893 Port Elizabeth Rabies Epidemic Lance van Sittert	111
Dogs, Poison and the Meaning of Colonial Intervention in the Transkei, South Africa Jacob Tropp	145
Fido: Dog Tales of Colonialism in Namibia Robert J. Gordon	173
Police Dogs and State Rationality in Early Twentieth-Century South Africa Keith Shear	193

'Gone to the Dogs': The Cultural Politics of Gambling—
    The Rise and Fall of British Greyhound Racing on the
    Witwatersrand, 1932–1949 217
    Albert Grundlingh

Social Subjects: Representations of Dogs in South African
    Fiction in English 235
    Wendy Woodward

The Canine Metaphor in the Visual Arts 263
    Meredith Palumbo

Dogs and Dogma: A Discussion of the Socio-Political
    Construction of Southern African Dog 'Breeds' as a
    Window onto Social History 267
    Sandra Swart

Index 289

LIST OF ILLUSTRATIONS

Cover illustration by Imke Rust.

1. Canine Census, 1911	15
2. Rhodesian ridgeback: 'Eskdale Connie', Bulawayo Show, 1925	17
3. South African Kennel Union Breed with Highest Annual Registration 1934–2001	19
4. RSA 21c Stamp, February 1991	21
5. Animals Destroyed by Cape Town and Johannesburg SPCAs, 1896–1961	25
6. National Party Minister of Co-operation and Development, Piet Koornhoff receives the freedom of Soweto, 15 October 1980	28
7. Willie Bester, Dogs of War, 2001	31
8. Lady Anne Barnard's sketch of a young Cape coloured woman caring for two young children, a dog at her feet, c. 1796–1803	77
9. Little Bess, c. 1888	114
10. The 'Guns': Easter hunt, Wycombe Vale, 1888	118
11. The Beaters, Easter hunt, Wycombe Vale, 1884	120
12. Port Elizabeth Municipal Dog and Hunting Licence Issues 1852–1902	126
13. The South African Kennel Club Committee, 1883 and 1893	128
14. Canicide in Little Bess, 1893	132
15. The commissioner of police saluting the Cato Manor Dog Memorial	210
16. The traditional role of the Africanis	274

NOTES ON CONTRIBUTORS

Robert J. Gordon teaches anthropology at the University of Vermont. He has published widely on Namibia and is currently developing a comparative perspective on the former mandates of New Guinea and South West Africa to be published as a book.

Elizabeth Green Musselman is associate professor of history at Southwestern University, just outside Austin, Texas, in the U.S. She specializes in the cultural and world history of science, and is writing a book-length comparative study of how colonial South African cultures circa 1750–1850 understood nature. Her previous book, *Nervous Conditions: Science and the Body Politic in Early Industrial Britain*, was published in 2006 by the State University of New York Press.

Albert Grundlingh is Professor and Head of the History Department at the University of Stellenbosch. He has published widely on South African social history and historiography.

Kirsten McKenzie has been Lecturer in History at the University of Sydney since 2002. She has published on the themes of British imperial bourgeois culture and respectability. Her book *Scandal in the Colonies: Sydney and Cape Town, 1820–1850* (Melbourne University Publishing, 2004) was awarded the Crawford medal by the Australian Academy of the Humanities.

Tim Maggs is former Head of the Department of Archaeology at the Natal Museum, and currently Honorary Professor in the Department of Archaeology at the University of Cape Town. He has worked on pre-colonial farming communities in South Africa, especially on the southern Highveld and in KwaZulu/Natal. He has kept African dogs for more than 20 years.

Susie Newton-King was educated at the universities of Cape Town and London. She teaches at the University of the Western Cape and researches the social history of the Cape in the seventeenth and eighteenth centuries. She is a keen participant in team research with colleagues from the University of Cape Town.

Meredith Palumbo received her Ph.D. in African art history from Indiana University. Her area of specialty is modern and contemporary Namibian art. Currently, Dr. Palumbo is an assistant professor of Non-Western art at the Kendall College of Art and Design of Ferris State University in Michigan in the United States.

Imke Rust is best known for raising political questions in Namibia through striking and unique images. Born 1975 in Windhoek, she studied visual arts through UNISA and has won the Namibia Biennale twice. She had several solo exhibitions in Namibia and Europe, has received the DAAD Berliner Künstlerprogramm and is the author of articles on Namibian art.

Judith Sealy is an Associate Professor in the Department of Archaeology at the University of Cape Town. Her principal research interests are in the archaeology of hunting and gathering people, and in the application of chemical analytical techniques to archaeological remains.

Keith Shear teaches African history and politics at the Centre of West African Studies, University of Birmingham, England. His contribution in this volume is derived from a larger work on policing and state formation in early twentieth-century South Africa, portions of which have also been published in *Gender and History* and in L.A. Lindsay and S.F. Miescher (eds.), *Men and Masculinities in Modern Africa* (2003).

Sandra Swart is an environmental and social historian. She received both a DPhil in history and MSc in environmental change from the University of Oxford. She is a senior lecturer at the University of Stellenbosch.

Jacob Tropp is Associate Professor of History and Spencer Fellow in African Studies at Middlebury College in Vermont (U.S.). He is the author of *Natures of Colonial Change: Environmental Relations in the Making of the Transkei* (Ohio University Press, 2006) and related journal articles on social and environmental history in the Eastern Cape.

Lance van Sittert is a senior lecturer in the Department of Historical Studies at the University of Cape Town working on the environmental history of the Cape.

Wendy Woodward is Professor in English Studies University of the Western Cape. She has published widely in the fields of gender and colonialism, and South African literature. At present she is working on a book length project, *The Animal Subject in southern African writing*.

CANIS FAMILIARIS: A DOG HISTORY OF SOUTHERN AFRICA*

Lance van Sittert and Sandra Swart

> You have talked so often of going to the dogs—and well, here are the dogs, and you have reached them...[1]
>
> George Orwell

Who Let the Dogs Out?

Dogs, like humans, are products both of culture and nature. For the past twelve thousand years they have been entangled with human societies. Dogs connect the wild with the tame. They occupy an ambiguous position, straddling the opposing spheres of nature and culture.[2] They occupy warm *stoeps*, follow their masters at night, track insurgents, patrol borders, sniff out strangers, hunt game, protect homesteads and leave their pawprints all over the archives. Yet, equally, they are often scavengers, liminal creatures in only loose association with human society, foraging at the peripheries of homesteads and nomadic groups, spreading disease and polluting civilized streets.

This suite of essays is a first step in recovering *Canis familiaris*' ubiquitous yet invisible presence in southern African history and, because of its relationship with humans, some of our own species's past as well. What is revealed is in many respects familiar territory, albeit illuminated in an unfamiliar light, but in others it is a *terra incognito* mapped here for the first time. The use of the dog to think about human society has a long scholarly pedigree and the recent animal turn in the humanities

---

* This chapter was first published in *SAHJ* 48 (2003), pp. 138–173 and has been used with permission of the South African Historical Journal.

[1] G. Orwell, *Down and Out in Paris and London*, Penguin, 1933, 2003, p. 18.

[2] M. Schwartz, *A History of Dogs in the Early Americas* (New Haven, 1997). See the seminal work of E. Leach, 'Anthropological aspects of language: animal categories and verbal abuse', in E. Lenneberg (ed.), *New Directions in the Study of Language* (Boston, 1964).

has sparked a florescence of canine studies.³ These have emphasised the relentless persecution of wild and feral canines⁴ and the concomitant reconstitution of their domesticated cousins in accordance with the human demands of utility and aesthetics.⁵

The two themes of extermination and domestication also animate the dog history of southern Africa, part of a broader process of 'bringing in the wild' first under the superintendence of Africans and, from the mid-seventeenth century onwards, European settlers.⁶ Each epoch of human-canine interaction produced its own peculiar animal, literally a pre-colonial, colonial and post-colonial dog, as well as its dark doppelgänger, the wild, 'Kaffir' or stray dog. The following essays show that the cynological world is invested with emotional, intellectual, financial, and political narratives, and that equally the human world can usefully be observed through canine eyes.

Pre-Colonial Dog

It is now generally accepted that the principal ancestor of the domestic dog (*Canis familiaris*) is the wolf (*Canis lupus*).⁷ The first primitive or *ur*-dogs appeared in present-day Germany 14,000 years BP.⁸ Dogs appear

---

[3] See, for example, J. Wolch and J. Emel (eds.), 'Bringing the Animals Back In', *Environment and Planning D: Society and Space*, 13 (1995), 631–730; J. Wolch and C. Philo (eds.), 'Animals and Geography', *Society and Animals*, 6 (1998), 103–202; J. Wolch and J. Emel (eds.), *Animal Geographies: Place, Politics and Identity in the Nature-Culture Borderlands* (London, 1998); C. Philo and C. Wilbert (eds.), *Animal Spaces, Beastly Places: New Geographies of Human-Animal Relations* (London, 2000).

[4] T.R. Dunlap, *Saving America's Wildlife: Ecology and the American Mind 1850–1990* (Princeton, 1988); V. Fogelman, 'American attitudes towards wolves: a history of misperception', *Environmental Review*, 13 (1989), 63–94; J. Emel, 'Are you man enough, big and bad enough? Ecofeminism and wolf eradication in the USA', *Environment and Planning D: Society and Space*, 13 (1995), 707–34; and R. Paddle, *The Last Tasmanian Tiger: The History and Extinction of the Thylacine* (Cambridge, 2000).

[5] See K. Thomas, *Man and the Natural World: Changing Attitudes in England 1500–1800* (London, 1984); H. Ritvo, *The Animal Estate: The English and Other Creatures in the Victorian Age* (Cambridge MA, 1987); K. Kete, *The Beast in the Boudoir: Pet-Keeping in Nineteenth Century Paris* (Berkeley, 1994); and P. Howell, 'Flush and the *banditti*: dog-stealing in Victorian London', in Philo and Wilbert (eds.), *Animal Spaces*, 35–56.

[6] K. Anderson, 'A walk on the wild side: a critical geography of domestication', *Progress in Human Geography*, 21(1997), 463–85.

[7] Based on studies of morphology, genetics and behaviour, see F.E. Zeuner, *A History of Domesticated Animals* (London, 1963); J. Clutton-Brock (ed.), *The Walking Larder: Patterns of Domestication, Pastoralism and Predation* (London, 1989).

[8] J. Clutton-Brock, 'Origins of the dog', in J. Serpell (ed.), *The Domestic Dog, Its Evolution, Behaviour and Interactions with People* (Cambridge, 1995), 8–20.

to have evolved in a number of sites where humans and wolves were sympatric, at the beginning of the Mesolithic period, when settled agriculture began to take hold. Archaeological evidence suggests that this coincided with early pastoralism, and that dogs probably served as guards and herders of livestock, as well as trackers and collaborators in hunting game.[9] Primitive dogs reveal a great deal of variation in skull shape and body size because of the wide geographic diversity of the initial sites of their evolution and the variations in local wolf foundation stock.[10] The first distinct and distinguishable dog 'breeds' date back to 3,000 to 4,000 BP in North Africa.[11] By 2,000 BP there were four breeds in evidence in Egyptian tomb paintings—a greyhound-like hunting dog, a short-legged 'terrier' variety, a larger prick-eared dog and a drooping-eared mastiff type, and the Romans had begun to breed particular dog types to serve particular social roles.[12] The ancestry of many modern dog breeds may be traced back to this period.[13]

The genetic plasticity of the dog facilitates the great number of variations of which the species is capable. New breeds are born and old breeds die. 'Breeds' should not be elided with the term 'species', which occur naturally under the influence of natural selection; dog breeds are artificially created by anthropogenic forces, with environmental factors playing a role. Although an estimated 400 human-made dog breeds exist today, 'primitive dogs'—those that have undergone little artificial selection—still occur, especially in the tropics. The most famous is the dingo, transported to Australia by seafarers from south-east Asia 3,000–4,000 BP.[14] Dogs showing little evidence of selective breeding are also common in North Africa, the Middle East and western Asia. Today many still live in a loose association with human society, scavenging around homesteads and nomadic groups. More discussion is provided by Tim Maggs and Judith Sealy, 'Africanis: The Pre-Colonial Dog of Africa' in this volume.

---

[9] J.R.A. Butler, 'The ecology of domestic dogs: *canis familaris* in the communal lands of Zimbabwe' (PhD thesis, University of Zimbabwe, 1998).
[10] J. Clutton-Brock, *A Natural History of Domesticated Mammals* (London, 1989). There are probably 32 subspecies of wolves across the species' Eurasian and North American range, and variations in early domestic dogs reflect those of their founders.
[11] Clutton-Brock, 'Origins of the dog'.
[12] P. Wapnish and B. Hesse, 'Pampered pooches or plain pariahs? The Ashkelon dog burials', *Biblical Archaeologist*, 56 (1993), 55–80 and Clutton-Brock, 'Origins of the dog'.
[13] Clutton-Brock, 'Origins of the dog'.
[14] L.K. Corbett, *The Dingo in Australia and Asia* (Sydney, 1995).

Little is known of the dogs of sub-Saharan Africa.[15] The first recorded reference to indigenous dogs in southern Africa was by the Portuguese explorer Vasco da Gama in 1497, who noted of a San community at St Helena Bay: 'They have many dogs like those of Portugal, which bark as do these.'[16] Between c. 1700 and 1800, explorers of the interior recorded dogs among various indigenous groups.[17] Reports tended to focus on the dogs' small and unattractive appearance, and their courage and usefulness in hunting.[18] Early ethnographers, like Soga on the Xhosa, and Bryant on the Zulu, provided descriptions of the various indigenous dogs and their social roles. Both ethnographers feared that these dogs were threatened with extinction.[19]

It is probable that the ancestors of these dogs were introduced into southern Africa around 2,000 BP by Bantu-speaking agriculturalists and/or Khoikhoi pastoralists.[20] Dog skeletal remains, for example, suggest the presence of dogs in several Iron Age and a few Stone Age sites. Plug argues that the earliest conclusive evidence dates to 570 AD.[21] Although earliest sites associated with Nguni and Sotho people have not revealed dog remains, it is hypothesised that dogs could have accompanied these communities via East Africa into the southern Africa. Hall contends that the earlier western-stream immigrants introduced both a small spitz-type dog from the equatorial environment (similar to the present-day basenji, found in the Congo) and a more slender

---

[15] J. Clutton-Brock, 'The spread of domestic animals in Africa', in T. Shaw, P. Sinclair, B. Andah and A. Okpoko (eds.), *The Archaeology of African Foods, Metals and Towns* (London, 1993) and T. Maggs and J. Sealy, 'The pre-colonial dog' in this volume.

[16] E.C. Boonzaier, C. Malherbe, P. Berens and A. Smith, *Cape Herders: A History of the Khoikhoi of Southern Africa* (Cape Town, 1996), 54.

[17] V.S. Forbes, *Pioneer Travellers of South Africa* (Cape Town, 1965).

[18] J. Stuart and D.M. Malcolm, *The Diary of Henry Francis Fynn* (Pietermaritzburg, 1986).

[19] J.H. Soga, *The Ama-Xosa: Life and Customs* (London, 1905) and A.T. Bryant, *The Zulu People as They were Before the White Man Came* (Pietermaritzburg, 1967).

[20] S. Hall, 'Indigenous domesticated dogs of southern Africa: an introduction', in R.M. Blench and K.C. MacDonald (eds.), *The Origins and Development of African Livestock: Archaeology, Genetics, Linguistics and Ethnography* (London, 2000), and Corbett, *The Dingo*. There are no wolves in the southern African sub-continent and dogs were thus introduced from elsewhere. There is an alternative, but less widely supported theory, suggested by Corbett: that the dogs arrived 1,000–2,000 BP via Madagascar, transported by the Melanesian seafarers that introduced the dingo to Australia. He bases his theory on the Basenji, a hunting breed from the Congo, which resembles the dingo in its inability to bark and its annual (rather than biannual) reproductive cycle.

[21] Quoted in Hall, 'Indigenous domesticated dogs', 302.

hound, like those typical of arid North Africa (like the modern saluki) into southern Africa.[22]

San rock paintings display both these morphological types and both varieties have been found in Iron Age sites dating to c. 1,000 BP.[23] Later paintings by traveller artists, like Baines, provide more visual evidence, which corresponds with these two types of dogs. Khoisan sites have not yielded dog remains, except possibly at a Cape St Francis site, dated to c. 1,200 BP.[24] Certainly active trade networks did exist with Iron Age farmers and they could have acquired their dogs in this manner. However, it is also possible that Khoisan groups introduced the dog into southern Africa independently of Iron Age farmers.[25]

Another possibility is that some dogs were introduced via the east coast between 900 and 1400 AD as part of the Islamic trading network. Islamic traders were accompanied by dogs in the vessels, as guards and vermin controllers.[26] Epstein even argues for a strong genetic presence in the dogs left by Islamic and Portuguese traders, arguing that the indigenous dogs reflected characteristics of Portuguese and middle eastern gazehounds (although these dogs would, in any event, have shared a common ancestor, which could explain their similar appearance).[27]

San rock paintings indicate the importance of dogs in their society. Hall hypothesises that dogs altered the subsistence pattern and therefore social institutions of other groups too, impacting heavily on the environment itself.[28] While dogs were initially probably used to control vermin—as evinced by the co-occurrence of dog remains with that of the earliest evidence of the house rat (*Rattus rattus*) on the eighth century site of Ndondonwane—their role in hunting impacted most heavily on social rituals. With dogs a new hunting strategy was developed. Prey formerly hunted with a bow and arrow could be more efficiently tracked and hunted with dogs.

---

[22] For more discussion see Tim Maggs and Judith Sealy, 'Africanis: The Pre-Colonial Dog of Africa', this volume.
[23] I. Plug and E.A. Voigt, 'Archaeozoological studies of Iron Age communities in southern Africa', *Advances in World Archaeology*, 4 (1985), 189–238.
[24] E.A. Voigt, *Mapungubwe: An Archaeozoological Interpretation of an Iron Age Community* (Pretoria, 1983).
[25] Hall, 'Indigenous domesticated dogs', 303.
[26] Hall, 'Indigenous domesticated dogs', 304.
[27] H. Epstein, *The Origins of the Domestic Animals of Africa* (New York, 1971).
[28] Hall, 'Indigenous domesticated dogs', 309.

This was particularly influential, Hall notes, for groups like the Zulu, who developed this hunting formation further into the cattle-horn formation used in combat, and which they were to use in their wars against colonial settlement. The importance of the canine revolution can also been seen in Xhosa culture, where 'dogs' were believed to ward off the *thikoloshe*, and became a colloquialism for 'commoners'. In one recollection, the millenarian prophetess Nongqawuse urged the Xhosa 'slaughter your cattle but save the dogs, for plenty of game is coming'.[29]

Colonial Dog

Canis familiaris was also an integral member of the 'portmanteau biota' that accompanied European settlement of the subcontinent from the mid seventeenth century onwards.[30] The settlers' domestic animals were of symbolic as well as practical importance to the survival of the colony, providing it with goods and services, but also serving as ubiquitous and highly visible markers of the boundaries between culture and nature, human and animal on the outer edge of a rapidly expanding European world. These boundaries were vigilantly and ruthlessly policed in accordance with the received Judeo-Christian wisdoms; inter-species sexual relationships being deemed even more subversive of a civilized order in the colony than miscegenation with the natives down to the end of the eighteenth century.[31]

The dog's ubiquitous and intimate presence on both sides of the frontier, in settler and indigene societies and bourgeois and underclass households, also made it a handy and frequently used mnemonic for evaluating its human owners in the increasingly racially and class stratified colonial society of the nineteenth century. This is trajectory is explored in the Cape context by Elizabeth Green-Musselman, 'What the dogs knew: intelligence and morality in the Cape Colony' and Kirsten McKenzie, 'Dogs and the public sphere: the ordering of social space

---

[29] M. Hunter, *Reaction to Conquest: Effects of Contact with Europeans on the Pondo of South Africa* (London, 1936), 297; J.B. Peires, *The House of Phalo* (Johannesburg, 1981), 32; and W.B. Rubusana, *Zemk' inkomo Magwalandini* (London, 1911), 271. Thanks to Helen Bradford for these references.

[30] A.W. Crosby, *Ecological Imperialism: The Biological Expansion of Europe, 900 to 1900* (Cambridge, 1986).

[31] S. Newton King, 'A short paper about a dog', in this volume.

in early nineteenth century Cape Town', while Rob Gordon, in 'Fido: dog tales of colonialism in Namibia', investigates the parallel process in an adjacent European colony at the end of the nineteenth century. The Scottish missionary, John Campebell, was one of many travelers who reported being

> Saluted with the barking of many dogs, which seem to abound in Africa more than men. These animals are only useful as watchers. A shepherd's dog from Britain would have assisted us more in driving our spare cattle than a thousand African ones. It would be well if some of these were sent over to instruct African dogs to be more useful to their masters. Perhaps were the people here to witness their sagacity, they would suspect they were rational beings.[32]

His contempt for the natives' want of industry, expressed through disdain for their slothful dogs, was noteworthy only for being directed against Boers rather than Africans in this instance.

Burchell confirmed the colonial dog's ubiquitous presence, but not its want of utility, reporting that '[E]very farm-house was apparently over-stocked with these animals, [but] the boors, knowing their value, could seldom be persuaded to part with any.'[33] Their primary value, according to Burchell (echoing Campbell), was as alarms and he regarded 'good pack of dogs, of different kinds...a very necessary part of the equipment' for travelling in the region.[34]

> Our pack of dogs consisted of about five-and-twenty of various sorts and sizes. This variety...was of the greatest service on such an expedition, as I observed that some gave notice of danger in one way, and others, in another. Some were more disposed to watch against men, and others against wild beasts; some discovered an enemy by their quickness of hearing, others by that of scent: some were useful only for their vigilance and barking; some for speed in pursuing game; and others for courage in holding ferocious animals at bay...their services were invaluable, often contributing to our safety, and always, to our ease, by their constant vigilance; as we felt a confidence that no danger could approach us at night without being announced by their barking.[35]

---

[32] Quoted in K. Parker, 'Fertile land, romantic spaces, uncivilised peoples: English travel-writing about the Cape of Good Hope, 1800–50' in B. Schwarz (ed.), *The Expansion of England: Race, Ethnicity and Cultural History* (London, 1996), 209.

[33] W.J. Burchell, *Travels in the Interior of Southern Africa*, vol. 1 (London, 1822), 176.

[34] W.J. Burchell, *Travels in the Interior of Southern Africa*, vol. 1 (London, 1822), 175. See also F. Galton, *Narrative of an Explorer in Tropical South Africa* (London, 1853), 8–9; C.J. Andersson, *Notes of Travel in South Africa* (London, 1875), 312.

[35] W.J. Burchell, *Travels in the Interior of Southern Africa*, vol. 2 (London, 1824), 174.

Burchell's favourite, *Wantrouw* (Mistrust), was the epitome of the colonial mongrel *boer hond*: 'a large white flap-eared dog having two or three brown spots, wiry hair, and a bearded muzzle'.[36] Such Dutch *vuil-* and *steekbaard* varieties were leavened during the nineteenth century with the dogs imported by the British military to hunt indigenes and game under the *Pax Britannica*. As one Eastern Cape settler recalled:

> In the early [eighteen] sixties, when military posts were scattered about the frontier...As a rule there were to be found at each post bloodhounds, staghounds, greyhounds, bulldogs, terriers, mastiffs, pointers, and occasionally foxhounds, and...the Boer dog was a cross between one or other or more of the dogs mentioned, for it was generally in the vicinity of military posts that the best Boer dogs were to be found.[37]

The *boer hond* also crossed the frontier, with Xhosa guerrillas operating in the Fish River bush during Mlanjeni's War in the early 1850s employing 'wolf hounds' trained to pull down British soldiers.[38] Thus when a detachment of newly arrived troops became lost in the area during a skirmish in September 1851, '[m]any of these brave men were caught alive, having been hunted down with dogs. They were heard calling for help. It has been a most murderous affair. The Kaffirs hunted after the poor fellows with dogs.'[39]

The growth of towns and closure of the frontier in the second half of the nineteenth century marked a major watershed in the canine history of the region. A new sensibility towards animals emerged among the urban middle class modelled on Victorian Britain.[40] The separation of town from countryside was achieved in part through the ever more extensive control and ultimately exclusion of animals from the new urban spaces.[41] An animal presence was tolerated in towns only

---

[36] W.J. Burchell, *Travels in the Interior of Southern Africa*, vol. 1 (London, 1822), vol. 1, 266.

[37] J.J.K., 'The Boer dog: another version', *Agricultural Journal of the Cape of Good Hope (AJCGH)*, 34 (1909), 188.

[38] J.B. Peires, *The Dead Will Arise* (Johannesburg, 1989), 18 and W. King, *Campaigning in Kaffirland* (London, 1853), 96 and 217–19. Thanks to Helen Bradford for these references.

[39] See *Graham's Town Journal*, 13 Sep. 1851 and Peires, *The Dead Will Arise*, 16 for a November 1851 action in the Fish River bush in which 60 British soldiers from the same regiment were killed. Thanks again to Helen Bradford for these references.

[40] See Thomas, *Man and the Natural World*, and Ritvo, *The Animal Estate*.

[41] See C. Philo, 'Animals, geography and the city: notes on inclusions and exclusions', *Environment and Planning D: Society and Space*, 13 (1995), 655–81; P. Brummett, 'Dogs, women, cholera and other menaces in the streets: cartoon satire in the Ottoman revolutionary press 1908–11', *International Journal of Middle Eastern Studies*, 27 (1995),

when servicing the food, transport and aesthetic needs of inhabitants, but even then was confined to specified routes, rendezvous and spaces (such as the market place, shambles and zoological garden). Although livestock animals remained a ubiquitous presence in the pre-industrial urban space, this too was gradually erased by railways, refrigeration and motorised road transport, which removed the need for towns to maintain their own resident populations of draught and food animals.

Urban civilisation defined itself not only in opposition to the animal countryside, but also to *backveld* (rural) sensibilities towards animals, deemed backward and brutish. The urban middle class thus championed a new sensibility embodied by the notions of 'humanitarianism' and 'sportsmanship' in their increasingly detached and ritualised relations with domestic and wild animals.

The new sensibility first found expression through the growing middle class activism against all forms of brutality towards the 'dumb creation' in the towns. Cruelty against animals was made a criminal offence in the Cape (1856), Natal (1874), the Orange Free State (1876) and the South African Republic (1888) and the urban middle class rallied to the standard of the new societies for the prevention of cruelty to animals that proliferated in their wake.[42] The mother SPCA was founded in Cape Town in 1872 and spawned both associate branches and allied organisations across the region in the final quarter of the nineteenth century.[43] Assisted by a steady increase in penalties and encouragement to public prosecution, the societies sought to civilise the towns by eradicating the innate brutality of the underclass and countryside from their public thoroughfares. Similarly, game law reform sought to rescue a wide range of wild animals from alleged imminent destruction at the hands of farmers through the imposition of a hunting licence and close season and substitution of the urban hunters' code of 'sportsmanship' for the brute demand of the market.[44]

438–43; and K. Mckenzie, 'Dogs and the public sphere: the ordering of social space in early nineteenth-century Cape Town', in this volume.

[42] See Cape of Good Hope Act No. 8, 1856; Natal, Act No.?, 1874; Orange Free State, Act No. 2, 1876; and South African Republic, Act No.?, 1888.

[43] For the animal anti-cruelty movement on the north Atlantic rim, see E.S. Turner, *All Heaven in a Rage* (London, 1964); Thomas, *Man and the Natural World*, 143–91; Ritvo, *Animal Estate*, 125–66; and Kete, *Beast in the Boudoir*, 5–21. The movement in southern Africa, exemplified by the formation of local SPCAs, has yet to find a historian.

[44] J.M. Mackenzie, *The Empire of Nature: Hunting, Conservation and British Imperialism* (Manchester, 1988) and Cape of Good Hope, Game Law Amendment Act No 36, 1886.

These new sensibilities found their ideal expression in the 'pets' of the new urban middle class.[45] This category initially included a wide menagerie of wild and domestic consorts, but was gradually narrowed to exclude all except canine and feline companions. A middle-class dog fancy boomed in the last quarter of the nineteenth century characterised by the importation of British standards and dog breeds through the formation of a South African Kennel Club (SAKC) in Port Elizabeth in 1883.[46] The 'underclass mongrel pack' was an anathema to the colonial breed clubs. The institutionalised dog breed was founded on Victorian typological thinking about race, quality, purity, and progress. Harriet Ritvo has described this process for English dogs in the nineteenth century, emphasising the developing urban professional classes, for whom the ideology of social position based on competitive merit was fundamental.[47] Ritvo has shown that the ideology of 'pure blood' permeated their thinking. Unlike the aristocratic breeding of horses, for example, breeding dogs necessitated only modest means and offered a useful way of demonstrating their breeder's status. Urban middle-class Victorians celebrated the power to manipulate the raw material of breeding dogs to manufacture something novel, to 'invent' a breed with standards divorced from the merely utilitarian.

Such capability, Ritvo argues, reinforced notions of instrumentalism, progress, earned wealth, and meritorious leisure. The ideal of the purified lineage was seen as an end in itself; accordingly, the studbook was structured to reflect and to enforce that ideal rigidly and absolutely. The value placed on breed purity was animated by older ideas of human aristocracies and thoroughbred horses; and was to resurface in the Nazi endeavour to breed an Aryan superman. As Ritvo has demonstrated, the power to sculpt dog flesh symbolically destabilised rank based on nature, adding support to the respect given to the hard-won status of the professional classes, while simultaneously reinforced

---

[45] Thomas, *Man and the Natural World*; Ritvo, *The Animal Estate*; and Kete, *The Beast in the Boudoir*.

[46] See J. Harpur, 'South African Kennel Club: its origin and development', *South African Kennel Club Gazette (SAKCG)*, 1 (Mar.–June 1908), 24–5, 37–9, 49–51 and 68–70. The *SAKCG* ceased publication in 1914 and was only re-launched a quarter of a century later in 1938 as the *South African Kennel Union Gazette (SAKUG)*. In May 1964 the name was shortened to *Kennel Union Gazette (KUG)* and in August 1992 to *KUSA*. Finally, in July 1996 the journal changed its name again to *Dogs in Africa*, which it still bears.

[47] H. Ritvo, 'Pride and pedigree: the evolution of the Victorian dog fancy', *Victorian Studies*, 29 (1986), 227–53; Ritvo, *The Animal Estate*, 82–121.

the nexus tying together race, blood, genealogy, merit, and purity in 'good breeding'. This ideology, permeated with the urgency of racial thinking found in colonies, was imported into the colonial discourses from the metropole.[48]

The new dog mania in southern Africa was closely associated with the rise of the 'urban sportsman', hunting breeds dominating both imports and the shows. The middle class demanded the same freedom of movement and protection in law for their dogs as themselves. The latter thus enjoyed the liberty of the town and protection from theft or assault through legal recognition as private property of their owners. The growing canine underclass, however, roaming the streets in packs and indulging its animal appetites in the public thoroughfares, threatened the social order of both class and town, and was relentlessly persecuted through a combination of punitive licensing and occasional pogroms of ownerless 'strays'.[49]

The closure of the frontier in the second half of the nineteenth century similarly transformed the dog's place in the countryside. The shift from transhumance to permanent settlement and emergence of commercial agriculture prompted efforts by self-styled 'progressive' farmers to contain the threat posed by the dogs of the rural underclass and wild canines to livestock, cultivation and game.

Canis familiaris menaced domestic stock both independently and as the accomplice of stock thieves. Sheep, goats and ostriches were particularly vulnerable to the depredations of 'vagrant dogs' and thieves in a still largely unenclosed countryside, the latter relying on their animals to consume all evidence of their crimes. Thus, according to one farmer, the 'Kaffirs'...idea in having a large number of dogs was, that when they took a sheep, the dogs would eat all the offal, and in that way there would be no trace of the animal left'.[50] Cultivated land was similarly vulnerable to damage by dogs at large and wine farmers in the south-western Cape were permitted to destroy canine trespassers out of hand in defence of their vineyards during the summer harvest.[51] Lastly, dogs poached game with or separately from their owners. An

---

[48] See S. Dubow, *Scientific Racism in Modern South Africa* (Cambridge, 1995).

[49] See L. van Sittert, 'Class and canicide in Little Bess: the 1893 Port Elizabeth rabies epidemic', in this volume.

[50] Cape of Good Hope, *Report of the Select Committee on the Destruction of Vermin*, 1904 (A2–1904), evidence of W. Rubidge, 19.

[51] Cape of Good Hope, Pounds and Trespass Act (No. 15, 1892), Clause 26(c).

initial attempt at checking rural canine population growth was made through taxation, dog tax acts being duly passed in Natal (1875), the Cape (1884), Orange Free State (1891), South African Republic (1892) and Namibia (1907).[52] Opposition from both settlers and natives and the cost of collection blunted the impact of punitive taxation as a population control mechanism and, as in the towns, canicide became the last resort of the rural gentry against the canine underclass.

Farmers shared little of the new urban sentimentality for 'man's best friend', being well aware of *Canis'* ability to slough off the thin veneer of domestication and revert to its wild prototype.[53] Suspicious even of their own dogs, few farmers regarded those of the underclass as domesticated at all, but likened them instead, in both discourse and action, to the indigenous wild canids that stalked the 'howling wilderness' beyond the fence lines of the farm.[54]

The wild dog (*Lycaon pictus*) was the most feared of the wild canids, but the black-backed and other associated 'jackals' were the most common.[55] With the wool boom in the nineteenth century the latter displaced the large wild cats (lion and leopard) from their pre-eminence on the earlier bounty lists of the cattle-keeping Dutch East India Company. In the wake of a sharp downturn in the wool price in the last quarter of the nineteenth century, progressive farmers in the Eastern Cape pastoral heartland formed wild animal poisoning clubs and initiated co-operative poisoning campaigns against the jackal and other carnivorous vermin in defence of their flocks and profits.[56] Their efforts were rewarded with an official subsidy from 1889 converted into public bounty system in 1895 and further enhanced by the state distribution of strychnine at cost and the subsidisation of vermin proof-fencing. In the twenty years after 1889 more than 350,000 jackal 'proofs' (the body part—tail, ears, full skin, etc—produced as proof of having killed the animal in order to claim the reward) were paid for, but even this represented only a

---

[52] Natal, Act No. 27, 1875; Cape of Good Hope, Act No. 23, 1884; Orange Free State, Act No. 2, 1891. For Namibia, see Union of South Africa, *Report of the Commission Appointed to Enquire into the Rebellion of the Bondelzwarts, 1923* (UG16-23), 8–9.

[53] See L. van Sittert, 'Keeping the enemy at bay: the extermination of wild carnivora in the Cape Colony 1889–1910', *Environmental History*, 3 (1998), 341–4.

[54] T. Hoole, 'Jackal proof fencing: its advantages and economies', *AJCGH*, 25 (1904), 561.

[55] See F.W. Fitzsimons *The Natural History of South Africa: Mammals*, vol. 2 (London, 1919) for wild canids, and Van Sittert, 'Keeping the enemy at bay', 338–41 for the generic 'jackal'.

[56] Van Sittert, 'Keeping the enemy at bay', 341–4.

fraction of the canine poisoning mortality in the countryside.[57] Indeed, strychnine was liberally employed against both wild and domestic dogs, extermination of the latter constituting in many instances a welcome and intended bonus of the official extermination campaign against the 'jackal'.[58]

The imperial canine class order was fired in the furnace of epidemic emergency in the two decades, 1892–1912. An urban rabies outbreak in Port Elizabeth in 1892–94 provided the pretext for a canicide of 2,000, mainly underclass, dogs and for disciplining the urban middle class in the priorities and practices of quarantine.[59] A second rural rabies pandemic, starting in Northern Rhodesia in 1902 and raging through Southern Rhodesia and the Bechuanaland Protectorate over the next decade, met with a similar response: the canicide of 100,000 'native dogs' and the imposition of a regional canine quarantine.[60] The spectre of disease both confirmed the need for the separation of the canine familiars of the urban middle class/rural gentry from those of the urban/rural underclass and legitimised the use of canicide to enforce an impermeable class/race quarantine.

The gradual withdrawal of direct British control over southern Africa after 1910 and the rising tide of settler nationalism both endorsed the fundamental tenets of the imperial canine order and forced a continual revision of the boundaries of class and quarantine to suit the requirements of an ever-changing imagined community. Fitzpatrick's *Jock of the Bushveld*, first published in 1907, signals the shift by pairing its young English proconsul with the runt of a mongrel (*boer* dog) litter and suggesting that the hybrid—not the thoroughbred—was destined to inherit the colonial earth by virtue of its Darwinian competitive superiority. The progeny of an imported father and colonial mother, Jock 'was not yellow like them, nor dark brindled like Jess [his mother], but a sort of dirty pale half-and-half colour with some dark faint wavy lines all over him, as if he had tried to be brindled and failed'.[61]

---

[57] Van Sittert, 'Keeping the enemy at bay', 345–51.
[58] See J. Tropp, 'Dogs, poison and the meaning of colonial intervention in the Transkei, South Africa', in this volume.
[59] Van Sittert, 'Class and canicide'.
[60] R. Mutwira, 'Southern Rhodesian wildlife policy (1890–1953): a question of condoning game slaughter?', *Journal of Southern African Studies*, 15, 1989, 250.
[61] P. Fitzpatrick, *Jock of the Bushveld* (London, 1907).

John Buchan, in a novel published the same year as Fitzpatrick's autobiography, also gave his fictional hero, David Crawfurd, a bastard canine 'second shadow', but with an explicitly colonial pedigree.

> It was an enormous Boer hunting-dog, a mongrel in whose blood ran mastiff and bulldog and foxhound, and Heaven knows what beside. In colour it was a kind of brindled red, and the hair on its back grew against the lie of the rest of its coat. Some one had told me, or I may have read it, that a back like meant that a dog would face anything mortal, even to a charging lion, and it was this feature which first caught my fancy.[62]

The faithful 'Colin' duly makes the ultimate sacrifice, dying in defence of Crawfurd, and thereby helping thwart an impending 'Kaffir Rising' against white rule in Africa.[63]

This new settler nativism inspired by Union initiated the rehabilitation of the *boer* dog from mongrel outcast to 'pure-breed' in order to have 'something South African as an addition to the breeds on the show bench'.[64] On the eve of Union, the 'old Boer hunting dog' was being lauded for its pluck, endurance and talent for killing leopards, baboons and other vermin, and it was deemed 'a great pity that no effort seems to have been made to keep this fine old South African dog pure-bred'.[65] In the mid-1900s the president of the SAKC initiated a futile search for a breeding pair 'of the well-known and useful Boer Hond...to breed to type and if possible improve the breed'. Farmers everywhere claimed the dogs had been 'exterminated during the late war'.[66] Another rural aficionado, signing himself 'A South African', writing in 1909 blamed the fancy for the *boer* dog's demise, claiming 'Useful dogs have been and are being discarded for many useless fancy-dogs, by dog-fanciers'.[67] Thus was the old imperial fear of degeneracy, expressed in the waking dread of the urban middle class and rural gentry for the underclass mongrel pack, given a new national inflection. Class and quarantine remained as urgent and integral to nation building as empire and *Canis familiaris*, because of its ubiquity, a key indicator of national health and well-being.

---

[62] J. Buchan, *Prester John* (London, 1910), 45.
[63] Buchan, *Prester John*, 239.
[64] 'The Boer hond', *SAKCG*, 2 (Mar. 1909), 24.
[65] Dog-fancier, 'The Boer hunting dog', *AJCGH*, 34 (1909), 96.
[66] 'The Boer hond', 24.
[67] A South African, 'The Boer hunting dog', *AJCGH*, 34 (1909), 187.

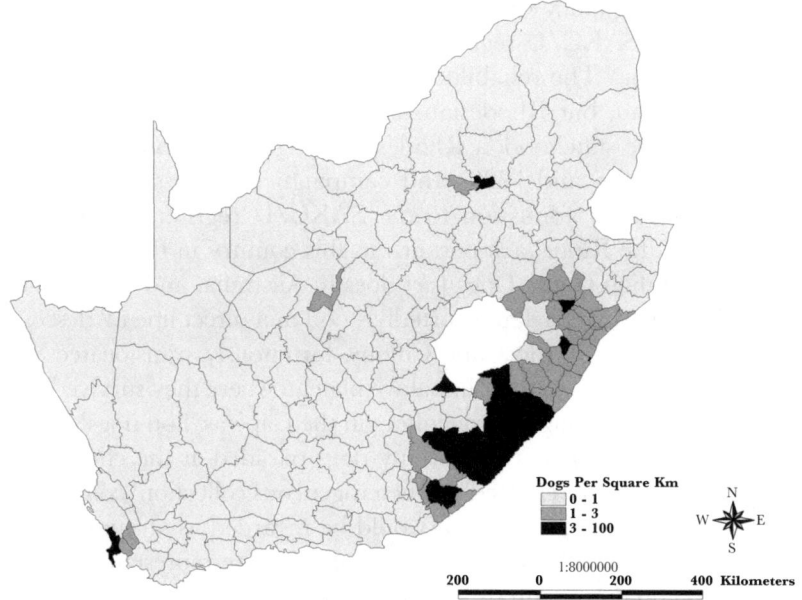

Figure 1. Canine Census, 1911[68]

Post-Colonial Dog

The 1911 census provides a unique glimpse of South Africa's canine geography at the start of the twentieth century (see Figure 1).

It revealed a total dog population in excess of 650,000 with heavy concentrations in both the major cities and overcrowded black reserves, separated by a largely dog-depopulated white countryside.[69] This colonial canine topography was entrenched over the course of the twentieth century through the continuation of the established practices of quarantine and extermination.

---

[68] Union of South Africa, *Census 1911 Annexures to the General Report Part 9: Live Stock and Agriculture* [UG32h-1912], 1222–25.

[69] See *Census 1911 Part 9*, 1222–25; C.H. Blaine, *Dog Law: A Compilation of the Law in South Africa relating to Dogs with Appendices: South West Africa, Southern Rhodesia* (Johannesburg, 1928), 4–7 and R.R. Byrne, 'Taxation of dogs', *SAKUG*, (Nov. 1945), 171. The 1911 census was the last to enumerate dogs, and thus just 17 years later Blaine grossly (under)estimated the national canine population at just 400,000 from licence and tax returns. Seventeen years later again, Byrne estimated it at just 150,000. The available proxy data from the SPCA lethal chambers and SAKU registrations suggest exactly the opposite trend.

The urban dog fancy was indigenised through the admission of the *boer hond* to the SAKC/U register in the 1920s and Afrikaners to club ranks after 1945.[70] The rehabilitation of the *boer* dog was secured, not by South African, but Rhodesian settlers, where, in the full flush of impending white statehood, a Rhodesian Ridgeback (Lion Dog) Club was formed in the mid-1920s and campaigned successfully for the 'fiddleback' breed's admission to the SAKC/U register in 1924 on grounds that 'the Ridgeback pertains to this country in the same way that the Australian Cattle Dogs [*sic*] does to Australia, and are equally valuable'.[71] The ridgeback purportedly stood in a direct line of descent from the *boer* dogs of the Cape Colony, fortuitously translocated via missionary endeavour to the Zimbabwe plateau where they survived the extinction of their mongrel progenitors in the Cape as 'lion dogs' in the service of settler hunters. The twenty dogs paraded at the club's first meeting in 1922 were reportedly 'a heterogeneous collection' comprised 'of all types and sizes, from what would be regarded as an undersized Great Dane to a small Bull Terrier; all colours were represented, Reds and Brindles predominating'.[72] Stressing a character forged in the bush and fitting it to a Dalmatian standard, its promoters invented a new indigenous breed as the appropriate canine companion for a florescent settler nationalism across the region (see Figure 2).

---

[70] See R.D.S. Gwatkin, 'Dogs and human migrations', *Journal of the South African Veterinary Medicine Association*, 5 (1934), 37–40; G.C. Dry and T.C. Hawley, *The Rhodesian Ridgeback: Its Origin, Development and Treatment* (Pretoria, 1949?); M. Yule, 'The Rhodesian Ridgeback', *SAKUG*, (Feb. 1951), 7; M.D.W. Jeffreys, 'The origin of the Rhodesian Ridgeback', *Africana Notes and News*, 11 (1953), 10; M. Wellings, 'The origin and short history of the Rhodesian Ridgeback dog', *SAKUG*, (June 1954), 102–4; T.C. Hawley, *The Rhodesian Ridgeback: The Origin, History and Standard of the Breed* (Pretoria, 1957); M.L. Arsenis, *Dog Tales and Trimmings* (Cape Town, 1957); J.N. Murray, *The Rhodesian Ridgeback 1924–74* (Verwoedburg, 1976); M.L. Arsenis, *Ridged Dogs in Africa* (Randburg, 1981); C.A. Hromnik, 'The Ari ridgeback of the Qurena', *KUG* (Nov. and Dec. 1991), 402–10 and 455–64; and M.R. Darwin, 'On the origin of the breeds: Rhodesian Ridgeback', *KUG* (Nov. and Dec. 1991), 412–17 and 464–7.

[71] G.F. Downes, 'Bulawayo dogdom 1909–1959: a brief history of the Bulawayo Kennel Club', *SAKUG* (Nov. 1959), 222.

[72] Wellings, 'The origin', 104, and B.W. Durham, 'Origin and standardisation of the Rhodesian Ridgeback', *SAKUG* (Dec. 1950), 246.

Figure 2. Rhodesian ridgeback: 'Eskdale Connie', Bulawayo Show, 1925[73]

The ridgeback enjoyed a surge in popularity in South Africa between 1945–50. The Transvaal Rhodesian Ridgeback Club became the first bilingual affiliate of the SAKU in 1945, the breed topped SAKU registrations between 1946 and 1948, it was presented to the royal family during their 1947 visit and lay at the feet of the first National Party prime minister.[74]

The ridgeback boom was a product of broader societal changes. The Second World War accelerated African urbanisation and the rise of militant black nationalism in the cities. Amidst rising fears of a *swart gevaar* on their doorsteps, a growing number of urban whites looked

---

[73] Hawley, *The Rhodesian Ridgeback*, 25.
[74] Dry and Hawley, *The Rhodesian Ridgeback*, 8; Figure 6 below; Downes, 'Bulawayo dogdom', 223; and Darwin, 'On the origin', 465.

to Afrikaner nationalism for political salvation and a dog breed forged on the frontier and sought after by the military during the war for 'a first-class house-guard'.[75] As a Potgietersrus ridgeback breeder confided in his fellow dogmen in 1946:

> I'm sure I would have considerable difficulty in finding a better watch-dog and I have often had to replace a native's whole rig-out which my dogs have torn to ribbons off his back and also to give the boys a few shillings to keep it quiet.[76]

Military and urban security required a bigger, heavier dog than the prototype developed for rural hunting and the war noticeably altered the breed's phenotype from Dalmatian towards Great Dane.

The destabilizing effect of wartime urbanization on form was further exacerbated by a post-war demand so great that purists held it to have briefly jeopardised the maintenance of the breed standard, with 'pirate catch-as-catch-can breeders' flooding the market with pups to capitalise on public demand and gullibility.[77] The wartime fame of *Just Nuisance* thus represented the swansong of the imperial canine order. The death of the drunken, dissolute Great Dane 'symbol of the British Navy in the Peninsula' in 1944, ceded the stage to Fitzpatrick's long-heralded indigenous hybrid and its accompanying new political order.[78]

Rising white affluence during the long post-Second World War boom, however, also popularised and commercialised the previously elite middle-class dog fancy, making fidelity to a single national breed impossible to maintain. The market introduced a democracy of personal taste that diluted the SAKU's authority over national dogdom and shifted local canine cultural reference points from Britain to the United States. The former was reflected in the number of recognised breeds, which doubled in the half century after 1945 from 88 to 177.[79]

---

[75] See 'Dogs wanted' advertisement, *SAKUG* (Oct. 1942), 105; V.H. Brisley, 'Rhodesian Ridgeback types', *SAKUG* (Nov. 1945), 170; and H.G. Mundy, 'Rhodesian Ridgebacks', *SAKUG* (Feb. 1946), 6 for the wartime increase in the minimum height and weight specifications in the breed standard in favour of the guard over the traditional sporting dog role. The quote is from Mundy.

[76] E. Trinder, 'Rhodesian Ridgebacks', *SAKUG* (Feb. 1946), 7.

[77] Hawley, *The Rhodesian Ridgeback*, 41, and Wellings, 'The origin', 104.

[78] L.M. Steyn, *Just Nuisance: Life Story of an Able Seaman Who Leads a Dog's Life* (Cape Town, n.d.), 35. See also L.M. Steyn, *Just Nuisance Carries On* (Cape Town, n.d.) and T. Sisson, *Just Nuisance AB: His Full Story* (Cape Town, 1985).

[79] 'Report of the Chairman of the Federal Council for the year 1946/47', *SAKUG*, 10 (Jan. 1948), 268 and 'Comment', *KUSA*, 59 (Jan. 1995), 14.

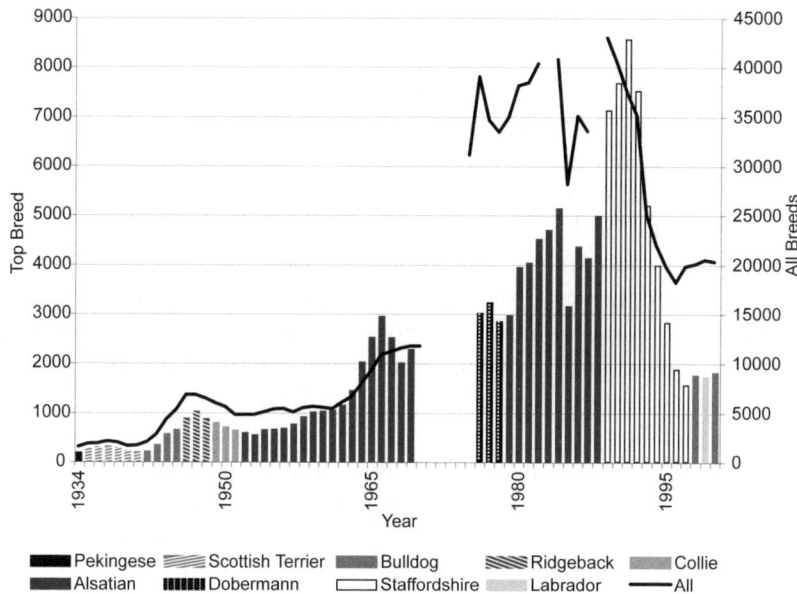

Figure 3. South African Kennel Union Breed with Highest Annual Registration 1934–2001[80]

The latter in the usurpation of the ridgeback's pride of place in popular affection by first the collie in 1949 and then the alsatian in 1952 following their immortalisation in Hollywood films and on television (see Figure 3).[81]

The enduring popularity of the alsatian (the top national breed 1952–89) and its brief displacement by the dobermann pinscher (1976–78) also reflected escalating black opposition to apartheid after 1960, producing a clear preference for large, fierce dogs on the part of the white public. By 1980 just four out of the 177 recognised breeds—alsatian, rottweiler, bull terrier and dobermann—accounted

---

[80] Compiled from *SAKUG, KUG, KUSA* and *Dogs in Africa*, 1938–2002. The SAKU's administrative capacity was overwhelmed by the surge in registrations in first half of the 1970s and it published no annual league table 1970–75. These could, however, be reconstructed from the monthly listings in the *SAKUG*.

[81] J. Walker (ed.), *Haliwell's Film Guide 8th Edition* (London, 1991). There were no fewer than seven *Lassie* films between 1943 and 1951, starting with *Lassie Come Home* starring Elizabeth Taylor; while the interwar Alsatian movie star Rin Tin Tin received a new lease on life with a five-year-long television reincarnation on ABC recycled as shorts in South African cinemas.

for a third of all SAKU annual registrations.[82] The Staffordshire bull terrier's final ousting of the alsatian in 1989 was the result of a neat congruence between international and domestic influences. The casting of a 'staffie' as the *boer* dog lead in the Hollywood version of Fitzpatrick's novel in 1986 started a trend, reinforced by the *glastnost* of the early 1990s, which produced a SAKC/U record of 8,557 'staffie' registrations in 1991.[83]

The resurrection of the old emblem of white nationhood at Union was short-lived, however, and the current popularity of imported breeds (bulldog and labrador) masks an underground preference for American pitbull terriers in both the white suburbs and countryside as the last line of defence against the barbarians loosed by democracy.[84] The popularity of the pitbull has been further enhanced by the post-apartheid promotion of casino capitalism in which dog-fighting has provided another outlet, albeit illegal, for the national gambling mania.[85]

More interesting still has been the ongoing attempt to substitute the ridgeback as national breed with its purported African ancestor.[86] Although the ridgeback never regained the brief national pre-eminence it enjoyed in the late 1940s, it was adopted as the SAKU emblem in 1968, tracked the upward curve of white paranoia over the subsequent two decades and appeared on the national postage in 1991 to mark the centenary of the SAKU (see Figure 4).[87]

---

[82] See, for example, A. Hazeldene, 'The Alsatian as tracker', *SAKUG* (Sep. 1954), 182 and 'Statistics of registrations for the period 1 September 1979–31 August 1980', *SAKUG*, 44, 10 (1980), 363–66.

[83] See Figure 6 above.

[84] The most (in)famous pitbull breeding establishment in the country is the Noupoort Christian Centre, ironically located in the purported nineteenth-century Karoo heartland of the ridged Hottentot/Boer dogs.

[85] See N. Jackson, 'The pitbull: a modern history' (BA History third-year essay, University of Cape Town, 2002).

[86] S. Swart, 'Dogs and dogma: a discussion of the socio-political construction of southern African dog breeds as a window on social history', in this volume.

[87] See L. Megginson, 'Kennel Union emblem and Rhodesian Ridgeback jubilee', *SAKUG* (Nov. 1984), 612; 'First South African dog stamp', *SAKUG* (Feb. 1991), 50 and Darwin, 'On the origin', 407. The stamp issue on 21 February 1991 included the Boer horse, bonsmara cattle, dorper sheep and putterie racing pigeon alongside the ridgeback while a poultry breed, the Potchefstroom koekoek (chicken), graced the commemorative envelope.

Figure 4. RSA 21c Stamp, February 1991[88]

The ridgeback's inventors always accepted that it was the product of canine miscegenation and proudly claimed the feisty, but extinct, 'Hottentot hunting dog' as its indigenous 'ridged' ancestor, rejecting counter-claims of an Asian origin for the breed's defining whorl.[89] They did, however, regarded the admixture of European canine blood as decisive and the resulting hybrid as a superior animal to its progenitors. The promoters of the 'Kaffir dog' rejected 'Hottentot' for 'Nguni' origin and claimed that, far from being extinct, 'the original Iron Age dog' could still be found in 'isolated rural areas'.[90] Hence 'the dogs we glance at while speeding past a township or rural kraal are the very same type of dogs which accompanied Shaka or Moshwesh on their

---

[88] The image is reproduced with the kind permission of the South African Post Office. Republic of South Africa, Philatelic Services and Intersapa, *Postage Stamp Programme 1991*, 4.
[89] See footnote 68 above for this debate.
[90] See S. Hall, 'Indigenous dogs of southern Africa', *KUSA* (July 1994), 283; J. Gallant, 'Exploring the pre-history of the Rhodesian Ridgeback', *Dogs in Africa* (Nov. 1996), 14; J. Gallant, 'The Africanis: the remarkable dog of Africa', *Dogs in Africa* (Aug. 1999), 15–16 and J. Gallant, *The Story of the African Dog* (Pietermaritzburg, 2002).

royal ceremonial hunts'.[91] In a call to action echoing the SAKU's alarm over the *boer hond* ninety years earlier they warned that:

> With the comparatively recent emphasis on urbanisation and westernisation, together with the protection of dwindling game resources and the introduction of foreign breeds, these dogs are becoming increasingly endangered. They should not be allowed to disappear and it is our responsibility to ensure their survival as part of the cultural and historical African heritage.[92]

An 'African Indigenous Dog Project' was duly established in 1995, under the aegis of the SAKU and National Cultural History Museum, to initiate a breeding programme.[93] The latter focused on the *Isiqha/Sica*, dubbed the 'thornveld German Shepherd', and deemed 'the perfect dog for the Third World: eager and obedient workers, adaptable, loyal, brave, tough and economical feeders'.[94] 'Homing' and DNA testing were duly employed to reinvent this 'mangy township mongrel' as *africanis*—'the dog of Africa'—a new national breed appropriate to a post-1994 rainbow-cum-pan-African nationalism.[95]

The success of this project was crowned, as with the ridgeback under the old apartheid regime, by the africanis' appearance (alongwith the boerboel and ridgeback) on the national postage in 2003. The rehabilitation of the 'Kaffir dog', however, remains an exclusively white project with no perceptible purchase on the popular imagination of the black majority for whom dogs remain perhaps alternatively a symbol of white oppression (see below) or animals prized for their utility rather than their bloodline.[96] African dog hunting, however, continues to be stigmatised as poaching and subject to canicide in defence of stock

---

[91] S. Hall, 'The African indigenous dog project', *KUSA* (Jan. 1996), 19.

[92] S. Hall, 'Indigenous dogs of southern Africa', *KUSA* (Oct. 1994), 420. See also Gallant, 'Africanis', 15–16 and Gallant *The Story*.

[93] See 'New project on dogs in Africa', *KUSA* (June 1994), 251; N.S. Kay, 'By the way', *KUSA* (July 1994), 282–3; 'The African indigenous dog project', *SAKCG* (Apr. 1995), 167; and Gallant, 'Africanis', 15–16. The AID comprised a small group of archaezoologists, anthropologists and canine entrepreneurs.

[94] Hall, 'African indigenous dog project', 22. Character and honing by natural selection in a harsh environment were, of course, also the purported attributes of the rehabilitated *boer hond* a century earlier.

[95] See Hall, 'African indigenous dog project', 19–22 and Gallant, 'Africanis', 15–16. The Africanis Society of Southern Africa was formed in 1998 and claimed its mandate was not the development of a breed, but rather to 'conserve a 'natural dog' threatened with extinction as 'a pure African breed' by admixture with European and Eastern breeds'.

[96] Similarly the rehabilitation of the *boer hond* was the project of the English-speaking dog fancy, not nascent Afrikaner nationalism.

and game with no indication of any change in official attitudes on this front. A particular post-apartheid flashpoint has been the Natal midlands where 'White farmers have always loathed hunting dogs...[and] for the last century...have shot hunting dogs, tried to outlaw them, evicted tenants for keeping them'.[97] A shift to game farming after 1994 has speeded enclosure, and the concomitant denial of African informal access to uncultivated parts of white farms in the region, and turned dog hunting into another front in a threatened black *jacquerie*.[98]

The deep and abiding enmities animating this rural class war intrude even into liberal efforts at fictional resolution. Thus a black character in a recent novel set in the Natal midlands with a *Canis africanis*, 'Gillette', as its hero, blames the death of his four dogs on the fact that 'Some of the farmers around here are putting out poison—you know they hate our dogs'.[99] This is confirmed when one of the white farmers, Henry Montgomery, publicly condemns 'Kaffir dogs' as 'Good-for-nothing mongrels. Look at them: skinny, flea-bitten, mangy. Probably all got rabies. They should be shot like vermin'.[100] Montgomery's subsequent conversion to their merits, through grudging participation in a sanctioned hunt on a neighbour's farm and 'Gillette's' finding his missing daughter, is only marginally less implausible than the novel's suggestion that peace in the midlands can be achieved through mutual respect rather than land redistribution.

The massive growth in white dog-keeping after 1960 also created a burgeoning market for specialist services and products. Private veterinary practices flourished in the white suburbs as vaccination against previously fatal diseases prolonged the life of middle-class pets and created a demand for a host of ancillary veterinary services to treat the effects of aging and protein-rich diets. Thus of the 333 registered vets in South Africa in 1962, more than half worked in some 140 private practices clustered around the major urban centres, a third being located on the Witwatersrand alone.[101] Thirty years later the number of private veterinary practices had more than tripled to over 500 and

---

[97] J. Steinberg, *Midlands* (Johannesburg, 2002), 225.
[98] See, for example, A. Abacar *et al.*, 'Traditional hunting with dogs: A contemporary issue in KwaZulu-Natal' (MA thesis, University of Natal, Durban, 1999).
[99] A. Ferreira, *Sharp Sharp, Zulu Dog* (Bellevue, 2003), 12.
[100] Ferreira, *Sharp Sharp*, 91. Ironically, Montgomery's own pure-bred Doberman pinscher is shown to be both undisciplined and decrepit, deaf to its owner's commands when hunting and suffering from hip dysphasia.
[101] Calculated from Republic of South Africa, Bureau of Statistics, *Special Report No. 267: Census of Veterinary Services years ending 30 June 1962 and 30 June 1963*.

fully two-thirds of them depended on domestic animals for more than 75 per cent of their annual gross income, which amounted to more than R9 million by 1978.[102] The urban middle class also extended its own birth control practices to its pets—sterilisation becoming standard and a mainstay of private veterinary practice—as prophylactic and more humane alternative to canicide. Vaccination also encouraged a new affection for and anthropomorphism of dogs among the middle class. This was reflected in a home-grown popular literature on dog psychology and rapidly expanding range of specialised dog products.[103] Anthropomorphism and commodification helped consolidate the dog's place as an integral member of the white middle-class household.

The growth of a middle-class dog culture was paralleled by the ongoing containment of the underclass mongrel horde. Urban local authorities continued to employ dog licenses and 'lethal chambers' to this end, assisted by the Societies for the Prevention of Cruelty to Animals (SPCAs) established in all the major urban centres. Thus the Cape Town municipality opened its 'dogs' home' in the rabies year 1893 and the local SPCA no fewer than eleven lethal chambers during the inter-war decades, which in 1939 destroyed more than 5,000 animals by electrocution rather than the coal gas still favoured by the municipality.[104] The number of animals destroyed in the major urban centres rose so alarmingly after 1945 that the Cape Town SPCA stopped disaggregating the statistics in 1951 and publishing them altogether in 1953 (see Figure 5).

---

[102] Calculated from Republic of South Africa Department of Census and Statistics, *Report No. 06–05–01: Census of Veterinary Services, Animal Hospitals and Care Centres, 1978* and Republic of South Africa Central Statistical Services, *Report No. 06–05–02: Census of Veterinary Services, Animal Hospitals and Care Centres, 1984.*

[103] See, for example, S. Shapero, *Dog Training's Easy This Way* (Johannesburg, 1964); J.K. Lowson, *Baz* (Johannesburg, 1965); S. Shapero, *Dog Training with Love* (Johannesburg, 1967); P.J. Whyte, *Who Wants a Dog?* (Cape Town, 1975); I.D. du Plessis, *Buster, Sally and Mark: The Story of Three Dogs* (Cape Town, 1978) and A. Markowitz, *This is Your Dog* (Johannesburg, 1978).

[104] Cape of Good Hope SPCA, *Annual Report*, 1939.

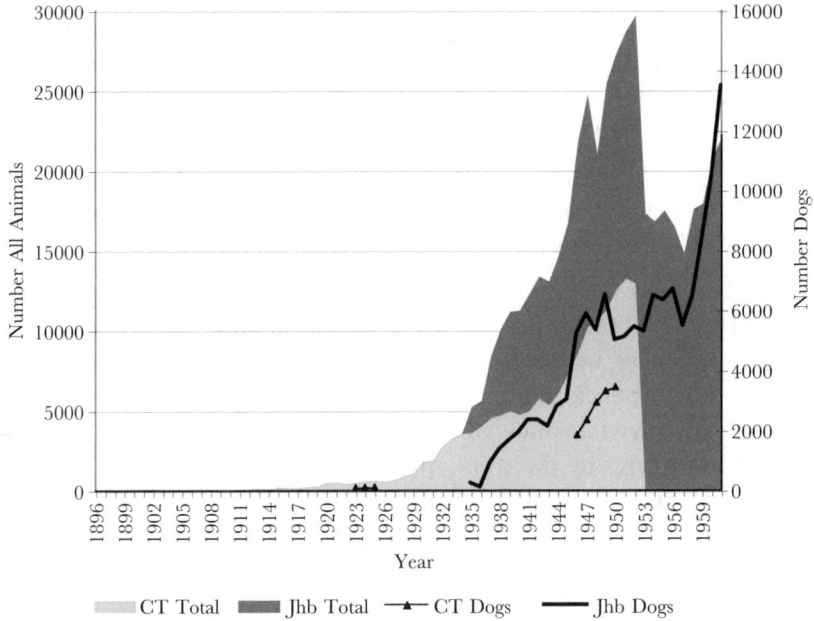

Figure 5. Animals Destroyed by Cape Town and Johannesburg SPCAs 1896–1961[105]

By the start of the twenty-first century, it was alleged that some half a million domestic animals were destroyed in South Africa annually at an estimated cost of R37.5 million and the SPCA was destroying nearly 80,000 dogs and 60,000 cats per annum nationally.[106]

Although horrified at the negligence and brutality of whites and coloureds towards their dogs, the middle class believed they could be reformed through the pedagogy of the classroom and courtroom. Africans, however, were deemed to lack reason and compassion and hence practise innate cruelty in obeisance to irrational superstition. As one dogman reminded others in the late 1940s:

---

[105] Compiled from Cape of Good Hope SPCA, *Annual Report* 1923–52 and Johannesburg SPCA, *Annual Report* 1935–61. The Cape Town SPCA data is complete as published, but that for Johannesburg only reflects the holdings available at the National Library Cape Town, omitting the periods 1902–34 and 1962–2002. The Cape Town SPCA only disaggregated dogs for the periods indicated.

[106] See 'Bodies pile up in pet cemetery', *Tabletalk* (29 Aug. 2002), 20.

> Most of us are aware of the prevalent superstition existing among natives that in order to cure a dog of its ills its ears must be cut off, or a cruel and senseless amputation must be made beneath its tongue in order to remove a so-called 'worm' which, as any enlightened person knows, is a muscular ligament necessary for the proper control and movement of the tongue. Well some scores, probably hundreds of dogs are roaming around these locations minus their ears and tongues that are lacerated by cruel natives under the mistaken notion that they are helping their dogs to recover from their illnesses.[107]

Then there was the 'charming native custom of winding wire tightly around pet's (?) jaws to prevent it stealing or barking' and the endemic neglect evidenced by 'the hordes of starving, mangy dogs in the native locations'.[108] 'Natives', the middle class agreed, 'have no thought...but for their own wretchedness' and hence 'Jim Fish' was best prevented from owning dogs by the strict application of the dog tax.[109]

The increasingly rigid segregation of urban space after 1948 also forcibly removed the 'gutter-hunting' mongrel stray to the urban periphery and quarantined it in the apartheid city's ghetto archipelago out of sight and mind of the middle class, thus reducing the need for the institutionalised urban canicide so offensive to the sensibilities of the bourgeoisie.[110] Thereafter the SPCAs and their growing number of imitators, whose earlier devotion to the defence of the urban work horse was rendered redundant by the combustion engine, undertook the management of the urban canine underclass by preaching and practising population control in the ghetto through both sterilisation and canicide. An interwar proletarian predilection for greyhound racing was also suppressed in the late 1940s by Afrikaner nationalists worried about its corrosive effects on *volk's* unity and morals.[111] The only permissible post-1945 public canine presence was utilitarian, the South African Guide-Dog Association being founded in 1953 and police patrol dogs appearing a decade later.

In the countryside, too, provincial dog taxes differentiated owned from stray/feral dogs and marked the latter for extermination. They

---

[107] G.R. Vivyan, 'Starving and wretched dogs', *SAKUG* (June 1942), 52–3.
[108] C.I. Cocker, 'Cropping dogs ears', *SAKUG* (Jan. 1947), 269.
[109] Vivyan, 'Starving and wretched dogs' and M. Vane, 'Cropping dogs ears', *SAKUG* (Dec. 1946), 241.
[110] For the quote, see 'Dogs in the home: thoroughbreds and mongrels', *SAKUG* (Aug. 1942), 79.
[111] A. Grundlingh 'Gone to the dogs: the cultural politics of gambling: rise and fall of British greyhound racing on the Witwatersrand 1932–1949', in this volume.

also imposed a disproportionate share of the cost of rural local government on blacks by specifically targeting their dogs, variously referred to as 'bastard greyhounds' (Cape) or 'Kafir hunting dogs' (Natal) with massively punitive annual licence fees and taxes in the name of game conservation.[112] So onerous were these demands that the extension of the dog tax to the new Namibian colony in 1922 pushed erstwhile black allies into open rebellion against the South African administration.[113] Rural canicide continued after Union, most vigorously in the Cape, where a host of wild canids remained proclaimed vermin with bounties on their heads until as late as the mid 1950s.[114] In the 45 years after 1910, the Cape provincial administration organised and subsidised their extermination, paying for no less than one million 'jackal' and more than 300,000 fox, wild dog and hyena proofs along with those of numerous other species.

The growth of wildlife tourism and a new ecological approach to environmental management after 1945 prompted the gradual rehabilitation of predators and abolition of official Cape vermin bounty in 1956, four years after the establishment of a provincial Department of Nature Conservation.[115] Farming practice, however, was much slower to change and the resurgence of rabies in Natal in the 1960s forced a resumption of the extermination of wild/feral dogs across a large swath in the south-east of the country. Dogs were also increasingly used to maintain social boundaries in post-colonial South Africa.[116]

Police dogs were first employed by the police in Natal in 1909 and a training centre established in the Transvaal in 1911.[117] Keith Shear, speculates, in 'Police dogs and state rationality in early twentieth-century South Africa', in this volume, that the dogs were used as 'trackers' in the rural areas where Africans understood their operating within

---

[112] Cape of Good Hope, Game Law Amendment Act 1908 (No. 11, 1908), Section 11 and Editorial: 'Dogs in Natal', *SAKUG* (July 1950).

[113] Union of South Africa, *Report of the Administrator on the Bondelzwarts Rising 1922* (UG30-22) and *Report of the Commission appointed to enquire into the Rebellion of the Bondelzwarts, 1923*.

[114] For Cape exceptionalism, see W. Beinart, 'The night of the jackal: sheep, pastures and predators in South Africa 1900–1930', *Past and Present*, 158 (1998), 172–206 and R. Bigalke, 'A biological survey of the Union', *South African Journal of Science*, 31 (1934), 396–401.

[115] D. Hey, *A Nature Conservationist Looks Back* (Cape Town, 1995), 74–99 and 160–75.

[116] See J.R. Lilly and M.B. Puckett, 'Social control and dogs: a sociohistorical analysis', *Crime and Delinquency*, 43 (1997), 123–47.

[117] M. de W. Dippenaar, *History* (Silverton, 1988), 41.

the idiom of witchcraft by 'sniffing out' the guilty.[118] *Spykerbekke* (nail mouthes) were first employed in an urban 'patrol' capacity only half a century later in 1962, to assist in containing a growing underclass youth rebellion of white ducktails and black nationalists and their scope of operation was expanded again in the early 1970s to include narcotics and explosives detection.[119] Over this period, the number of police dogs rose sharply from around 167 in 1960 to near more than 1,000 by the mid 1980s, in direct relation to the escalation of black rebellion against the apartheid state (see Figure 6).[120]

Figure 6. National Party Minister of Co-operation and Development, Piet Koornhoff, receives the freedom of Soweto, 15 October 1980[121]

---

[118] See Keith Shear, Police Dogs and State Rationality in Early Twentieth-Century South Africa, in this volume.

[119] Dippenaar, *History*, 297, 304–5 and 483. See also Republic of South Africa, *Prisons Department Report for the period 1963–1966* (RP71/1967), 24 for the experimental deployment of 'service dogs' trained by the police dog school in prisons particularly to control 'the gangster type of prisoner'.

[120] Compare Republic of South Africa, *Annual Report of the Commissioner of the South African Police for the year 1960* (RP19/1961), 2 and Republic of South Africa, *Annual Report of the Commissioner of the South African Police 1 July 1985 to 30 June 1986* (RP91/1987), 26. The actual number of police dogs employed in 1985–86 was 1137.

[121] Photo with kind permission of Howard Barrell. From J. Frederikse, *South Africa: A Different Kind of War* (Johannesburg, 1986), 55.

A military dog unit was also established in 1964 to assist the army in 'sniffing out' guerrillas in its escalating counter-insurgency wars against nationalist movements in the region.[122] The South African practice was replicated in its neighbouring settler states and colonies by both export and example. The police and military employed a range of existing dog breeds, but also experimented with the creation of new breeds closer to the animal's wild ancestors. Thus the police dog school experimented with Israeli Canaan dogs in the 1970s and the Roodeplaat Breeding Enterprises developed a 'wolf-dog' to track down insurgents in the 1980s.[123] The 'howling, yellow-eyed animal' was the product of a South African Defence Force experiment to improve the patrol dogs used in Angola and Namibia. The breeder observed of his first wolf-dog: 'One problem is that he doesn't like blacks because he was trained in the army—and he's become temperamental in his old age.'[124] Although bred to be *über* dogs, many of these animals suffered from an Achilles heel that embarrassed the apartheid state. They had soft paws, better suited to the tundra than the desert and they had purportedly to wear custom-designed booties.[125]

Dogs were also widely employed in defence of private property, many of them trained or even manufactured by the state security apparatus. By the 1970s the police dog school was graduating 300 animals per annum, which, together with a proliferation in private obedience training schools, produced a large pool of dogs for corporate and private security.[126] De Beers pioneered the corporate practice by deploying police dogs to patrol its Kimberley compounds in the inter-war period to detect and deter illicit diamond buying and their use was generalised to the rest of the mining industry thereafter.[127] The canine defence of white privilege and property was miniaturised to the private farm and home where breeds renown for their fierceness were kept or

---

[122] H.-R. Heitman, *South African War Machine* (Johannesburg, 1985), 38.
[123] A German geneticist, Professor Peter Geertshen, introduced Russian wolf genes into alsatians in an effort to improve the strain. Dippenaar, *History*, 626–7 and M. Soggot and E. Koch, 'A trip around the bizarre world of Apartheid's mad scientists', *Mail and Guardian*, 27 June 1997.
[124] Soggot and Koch, 'A trip'.
[125] Soggot and Koch, 'A trip'.
[126] Dippenaar, *History*, 483.
[127] H.A. Chilvers, *The Story of De Beers* (London, 1939), 38–9.

created—such as the *boerboel*—as deterrent to the real and imagined threat of black revolt and redistribution.[128]

Thus dogs, as much as people, patrolled and maintained the white cities and countryside of post-colonial South Africa, repeatedly acting as both catalysts and actors along its social frontiers. The 1976 Soweto revolt, in one recent retelling, was sparked by the killing of a police dog.[129] The first six police patrol dogs with black handlers graduated from the police dog school in 1971 and deployed to the Soweto and Jabulani police stations.[130] A witness to events five years later explained:

> A police dog kept chasing the kids until they went inside the yard of the school. And then immediately they went in, turned and then the others just grouped against the dog. The kids started stoning this dog. Some with knives were stabbing the dog.[131]

Once the dog was dead, 'everything started, and there was fire all over, and there was teargas all over that is why I say it started with a dog'. An icon of authority, the proxy of state power in the township, had been assaulted in the canicide. Similarly, in a telling court case in 1994, shortly before the first democratic elections, a white magistrate caused a storm of protest by merely fining a right-wing couple who had been accused of beating to death a black farm labourer for letting his dog mate with their bitch.[132] He merely fined the defendants a total of R2 200, payable in instalments, for assault. The couple explained that they 'did not want a kaffir dog mating with a white man's dog [a Rhodesian ridgeback]'.[133] The African National Congress (ANC) commented: 'Once again, white man's justice was dispensed in a white man's court, where a black man's life is worth less than a dog's.'[134]

Given its prominent role in the defence of white power and property, the dog became an easy metaphor for apartheid. The canine metaphor has also been employed to emphasise the rainbow nation's enduring continuities with the past. Thus Steven Paswolsky's film, *Inja* (dog), deals

---

[128] *Standard Encyclopaedia of Southern Africa*, vol. 4 (Cape Town, 1971), 55–7.
[129] E. Brink *et al.*, *It All Started With A Dog* (Johannesburg, 2001).
[130] Dippenaar, *History*, 483–4.
[131] Brink *et al.*, *It All Started With A Dog*, 58–9.
[132] http://www.anc.org.za/anc/newsbrief/1994/news0107.
[133] http://www.anc.org.za/ancdocs/pr/1994/pr0105a.html.
[134] The defendants were both members of the AWB, and uniformed members of the AWB paraded in the halls of the Vereeniging court during the trial.

with a farmer who teaches his *boerboel* puppy to hate black people and explores the tragic consequences of this as the dog reaches maturity.[135] More provocatively still, Willie Bester's sculpture *Dogs of War* equates the new with the old government for its prioritising of military over social expenditure (see Figure 7).[136]

Figure 7. Willie Bester, Dogs of War, 2001[137]

---

[135] 2002 Sundance Film Festival, *Inja* (Dog) (Steve Pasvolsky, 17 min., South Africa/Australia, 2001).

[136] For more on dogs and art in the southern African context, see Meredith Palumbo, 'The Canine Metaphor in the Visual Arts'.

[137] G. Thiel, 'Not African enough artist told', *Cape Times*, 16 Feb. 2001. Used with kind permission of *The Cape Argus*.

The work, when displayed at the parliamentary club, so offended the ANC's preference for 'decorative' art that the chief whip ordered its removal. Paswolsky and Bester's art were also merely imitating life in post-apartheid South Africa where a shockingly graphic demonstration of the dog's iconic role was provided when four white policemen 'trained their dogs' on three black Mozambican illegal immigrants in 1998. A video, made by one of the officers, showed them laughing as their dogs savaged the men. Before broadcasters got hold of the video, it was apparently popular at police parties.[138]

Paws for Thought

Social history revolutionised historical enquiry in southern Africa through enlarging its remit to include a variously constituted 'underclass'. By refracting the received wisdom about the past through this new lens—'from the bottom up'—much of the existing orthodoxy was revised or rejected. The animal turn holds a similar potential for southern African studies. The essays in this volume all argue against universalizing and essentialising histories of species, but remain preliminary reconnaissances of a vast and unexplored terrain.[139] They point out many rich and varied trails to be followed further, but also hinting at others lost or still to be explored. What might some of the latter be?

Firstly, the essays all survey and map the region's shifting canine geography from the vantage point of the settler/white middle class and there is still no social history of African hunting that would reveal the changing place and meaning of the dog in African cultures across the region.[140] Without it, the canine history of the majority of the region's population remains an ahistorical caricature culled from archaeological middens, ethnographic asides and settler diatribes onto which the shifting prejudices of the moment can be projected freely.

---

[138] See http://artthrob.co.za. Bester subsequently used the video in his 'Dogs of War' series.

[139] See for example S. McHugh, *Dog* (2004) for a recent attempt to treat the species history universally.

[140] Shear, 'Police dogs' and Tropp, 'Dogs' in this volume. Both allude to the place and social meaning of dogs in African society, but through the eyes of white observers. No comparable historical work has been attempted to the rich contemporary sociology of Abacar *et al.'s*, 'Traditional hunting', supervised by the late Ruth Edgecombe.

The second lacuna where caricature substitutes for analysis is the dog's place in Afrikaner society, for the essays in this collection are not only middle class, but also mainly urban, English-speaking in perspective—the location and language of the state and organised dog fancy in the region. Afrikaans dog culture presumably found an outlet and expression elsewhere. Albert Grundlingh and Sandra Swart's explorations of this subject hint at the creation of polite and popular dog-cultures among the Afrikaner and landed gentry urban proletariat around mid century.[141] The origin and trajectory of the *boerboel*, for example, remains still largely unknown, but suggests at an alternative, possibly rural-based canine nationalism to the English promoters of the ridgeback.[142]

Thirdly, the literary and artistic signals of the region's canine presence have barely begun to be studied systematically.[143] We have alluded above to some of their more obvious manifestations and Wendy Woodward and Meredith Palumbo consider these and others in more depth in this collection, but much remains to be explored.[144] Our readings of Fitzpatrick's novel and contemporary visual art both suggest the metaphoric power of the dog and that its pursuit in this form is a potentially rich line of enquiry, especially if it were done across class, race, language and national divides.[145]

Finally, the work of Susie-Newton King suggests the need to broaden the focus on the animal moment beyond *Canis familiaris* to include the cultural construction of all humanity's non-human consorts in the region.[146] The trajectory of the *boer* dog from pariah to totem was one followed by the colonial mongrel progeny of a host of other species in southern Africa—from horses to sheep, cattle and chickens—each with its maligned, usually 'Kaffir' or 'Boer' doppelgänger. The synchronicity

---

[141] Grundlingh, 'Gone to the dogs'.

[142] *Standard Encyclopaedia*, vol. 4, 55–7.

[143] For the social history potential of such inquiry, see, for example, S. Kaul, 'Why Selima drowns: Thomas Gray and the domestication of the imperial ideal', *PMLA*, 105 (1990), 223–2 and L. Wyett, 'The lap of luxury: lapdogs, literature and social meaning in the long eighteenth century', *Literature Interpretation Theory*, 10 (2000), 275–302.

[144] W. Woodward, 'Social subjects: dogs in southern African fiction', and Meredith Palumbo, 'The Canine Metaphor in the Visual Arts', in this volume.

[145] See for example *De Hond in de Boekenkast* (Amsterdam, 1992). Thanks to Etienne van Heerden for bringing the collection to our attention.

[146] Newton-King, 'A short paper' in this volume and L. Witz, 'The making of an animal biography: Huberta's journey into South African natural history, 1928–1932', *Kronos*, 30 (2004), 138–66.

of the cycles of rejection and rehabilitation with the rise and fall of competing nationalisms suggests the central place of the animal in the imagining, construction and maintenance of human society in the region.

Dogs are invested with human identity—both individual identity as part of a human family and domestic unit, and an identity derived from belonging to a group or community. Dogs thus serve as a *proxy*—and a blow against them therefore serves as a blow against their owners. The emotional investment people made in their dogs in smaller communities in pre-colonial and colonial society has not disappeared in hyperstratified globalised modern South Africa. Dogs of the past were fewer and hungrier, but equally integral to identity politics and practical workings of society.

AFRICANIS: THE PRE-COLONIAL DOG OF AFRICA

Tim Maggs and Judith Sealy

Yellow cur, *brak, godoyi*—many harsh words of insult and opprobrium have been poured scornfully on the head of the African dog by colonists and their descendants. Even in academic circles, African dogs have fared little better. They have most commonly been referred to as 'pariah dogs' in the literature. Typical of European observers are phrases like: '...the native fox-like breed are awful-looking creatures'[1] and 'he [i.e. the dog of Khoisan people] was an ugly creature, his body being shaped like a jackal...'.[2] Yet even these nineteenth-century gentlemen were forced to attest to virtues: '...but he was a faithful, serviceable animal of his kind'[3] and 'I have never found any others equal to them for daring or pertinacity'.[4] The lowly African dog has even found an honourable place in South African literature, for loyalty beyond the call of duty, in that excellent canine tale 'Unto Dust' by Herman Charles Bosman.[5]

Dogs and Their Ancestors

Dogs are derived from wolves, and were the earliest animal species to be domesticated. Analyses of DNA clearly indicate wolf ancestry.[6] Clutton-Brock emphasises the importance of behavioural traits in the successful domestication of the wolf, rather than other types of wild canids.[7] She points out that wolves' pack structure, and their

---

[1] C.J. Andersson, *Notes of Travel in South Africa* (London, 1875), 180.
[2] Theal quoted in J. Gallant, *The Story of the African Dog* (Pietermaritzburg, 2002), 8.
[3] Gallant, *The Story*, 8.
[4] Andersson, *Notes of Travel*, 180.
[5] From the outset, we should admit to a bias, since we are fond owners of African dogs. Tim Maggs has kept Africanis since 1985, and admired them for longer still from acquaintance in deep rural parts of South Africa.
[6] C. Vilà *et al.*, 'Multiple and ancient origins of the dog', *Science*, 276 (1997), 1687–9.
[7] J. Clutton-Brock, *A Natural History of Domesticated Mammals* (Cambridge, 1999), 49–60.

communication by means of facial expression and posture, make them particularly receptive to similar cues from humans. There have been claims for very ancient dogs, at around 100,000 years ago, but these are based solely on genetic evidence,[8] and are not widely accepted. The earliest recognizable bones of domesticated dogs (i.e. bones of a shape and size significantly different from those of wolves) appear between 15,000 and 10,000 years ago, and most specimens thus far come from the Near East.[9] These animals were physically very similar to their wolf ancestors, but tended to be smaller, with shorter muzzles, leading to some crowding of the teeth. The animals that thrived in close contact with humans must also have had particular behavioural characteristics, including sociability and willingness to submit to human authority. Domestic dogs can breed twice a year, compared with only once for wolves, and this feature may have evolved early on.[10]

African Dogs

Distributed all over Africa is a basic variety of dog, generally considered to represent an ancient form. This is a medium-sized, lightly-built animal with a long slender muzzle, usually with a short coat, frequently fawn in colour but varying from white through browns and brindle colouring to black.

Within this broad spectrum, there are some regional variations that we think are the result of isolation and a limited degree of deliberate breeding. The degree of variation among traditional dogs in Africa is, however, far less than that seen in Europe or Asia, where selective breeding has a long history and has produced highly differentiated varieties of dog such as the Great Dane and the Pekingese.

Looking at the earlier scientific literature on African dogs, particularly that covered in the classic review of Epstein,[11] one gets the impression that there are many different 'types' or 'breeds'. Many different names

---

[8] Vilà *et al.*, 'Multiple and ancient origins'.

[9] T. Dayan, 'Early domesticated dogs of the Near East', *Journal of Archaeological Science*, 21 (1994), 633–40 and S.J.M. Davis and F.R. Valla, 'Evidence for domestication of the dog 12,000 years ago in the Natufian of Israel', *Nature*, 276 (1978), 608–10.

[10] D.F. Morey, 'The early evolution of the domestic dog', *American Scientist*, 82 (1994), 336–47.

[11] H. Epstein, *The Origin of the Domestic Animals of Africa*, vol. 1 (New York, 1971), 3–184.

are recorded, both those used by African communities and terms introduced from other continents. Much of the work on which these divisions were based was done in the early part of the twentieth century, at a time when taxonomy was much concerned with 'types' and 'races'. This approach to classifying biological diversity sought to identify pure 'types', on the basis of physical appearance, and to assign specimens to these 'types'. It did not consider variation within 'types' and specimens that did not fit neatly into a defined 'type' were considered to be cross-breeds. This approach to biology has long been recognised as fundamentally flawed; today biologists assess variability in the light of the range of genetic make-up of organisms in a breeding population. Some of the more recent publications on African dogs appear, however, still to be influenced by older 'typist' approaches.[12] By contrast, we take the view that, at least in southern Africa, the pre-colonial dog population was essentially one, albeit large and diverse, gene pool.

We make this argument because most homesteads in rural African communities do not have the facilities for effective segregation of bitches on heat. The structure of the buildings and the ways in which they are used does not allow for secure confinement of dogs and, although preferred matings can be facilitated, it is almost impossible to prevent couplings that the owners may consider less desirable. Gallant notes that bitches normally choose their mate(s) themselves, rather than the owners choosing for them.[13] The old African reserves today are unfenced and dogs are largely free to roam at will. We infer that these limitations applied also in pre-colonial societies, where homesteads were constructed in very similar fashion.

It is, therefore, impossible for pure 'breeds' of dogs, as understood by Western dog-breeders, to exist in rural black southern Africa. We believe that the variation seen in rural areas today and in the past is the result of a diverse gene pool that most often yields medium-sized, short-haired etc. dogs, as described above, but can produce a range of animals of different appearance around this norm. Rather than 'breeds', the concept of a 'land race' as used by Gallant is a more appropriate one. We therefore feel that the terminology used by many previous authors needs to be critically re-examined; for example, the

---

[12] For example S. Hall, 'Indigenous domesticated dogs of southern Africa: an introduction', in R.M. Blench and K.C. MacDonald (eds.), *The Origins and Development of African Livestock: Archaeology, Genetics, Linguistics and Ethnography* (London, 2000), 302–11.

[13] Gallant, *The Story*, 103

word 'greyhound' has frequently been used to describe dogs in Africa, yet the term should probably be reserved strictly for the selectively-bred racing dogs of European origin. The term 'graioïd' as used by Gallant to denote 'a slender dog of greyhound type' is preferable.

Courser-like dogs of this general appearance are frequently depicted in ancient, classical and medieval art works, and resemble, in many respects, the africanis we discuss here. Modern breeds of dogs, such as greyhounds and whippets, were produced by selective breeding from a more diverse ancestral population. Today, in the Western world, hound breeds are stereotypically divided into sight or scent hounds, according to the primary sense used in pursuit. For example, the greyhound is a sight hound. These categories are inappropriate for africanis, which uses both senses extensively, scent dominating in the early stages of pursuit, until the prey is clearly within sight, or when the prey is an underground animal. This is in accordance with the basic, undifferentiated nature of africanis (and other ancestral land races).

Of all terms used for Africanis, the most common and most inappropriate is 'pariah'. This word is firmly entrenched in the literature to mean an outcast dog: one not attached to a particular owner or homestead. This may be true in India, where the term originated, and perhaps in Islamic communities where dogs are considered unclean; it is definitely not the case in southern Africa, as we shall see below.

In recent years, a number of people (several of them academics with a background in archaeology) have attempted to increase appreciation of, and foster interest in African dogs. This growing interest was formalised in 1998 with the founding of the 'Africanis Society of Southern Africa, for the conservation of the early domesticated dogs [sic] of southern Africa'. Its objectives are 'to promote the well-being of the early domesticated dogs of southern Africa; to develop a body of knowledge and to foster and encourage the study of these dogs; to conserve these dogs by promoting the breeding and rearing....'[14] The name 'africanis' was chosen as a neutral term, not derived from any particular African language or community. Membership remains modest, and it remains to be seen whether, in time, africanis becomes accepted by the middle-class dog-loving establishment, with its emphasis on 'breeds' and 'pedigrees'.

---

[14] Africanis Society of Southern Africa (http://www.sa-breeders.co.za/org/africanis).

Early Dogs in North and West Africa

It is likely that the first dogs entered Africa from the Middle East, whence comes the earliest evidence for dog domestication. The earliest securely identified domesticated dog in Africa is from Merimde, in the Nile delta, dated to the late 5th millennium BC. Recognition of dog bones is difficult, because of their close resemblance to those of jackals, and in only a few parts of the skeleton is it possible to differentiate clearly between dogs and jackals. The diagnostic parts are not always preserved in archaeological sites. The dates below are, therefore, minimum estimates for the antiquity of domesticated dogs. Once they had arrived in Africa, dogs spread rapidly through the Saharan region. They were probably present at the site of Kadero, near Khartoum in present-day Sudan, during the 4th millennium BC, and there are dog burials at Kerma, further north in the Sudan, in the second half of the third millennium BC.[15] At the same time, dogs are also found much further west, in the Agadez region of the central Sahara.[16] South of the Sahara, the earliest dates are considerably later: around 400 AD at several sites in Mali.[17] We should, however, heed MacDonald's warning that, because of the relative scarcity of well provenanced and researched specimens, we do not yet have 'a convincing picture of the origins of African dogs'.[18]

Even with our present incomplete picture it is clear that the earliest dogs of Egypt and the Sahara were not regarded as pariahs. They were frequently depicted in Egyptian mural art, particularly in hunting scenes where graioïds are common. Dynastic Egypt clearly had the facilities to maintain several different breeds of dog such as the tesen, saluki and, imported from Asia, the mastiff.[19] A wall painting of about 1,500 BC shows a pack of Ethiopian hounds sent to Pharaoh Totmes III and 1,200 years later another pack of specialised hounds, also from

---

[15] F. Marshall, 'The origins and spread of domestic animals in East Africa', in Blench and MacDonald, *The Origins*, 191–221.

[16] F. Paris, 'African livestock remains from Saharan mortuary contexts', in Blench and MacDonald, *The Origins*, 111–26.

[17] K.C. MacDonald and R.H. MacDonald, 'The origins and development of domesticated animals in arid West Africa', in Blench and MacDonald, *The Origins*, 127–62.

[18] K.C. MacDonald, 'The origins of African livestock: indigenous or imported?', in Blench and MacDonald, *The Origins*, 2–17.

[19] R.M. Blench, 'African minor livestock species', in Blench and MacDonald, *The Origins*, 314–38; Epstein, *The Origin*, 71 & 78.

Ethiopia, was sent to Alexander the Great.[20] The early evidence from the central Sahara is from deliberate burials of dogs, for example at Chin Tafidet, dated between 2,600 and 1,300 BC, three articulated dog skeleton of graioïd type were excavated from a cemetery with numerous burials of humans, as well as bones of cattle and sheep or goats.[21] As with the Egyptian mural art, there are widespread depictions of dogs, in association with people, hunting wild animals or herding cattle in the rock art of the Sahara. All these examples show that, far from being pariahs, dogs were widely appreciated and valued millennia ago in North Africa.

Early Dogs in Southern Africa

The earliest evidence for domesticated dogs in southern Africa consists of fragments of dog skeletons from the archaeological sites of Diamant, in Limpopo Province, dating to about 570 AD, and Bosutswe in eastern Botswana, at around 700 AD.[22] These sites were occupied by 'Iron Age' farming communities, who kept domesticated sheep and cattle, and grew sorghum, millets, various kinds of legumes and squashes. Dogs may have been present earlier, but the picture is inconclusive: we have very few bones, of any kind, preserved on Iron Age sites from the first half of the first millennium AD. Future research may yet reveal that southern African farming communities kept dogs at earlier dates.

The farming way of life in South Africa dates back only about 2,000 years, with a slightly greater time depth in countries immediately to the north. Before that time, the population of southern Africa lived entirely by hunting wild animals and gathering wild plant foods. The first farmers were an immigrant population who spread rapidly from equatorial Africa southwards, bringing with them knowledge of crop and animal farming, iron-working, settled village life and much more. This new way of life rapidly took hold in the northern and eastern parts of South Africa, where summer rainfall allowed the cultivation of sorghum and millets, the staple foods that provided the economic basis of these societies. In the Cape, with its pattern of winter rainfall, and in the

---

[20] Epstein, *The Origin*, 80.
[21] Paris, 'African livestock remains', 112.
[22] I. Plug, 'Domestic animals during the Early Iron Age in southern Africa', in G. Pwiti and R. Soper (eds.), *Aspects of African Archaeology. Papers from the 10th Congress of the Pan African Association for Prehistory and Related Studies* (Harare, 1985), 515–20.

dry western parts of South Africa, agriculture was impossible without irrigation. Pre-colonial farmers never settled in these areas.[23] In the last 2,000 years, however, some groups of people in the western parts of the country herded domesticated sheep and later cattle, although they did not grow crops. In the seventeenth and eighteenth centuries, we have written and pictorial records of Khoekhoe herders left by European visitors to the Cape. These herders were of particular interest to the colonists, as the suppliers of the sheep and cattle that furnished fresh meat to ships rounding the Cape. Although we know a certain amount about the Khoekhoe at the time of contact with Europeans, we do not yet understand the historical roots of these societies—what were herding communities at the Cape like 1,000 years ago or 1,500 years ago? These questions are the topic of active ongoing research.

Dogs in Hunter-gatherer and Pastoralist Communities

There is no evidence that the hunter-gatherer (or forager) peoples who lived in southern Africa prior to 2,000 years ago had dogs. A dog skeleton found at Cape St Francis has been dated to 800 AD, associated with a grave containing the remains of someone who was either a herder or a forager.[24] Dog bones are very rare in sites from the western parts of South Africa. The site of Die Kelders, near Gansbaai, has yielded two possible dog bones from the first half of the first millennium AD.[25] This scarcity is not altogether surprising: most animal bones in archaeological sites are food remains, and there is no evidence that dogs were eaten in these communities. Dogs that were sick or injured would have crept away to a quiet spot to die, so their bones would be unlikely to become incorporated into the archaeological deposits.

The best archaeological evidence for the presence of dogs in forager or herder sites comes from gnaw marks on other bones, where these are sufficiently common to make it unlikely that they derive from wild animals. We have large assemblages of archaeological bones that

---

[23] T.M.O'C. Maggs, 'The Iron Age sequence south of the Vaal and Pongola Rivers: some historical implications', *Journal of African History*, 21 (1980), 1–15.

[24] C.A. Chappel, 'A strandloper skeleton found at Cape St Francis', *Diastema*, 2 (1968/69), 37–9. E.A. Voigt, *Mapungubwe: An Archaeozoological Interpretation of an Iron Age Community* (Pretoria, 1983), 67.

[25] F.R. Schweitzer, 'Excavations at Die Kelders, Cape Province, South Africa: the Holocene deposits', *Annals of the South African Museum*, 78 (1979), 101–233.

represent discarded human food-waste, from archaeological sites both before and after 2,000 years ago. Gnaw marks are reported to be common at only three sites: Smitswinkel Bay Cave, on the Cape Peninsula, Kasteelberg B, on the Vredenburg Peninsula and Dunefield Midden, near Elands Bay.[26] At all three sites, there are also sizeable numbers of sheep bones, indicating that the inhabitants kept domestic stock. All three sites date between 1,500 and 500 years ago. It is interesting that at two slightly earlier sites that have also yielded important collections of sheep bones, Die Kelders and Boomplaas, gnawing does not appear to feature significantly.[27] We need to acknowledge the limits of the rather slender archaeological evidence, but we may be able to infer that dogs became an important part of herder society in the second half of the first millennium AD. By 1497, we have eyewitness accounts of the dogs owned by the inhabitants of the Western Cape. Vasco da Gama wrote that the people of St Helena Bay '…have many dogs like those of Portugal and they bark the same as they do'.[28]

Where did these dogs come from? This question is related to the issue of where herders obtained their sheep. Current hypotheses are that sheep were acquired from East African herders before the arrival of mixed ('Iron Age') farmers, or that they came from these farmers. It is, at present, not possible to distinguish clearly between these two possibilities. If, however, herders acquired dogs only in the second half of the first millennium AD, once Iron Age farmers were well established on the South African landscape, then farming communities may be a likely source.

---

[26] K. Cruz-Uribe and R.G. Klein, 'Chew marks and cut marks on animal bones from the Kasteelberg B and Dune Field Midden Later Stone Age sites, Western Cape Province, South Africa', *Journal of Archaeological Science*, 21 (1994), 35–49.

[27] H.J. Deacon, J. Deacon, M. Brooker and M.L. Wilson, 'The evidence for herding at Boomplaas Cave in the southern Cape, South Africa', *South African Archaeological Bulletin*, 33 (1978), 39–65.; R.G. Klein, 'A preliminary report on the larger mammals from the Boomplaas Stone Age Cave site, Cango Valley, Oudtshoorn District, South Africa', *South African Archaeological Bulletin*, 33 (1978), 66–75 and Schweitzer, 'Excavations at Die Kelders'.

[28] E. Axelson, *Vasco da Gama: The Diary of his Travels through African Waters, 1497–1499* (Somerset West, 1998), 23.

Dogs in Southern African Rock Art

Another source of information about pre-colonial dogs is rock art. In southern African rock art, dogs appear only rarely, except in the southern Drakensberg region where they are more common. Isolated examples are known from Zimbabwe, Namibia and the Western Cape[29] but little can be said about their distribution as there are so few examples. In the southern Drakensberg, however, more than a dozen sites with images of dogs are known. The frequency of painted dogs here is more on a par with that of other domesticated animals such as sheep; indeed, in the Underberg area, dogs outnumber sheep by 41 to seven.[30] Even here, however, dogs comprise only 1.1 per cent of all painted images.

Rock art is notoriously difficult to date, since the pigments contain too little carbon to be readily amenable to radiocarbon dating. Paintings of domesticated sheep and cattle must, however, date to within the last 2,000 years. Images of dogs in rock art are not very helpful in establishing the antiquity of dogs in South Africa. They demonstrate, however, that pre-colonial foragers (not herders) in the Drakensberg had dogs, and the fact that they were depicted in rock paintings is significant.

Some of the images of dogs are unclear; small animals in general were often not painted very precisely. The better paintings do, however, give quite a clear picture of the type of dog familiar to the artists. It was a relatively small, lightly built animal with a deep chest—essentially a small graioïd like so many africanis. The tail describes an arc with the tip curled upwards. It is this curved tail that often appears to be the diagnostic characteristic of painted dogs.

Some authors have discussed the difficulty of separating domestic from wild dogs in paintings, as the Cape hunting dog, *Lycaon pictus*, is known to adopt this tail position in certain circumstances.[31] Woodhouse has argued that paintings of dogs with large round ears represent wild dogs, while those with pointed ears are intended to show domesticated

---

[29] W. Batiss, *The Artists of the Rocks* (Pretoria, 1948); J. Rudner and I. Rudner, *The Hunter and His Art* (Cape Town, 1970); T.M.O'C. Maggs, 'A quantitative analysis of the rock art from a sample area in the western Cape', *South African Journal of Science*, 63 (1967), 100–4 and H.C. Woodhouse, 'Dogs in the rock art of southern Africa', *South African Journal of Ethnology*, 13 (1990), 117–24.

[30] P. Vinnicombe, *People of the Eland* (Pietermaritzburg, 1976), 153.

[31] J.D. Skinner and R.H.N. Smithers, *The Mammals of the Southern African Subregion*, (Pretoria, 1990), 432.

animals.³² We find this distinction difficult to apply, and since there are few, if any images that can clearly be identified as wild dogs, we are inclined to interpret most of the images as those of domestic dogs. Some depictions previously labelled 'dogs' may not be dogs at all: the engraving of a 'hunting dog' from Klipfontein, near Kimberley has a long slender neck and a buck-like head, and is in our opinion at least as likely to be a small antelope.³³

Within the painted panels, animals that are unequivocally dogs are frequently shown in close association with humans and groups of humans, and some scenes afford insight into the relationships between artists and dogs. Some paintings depict dogs accompanying men or women; some have a hunting theme, with dogs shown in pursuit of eland,³⁴ while there are also examples of humans and dogs attacking baboons.³⁵

Whilst a literal interpretation can be applied to some of the panels just mentioned, others can be understood only in terms of the artists' belief systems. Several panels incorporate painted elements related to supernatural experiences, including human figures with animal heads walking along lines.³⁶ Two images are especially tantalising: one the dog-like creature from Diana's Vow, in Zimbabwe, embellished with non-realistic white lines like those that mark some of the human figures in the panel, and tusks.³⁷ The other is the canine image on the 'Linton panel', from the Maclear District of the Eastern Cape (now in Iziko Museums of Cape Town).³⁸ This has superimposed white spots that also appear on an adjacent human figure, and that fringe a red line meandering between the nearby images, linking them together. David Lewis-Williams has argued that red lines fringed with white dots, a recurring feature in Drakensberg rock art, depict the spiritual potency that was activated in San medicine dances.³⁹ Medicine men harnessed

---

³² Woodhouse, 'Dogs in the rock art', 118–9.
³³ M. Wilman, *The Rock Engravings of Griqualand and Bechuanaland, South Africa* (Cape Town, 1968), fig. 41.
³⁴ Vinnicombe, *People of the Eland*, 89; H.C. Woodhouse, *The Bushman Art of Southern Africa* (Cape Town, 1979) and Woodhouse, 'Dogs in the rock art', 121–2.
³⁵ Vinnicombe, *People of the Eland*, 227.
³⁶ Vinnicombe, *People of the Eland*, 71 and N. Lee and H.C. Woodhouse, *Art on the Rocks of Southern Africa* (Cape Town, 1970), 62.
³⁷ P. Garlake, *The Hunter's Vision: The Prehistoric Art of Zimbabwe* (London and Harare, 1995), plate 35 and Woodhouse, 'Dogs in the rock art' fig. 16.
³⁸ Voigt, *Mapungubwe*, plate 6.26.
³⁹ J.D. Lewis-Williams, 'The thin red line: southern San notions and rock paintings of supernatural potency', *South African Archaeological Bulletin*, 36 (1981), 5–13.

this potency to cure the sick, influence the game, capture the rain animal to bring on rain, and achieve other ends. Lewis-Williams has developed a detailed interpretation of the Linton panel, arguing that it shows San shamans in trance, a state in which potency was activated or accessed. He has pointed out that the canine image is painted with two additional legs shown in white pigment, just as the large central human figure has an extra white arm. In addition, both have hairs standing on end, a feature associated with trance experience.[40] We have here a clue that canids held meaning in the complex spiritual and symbolic world of San hunters.

The paintings at Diana's Vow and on the Linton panel are undated. We cannot be certain that the canids depicted are domesticated dogs; their tails are more dog-like than jackal-like, but because animals in rock paintings are sometimes shown with non-natural features, we must be cautious. Marshall has, however, pointed out that dogs are probably the easiest domesticated animal for hunter-gatherers to adopt, since they are useful in hunting, and do not necessitate fundamental re-adjustments to the hunter-gatherer way of life (unlike, for example, the adoption of stock-herding).[41]

By the nineteenth century, dogs were involved in at least one aspect of the complex of rituals performed when a /Xam San girl reached puberty. The ceremonies were intended, in part, to harness the extraordinary potency that the girl was believed to embody at this time, and to channel this in beneficial, rather than harmful directions; desirable goals included bringing rain and promoting men's success in the hunt. To ensure good hunting by the dogs of the camp, the girl was given a piece of meat to chew from an animal that the dogs had killed. She then 'sucks off her knee's dirt; when her knee's dirt is with the meat she tells the people to catch hold for her of the dog...She spits the meat into his mouth with her saliva on it'.[42] Saliva, like other body fluids, held potency.

Another /Xam San observance involving dogs had to do with the disposal of parts of the hunted animal:

---

[40] J.D. Lewis-Williams, 'The world of man and the world of spirit: an interpretation of the Linton rock paintings', Margaret Shaw Lecture 2, South African Museum, Cape Town, 1988.
[41] Marshall, 'The origins and spread', 213.
[42] J.D. Lewis-Williams, *Believing and Seeing: Symbolic Aspects of Southern San Rock Paintings* (Academic Press, 1981), 51.

Thus my grandfather was the one who put away (in the sticks of the hut [i.e. in the framework]) the upper bones of the fore leg, and the shoulder blades, and the springbok's //khúruken; because the first finger (of our right hand) is apt to get a wound when we are shooting, if the dogs eat the springboks' //khu//khúruken, our first finger has a wound; we do not know how to manage with it, when we pull the string as we are shooting.[43]

These examples show clearly that, by the nineteenth century, dogs had already been incorporated into the web of symbolic meanings and associations of hunting, an activity with resonances that permeated San society. The implication is that foragers had had dogs for some considerable time, and attached social and cultural, as well as economic importance to them.

Dogs in the Black Farming Communities of Southern Africa

As we have seen above, dogs were incorporated into Early Iron Age communities in southern Africa by 500 AD, if not from the first appearance of such communities several centuries earlier. The faunal remains from early farming sites regularly include bones of domestic dogs, but usually in small numbers. The bones indicate mainly gracile animals with long legs and muzzles, i.e. coursers, though some individuals are more compact and robust.[44] Plug sees the difference as variation within a broad gene pool, rather than an indication of different breeds.[45] The existing evidence for the first millennium AD therefore suggests that, from their initial introduction into southern Africa, there was a range of dogs something like the range within the modern Africanis population.

Most published information on southern African dogs of more recent times stresses their use in hunting. Quin's comment about Pedi dogs: 'The Pedi have no specific breed of dog, but since it is used primarily for hunting, the whippet or greyhound type is favoured for obvious reasons' applies generally in the subcontinent.[46] Dogs may be treated by traditional doctors to improve their effectiveness as hunters. Among the BaVenda, dogs sometimes had medicine rubbed on their eyes and noses to make them see and smell better. A dog that sank its teeth into

---

[43] W.H.I. Bleek and L.C. Lloyd, *Specimens of Bushman Folklore* (London, 1911), 283.
[44] Plug, 'Domestic animals during the Early Iron Age', 518.
[45] Plug, personal communication 2004.
[46] P.J. Quin, *Food and Feeding Habits of the Pedi* (Johannesburg, 1959), 106.

an antelope and then let go had its teeth well rubbed with medicine to prevent this happening again.[47] Less is recorded about Africanis's skill as a herder of livestock, though this too is important.[48] We have been impressed by these dogs' herding skills. On one occasion, during an archaeological excavation in KwaZulu/Natal, cattle were threatening to walk through the site and damage the neatly-dug trenches. One of the labourers employed on the excavation, a man who lived nearby, appreciated the problem and called his dogs to keep the cattle at a distance, which they did over a period of several weeks with very few orders and no fuss. Dogs are also important as watch-dogs, guarding both home and herds. The latter function must have been particularly important before the days of guns and fences when wild animals were a serious threat to livestock. Today Africanis still serves as an alert early warning system in many rural and urban homes.

There are some regions of Africa where the dog is a regular item of peoples' diet, such as southern Nigeria, where there is a flourishing trade in dog meat. It is, however, not simply an everyday food: in most African societies in which it is consumed, dog meat is a high-status food, and is often incorporated into ritual or magical practices (see below).[49] In southern Africa, during the period for which we have a written history, dogs were not a part of peoples' diet; Casalis recorded a nineteenth-century Basotho saying that 'to eat a man and a dog is one and the same thing'.[50] The situation in the first millennium AD Early Iron Age is, however, less clear. Broken up dog bones, albeit in small quantities, are regularly found in middens on sites of this period, along with a variety of food waste. At Ndondondwane on the Thukela River,[51] and perhaps other sites, some of the dog bones show chop marks which are normally regarded as evidence of butchery. Dogs may indeed have been eaten in South Africa in the first millennium AD: a taboo against this practice perhaps started with the beginning of the Late Iron Age in the early second millennium AD—a time when many important cultural and ritual changes took place.

---

[47] H. Stayt, *The BaVenda* (London, 1931), 45.
[48] Gallant, *The Story*, 30.
[49] Blench, 'African minor livestock', 319–320.
[50] E. Casalis, *The Basutos, or Twenty-Three Years in South Africa* (Cape Town, 1965), 177.
[51] E.A. Voigt and A. von den Driesch, 'Preliminary report on the faunal assemblage from Ndondondwane, Natal', *Annals of the Natal Museum*, 26 (1984), 95–104.

The only exception to this evidence that we have come across for southern Africa is recorded from the Ovambo of northern Namibia. Here, in cases of illness or other misfortune, a dog might be sacrificed and eaten,[52] but dogs were not ordinarily consumed. Dog sacrifices do or did occur in some other regions of Africa, but in southern parts the only other instance we have been able to trace is among the Shona of Zimbabwe, where a black dog might be sacrificed in crop planting ceremonies, although people did not eat it.[53]

The rarity of dog sacrifice may, in part, relate to the generally low status accorded to dogs, in contrast with cattle or goats, which are highly valued for sacrifice. This can be seen in a range of proverbs, for example: 'a dog's tears drop inside' which means that a poor man's misfortune knows no remedy; he has no means of expressing his grief, so as to obtain help.[54] In such proverbs, the dog is a metaphor for a poor or subordinate man. Yet despite the generally low status, there are exceptions within South African folklore where the dog may be accorded greater recognition. In the story of the ruling Venda lineage, one version has it that Chief Dimbanyika went hunting dassies and followed his dog into a deep cave. A rock then fell, blocking the entrance and trapping him inside. His son, Popi, searched for him for a long time, and eventually found the dog guarding the entrance to the cave. Popi called to his father, who answered 'Take care of the dog and leave me here. I shall not return. I am quite content.' Popi thereby became chief, and moved his abode to Dzata which is regarded as the ancestral home of the ruling lineage.[55] This tale glosses an episode of apparent patricide, but the dog emerges with honour.

Dogs sometimes play a larger social role in communities further north in Africa. Dog totems and sacrifices occurred in parts of eastern, central and western Africa,[56] while Blench says that dogs are widely used to pay bride price,[57] although we do not know of any evidence of this in southern Africa. Here again, perhaps the dog's lowly status precludes this, since cattle are usually the preferred medium of exchange in such transactions. On the negative side, dogs can be suspected of

---

[52] S.S. Dornan, 'Dog sacrifice among the Bantu', *South African Journal of Science*, 30 (1933), 628–32.
[53] Dornan, 'Dog sacrifice', 631.
[54] H.P. Junod, *Bantu Heritage* (Johannesburg, 1938), 48.
[55] Stayt, *The BaVenda*, 12.
[56] Dornan, 'Dog sacrifice', 631.
[57] Blench, 'African minor livestock', 318.

being familiars of witches. Among rural Zulu, Berglund records that dogs that show particular traits, such as markedly nocturnal habits or abnormal interest in peoples' anatomy or faeces, are suspected of being implicated in witchcraft and may therefore be put down.[58]

While africanis in rural African homesteads may well receive harsher treatment and less in the way of nourishment and care than in contemporary middle-class households, s/he is by no means a pariah. Each will be recognized in the neighbourhood as belonging to a particular individual or family. Each will have a name, although this name will *not* be that of an admired or respected person. A few years ago a White admirer, thinking it was complimentary, named his favourite dog after Mangosuthu Buthelezi, an act that caused great consternation and resentment in Zulu circles.

Africanis in the Wider Canine World

As we have seen, there is a considerable range in size, shape and colouring contained within the Africanis population. An early study on a sample from Cofimvaba in the Eastern Cape recognised three 'types' with intermediate examples. Following the thinking of his time, Petters interpreted these as three distinct races rather than parts of a single but heterogeneous population as we have argued above. Petters thought that some of this variation was due to the introduction by colonists of European breeds; i.e. mongrelisation.[59] This mongrelisation issue crops up frequently and we therefore need to consider it. Africanis are still widely considered by White South Africans to be mongrels, as witness our opening sentence and the introductory essay above. It is certainly true that, today, interbreeding between Africanis and dogs of imported breeds is common, especially in peri-urban areas, and even in more remote rural parts. There is, however, enough evidence on Africanis prior to this process to give us a clear picture of its true characteristics. Part of the mongrelisation issue arises out of the 'greyhound' concept. For example, Blench sees two distinct dog populations, the 'pariah' and the 'greyhound', spreading widely from North Africa over most of the continent. He believes that 'in many places it [the greyhound]

---

[58] A.I. Berglund, *Zulu thought-patterns and symbolism* (Bloomington, 1976), 284–5.
[59] Petters in Epstein *The Origin*, 46–49.

crossed with the pariah thereby diluting its distinctive body shape'.[60] Hall goes even further than this, believing that elegant graioïds like the *iTwina* of the Eastern Cape are descended from Mediterranean or Middle Eastern gazehounds brought southwards by early Portuguese or Islamic mariners.[61] We would disagree with this suggestion, since even in the unlikely event of individual such dogs becoming part of Africanis communities, their genetic contribution would be the merest drop in the Africanis gene pool. Far more significant has been the recent crossing that has taken place with British greyhounds, which became popular in South Africa with the development of greyhound racing in the second quarter of the twentieth century.[62] Clearly, there are now many dogs, especially in KwaZulu/Natal, that combine Africanis and imported greyhound blood.

We must not, however, allow this recent interbreeding with imported dogs to deflect us from the path of investigating the real African dog. On this issue, the ever-cautious Epstein makes it clear that '...a high degree of variability characterizes the majority of African pariah dogs. This applies also to regions where an influence of modern European breeds cannot possibly be suggested' and '...in several African pariah populations a tendency towards the slender greyhound type is observed'.[63] In fact, reading Epstein's review one gains the impression that graioïds are found in virtually every part of Africa. Furthermore, Epstein readily accepts that 'greyhounds' are derived from 'pariah stock' and that no '...line of demarcation can be drawn between slender greyhound-like pariahs and coarse greyhounds proper'.[64] We would go one step further and argue that the graioïds widely observed throughout Africa are an intrinsic part of the Africanis gene pool—a claim that it should be possible to test through DNA, hopefully in the not-too-distant future.

Taking an even broader geographical perspective, we note that dog populations labelled 'pariah' are distributed not only throughout Africa but also in southern Europe, Asia, Indonesia, Australia and many Pacific islands.[65] 'Pariah' in this context is defined as a 'dog of a primitive,

---

[60] Blench, 'African minor livestock', 317.
[61] Hall, 'Indigenous domestic dogs', 304 and 308.
[62] Gallant, *The Story*, 78–81 and A. Grundlingh, 'Gone to the dogs: the cultural politics of gambling: rise and fall of British greyhound racing on the Witwatersrand, 1932–1949', in this volume.
[63] Epstein, *The Origin*, 49.
[64] Epstein, *The Origin*, 170.
[65] Epstein, *The Origin*, 12.

generalised racial type' rather than on the status of its attachment to people.[66] A few further points, drawn from Epstein's survey, are revealing. First, while the dog populations from these different regions of the world do vary somewhat, they show a number of common features. In particular, they tend to be similar in body size and they show the considerable range of variability that we have already noted among Africanis.[67] As in Africa, wherever dog-owning communities have had limited or no facilities for confining bitches in oestrus, the result is a heterogeneous population with many parallels to Africanis.[68] This also applies to some of the earliest domestic dogs on record: those from the Eurasian Mesolithic which date back to around 10,000 years ago.[69] Another insight from Epstein is that 'It should be possible...to breed from them [i.e. 'pariahs'], in a comparatively short time, nearly every Northern type of dog'.[70]

Seen in this broader light, Africanis becomes an honourable member of a canine society with branches in many parts of the world: a society, moreover, with a pedigree more ancient than the pyramids (upon which later generations gazed as they were being constructed). Furthermore, this society holds the genetic blueprints of the many distinct breeds of dog we see around the world today.

---

[66] Epstein, *The Origin*, 28.
[67] Epstein, *The Origin*, 120.
[68] Clutton-Brock, *A Natural History*, 59.
[69] Epstein, *The Origin*, 136.
[70] Menzel and Menzel in Epstein, ibid., 121.

A SHORT PAPER ABOUT A DOG

Susie Newton-King

This is the story of Claas Holder and of my attempts to understand the circumstances of his lonely death. I had discovered that he was much older than I had at first thought and his name, I was now sure, **was** Holder, not Holdoem or Ondom. I had assumed, because of the nature of the allegation made against him, that he was young. 'Bestiality...was not uncommon among adolescent males in rural Europe at the time.'[1] But Claas Holder was 69 when he died, or so it now seemed. Marooned in the Witsenberg mountains on Jacobus Mostert's farm, without family or property, alone with his young Huguenot mistress, her Khoisan servants and infant child, he had, one hot November morning in 1713, given in to his desire and sought sexual satisfaction with a dog belonging to his master. And then, discovered, he shot himself on the bank of the Breede River which ran through Mostert's land.

Claas Holder's death is mentioned only twice in the records left by the Dutch authorities at the Cape.[2] The first entry covers only one page, but it is by far the longest. The second is no more than a scratch in the muster rolls of Drakenstein district. Each year from 1710 to 1713, 'Claas Oudom' was listed as a member of a burgher infantry division led by Captain Abraham de Villiers, but his name was crossed off the list for 1713 (the list was compiled in September) and someone had pencilled the word '*dood*' in the margin.[3]

There was a sentence in the first entry which proved puzzling. The entry comprises a deposition by Maria de Péronne, 18 year old bride of Jacobus Mostert, concerning the death of her *knegt* (servant), Claas

---

[1] J. Liliequist, 'Peasants against nature: crossing the boundaries between man and animal is seventeenth- and eighteenth-century Sweden', in J.C. Fout (ed.), *Forbidden History: The State, Society and the Regulation of Sexuality in Early Modern Europe* (Chicago, 1992), 60, note 5.
[2] The Cape of Good Hope was in the possession of the Dutch East India Company from 1652 to 1795.
[3] Cape Archives (CA), 1/STB, 18/156, Muster Rolls, 1700–16.

Ondom. 'On the eleventh of this month November [1713]' wrote secretary Mahieu of Stellenbosch, who was recording De Péronne's statement in the third person, 'she had washed some linen and hung it out to dry on bushes behind the house.' She went to gather it up and as she was doing so, she saw Claas Ondom behind the bushes 'with a big dog, committing sodomitical atrocities and sins!' When asked by Ondom not to betray him, she responded ('since her husband was at the Cape and she was alone in the house with just the child'): 'I have no proof, how could I betray you, **but the dog will eat no more bread [and] as soon as my husband comes home we will shoot the dog dead**.'[4]

Why the dog? In Leviticus, third book of the Jewish *torah*, or the *Pentateuchus*, as it was known to Greek-speaking Jews and Christians in the ancient world, it is written in 20:15–16:

> The man who has intercourse with an animal will be put to death; you will kill the animal too. The woman who approaches any animal to have intercourse with it: you will kill the woman and the animal. They will be put to death; their blood will be on their own heads.[5]

Leviticus 18:23 provides some insight into why it should be necessary to kill the animal: 'You will not have intercourse with any kind of animal; you would become unclean by doing so. Nor will a woman offer herself to an animal, to have intercourse with it. This would be a violation of nature.'[6] The defiling effects of this and other sexual transgressions are further spelt out in the final verses of chapter 18:

> Do not make yourselves unclean by any of these practices, for it was by such things that the nations that I am driving out before you made themselves unclean. The country has become unclean; hence I am about to punish it for its guilt, and the country itself will vomit out its inhabitants.[7]

The sexual prohibitions in Leviticus form part of a much larger set of positive and negative commands which together make up the 'the law of holiness'. According to the anthropologist Mary Douglas, the root

---

[4] CA, 1/STB 18/156, Judicial Declarations, statement of Maria Piron, 24 Nov. 1713. Emphasis added.
[5] *The New Jerusalem Bible*, study edition (London, 1994), 160.
[6] *The New Jerusalem Bible*, 158.
[7] *The New Jerusalem Bible*, 158.

meaning of 'holy' is 'separate' or 'set apart'.[8] But Douglas has shown, in an illuminating analysis of the dietary rules in Leviticus, that, in the context of the *torah*, 'holiness' means much more than that. In Leviticus the idea of holiness is associated with perfection, completeness and order. And order requires 'that individuals shall conform to the class to which they belong... To be holy is to be whole, to be one; holiness is unity, integrity, perfection of the individual and of the kind.'[9] The opposite of holiness is confusion, the mixing of categories and the blurring of boundaries between species. 'Hybrids and other confusions are abominated.'[10] Lying, cheating and theft are likewise outlawed in this section of Leviticus because they involve deception and dissimulation, which 'are clearly contradictions between what seems and what is' (a lack of integrity, that is).[11] Therefore, Douglas contends, Leviticus 19 can move easily from an injunction against stealing and dealing deceitfully with one's neighbour to a prohibition against mating one's cattle with those of another kind or sowing 'two kinds of grain' in one field: 'You will not mate your cattle with those of another kind; you will not sow two kinds of grain in your field; you will not wear a garment made from two kinds of fabric.'[12]

The dietary laws, which at first reading appear to be without system or logic, represent, in Douglas's view, an extension of these principles. Animals, sea creatures, birds, reptiles and insects which did not conform to the typical and proper characteristics of their class (as then understood), and those, like eels, worms and reptiles, whose characteristics were indeterminate, were deemed unclean and were not to be eaten.[13]

From this perspective it is not difficult to see why sexual behaviours such as intercourse between humans and animals, or between persons of the same gender, or between persons defined as members of the same family, should be considered 'hateful things'. They involved a confusion of categories—human and animal, male and female, family and non-family—and a violation of the order of creation. Obedience

---

[8] M. Douglas, *Purity and Danger: An Analysis of Concepts of Pollution and Taboo* (London, 2000), 51–2; *New Jerusalem Bible*, 157, note 17a.
[9] Douglas, *Purity and Danger*, 54–5.
[10] Douglas, *Purity and Danger*, 54.
[11] Douglas, *Purity and Danger*, 55.
[12] *New Jerusalem Bible*, 158.
[13] Douglas, *Purity and Danger*, 51–5.

to the laws of holiness was rewarded with God's life-giving blessing. 'Speak to the Israelites', said God to Moses as he led his followers through the desert towards the promised land, 'and say: ... I, Yahweh, am your God: hence you will keep my laws and my customs. Whoever complies with them will find life in them.'[14] By contrast, disobedience to these commands brought disease, death and chaos. Deuteronomy, which, despite its position as the fifth and last book of the *torah*, was compiled in Judah by exiled Levites some 100 years before Leviticus acquired its final form,[15] contains an eloquent and terrifying recitation of the disasters which would befall those who defied God and failed to respect the order of His creation. Framed as part of a discourse given by Moses at Moab as the Israelites were poised to enter Canaan, Deuteronomy 28:1–14 describes the life-giving bounty which will accrue to those who keep Yahweh's commands:

> From you Yahweh will make a people consecrated to himself, as he has sworn to you, if you keep the commandments of Yahweh your God and follow his ways... Yahweh will make you abound in possessions: in the offspring of your body, in the yield of your cattle and in the yield of your soil, in the country which he swore to your ancestors he would give you. For you Yahweh will open his treasury of rain, the heavens, to give your country its rain at the right time, and to bless all your labours. You will make many nations your subjects, yet you will be subject to none.[16]

Those who turned away from God, ignored His laws and polluted His creation through disorderly and undiscriminating behaviour could expect multiple afflictions. Their crops would wither and their bodies and minds would become corrupted and diseased. 'Where the blessing is withdrawn and the power of the curse unleashed, there is barrenness, pestilence, confusion':[17]

> You will be accursed in the town and accursed in the countryside; accursed, your basket and your kneading trough; accursed, the offspring of your body, the yield of your soil, the young of your cattle and the increase of your flock. You will be accursed in coming home and accursed in going out. Yahweh will send a curse on you, a spell, an imprecation on all your labours until you have been destroyed and quickly perish,

---

[14] Leviticus 18:5, in *The New Jerusalem Bible*, 156.
[15] See J. Rhymer, *Atlas of the Biblical World* (New York: 1982), 104–5.
[16] Deuteronomy 28:11–12, in *The New Jerusalem Bible*, 256.
[17] Douglas, *Purity and Danger*, 51.

because of your perverse behaviour, for having deserted me. Yahweh will fasten the plague upon you, until it has exterminated you from the country you are about to enter and make your own. Yahweh will strike you down with consumption, fever, inflammation, burning fever, drought, wind-blast, mildew, and these will pursue you to your ruin. The heavens above you will be brass, the earth beneath you iron. Your country's rain Yahweh will turn into dust and sand; it will fall on you from the heavens until you perish...You will be a terrifying object-lesson to all the kingdoms of the world.[18]

Deuteronomy 27 briefly rehearses the sexual prohibitions of Leviticus 18, this time framed as curses to be uttered by the Levites when the Israelites have crossed over the Jordan into Canaan. Verse 21 reads: 'accursed be anyone who has sexual intercourse with any kind of animal.'[19] There is no mention of the fate of the animal, but an Israelite audience would have understood that both human and animal were so polluted by their illicit union that both were beyond redemption and both must die. Only death could wipe out the stain on creation and atone for the affront to God.

When Maria de Péronne warned Claas Ondom that the dog would be shot on her husband's return, was she knowingly citing Leviticus 20:15? Her parents were Huguenots, but both died while she was still a child.[20] She may have acquired a religious education in the house of

---

[18] Deuteronomy 28:16–24, in *The New Jerusalem Bible*, 257.

[19] Deuteronomy 27:21 in *The New Jerusalem Bible*, 256.

[20] Born Marie Madeleine de Péronne in 1695, her father was Louis de Péronne of Nazareth near Ghent in Flanders. De Péronne sailed for the Cape as a soldier on the *Eemland* in 1687 and in 1692 he married Marie le Fèvre, widow of the Huguenot immigrant Charles Prévot. Little is known about his background, but he was almost certainly a Calvinist, like other French immigrants from Flanders, the Calaisis and the Boulonnais. In 1694 it was alleged that he had a wife and children in the Netherlands, though he denied this. M. Boucher, *French Speakers at the Cape in the First Hundred Years of Dutch East India Company Rule: The European Background* (Pretoria, 1981), 276. Marie le Fèvre and her first husband Charles Prévot were members of the devout Calvinist congregation at Guines near Calais. Marie was 41 when she married Louis de Péronne, her third husband. Boucher, *French Speakers at the Cape*, 253. When their daughter Maria was one year old, Marie le Fèvre apparently took a fourth husband, the 24 year old Hercules du Preez. Du Preez's parents, Hercule des Prez and Cécile Datis, had emigrated from Flanders via Vlissingen on the same ship as Marie le Fèvre and her first husband Charles Prévot. Boucher, *French Speakers at the Cape*, 270 and J.G. le Roux, *Hugenote Bloed in Ons Are* (Pretoria, 1988), 22–3. Hercules du Preez subsequently married Cornelia Viljoen and their second child was born in 1704, so Marie le Fèvre must have died some years before. C.C. de Villiers and C. Pama, *Geslagsregisters van die Ou Kaapse Families* (Cape Town, 1966), 2, 728–9.

her stepfather, Hercules du Preez,[21] but it seems unlikely that she would have been introduced to the obsessive liturgical concerns of Leviticus, though the sexual prohibitions and moral regulations of Leviticus 18–20 may have been an exception. She was probably more familiar with the commandments in Exodus, including Exodus 22:18: 'Anyone who has intercourse with an animal will be put to death'. Failing this, we can at least assume that she knew the founding text of the Hebrew Bible, the story of creation in Genesis 1–3, from which the sense of order underlying the Levitical prohibitions was derived. The first chapter of the Book of Genesis explains how God deliberately created an ordered universe from the formless void. First He separated day from night and established regularity in their succession. Then He separated the waters above from the waters below and set heaven between them. Then he created earth and its vegetation, 'seed-bearing plants, and fruit trees on earth, bearing fruit with their seed inside, each corresponding to its own species.'[22] Sea creatures and birds were likewise created each 'in their own species'. On the sixth day, God made animals, lizards, snakes and insects, 'every kind of living creature in its own species': 'God made wild animals in their own species and cattle in theirs, and every creature that crawls along the earth in its own species. God saw that it was good.'

Man alone was made in God's own image, separate from and dominant over all other living creatures:

> God created man in the image of himself,
> in the image of God he created him,
> male and female he created them.[23]

These powerful lines have echoed down the ages, ultimately underpinning modern campaigns for universal human rights, the abolition of slavery and gender equality. But they also establish a clear boundary between humans and animals. 'Be fruitful, multiply, fill the earth and subdue it', said God to the newly created human beings. 'Be masters of

---

[21] In 1715 Hercules du Preez retired from his position as deacon of the church at Drakenstein. H.C.V. Leibrandt, *Precis of the Archives of the Cape of Good Hope: Requesten, 1715–1806* vol. 1 (Cape Town, 1905–6 and 1984–9), 346. For an illuminating discussion of the religious books in use in colonial households at the Cape, see J.N. Gerstner, *The Thousand Generation Covenant: Dutch Reformed Covenant Theology and Group Identity in Colonial South Africa, 1652–1814* (Leiden, 1991), chapter 6.

[22] Genesis 1:11 in *The New Jerusalem Bible*, 17.

[23] Genesis 1:27 in *The New Jerusalem Bible*, 18.

the fish of the sea, the birds of heaven and all the living creatures that move on earth.' He did establish the human diet as vegetarian[24]—meat-eating came after the flood[25]—but there was no doubt that humans were superior to animals. Only humans were animated by spirit, though their bodies, like those of animals, were made from earth.[26]

The incompatibility between humans and animals is further implied in Genesis 2:4–25, an older and more accessible version of the creation story. Man, *adam*, was living alone in the garden of Eden when God decided to find him a mate. 'It is not right that the man should be alone', said Yahweh God, 'I shall make him a helper.'[27] He made cattle, wild animals and birds from the soil of the earth and brought them to the man and the man gave them names, 'but no helper suitable for the man was found for him.' Only when God created woman from the man's own rib did the man say:

> This one at last is bone of my bones
> and flesh of my flesh!
> She is to be called Woman
> because she was taken from Man.
>
> This is why a man leaves his father and mother and becomes attached to his wife. And they become one flesh.[28]

This evocative account of 'the first marriage' in Genesis 2 became the model for 'natural' sexual relations and heterosexual marriage in the Judaeo-Christian tradition. 'Nature' in this context was not an unconscious process driven by natural selection, but a universe deliberately created and ordered by God. A 'natural' act was an act 'desired by God' and in accordance with His design, and an 'unnatural' act was 'a perversion of God's work'.[29]

---

[24] Genesis 1:29 in *The New Jerusalem Bible*, 18.
[25] Genesis 9:3–4 in *The New Jerusalem Bible*, 26.
[26] Genesis 2:7 in *The New Jerusalem Bible*, 18. J. Boswell's book, *Christianity, Social Tolerance and Homosexuality: Gay People in Western Europe from the beginning of the Christian Era to the Fourteenth Century* (Chicago, 1980), contains a complex discussion of the many ways in which nature was understood by Christian theologians from antiquity to the Middle Ages, but, in my view, the meaning given here is the most fundamental and the one which underpinned Christian hostility to homosexuality.
[27] Genesis 2:18, in *The New Jerusalem Bible*, 19.
[28] Genesis 2:24, in *The New Jerusalem Bible*, 20.
[29] J.L. Flandrin, *Sex in the Western World: The Development of Attitudes and Behaviour* (Philadelphia, 1991), 119.

Despite the common ground of both Jewish and Christian ideas concerning marriage and sexuality, there were significant differences in the way the two traditions interpreted the guidelines laid down in Genesis 1–3. Jewish moralists read the story of the first marriage in conjunction with the prior command to 'be fruitful, multiply and fill the earth...' This command took precedence 'even over marital obligations'. Procreation was a sacred duty. Thus where a marriage was barren, divorce or, alternatively, polygamy, were permissible.[30] Sexual relations 'not conducive to procreation', especially prostitution, homosexuality and bestiality, were abhorrent, but even masturbation and *coitus interruptus* were considered serious sins.[31] Within these constraints, however, sexual pleasure was quite acceptable. Indeed, many authors observe that Jewish tradition generally regarded physical love in a positive light.[32] By contrast, the Christian attitude to sexual pleasure, even within marriage, was much more ambiguous. Medieval and early modern theologians seem to have tolerated or even encouraged it insofar as it was deemed necessary for conception to take place, but in any other context it was sinful.[33] But Christian attitudes to 'fornication' evolved over many centuries. More shocking, from the viewpoint of contemporary Jewish and pagan cultures, was the ambiguity in the Christian attitude to marriage itself. This ambiguity was there from the start. Asked by a group of Pharisees whether there were any legitimate grounds for divorce, Jesus answered that there were none. Quoting Genesis 2:24, he concluded: '...what God has united, human beings must not divide...It was because you were so hard-hearted that Moses allowed you to divorce your wives, but it was not like this from the beginning.'[34] When his disciples objected that 'If that is how things are between husband and wife, it is advisable not to marry', Jesus answered cryptically:

> It is not everyone who can accept what I have said, but only those to whom it is granted. There are eunuchs born so from their mother's womb,

---

[30] E.H. Pagels, *Adam, Eve and the Serpent* (New York, 1988), 11–12.

[31] Pagels, *Adam, Eve and the Serpent*, 11 and 13. See also E. Cantarella, *Bisexuality in the Ancient World* (New Haven, 1992), 202.

[32] Flandrin, *Sex in the Western World*, 90; Cantarella, *Bisexuality in the Ancient World*, 208; Pagels, *Adam. Eve and the Serpent*, 12.

[33] Flandrin, *Sex in the Western World*, chapter 8.

[34] Matthew 19:6–8 in *The New Jerusalem Bible*, 1640. This uncompromising rejection of divorce was qualified by the phrase 'except in the case of an illicit marriage', but this phrase was apparently added by later editors of Matthew. See Pagels, *Adam, Eve and the Serpent*, 22 and *The New Jerusalem Bible*, 1641, note 19b.

there are eunuchs made so by human agency and there are eunuchs who have made themselves so for the sake of the kingdom of Heaven. Let anyone accept this who can.[35]

Eunuchs, as the theologian Elaine Pagels explains, were particularly despised by Jewish teachers 'for their sexual incapacity'.[36] Later, in the context of a debate about the resurrection of the dead, Jesus reportedly said:

> The children of this world take wives and husbands, but those who are judged worthy of a place in the other world and in the resurrection from the dead do not marry because they can no longer die, for they are the same as the angels, and being children of the resurrection, they are children of God.[37]

These passages clearly associate marriage with the corruptible things of this world and celibacy with the incorruptible Kingdom of Heaven. They were much quoted by early Christian ascetics who sought through fasting and chastity to recover 'the lost body of paradise' and to free themselves from the insistent needs of the flesh so as to focus on communion with the divine.[38] Ascetics sought through fasting and sexual renunciation to undo the sin of Adam and Eve and to imitate the angels, who have no physical bodies and who neither eat nor marry.[39] Paul's tentatively expressed preference for celibacy in 1 Corinthians 7 derived from a similar motive.[40]

These radical doctrines were modified by later generations and marriage was re-established as the norm for most Christians.[41] But Christian theology preserved an abiding mistrust of the human sexual urge and the implication that celibacy was a higher (and holier) state than marriage never completely disappeared from Christian thought.

There were thus important differences between the views held by Jews and Christians regarding the place of human sexuality in God's creation. Christian doctrine tended towards the view that although sexual desire was 'natural', that is, part of human nature, it belonged

---

[35] Matthew 19:11–12, in *The New Jerusalem Bible*, 1641.
[36] Pagels, *Adam, Eve and the Serpent*, 14–15.
[37] Luke 20:34–36, in *The New Jerusalem Bible*, 1724.
[38] T.M. Shaw, *The Burden of the Flesh: Fasting and Sexuality in Early Christianity* (Minneapolis, 1998), chapter 5.
[39] Shaw, *Burden of the Flesh*, 171–214.
[40] See 1 Corinthians 7, especially verses 28 and 32–35 in *The New Jerusalem Bible*, 1898–9 and Pagels, *Adam Eve and the Serpent*, 17.
[41] Pagels, *Adam, Eve and the Serpent*, 21–31.

only to the condition of fallen man, whereas Jews believed that it was part of God's plan for humanity from the beginning.

Despite these differences, both Jewish and Christian teachers (from the time of Paul onwards) agreed that certain expressions of sexual desire were entirely 'against nature', whether fallen or not. When sexual intercourse was directed away from its intended procreative purpose, the order of nature was violated and contamination was the result. 'You...must keep my laws and customs and not do any of these hateful things...' said Yahweh.

> For all these hateful things were done by the people who lived in the country before you, and the country became unclean. If you make it unclean, will it not vomit you out as it vomited out the nations there before you?[42]

* * *

On Saturday 4 August 1714, Nanning Willemsz (also known as Jan Willemsz) of Muiden in Het Gooi stood before a special evening session of the Court of Justice in the Castle of Good Hope. He was 51 years old and stood accused of 'sodomy, or indecency against nature'.[43] By his own admission (he had not been tortured though he may have been in custody at the Castle for some time before making his confession)[44] he had had sexual intercourse ('*zig vleeschelijk vermengt*') with a young white foal (three months old) belonging to his master, the brewer Roedolph Fredrik Steenbok.[45] Furthermore, according to the joint testimony of Sijmon Huijbert of Zevenhoven, a thatcher in the Company's employ, and Steenbok the brewer, Steenbok's slaves had seen Willemsz 'three or four times' having sex with the horses in the stable. In particular, they had described an encounter with a certain mare, the mother of the foal

---

[42] Leviticus 18:26–28, in *The New Jerusalem Bible*, 158.

[43] CA, CJ 6, Minutes of the Court of Justice, 4 August 1714.

[44] For a discussion of criminal procedure at the Cape in the eighteenth century see S. Newton-King, 'For the love of Adam: two sodomy trials at the Cape of Good Hope', *Kronos* 28 (2002), 24–29.

[45] CA, CJ 318, Documents in Criminal Cases, '*Eijsch ende conclusie*' of the Fiscal, Cornelis van Beaumont, 4 August 1714, 326. The brewery was situated on the farm Papenboom in Newlands. Steenbok had bought it on 19 Aug. 1713 from the sequestrated estate of his disgraced predecessor, Willem Menssink. See N. Penn, *Rogues, Rebels and Runaways: Eighteenth Century Cape Characters* (Cape Town, 1999), 62. Nanning Willemsz had arrived at the Cape as a soldier 'at least four years before' and had been in Steenbok's employ for 'about two months'. CA, CJ 318, Interrogatory of Nanning Willemsz, 21 July 1714.

in question. Confronted with the slaves' testimony, Willemsz had (again by his own admission, as well as the testimony of both witnesses) thrown himself at Steenbok's feet, and begged Steenbok not to bring shame or misfortune upon him. To which Steenbok replied 'pray to God for forgiveness, but not to me; I am just a sinful human being.'[46]

Nanning Willemsz's arraignment was largely the work of Sijmon Huijbert the thatcher. In June that year, Huijbert had been working on the roof of the brewery when he was drawn into a conversation between two of Steenbok's slaves. He had overheard the boy Bastiaan telling Cupido, who was helping Huijbert on the roof, how Willemsz had tied up the foal and 'fucked it'. '*Sijmon, hoor je dat wel?*' (Simon do you hear that?) said Cupido, '*dat hebben wij nu al drie of vier maalen gesien*' (We have now seen that three or four times). 'Have you seen it so many times?' asked Huijbert. 'Why didn't you tell your master?' 'We didn't dare,' said Cupido.[47]

So Huijbert took it on himself to tell the brewer. 'Monsieur Steenbok,' he said grandly, while the two men were sharing a drink, 'do you know what's going on in your place?' This was a rhetorical question, to which the brewer could only reply: 'Be kind enough to enlighten me.' 'Your slaves say that your *knegt* Jan is fucking the horses', responded Huijbert, apologising for his language when he later recounted these events to the Commissioners of the court.[48] Steenbok's response to the thatcher's revelations is not recorded, but a few days later, while he was sharing a midday meal with the thatcher and the *knegt*, an argument over wine became the pretext for the eruption of his anger. Calling Willemsz a '*verdoemde paarde pikeur*' ('a damned horse fucker'), he called his slaves into the room and confronted Willemsz with their testimony. This they willingly gave, adding details not initially divulged to Huijbert.[49] The *knegt*'s denials (supported by the display of a hernia in his lower abdomen, which, he implied, would have impeded the commission of such

---

[46] CA, CJ 318, Joint statement of Sijmon Huijbert of Zevenhoven and Roedolph Fredrik Steenbok, 10 July 1714.

[47] CA, CJ 318, Joint statement of Sijmon Huijbert of Zevenhoven and Roedolph Fredrik Steenbok, 10 July 1714.

[48] CA, CJ 318, Joint statement of Sijmon Huijbert of Zevenhoven and Roedolph Fredrik Steenbok, 10 July 1714. A *knegt* was a hired servant, usually, but not always, of European descent. Nanning Willemsz was employed as a gardener at Steenbok's brewery.

[49] CA, CJ 318, Joint statement of Sijmon Huijbert of Zevenhoven and Roedolph Fredrik Steenbok, 10 July 1714.

an act) collapsed in the face of the slaves' graphic descriptions and it was then that he fell at his master's feet.

Who eventually reported these events to the authorities and why? Not much has been written about contemporary attitudes to bestiality in the Netherlands, but a detailed study of similar transgressions among peasants in early modern Scandinavia has shown that witnesses, especially eyewitnesses, felt themselves to be morally compromised by what they had seen. It was as though the act was 'contagious':

> If not revealed, the mere viewing of an act of deadly sin such as bestiality implicated the witness morally and made him or her subject to God's condemnation...the bugger not only endangered his own soul but also, through exposure to his action, violated and injured the soul of any eyewitness.[50]

Witnesses faced a difficult decision. A lone witness might find himself accused of giving false testimony, or he might invite retaliation. Yet to keep silent was to risk his own soul, since bestiality was commonly seen as the devil's work ('crossing the boundaries between man and animal was something characteristic and inherent in the devil's nature').[51] Suspected 'buggers' were shunned, especially by their sexual partners, who feared physical defilement. Relatives and work mates avoided their company and refused to share food or drink with them.[52]

The first formal statement on the matter was made on 10 July 1714, some weeks after the confrontation between Steenbok, Willemsz and the slaves. At the request of the Fiscal, Sijmon Huijbert testified before two commissioned officers of the Court and Roedolph Steenbok confirmed what he had said.[53] Nanning Willemsz was arrested (I am not sure when) and interrogated on 21 July. The statements of the two witnesses (who, it must be emphasised, were not eye-witnesses) were read aloud to him on the day of his trial (4 August 1714) and reconfirmed by both men under oath.[54] The slaves were not called to make a formal statement, though they were, it seems, brought to the Castle to confront

---

[50] Liliequist, 'Peasants against nature', 65.
[51] Liliequist, 'Peasants against nature', 65–6.
[52] Liliequist, 'Peasants against nature', 68–9.
[53] CA, CJ 318, Statement of Sijmon Huijbert van Zevenhoven and Roedolph Fredrik Steenbok, 10 July 1714.
[54] CA, CJ 318, Statement of Sijmon Huijbert van Zevenhoven and Roedolph Fredrik Steenbok, 10 July 1714, *Recollement*, 4 Aug. 1714. This was probably the first time he had heard their evidence in full.

the prisoner, in an attempt to make him admit to having buggered the mare.[55] But Willemsz, who was facing some of the leading men in the colony, all members of the Dutch Reformed Church, persisted in his denial of everything except the single incident with the foal. He had been half drunk at the time he said, and he had not ejaculated ('*zijn zaat niet geschooten heeft*').[56] He begged for his life, saying he was willing to undergo 'all other punishments'.

In his opening statement, the Fiscal, Cornelis van Beaumont, cast doubt on the prisoner's claim that he had had no congress with the mare. His behaviour when first confronted by the slaves suggested otherwise, the Fiscal said, though he steadfastly refused to confess. He had, however, admitted to carnal congress with the foal ('*met een kleijn merrij vulle...sig vleeschelijk heeft vermengt*') and this admission was sufficient to condemn him.[57] With respect to Willemsz's claim that he had not released his semen inside the animal, Van Beaumont appealed to the authority of unnamed jurists and theologians who said that in such cases the intention counted as much the deed. He cited the sixteenth century Flemish jurist, Joost de Damhouder, who had written that 'even the attempt to commit this horrible sodomitical sin was to be punished as heavily as the deed itself'. Invoking the law of God in Leviticus 18:23, he called the lying of man with beast 'a horrible mixture' and he reminded his audience that, as laid down in Leviticus 20:15 and Exodus 22:18, God's law required that both the man and the animal should be put to death.[58] This, he said, was the practice 'in all of Christendom'.

After careful consideration of the documents before them, the assembled notables concurred. Passing sentence, the court condemned the prisoner to be taken on board one of the galliots then lying in the roadstead,[59] there to be thrust alive into a sack, to which sufficient weight would be attached, and drowned in the sea by the executioner.[60]

---

[55] CA, CJ 318, *Eisch ende conclusie* of Fiscal van Beaumont, 4 August 1714.

[56] CA, CJ 6, Minutes of the Court of Justice, 4 August 1714; CA, CJ 318, Interrogatory of Nanning Willemsz, 21 July 1714.

[57] CA, CJ 318, *Eijsch ende conclusie* of Fiscal van Beaumont, 4 August 1714.

[58] CA, CJ 318, *Eijsch ende conclusie* of Fiscal van Beaumont, 4 August 1714. 'A horrible mixture' is in fact a correct translation of the last sentence of Leviticus 18:23. It is more accurate than the phrase 'violation of nature' used by the translators of the *New Jerusalem Bible*. See Douglas, *Purity and Danger*, 54.

[59] A galliot was a small, fast, round-backed ship, used for carrying dispatches and receiving the incoming fleet.

[60] CA, CJ 6, Minutes of the Court of Justice, 4 August 1714

The two horses were also to be put to death.⁶¹ The governor, a 'very devout and quiet' man, ratified the sentence.⁶²

* * *

Are we to assume, then, that there was a direct line from Judah in the first millennium BC, via Babylon (where the exiled priests of the Jerusalem Temple patiently compiled and rearranged the ancient laws and regulations), Jerusalem and Roman Judea to the Protestant states of northern Europe in the seventeenth century and colonial Cape Town in the eighteenth? This is a difficult question because it spans such enormous variation in time and place. Nonetheless, the answer would have to be a qualified 'yes': the line was unbroken, though not direct. Christian attitudes to non-procreative sex remained consistently hostile from Roman times to the twentieth century, and sexual behaviour which transgressed what was understood as 'nature' was singled out for particular condemnation. However, as John Boswell has shown, at least with respect to homosexuality, there were periods of relative tolerance and, among a literate urban minority in the High Middle Ages, even celebration.⁶³ Despite the consistently repressive stance of Catholic moral theology, there were countervailing tendencies, even within the church itself.

As we have seen, the Christian understanding of human sexuality was absorbed from the Hebrew tradition which saw appropriate sexual relations as an integral part of a universe created and ordered by God.

The repressive laws of the Late Middle Ages remained in existence, with minor amendments, until the nineteenth century, though they were unevenly enforced. In the Netherlands, as elsewhere, the penalties inflicted on those convicted of sodomy varied from one region to another, but death by fire seems to have been the most common.⁶⁴ Greater uniformity in the treatment of sodomy in the Netherlands

---

⁶¹ CA, CJ 6, Minutes of the Court of Justice, 4 August 1714.
⁶² CA, CJ 6, Minutes of the Court of Justice, 4 August 1714. The Governor was Maurits Pasques de Chavonnes, of Bergen op Zoom in North Brabant. His great-grandfather, Joachim Pasque, Marquis de Chavonnes, had fled France after the massacre on Saint Bartholomew's Day in August 1572. *Dictionary of South African Biography* vol. 2 (Cape Town: 1972), 168–9.
⁶³ Boswell, *Christianity, Social Tolerance and Homosexuality*, especially chapters 8 and 9.
⁶⁴ D.F. Greenberg, *The Construction of Homosexuality* (Chicago, 1988), 270, note 145; T. van der Meer, *Sodoms Zaad in Nederland: Het Ontstaan van Homoseksualiteit in de VroegmoderneTtijd* (Nijmegen, 1995), 29, note 82.

was established in the sixteenth century, with the introduction of the Charles V's imperial criminal code, the *Constitutio Criminalis Carolina* in 1532. The *Carolina* stipulated that 'unchastity contrary to nature' with man, woman or beast was to be punished by burning.[65] According to the Dutch historian Theo van der Meer, 'well-known sixteenth and seventeenth century Dutch jurists, such as Philips Wielant, Joost de Damhouder, Antonius Mattheus II, Ulrik Huber, Simon van Leeuwen and Simon Groenewegen followed the *Constitutio*' and 'were unanimous in their opinion that sodomy, as the most serious of all carnal crimes, merited the death penalty.'[66] They agreed too that bestiality was 'the most horrible kind' of sodomy and felt that the animal should also be put to death. They were less sure of the status of heterosexual anal intercourse and masturbation. With the exception of Ulrik Huber, all were agreed that the appropriate penalty for sodomites was death by fire, but, in practice, strangulation '*binnenskamers*' (behind closed doors) seems to have been the penalty of choice in the early modern Netherlands.[67]

At the level of law and moral theology, then, we can trace a more or less unbroken line from the ancient Hebrews, via Byzantium, Rome and the early medieval church, to the states of post-Reformation Europe, including the Netherlands, and thence to the colonies established by the Dutch East India Company.[68] There were periods of relative tolerance, as Boswell has shown, and secular authorities took little action against sodomy until the Late Middle Ages, but Christian theology consistently maintained that sodomy was the gravest and most dangerous of all the sins of the flesh. However moral and legal continuities must not be mistaken for continuities in practice. We have already seen that, until the twelfth century, the church acted leniently towards sodomites in its own ranks. Secular law was also selectively applied. In fourteenth century Florence, for example, the laws were harsh and gave 'an impression of tight surveillance and unrelenting suppression of sodomy'.[69] But in

---

[65] Greenberg, *Construction of Homosexuality*, 303.
[66] Van der Meer, *Sodoms Zaad*, 29–30. The works of these jurists were regularly consulted by the Cape Court of Justice.
[67] Van der Meer, *Sodoms Zaad*, 30.
[68] I am not qualified to assess the effects of the Reformation upon the treatment of sodomy. But David Greenberg suggests that Calvinism inclined the Dutch authorities to a peculiarly unforgiving approach. Greenberg, *Construction of Homosexuality*, 314.
[69] M. Rocke, *Forbidden Friendships: Homosexuality and Male Culture in Renaissance Florence* (New York, 1996), 22.

practice men involved in consensual sodomy were rarely prosecuted, unless they were deemed to be 'public and notorious sodomites', or had committed rape or abused girls or boys under twelve years of age.[70] Sodomy remained extremely common in Florence throughout the sixteenth century. There could also be considerable regional variation in the type of sodomy which the authorities decided to pursue. Thus few people were prosecuted for bestiality in northern Europe (outside Sweden) in the early modern period, but many were prosecuted in southern Europe at the same time.[71] And within one region, attitudes to the prosecution of sodomy could vary markedly over time. Thus in the Netherlands, after several centuries of silence and secrecy surrounding the infrequent prosecution of sodomy, there was a sudden spate of highly publicised prosecutions and an outpouring of public concern in the fourth decade of the eighteenth century.[72]

In both the Dutch and Swedish cases, the sudden upswing in the number of sodomy prosecutions seems to have been linked to the surfacing of specific (and very different) social anxieties, which in turn were the product of circumstances specific to the regions concerned. In Sweden, as Jonas Liliequist explains, the growing number of prosecutions for bestiality seems to have been linked to deep anxieties about the nature of adult male sexuality. Herding in Sweden was traditionally the work of children, and adolescents and young boys developed a close familiarity with the animals in their care. As the Superior Court reported disapprovingly to the king in 1686, these herd-boys sometimes lived 'all summer in the woods together with the cattle, seldom or never attending church...'[73] Sexual play and experimentation were the inevitable result. In Liliequist's words:

> Boyhood in seventeenth- and eighteenth-century Sweden offered a natural and close relation with farm animals, providing the first demonstrations and knowledge of sexual functions and also opportunities for sexual experiences, and thus a psychological basis for continuing or later resumed sexual contacts with animals in adult life. This has presumably been known to most agrarian and stock-farming cultures, but the extent to which it became a problem has varied according to cultural and social conditions.[74]

---

[70] Rocke, *Forbidden Friendships*, 22–6.
[71] Liliequist, 'Peasants against nature'.
[72] T. van der Meer, 'Sodom's seed in the Netherlands: the emergence of homosexuality in the early modern period', *Journal of Homosexuality*, 34 (1997), 1–3.
[73] Liliequist, 'Peasants against nature', 78.
[74] Liliequist, 'Peasants against nature', 82–3.

When Swedish boys reached maturity, their close contact with cattle came to an abrupt end. Milking and tending the cattle in the cowshed was 'considered improper for a man'. It was strictly marked off as women's work 'and was not done by men unless necessitated by the absence of the wife or the female servants'.[75] According to Liliequist, it was this 'conflict between boyhood's close relations with farm animals and the adult males' restricted and problematic relations with cattle that constituted the roots of ambivalence and helped to make bestiality such a burning and ambiguous issue in seventeenth- and eighteenth-century Sweden. In the absence of 'a professional corporation of male herders', on whom society's fears could be projected, 'the potential bugger could be any man and former herdsboy.'[76]

In the case of the Netherlands, Van der Meer has suggested a link between popular anxieties about a perceived decline in the fortunes of the Dutch Republic in the early eighteenth century and the discovery in 1730 of 'networks of sodomites in which men of all social strata participated'. In earlier centuries, same-sex practices had (as elsewhere in Renaissance Europe) apparently been confined to encounters between persons of unequal age and social status, with the active role generally taken by the older man.[77] Same-sex relationships may have endured over a number of years, but there was no indication that the protagonists participated in a network or subculture of any sort. Now it was revealed that there were groups of men who had made what in modern terms would be called 'a lifestyle choice'—men who loved men, independently of age and status differences—and who participated as equals in same-sex practices, sometimes exchanging active and passive roles. Drawing on the ancient moral category of *luxuria*, with its associations between gluttony and unbridled sexual desire, eighteenth century Dutch moralists concluded that the emergence of these groups was symptomatic of a growing hedonism in Dutch culture.[78] Sodomy (as medieval moralists had long held) was but the most extreme consequence of the unchecked indulgence of the passions, the ultimate expression of a failure of self-restraint. Sodomites were men whose desires had become insatiable. They were habituated to excess, but anyone could succumb if they failed to keep a check on themselves:

---

[75] Liliequist, 'Peasants against nature', 80.
[76] Liliequist, 'Peasants against nature', 83.
[77] Van der Meer, *Sodoms Zaad*, 217–21 and 280–83.
[78] Van der Meer, 'Sodom's seed', 7. For a fascinating explanation of ancient theories of desire, see Shaw, *The Burden of the Flesh*.

'the seed of sodomy hid in each and everybody'.[79] The vigorous (and public) prosecution of sodomites thus served to recall the nation as a whole from its dangerous tendencies to excess and thereby restore it to favour in the sight of God.

What of Dutch colonies in other parts of the world? Is there any indication that the prosecution of 'sodomites' was informed by the social anxieties of the motherland? Or was the pattern of prosecutions linked to purely local concerns? Was there a pattern at all? With respect to the Cape, we are just beginning to find answers to these questions. There are as yet no sequential studies of sodomy prosecutions over a long period.[80] Where historians have touched on the subject they have suggested that homosexuality and bestiality were primarily a response to the scarcity of female sexual partners, especially among slaves.[81] It is also possible that the governors of a colony so closely linked to the sea (and to the hierarchical masculine milieu of sailors and mercenary soldiers) had a special concern with same-sex behaviour.

But there is another line of inquiry which might prove fruitful, especially with respect to the prosecution of bestiality at the Cape. This concerns the centuries-old Christian preoccupation (to which I have already alluded) with the uneasy relationship (some would say 'war') between 'flesh' and 'spirit' within the human person. This is a difficult and complex area upon which I am scarcely qualified to intrude, so I will tread carefully, relying for the most part on the wisdom of the scholarly editors of the *New Jerusalem Bible*. 'The primary meaning of "flesh"' it seems, is 'the matter of which the body is made.' As such, 'it is the opposite of spirit...it is the body with its senses...and especially the medium of sexual union...Thus "flesh", like *basar*, in biblical usage, emphasises the weak and perishable side of human beings...and

---

[79] Van der Meer, 'Sodom's seed', 8.

[80] H. Heese's book, *Reg en Onreg: Kaapse Regspraak in die Agtiende Eeu* (Bellville, 1994) is very helpful, but since its data is derived from the sentences of the Court of Justice, and the sentences imposed on sodomites were not always recorded in the sentence books, its list of cases is incomplete for my purposes. I am presently studying sodomy trials at the Cape from 1700 to 1770. Robert Ross has kindly given me access to his notes concerning slave trials and these do suggest that prosecutions for bestiality were more frequent in the 1730s, when the wave of Dutch sodomy trials was at its height, than in earlier decades. (Ross, personal communication, March 1999.)

[81] R. Ross, 'Sexuality and slavery at the Cape in the eighteenth century', *Collected Seminar Papers on the Societies of Southern Africa*, 22 (1976–77), N. Worden, *Slavery in Dutch South Africa* (Cambridge, 1985), 96.

their insignificance in comparison with God.'[82] The phrase 'according to the flesh' thus distinguishes 'what belongs to human nature from what belongs to grace.' In the letters of Paul, 'the "flesh" is especially the sphere in which the passions and sin operate...condemned to corruption...and to death, ...so much so that "flesh" becomes personified as a Power of evil hostile to God...and to the Spirit.'[83] The flesh can however be redeemed and made new by the gift of grace. When this happens (according to Paul) human beings achieve mastery over the flesh. 'They are still "in the flesh" as long as they remain in this world...but are not slaves to the flesh any more.'[84] In those who have faith, the human spirit—'the highest element in a human being',[85] in which reason dwells[86]—is guided and renewed by the Spirit of God and the body of the Christian is transformed from within.

The struggle for mastery of the flesh has thus been a central concern of Christian teaching from ancient times to the present. As Saint Jerome observed, if Paul himself had feared the power of the flesh, how could anyone else be confident of victory?[87] By the early eighteenth century, as we have seen, Dutch moralists were afraid that many in the Netherlands were losing the battle. How much greater, then, one may suppose, would be the fears of a tiny group of Dutch officials and freeburgher notables in an African colony where the scattered and semi-literate colonists were surrounded by untamed wilderness and outnumbered by heathen people? Was there not an even greater risk that the flesh would triumph and the colonists give themselves over entirely to the satisfaction of their bodily desires?

A careful study of the arguments of prosecutors and the language used by interrogators in colonial sodomy trials may throw some light on this question. Was there, for example, a difference in their approach when the accused was not a Christian? Did interrogators in such cases dispense with their usual efforts to elicit from the accused an admission of the gravity of his sin and the deservedness of his punishment?[88]

---

[82] *The New Jerusalem Bible*, 1877, note 7c.
[83] *The New Jerusalem Bible*, 1877, note 7c.
[84] *The New Jerusalem Bible*, 1877, note 7c.
[85] *The New Jerusalem Bible*, 1867, note 1f (Romans 1:9).
[86] But which is not the same as reason or *nous* (*The New Jerusalem Bible*, 1879, note 7m).
[87] Shaw, *Burden of the Flesh*, 98.
[88] Thus Nanning Willemsz was asked 'what was the matter with him that he dared to commit such a godless deed?' See also Van der Meer, *Sodoms Zaad*, 185–6.

This remains to be seen. In the meantime, one can note suggestive comments by educated visitors to the colony. In the 1770s Hendrik Swellengrebel, the Dutch-educated son of a former Cape governor, wrote of European settlers in the Camdebo (in the eastern Cape), who lived in 'tumble-down barns' which 'held on some farms, two or even three families and their children', that 'it may be prophesied that these people will wholly sink back into savagery.'[89] And Otto Mentzel, a German who wrote with hindsight of his experiences at the Cape in the 1730s, 'observed that "these shepherds live little better than the Hottentots" among whom they were raised, and asked rhetorically whether they would not "with the passing of time, forget that there is a God who created them?"'.[90]

Human nature, of course, was different from that of animals. Humans had been given the gift of reason. But human nature had been corrupted by the Fall. 'The whole human race perished in the person of Adam', wrote John Calvin in 1536, echoing the views of Augustine.[91] And reason itself could succumb to the promptings of a disordered nature. Saint Paul had written eloquently of the frailty of human reason in the face of the passions of the flesh. 'I am a creature of flesh and blood', he wrote, 'sold as a slave to sin. I do not understand my own behaviour. I do not act as I mean to, but I do things that I hate...where I want to do nothing but good, evil is close at my side...I see that acting on my body there is a different law which battles against the law in my mind. So I am brought to be a prisoner of that law of sin which lives inside my body.'[92] Saint Thomas Aquinas had characterised the Sodomitic vice as 'bestial'.[93] Was it not possible that, in the absence of Christian influences and in situations where human beings lived alone and close to nature, human behaviour might so approximate that of animals that the animal in the human might triumph altogether?

---

[89] CA, A 447, Hendrik Swellengrebel, *Journal eener landtogt gedaan in het noord oosten der Colonie tot in 't Kafferland en langs de zuid oostkust weder terug*, 21–4, cited in V.S. Forbes, *Pioneer Travellers in South Africa* (Cape Town, 1965), 68.

[90] O. Mentzel, *A Complete and Authentic Geographical and Topographical Description of the Famous and (all things considered) Remarkable African Cape of Good Hope* vol. 3 (Cape Town, 1944), 115–6, cited in S. Newton-King, *Masters and Servants on the Cape Eastern Frontier, 1760–1803* (Cambridge, 1999), 206.

[91] H.T. Kerr (ed.), *Calvin's Institutes: A New Compendium* (Louisville, 1989), 63.

[92] Romans 7:14–23, in *The New Jerusalem Bible*, 1876–7.

[93] Mark Jordan, *The Invention of Sodomy in Christian Theology* (Chicago, 1997), 149.

Certainly in the Swedish case it appears that contemporaries believed this was possible. Suspected buggers were often likened to 'brute beasts'.[94] They were shunned by relatives and neighbours and repudiated by their sexual partners. And the animals with which they had allegedly had intimate relations were avoided or disposed of. This aversion derived in part from the sense of sin and demonic presence with which the act of buggery was associated. But underlying it, as we have seen, was the popular (and ancient) belief that both the bugger and his animal partner had become corrupted in their very nature. Through the mixing of bodily fluids in the act of sexual intercourse, so it was believed, the animal was humanised and the human animalised.[95] Monstrous offspring could be the result, but the very act contaminated both parties irrevocably. Hence Nanning Willemsz's insistence that he had not ejaculated. Hence the necessity to execute the animal as well as the human perpetrator. And hence the murderous shame, which, I think, led Claas Holder to kill himself.

* * *

Claas Holder was born in Bremen in 1644. Initially, I thought he was a younger man. I thought his name was Claas Ondom, because that is what he is called in the statement made by Maria de Péronne, wife of Jacobus Mostert. It was she who surprised him behind the bushes with the dog and she who found his body later by the river. I looked for him everywhere: in the muster rolls of the VOC, in the inventories and *opgaafrollen* of the district of Stellenbosch, in the contracts, the judicial declarations and the notarial obligations. There was nothing in the inventories, nothing in the auction rolls, nothing in the wills. What became of his possessions when he died? Did he have any? A chest? A gun? An iron pot? A bedding roll? A silver buckle and a hat? An ABC or a book of hymns? He could write his own name.[96] Who took his things when he died? Later, when I found his name was Holder, I concluded that he had relatives at the Cape.

Claas Ondom was named in the muster rolls of freemen at the Cape. He was listed as a burgher in the district of Stellenbosch in 1711.[97] And

---

[94] Liliequist, 'Peasants against nature', 66.
[95] Liliequist, 'Peasants against nature', 70.
[96] CA, CJ 2873, Contract Book, 1698–1703, 3 March 1698.
[97] CA, VC 49, *Monsterrollen van de vrije lieden*, 1702–25.

he was there again in the rolls of the burgher infantry in Drakenstein, each year from 1710 to 1713, but in 1713 someone had crossed out his name and written *dood* in the margin.[98] And then, one day, in Hoge's *Personalia of the Germans at the Cape* I spotted the name of Claus Holder of Bremen.[99] In the list of freemen, the name Ondom changes to Houten and then to Holtum as one goes down the years. Then, in 1713, neither Ondom nor Houten nor Holtum appear (the list must have been drawn up in December). Moreover, among the civil attestations in the archive of the Court of Justice there is a statement made by one Claas Holdoem in October 1712. He tells how, some time ago (he is not specific), he had been working for Francois du Preez on the latter's farm in the Limieten Vallij (near present-day Wellington in the Cape). Francois du Preez had sent him inland over the mountains to a grazing farm on the Breede River which he was to occupy on behalf of Francois and his elder brothers, Philippe and Hercules, ahead of its rightful claimant, Claas Janse van Rensburg. He had spent many months alone on the farm, tending the sheep and cattle of Hercules and Philippe du Preez, but then Van Rensburg had arrived to claim the place and Holder had moved on. From there he had gone to work for Jacobus Mostert, 'his present master', who farmed further up the river at the Duiwelsberg, where the river breaks through the mountains between the Witsenberg and the Waaihoek range.[100] The statement was unsigned, but clearly this was the same Claas Ondom who died on Mostert's farm in 1713. From there it was but a short leap to Claus Holder of Bremen.

* * *

Claus Holder was born in Bremen in 1644. He came to the Cape as a midshipman at a wage of 10 guilders per month.[101] It is not clear when he arrived, but in 1690 he was listed for the first time as a freeman in the district of Stellenbosch. In 1693 his name was entered in

---

[98] CA, 1/STB 13/21, Muster rolls, 1700–16.

[99] J. Hoge, 'Personalia of the Germans at the Cape, 1652–1806', *Archives Year Book of South African History* (Pretoria, 1946), 170.

[100] CA, CJ 2966, Civil attestations, statement of Claas Holdoem, 25 October 1712. For Mostert's occupation of land *aan de duiwels bergh tegen de breede rivier*, see CA, RLR 1, 312 and 351 and RLR 2, 27 and 53.

[101] Hoge, *Personalia*, 170. For the wages of seamen in the employ of the Dutch East India Company, see J.R. Bruijn, F.S. Gaastra and I. Schöffer (eds.), *Dutch-Asiatic Shipping in the Seventeenth and Eighteenth Centuries* (The Hague, 1987), 210–13.

the muster rolls beneath that of Albert Holder, also of Bremen, who may have been a relative.[102] In 1696 his name appeared on a list of '*vrijknegten* (free servants) who lived with other people'.[103] But by 1698 he seems to have acquired land of his own, for in March that year he hired the soldier Jan Croese as his *bouwknegt* (farm servant) at a wage of 10 guilders per month (4½ guilders of which was to be paid into the Company's treasury).[104] In 1702 the contract was renewed for a year.[105] Thereafter Claus Holder disappears from the records, reappearing in the muster rolls as Claas Ondom in 1710. By that time, he was 66 years old and probably already a hired servant on Francois du Preez's farm in the Limieten Vallij. He was a single man, or so it seemed.[106] Some time in 1711 or 1712, he went to work for Jacobus Mostert, on the farm Duiwelsbergh in *'t Land van Waveren*. Mostert's wife, Maria de Péronne, whom Mostert had married in December 1712, was related by marriage to the brothers Philippe, Hercules and Francois du Preez. Her half-sister Elizabeth (Isabeau) Prévot had married Philippe du Preez and her mother, Maria le Fèvre, had taken his younger brother Hercules as her fourth husband after the death of Louis de Péronne in 1696.[107]

* * *

On Saturday morning, 11 November 1713, Maria de Péronne, of Huguenot parentage, but born in Stellenbosch, was gathering up the washing from the bushes behind her house when, 'to her utmost dismay' (as she later told the district secretary), she saw her *knegt*, Claas Ondom, behind the bushes with a big dog, 'committing sodomitical atrocities and sins! [the secretary added the exclamation mark]'. Seeing this, 'she turned around and went into the house.' After two hours, when Claas Ondom had not returned, she sent a child to fetch him. '*Basin*', he said,

---

[102] CA, VC 39, vol. 1; Hoge, *Personalia*, 170. Albert Holder became a burgher in Stellenbosch in 1687. In 1688 he married Adriaantje Jansen, an orphan from Rotterdam.
[103] CA, VC 39, vol. 1.
[104] CA, CJ 2873, Contract-book, 1698–1703, 3 March 1698.
[105] CA, CJ 2873, 27 October 1700. Holder agreed to pay Croese 11 guilders per month, plus board and lodging and a worsted smock.
[106] In 1698 Claas Holder's name appeared on a list of men allowed to draw their pay in Holland. Had he intended to return to Europe? H.C.V. Leibbrandt (ed.), *Precis of the Archives of the Cape of Good Hope: Letters Despatched, 1696–1708* (Cape Town, 1896), 8 March 1698.
[107] See above, note 23.

'I hope you won't betray me.' To this she replied ('since her husband was at the Cape and she was alone in the house with the child'): 'I have no proof of it; how could I betray you? But the dog will eat no more bread and as soon as my husband comes home we will shoot it.' '*Basin*', said Claas Ondom, 'the hartebeest have done much damage in the corn. I'm going to chase them away.' And he left the house with a gun. He stayed out until evening, when the dogs began barking down by the river. Accompanied by her 'Hottentot' servants, who had now returned to the house, Maria de Péronne went down to the river. Guided by the dogs, she found Claas Ondom lying dead on the river bank, covered in blood, with the rifle on his chest.[108]

---

[108] This account is taken almost verbatim from the statement of Maria de Péronne, CA, 1/STB 18/156, 24 November 1713.

WHAT THE DOGS KNEW: INTELLIGENCE AND MORALITY IN THE CAPE COLONY

Elizabeth Green Musselman

Historians find it difficult to say much with certainty about southern Africa before the mid-nineteenth century. Among those things we can know, there is this: dogs were everywhere (see Figure 8).

Figure 8. Lady Anne Barnard's sketch of a young Cape colored woman caring for two young children, a dog at her feet, c. 1796–1803[1]

---

[1] Reprinted with kind permission from the Department of Manuscripts, National Library of South Africa [MSB 68 (7055)]

Domesticated and feral dogs roamed the streets of Cape Town. People from every ethnic background kept dogs to hunt, to protect and herd their livestock, or to warn against intruders. Among the most irksome intruders were those dogs' closest relatives: jackals, wild dogs, and hyenas.

Dogs were ubiquitous and powerful communicators in Cape society. They could detect key details that human senses missed. Their tracking skills made them indispensable assistants in hunting and stock herding for virtually every subculture in colonial southern Africa. Dogs could even clarify whatever humans failed to convey to each other during their interactions. When cultures misunderstood each other, layers of human complexity could be reduced metaphorically to the apparently simple loyalty or treachery of the dog. Across a variety of Cape cultures, the dog spoke either simple, true messages or bald-faced lies. But whatever dogs said, it always merited attention.

Where canines fell in humans' moral universe differed across the cultures that populated the colonial Cape. In this brief exploratory essay, I will use stories about dogs from the late eighteenth and early nineteenth century to illustrate some of that variety. I will also make some general observations, though, that hold true across these cultures. First, southern African societies broadly valued dogs and believed they had access to special kinds of knowledge. Second, each culture distinguished between domesticated and wild canines: the former were knowledgeable and could be trusted; the latter were knowledgeable but could not be trusted. These beliefs in the power of canine knowledge and the veracity of different species typically reveal themselves as thinly veiled commentary on the knowledge and trustworthiness of fellow humans. Evaluating dog knowledge and trustworthiness teaches us a great deal not only about southern Africans' understanding of nature but also about how southern Africans understood each other. It seems that in colonial Cape cultures, among dogs and humans alike, intelligence was more widely spread than reliability, the latter bestowed through an accrual of trust within a domestic environment.

The colonial nomenclature for southern African canines, like the colonial nomenclature for human ethnicities, looks very confused to a modern eye. Some referred to the various types of jackals as foxes. In many sources, Europeans called hyenas 'wolves'. Wild dogs (Lycaon pictus)—also known as Cape hunting dogs—were easily confused with hyenas, even though the director of the South African Museum definitively distinguished the two as early as 1833.[2] Modern classification places hyenas in a separate family from canines. In this paper I refer to domesticated and wild dogs, hyenas, and jackals collectively as 'canines' because in the colonial period at least one significant group—Europeans—grouped them as such. And, as I will show, a variety of southern African cultures considered these animals exemplars of the moral ambiguity of intelligence.

The Dog Who Would Be Naturalist

Much of the early information available about dogs does not concern individuals, but we do have a few rich narratives about particular dogs—especially those who were beloved companions to published European residents and visitors. My favorite tale hails from William Burchell, an English botanist and gardener's son who explored southern Africa extensively from 1811–15. His travel narrative has become a staple read for those interested in the early years of British colonial rule. Justifiably so, for a wealth of rich detail resulted from the naturalist's keen eye for detail and the liberal Anglican's sharp (if, we might now think, imperialistic) sense of tolerance.

Burchell's journal, in both its published and unpublished versions, speaks in a tone that is almost unwaveringly earnest.[3] Then, about a quarter of the way into his journey, he shifts suddenly to a few pages of unbridled whimsicality. The inspiration for this change of mood came from a large, white dog in his company named Wantrouw. While Burchell had many companions on his four-year excursion—a fluctuating group of Africans that usually numbered about a dozen, a European companion or two for several stretches, multiple oxen, and anywhere from three to a couple dozen dogs—Wantrouw merited special attention. 'As he afterwards became, of the canine species, the greatest traveller I am acquainted with', the naturalist wrote, 'it is a tribute justly due to his memory, to record his history and exploits in

---

[2] A. Smith, '[Continuation of] an epitome of African zoology; or, a concise description of the objects of the animal kingdom inhabiting Africa, its islands and seas', *South African Quarterly Journal*, 2, 2 (1833), 81–96, on 92.

[3] Burchell's unpublished journal is housed in the Oxford Museum of Natural History's Hope and Arkell Libraries.

these pages, for the imitation of all future dogs who may hereafter accompany any scientific expedition'.[4]

Burchell gave only a sketchy physical description of his favorite dog—we learn that he was large and had wiry, white hair with a few brown spots, a bearded muzzle, and floppy ears[5]—but this tells us enough to suggest strongly that Wantrouw was not one of the Cape domesticated variety recently dubbed *Canis Africanis*; instead, Wantrouw may have been an Irish wolfhound.[6] However, what Burchell believed most deserved comment was not his dog's physique, but his character. Wantrouw, it seemed, had a penchant for natural history and thus made an ideal companion for a scientific expedition. Where Burchell's attentions turned mainly to botany, the dog's tastes (literally) ran toward zoology. 'Having already acquired some knowledge of zoology, (of botany he knew very little, and of entomology nothing at all), he sighed for an opportunity of improving himself in that science; and in the hope of becoming acquainted with the interior of many rare and nondescript animals, he offered himself to me as comparative anatomist on the expedition'. As proof of Wantrouw's precocious achievements as a comparative anatomist, Burchell offered the fact that his dog 'had prepared and cleaned a large collection of bones of rare quadrupeds, which would have been to any museum a valuable present'. The botanist bemoaned only that Wantrouw would almost certainly never publish a memoir of his intriguing life and observations.[7]

Of course, Burchell meant his readers to laugh at the idea that the dog's intense curiosity about animal innards verged anywhere remotely close to the scientific. But, cultural historians tell us, there is always more to getting the joke than a surface reading would suggest.[8] Why, in the middle of this otherwise virtually humorless investigation of Cape natural history and social mores, does this botanist decide to jest about his dog? If we try harder to get the joke, we will find much more than a cheap chuckle at a canine's expense.

---

[4] W.J. Burchell, *Travels in the Interior of Southern Africa*, vol. 1 (Cape Town, 1967), 382.

[5] Burchell, *Travels*, vol. 1, 382.

[6] For an explanation of the designation *Canis Africanis*, see J. Gallant, *The Story of the African Dog* (Pietermaritzburg, 2002), 3–4.

[7] Burchell, *Travels*, vol. 1, 383.

[8] See the title essay of R. Darnton, *The Great Cat Massacre; and Other Episodes in French Cultural History* (New York, 1984).

For one thing, it seems that Burchell may have meant the paean to Wantrouw to be taken with some seriousness. A good dog could serve as a relief from what many European travelers viewed as the unpredictable and even obnoxious behavior of one's human African companions. Much later in his narrative, Burchell lamented that he counted the expedition's dogs as his only friends, particularly at those times when he felt 'oppressed with vexation and distress at the conduct of my own men'.[9] For much of his expedition, Burchell had no European human companionship. Under those circumstances, he found that he often took more comfort in a dog of a familiar European breed than an African of his own species. In Burchell's eyes, Wantrouw deserved praise because he understood the expedition in a way that his African companions apparently did not. Wantrouw demonstrated that understanding in two ways: faithfulness and curiosity. The first sustained any expedition; the second sustained a scientific one.

So, we find that under the surface of this joke lies a deeper set of beliefs about European, African, and canine epistemology and morality. That complex of beliefs is not as simple as we might think at first. Burchell, far from being one of the more vehement bigots of his day, cultivated an optimism and open-mindedness about southern African cultures that was unusual for the nineteenth century, though certainly not unheard of. In fact, while back in Cape Town before beginning his expedition, he was pleased to find a Mozambican slave interested in his botanical work. The young man, Jak, proved a valuable plant collector in Burchell's initial, short excursions around Cape Town. 'My sable companion, witnessing the care with which I collected specimens of every thing we passed, caught at last some feelings of botanical pleasure, and good-naturedly plucked for me every showy flower he saw; and among them some which otherwise might, perhaps, have escaped my notice'.[10]

Jak's curiosity and assistance was, to his employer, both commendable and somewhat surprising. Like many liberal Britons, Burchell did not dismiss either the possibility or the supreme importance of improvement—but like many Europeans with colonial experience, he also had his doubts as to how receptive African blank slates were to enlightened

---

[9] Burchell, *Travels*, vol. 2, 243–245.
[10] Burchell, *Travels*, vol. 1, 35–36. For further discussion of African and European plant knowledge, see E. Green Musselman, 'Plant knowledge at the Cape: a study in African and European collaboration', *International Journal of African Historical Studies*, 36 (2003), 367–392.

inscription. His expedition thus became one long exercise in renewed hopes and deepening frustration. Burchell attempted to reproduce the darker thoughts that he had on this subject during the expedition:

> Draw but the picture of the solitary European, wandering, unsheltered, over the vast plains of Africa, deep in the interior eleven hundred miles; without a friend or companion from whom to seek advice, or to whom to communicate his thoughts; surrounded by savages, men of another color, of a strange and almost unintelligible language, often of hostile inclinations, or of suspicious manners, awakening every day some new anxiety for his personal safety; unprotected from the caprice of lawless tribes, whom no visible restraint withheld from making his property their own, and to whose power his life, either sleeping or waking, lay at all moments exposed; daily vexed and thwarted by those men on whom he had placed his only dependence for assistance; exhausted by corporal and mental labor without respite; and, through want to suitable food, reduced even to the lowest degree of bodily weakness; draw but this picture, and it will then present no more than the outlines of the history of the following year [1812]. Yet, in the midst of all these troubles and dangers, the highest enjoyments may be found by all who are not insensible to those charms.[11]

Burchell chiefly complains here of lacking like-minded and loyal companionship. In this context, the adventures of a faithful, curious dog could speak volumes. It offered the hope that exposure to civilization would, over time, produce many more companions in Africa. If it took thousands of years to domesticate another species, surely members of one's own could become 'civilized' more quickly under enough patient tutelage.

In the meantime, the untutored natural knowledge of the dog or the 'savage' would improve the success of many a European hunting or scientific expedition. As one early Victorian hunter put it, there were 'even situations in which the rational and civilized being will be inwardly sensible of his inferiority in some respects to the uncultivated child of nature', situations in which he would trade all his cultivation for 'the eye that ranging over the tradeless waste, or the barren mountain side, can distinguish landmarks to direct the course, where to his unpractised gaze, all around assumes one uniformly perplexing exterior'.[12]

---

[11] Burchell, *Travels*, vol. 1, 506–507.

[12] W.C. Harris, *Portraits of the Game and Wild Animals of Southern Africa, in Their Native Haunts, Delineated from Life in Their Native Haunts during a Hunting Expedition from the Cape Colony as Far as the Tropic of Capricorn, in 1834 and 1837, with Sketches of the Field Sports* (London, 1840), 39–40.

To nineteenth-century Britons, dogs modeled the keen deference needed for such a project. One naturalist considered their propensity to domestication as evidence that some animals were 'not entirely devoid of reason'.[13] According to Harriet Ritvo, who has written extensively on the place of animals in British society, dogs rivaled apes on the Victorians' scale of animal intelligence. Furthermore, dogs used their wits to moral ends: 'the relation between humanity and its dogs...epitomized the appropriate relationship between masters and subordinates. So natural was it for the dog to serve humankind that, unlike other long-domesticated animals, dogs did not need to be trained or broken to their primary allegiance'.[14]

How very similar this sounds to the words of those colonists who would attempt to break the 'savage' spirit and rebuild southern Africans as loyal Christian soldiers, farmers, and servants.[15] Which brings us to one final irony to this story: *Wantrouw* means 'distrust' in Dutch. Burchell reported that before Wantrouw came into his possession, his dog had fled the Tulbagh family who raised him. The man who found the runaway dog gave it the name Wantrouw 'on account of his apparent want of confidence in his first master'.[16] The fact of Wantrouw's distrust invoked a classic Enlightenment paradox: how would the independent-minded curiosity born of education mesh with the deference and loyalty required of 'inferiors'?[17] If the Mozambican slave Jak and all of his brothers and sisters became botanists in their own right, what help could a naturalist afford to hire? What if one day Wantrouw decided that he distrusted not only his previous master, but Burchell—or any other human? Distrust in the form of a healthy skepticism could be a virtue in the enlightened subject, but distrust could also intolerably subvert social order. These problems—suggested by the mismatch between Wantrouw's name and behavior—indicated that there would be no easy solution to the problems of subaltern epistemology.[18]

---

[13] T.W. Barlow, 'A few words on the question, do the inferior animals possess intellectual powers or not?', *Zoologist*, 3 (1845), 907; quoted in H. Ritvo, *The Animal Estate: The English and Other Creatures in the Victorian Age* (Cambridge, Mass., 1987), 17.

[14] Ritvo, *The Animal Estate*, 20, 35–39.

[15] For example, see R. Ross, *Status and Respectability in the Cape Colony 1750–1870: A Tragedy of Manners* (Cambridge, 1999), especially 114–124.

[16] Burchell, *Travels*, vol. 1, 382.

[17] For a succinct explanation of this paradox, see D. Outram, *The Enlightenment* (Cambridge, 1995).

[18] On trust and subaltern epistemology, see S. Shapin, *A Social History of Truth: Civility and Science in Seventeenth-Century England* (Chicago, 1995).

Tricksters: Wild Dogs, Hyenas and Jackals as Formidable Foes

Wantrouw's case invoked deeply consequential questions about the level of trust attainable in a society that, to a European eye, had not been fully domesticated. If we turn our attention from domesticated to the other canines that roamed the southern African countryside, we confront a different, equally fascinating question: How do you handle those who are cunning but fundamentally deceitful? To see how different colonial Cape cultures answered this question, we turn now to stories that they told about wild dogs, hyenas and jackals. Settlers, at least, sometimes lumped the three together into one pernicious, formidable menace. For example, the Abbé Nicolas de la Caille, who headed a mid-eighteenth century astronomical expedition to the Cape, complained of the wild animals that most plagued the farm country surrounding Cape Town: 'Animals which do wrong to people are wolves [hyenas], wild dogs, and foxes called Jackals'.[19]

From the colony's earliest days, though, Europeans did distinguish between domesticated and wild dogs. The latter, said Johannes de Grevenbroek, 'hunt up and down in packs of ten or twenty; when they come on sheep or calves, with the utmost savagery they promptly disembowel some and tear the udders and bellies of others with their long sharp teeth. In a moment they destroy a whole flock unless the watchful herds or trusty dogs can keep them off'.[20] Notice that Grevenbroek made a point of calling domesticated dogs 'trusty' and wild dogs 'savage'. The moral contrast could hardly be clearer, and yet he also portrayed the two kinds of dog as evenly matched in wits. A century later, Anders Sparrman expanded upon the clever-but-cruel image in his own account of wild dogs along the southern Cape coast:

> These wild dogs are some of the most pernicious beasts of prey, particularly with respect to sheep and goats, that either the African colonists or the Hottentot hordes are exposed to. They are reported not to be content merely with satisfying their hunger but even to destroy and wound everything they meet with.... It is asserted that they even have

---

[19] National Library of South Africa, MSB 297, 1 (1), part 3, E. Melck translation of N.L. de Lacaille, 'Historical journal of the voyage made to the Cape of Good Hope by the Abbé de la Caille', 1750–54.

[20] I. Schapera and B. Farrington (eds.), *The Early Cape Hottentots; Described in the Writings of Olfert Dapper (1668), Willem Ten Rhyne (1686), and Johannes Gulielmers de Grevenbroek (1695)* (Westport, 1970), 269; C.J. Skead, *Historical Mammal Incidence in the Cape Province*, vol. 1 (Cape Town, 1980), 62.

the courage to try their strength with larger dogs, as well tame as wild, and that they were once bold enough, in their turn, to pursue a sportsman who was out after them on horseback, but was unlucky enough to misfire. It has been observed that they hunt with great sagacity, acting perfectly in concert with each other; at the same time that each of them in particular does his best to overtake or meet the game till at length it falls prey to the pack.[21]

To Sparrman, wild dogs had both admirable qualities (courage, boldness, sagacity) and loathsome ones (a savage and wanton appetite). An English lieutenant named J.W.D. Moodie admired 'wolves' (hyenas) for their 'great sagacity' in concealing a fresh kill from other predators.[22]

Such language reminds us of something easily forgotten in imperial history: that Europeans and the colonists who descended from them did not predicate intelligence on morality and civilization. In their minds, not only could wild dogs combine savagery with sagacity, but so could Aztecs, South Asians, and Xhosa.[23] Though we have very little information about this, it would seem that at least some southern Africans had roughly similar beliefs. For example, Nathanael Morgan, an assistant staff surgeon in the colonial army and leader of one of the 1820 British settler groups, claimed that the Xhosa took wild dogs' howling as a sign of pending bad news.[24] The Barolong Tswana understood howling to mean a very specific type of bad news, namely the approach of a commando.[25] Wild canines were not just fearsome and unwelcome in the community; they also provided signs important for human survival—even if they did so unwittingly.

---

[21] A. Sparrman, *A Voyage to the Cape of Good Hope, towards the Antarctic Polar Circle, and Round the World: But Chiefly into the Country of the Hottentots and the Caffres, from the Year 1772, to 1776*, vol. 1 (London, 1785), 157; Skead, *Historical Mammal Incidence*, vol. 1, 67.

[22] J.W. Dunbar Moodie, *Ten Years in South Africa; including a Particular Description of the Wild Sports of That Country*, vol. 1 (London, 1835), 252; Skead, *Historical Mammal Incidence*, vol. 1, 90–91.

[23] For example, see H. Cortés, *The Dispatches of Hernando Cortés, the Conqueror of Mexico, Addressed to the Emperor Charles V, Written during the Conquest, and Containing a Narrative of Its Events* (New York, 1843); T.R. Metcalf, *Ideologies of the Raj* (Cambridge, 1994) and A. Smith, *Andrew Smith's Journal of His Expedition into the Interior of South Africa, 1834–36; An Authentic Narrative of Travels and Discoveries, the Manners and Customs of the Native Tribes, and the Physical Nature of the Country* (Cape Town, 1975).

[24] N. Morgan, '[Continuation of] an account of the Amakosae, a tribe of caffers adjoining the eastern boundary of the Cape Colony', *South African Quarterly Journal*, 2, 1 (1833), 33–48, on 41.

[25] South African Museum, Andrew Smith notebooks, Memoranda, vol. A, T.fol.1c, A. Smith, 'Notes on Tswana, Sotho....'

If the perceptiveness of wild dogs, jackals, and hyenas was not in question, this did not mean that southern African cultures found them trustworthy. Having spent a few years at the Cape in the late 1730s, O.F. Mentzel noted that the Dutch word *jakhals*, applied to several southern African fox and fox-like species, had become 'a term of abuse and means a liar or a person given to lying'.[26] But to many settlers, feral dogs and dogs that belonged to the poor (called curs) were as bad as, if not worse than, the wild canines who ravaged their livestock. Dogs had a strong association with sheep-stealing not only in the Cape Colony, but also in Britain. Many poachers and sheep-stealers in Britain used dogs called lurchers. Britain enforced strict game laws after the Napoleonic Wars, criminalizing not only the deed and the human perpetrator but also the dogs who aided them. The laws exacerbated class conflict in many parts of Britain and Ireland.[27] Around Cape Town, the proliferation of feral dogs and 'wolves' led one journalist to half-jokingly propose that the government set the former—'those lazy troops which infest our neighbourhoods'—on the latter, in the hopes that both populations would diminish in the mêlée. Elsewhere, the author made it clear that his loathing for these feral dogs was a blatant metaphor for 'vagrant' laborers, whose laziness and cowardice were no match for the wolf.[28]

'Twas worse, apparently, to know the taste of civilized behavior and reject it than to act the trickster when that was all one knew. As another journal would put it a decade later, Cape Town boasted only a few well-bred dogs, but all too many 'mongrel mangy and sneaking curs, too cowardly to attack you fairly, and too surly, and suspicious, to wag their tails, fawn, or fondle, or exhibit other signs of friendly recognition. In short, like Cape servants, they come to us, often *without a character*, and leave sans ceremonie without gratitude or obedience'.[29] Here again, the imputation of savage ingratitude adhered to both feral dog and urban African. But here again, we might easily mistake the journalist's insult

---

[26] O.F. Mentzel, *A Complete and Authentic Geographical and Topographical Description of the Famous and (All Things Considered) Remarkable African Cape of Good Hope*, vol. 3 (Cape Town, 1944), 232; Skead, *Historical Mammal Incidence*, vol. 1, 55.

[27] C.I.A. Ritchie, *The British Dog: Its History from Earliest Times* (London, 1981), 157–161.

[28] Vivian [A.J. Jardine?], 'Cape of Good Hope. Notes of the month', *Cape of Good Hope Literary Gazette*, 3, 9 (1833), 146–148.

[29] [W.L. Sammons?], 'Dogs', *Sam Sly's African Journal*, 2, 81 (1845), 2. Emphasis in original.

of cur and servant: he does not malign their intelligence, merely the ingratitude of rejecting a 'civilized' life.

Though undoubtedly Cape Africans would not have appreciated the colonists' feral metaphor, they did tend to share the sense that wild dogs were clever tricksters. For example, among the myriad stories that linguists Wilhelm Bleek and Lucy Lloyd collected from /Xam San prisoners and their families in the 1870s, some give us a picture of dogs' place in this social order.[30] A young man named ǂKasin told Bleek a tale of the lion and the jackals, in which a jackal repeatedly outsmarted the lion pestering his kin for food and water. The jackals finally rid themselves of the lion by tricking him into swallowing a scalding-hot stone. 'They said that the lion was a strong man', ǂKasin said at the close of his story. 'How was it then that he was not strong with fire? The jackals said that he had seemed to be a strong thing, but he was really only a little thing who had not been able to resist a small stone. They said that they, the jackals, are little things, but the lion has a large body. That they are like a little stone'.[31] More than in some other San tales, the lessons here seem clear: jackals were deceptive, but no fools. More importantly, the story taught that brute strength could not (always) trump the force of a sharper wit. One cannot help wondering if by the colonial period the story had come to speak of the relationship between the /Xam on the one hand and livestock-richer Khoisan, Tswana, and colonists on the other. Certainly the jackal's maneuver seems reminiscent of the clever tactics the San used to take livestock from pastoralists and settlers, who typically had more resources at their disposal.[32] Given the jackal's symbolic importance in a number of southern African cultures, we are left to wonder at the reasons that the Batlapin Tswana, Korana, and other northern neighbors of the Cape Colony preferred to make their karosses (a kind of sleeveless cloak) of jackal hide.[33] Did they simply serve a function as the largest hides available, or did jackals' cleverness give the human wearer a similar power?

---

[30] I am operating on the assumption that though these stories were recorded in the 1870s, they most likely stemmed from variants that existed in the earlier nineteenth century.

[31] J.D. Lewis-Williams (ed.), *Stories That Float from Afar: Ancestral Folklore of the San of Southern Africa* (Cape Town, 2000), 165–167.

[32] For example, see S. Newton-King, *Masters and Servants on the Cape Eastern Frontier* (Cambridge, 1999), 65–66; R. Ross, *A Concise History of South Africa* (Cambridge, 1999), 22–23.

[33] Smith, 'Notes on Tswana, Sotho....'. Also see vol. 4 of these notebooks.

In both European and African sources, hyenas endured the most abuse; tales about them tend to emphasize much more negative qualities, where stories about wild dogs and jackals painted a more positive, if still mixed, picture. Due to William Buckland's paleontological work in the 1820s, European scientific circles changed their depiction of hyenas from cowardly, solitary scavengers to well-organized social animals who hunted in packs. This, however, did not seem to change everyone's mind.[34] The English naturalist and artist William Daniell, for instance, claimed that whereas jackals could be tamed, hyenas were irrepressibly despicable.[35]

Hyenas' scavenging habits, however, made them in the end more rather than less valuable to some of their human neighbors. Among several southern African cultures, hyenas served as agents of a kind of euthanasia for the infirm. In the early seventeenth century, Edward Terry said that some of his party's guard had discovered an old man on shore. Terry later learned from a local Khoikhoi man named Cooree that 'it was their custom...thus to be rid of them'.[36] The Xhosa of the eastern Cape seem to have practiced this as well.[37] Andrew Smith, who led a particularly lengthy expedition in the 1830s around southern Africa, observed this practice among the Amatembo, and in his notes had a more sympathetic (or at least, less horrified) reading than earlier observers: 'Dying people carried out to the bush to be destroyed by Hyaenas and if die in house it is burned'.[38] One would guess that the hyenas' particular speed and cunning at locating a vulnerable meal made them the ideal—that is, most merciful—choice for this ritual. By the 1970s, the !ko San of the central Kalahari admired hyenas' clever practice of following vultures' flight toward new sources of food.[39] Though we obviously cannot extrapolate with confidence from 1970s

---

[34] P.J. Boylan, 'William Buckland (1784–1856) and the foundations of taphonomy and palaeoecology', *Archives of Natural History*, 24, 3 (1997), 361–372, on 362–364.

[35] W. Daniell, *Sketches Representing the Native Tribes, Animals, and Scenery of Southern Africa, from Drawings Made by the Late Mr. Samuel Daniell* (London, 1820), 8.

[36] R. Raven-Hart, *Before Van Riebeeck: Callers at South Africa 1488 to 1652* (Cape Town, 1967), 82; Skead, *Historical Mammal Incidence*, vol. 1, 99–100.

[37] J. Barrow, *An Account of Travels into the Interior of Southern Africa, in the Years 1797 and 1798*, vol. 1 (London, 1801), 200; L. Alberti, *De Kaffers aan de Zuidkust van Afrika, Natuur en Geschiedkundig Beschreven* (Amsterdam, 1810), 94 and Skead, *Historical Mammal Incidence*, vol. 1, 100.

[38] South African Museum. A. Smith, [Notebook title missing in original], vol. 4.

[39] H.J. Heinz, 'The Bushmen's store of scientific knowledge', in P.V. Tobias (ed.), *The Bushmen: San Hunters and Herders of Southern Africa* (Cape Town, 1978), 154.

!ko understandings to their nineteenth century attitudes, we at least have here another hint that southern Africans may have long acknowledged hyena intelligence.

Colonists acknowledged the hyena's cleverness by constructing unusually elaborate traps to hunt them. A *wolfhuis* often had two trap doors, each of which collapsed into a pit when pulled by a lever. Moodie explained the rationale: 'The hyena is exceedingly cunning and suspicious, particularly after an unsuccessful attempt to ensnare him, and it is therefore a better plan to have a door at each end of the trap which gives him more confidence to enter. I have often known them to go round and round a baited trap and not venture within the doorway'. To punish the 'captured enemy' for its 'misdeeds'—marauding their livestock and scavenging shallow graves—colonists would sometimes torture a trapped hyena with their bayonets and dogs before killing it.[40] If it was tempting to see the /Xam story about the jackal and the lion as a morality tale of size not correlating to wit, here one cannot help but think of 1830s settlers channeling some of their mounting frustrations on canine avatars. Once again, examining human relationships through the stories they tell about dogs shows us that neither Europeans nor southern Africans fully equated intelligence with morality. These cultures' frustrations with each other's 'misdeeds' and 'savagery' could be grounded in a begrudging respect for the Other's cleverness.

Conclusion

I have argued here that despite vast cultural differences otherwise, southern African societies tended to share some common beliefs about the intelligence and moral quality of dogs, both wild and domesticated. Domesticated dogs lived a symbiotic existence with a set of human cultures dependent on their skills in hunting and herding. Even canines who acted as tricksters had admirable wits and served valuable social functions for humans.

In many of the tales that southern Africans told about dogs, the storytellers also made thinly veiled comments about human behavior. Dogs lived in such cheek-by-jowl conditions with humans that they tended to take on similar social hierarchies. So we find European breeds

---

[40] Moodie, *Ten Years in South Africa*, vol. 1, 252; Skead, *Historical Mammal Incidence*, vol. 1, 101–102.

outperforming Africans as naturalists. We find feral dogs scavenging in the same spaces occupied by unemployed and underemployed workers and dispossessed Khoisan. We find hyenas executing the brutal life-and-death choices required in subsistence communities. We find jackals outsmarting their larger, more sedentary neighbors. To get the joke about Wantrouw or the jackals and the lion or the others, we must recognize that their stories served as analogues to ever-building social tensions within and beyond the Cape Colony.

Once we recognize the shallowly buried subtext of dog tales, we uncover some of the prehistory behind the colony's brutal actions toward canines after the mid-nineteenth century. Jacob Tropp, in 'Dogs, poison and the meaning of colonial intervention in the Transkei, South Africa', in this volume, has described how Cape colonial officials in the 1890s and 1900s tried to limit African men's hunting activities in the Transkei by killing their dogs. Lance van Sittert and William Beinart detail how the colony's vermin extermination programs dramatically affected jackal populations in the late nineteenth and twentieth centuries.[41] Such policies must have arisen not only as pragmatic protections of the colony's interests, but also from a recognition of dogs' symbolic importance in the social order. For the human victims of these colonial extermination policies, the symbolism would have been no less clear.

Given the paucity of traditional historical sources about southern Africans in the earlier colonial period, this paper suggests that we might try reading more closely the documentation that we do have about humans' interactions with their natural environments. Scrutinizing how southern African societies talked about predators, weather, flora, pests, and the heavens can help us understand a great deal more about human life in this under-documented period.[42] Of course, natural environments are well worth understanding for their own sake; we should not exclusively mine them for information about ourselves. But as the example of dogs makes clear, people also bury treasures about their lives within their tales about the natural world.

---

[41] L. van Sittert, 'Keeping the enemy at bay: the extermination of wild carnivora in the Cape Colony, 1889–1910', *Environmental History*, 3 (1998), 333–356 and W. Beinart, 'The night of the jackal: sheep, pastures and predators in the Cape', in this volume.

[42] For a rich example of this type of history in action, see N. Jacobs, *Environment, Power, and Injustice: A South African History* (Cambridge, 2003).

DOGS AND THE PUBLIC SPHERE: THE ORDERING OF SOCIAL SPACE IN EARLY NINETEENTH-CENTURY CAPE TOWN*

Kirsten McKenzie

During the 1820s and 1830s, the readers of Cape Town's *South African Commercial Advertiser* (*SACA*) were much discomforted by the packs of stray dogs which infested their city. The local bourgeoisie considered both the dogs and the means used to control them a threat to health and safety and a source of disorder on the streets over which they were seeking to assert the principles of rational improvement. As the Cape Colony's first independent newspaper, the *Advertiser* was selfconscious in its promotion of a particular kind of discourse, one that was based on enlightenment principles of the public sphere. The ultimate aim of the newspaper and its supporters was the establishment of representative government in the colony. This would place the destiny of the community in the hands of the 'respectable', defined in this instance as propertied men.

Dogs, and their control, played an ambiguous role in the mental map of order and disorder being drawn across the city by its respectable inhabitants. This essay traces concerns about stray dogs in the letters written to the *Advertiser* as a route towards understanding an emergent bourgeois culture in Cape Town. The concepts of social improvement and political rights articulated by the *Advertiser* were intimately connected to the control of social space and the material world. The worries over dogs, however, confirm that the colonial bourgeoisie was by no means in control of their city. The *Advertiser* is a somewhat uneasy record of bourgeois anxiety juxtaposed with bourgeois self-confidence. The ideal is constantly disrupted by the real, and the shores of the ordered world

---

* This chapter was first published in *South African Historical Journal* 48 (2003) pp. 235–51 and has been used with permission of the *SAHJ*. My thanks to Nigel Worden, who supervised the thesis for which the research in this chapter was originally conducted, and for all his continued support. Andrew Bank and Anthony Whyte kindly provided references from their own research. Kerry Ward checked archival details. Shane White and Jim Masselos pointed the way to wider concerns about dogs and racial conflict.

are continually lapped by a surrounding sea of perceived disorder. Throughout this contrast enacted within the pages of the newspaper, the physical landscape of the city is intimately connected to its moral landscape. The essay argues that dogs were a lightning rod for a whole series of contemporary concerns in colonial Cape Town. The place of dogs in the assertion of bourgeois values and the control of urban space in Cape Town needs to be understood within an emergent bourgeois emphasis on improvement in political discourse, labour relations and the physical space of the city.

In the letters written to the *Advertiser* about dogs and their control, dogs emerge as animals that are tailor-made for cultural ambiguity. They are liminal figures that cross the boundaries so central to the nineteenth-century bourgeois psyche. They disrupt the division between the home and the wider world. Dogs in early nineteenth-century Cape Town were simultaneously valued members of the respectable household and sources of dirt and disorder on the street. The division was dependent upon the dog's material location and symbolic associations.

While opinion was divided as to how to deal with stray dogs in Cape Town, there was no debate at all about the scale or existence of the problem. William Wilberforce Bird, British colonial comptroller of customs, felt that no-one in the city could be safe from 'hydrophobia' given the enormous number of dogs in the city. His influential published account of the Cape in 1822 touched on three of the key elements in bourgeois discussion of dogs in this period. He linked dogs to the dirt of the city, he drew a crucial distinction between household dogs and the strays of the street, and he symbolically associated stray dogs with their human equivalent—the disorderly underclass:

> In addition to the most extraordinary breed of diminutive lap-dogs, of which each house as a portion, whose long hair is combed and washed almost daily, numerous unowned dogs, of a larger description, roam around in packs. These animals live and grow fat on the offal of the fish market, and of the butchery; and after a nightly repose under the warm covert of the outhouses, rush tumultuously at dawn to the sea-shore, with the cry, but not the melody, of a pack of hounds. There they are gorged with the offal; and during the day, except their haunts suffer from intrusion, they are quiet...Numerous as the beggars in Europe, they are not so importune, but the whip will dismiss these, whilst the pertinency of the beggar can only be conquered by a gift.[1]

---

[1] W.W. Bird, *State of the Cape of Good Hope in 1822* (London, 1823), 162.

Dogs were well placed to be central to the respectable classes' cosmology in this period. By the second half of the nineteenth century, Harriet Ritvo has argued, the breeding of pedigreed dogs was an established means of consolidating urban bourgeois status in England.[2] This was of particular significance to the Cape, given that the urban bourgeoisie was increasingly taking its cultural cues from English society in this period.[3] Rather than for their utility, dogs owned by the bourgeoisie were bred for their looks and for their correspondence to an artificially determined standard of physical attributes. Representative of 'the power to manipulate and the power to purchase', the pedigree dogs of the English bourgeoisie, Ritvo argues, 'were emblems of status and rank as pure commodities'.[4] It was a fitting metaphor for a class which was by this time assured of a secure place in the nation's power structures. In both symbolic and practical terms, dogs were a suitable avenue through which to assert this discourse. By the eighteenth century, the dog was already established in English popular thinking as humanity's closest companion. By the middle of the nineteenth century, the liking of the British for dogs was considered to be above that of every European nation.[5] Unlike horses and domestic stock, dogs did not require more land or money than the urban bourgeoisie (in either the Cape or England) possessed in order to make the requisite point about respectability and pedigree. Furthermore, the designated clay was perfectly designed for human moulding. The foetal development of dogs allows them greater physical variation than any other mammalian species.

If dogs were a marker of class status, in societies structured by racial inequality struggles over dogs could also resonate with broader social tensions associated with race. In 1832, as Cape Town's bourgeoisie was mulling over the means of control over the city's dogs, the colonial authorities in Bombay were faced with a full-scale riot over their attempt to regulate the vast number of strays in that city.[6] The systematic killing

---

[2] H. Ritvo, 'Pride and pedigree: the evolution of the Victorian dog fancy', *Victorian Studies*, 29 (1986) 227–53.

[3] This argument is elaborated in K. McKenzie, 'Gender and honour in middle-class Cape Town: the making of colonial identities 1828–1850' (Ph.D. thesis, Oxford University, 1997).

[4] Ritvo, 'Pride and pedigree', 243–5.

[5] K. Thomas, *Man and the Natural World: Changing Attitudes in England, 1500–1800* (London, 1983), 108.

[6] J.S. Palsetia, 'Mad dogs and Parsis: the Bombay dog riots of 1832', *Journal of the Royal Asiatic Society*, 11 (2001), 13–30.

of dogs was prompted by health concerns and exacerbated by the incentives offered of payment per dog dispatched. Some idea of the scale of the operation is suggested by the fact that between 1823 and 1832, some 63,000 Bombay dogs met an untimely end. As in Cape Town, as we shall see, the dog killers tended to be less than discriminating about which dogs they captured and many were removed from protesting Indian owners, although in this case the status and racial axes of the conflict were different. In a wider perspective the dog massacres offended a variety of Indian religious beliefs, particularly those of the Parsis, a prominent community of the city. Dog killers entering Parsi houses to take their dogs away were an especial source of outrage since Parsi women kept Purdah.[7] Although a major ally of the British colonial endeavour in Bombay, the Parsi leadership were unable to control the widespread rioting and strikes in protest against the dog killings, which caused massive disruption in the city. The response of the British in the face of Indian dissent was to insist on dispatching the dogs as a matter of principle. To do so was symbolic of their political authority in a threatening colonial situation.

Undesirable dogs were a persistent problem for colonial authorities in Melbourne, where the police were also used to destroy unwanted animals. Most white families, however, owned dogs as pets and as a look-out for intruders. A key role for settler dogs was to warn of encroachment by Aborigines. By the 1840s the original inhabitants of the Melbourne district had been dispossessed and were as far as possible kept outside the confines of a city reserved for whites. Aborigines themselves had numerous dogs, of which they were notoriously fond, but which the authorities considered a threat to order and white health. The regulation of stray dogs in colonial Melbourne was specifically designed to control the dogs of Aborigines and these animals would remain the target of Australian police well into the twentieth century. Reports from the 1840s suggest that even when Aborigines received permission to enter Melbourne, their dogs were forbidden from accompanying them, much to the chagrin of their owners.[8]

John Campbell's study of the laws controlling slaves' dogs in South Carolina demonstrates the symbolic and material association between

---

[7] G.N. Madgoakar, *Maumbaiche Varnan* (Bombay, 1863), 126. With thanks to Jim Masselos.

[8] On dogs in colonial Melbourne, see A. Brown-May, *Melbourne Street Life: The Itinerary of Our Days* (Melbourne, 1998), 68–9.

slave ownership of dogs and white perceptions of the disruption of the racial order. Dogs helped slaves to assert their humanity as well as assisting in practical ways by protecting them from white patrols and supplementing their diet through hunting and theft. The movement which culminated in a mass destruction of slave-owned dogs in South Carolina in the years immediately proceeding the Civil War was part of a 'much larger campaign' by whites 'to reassert, expand, and intensify their control and domination of their slaves'.[9]

Dogs and their control thus had the potential to intersect profoundly in the battles of race and class enacted through a variety of nineteenth-century societies. In Cape Town we have little information about the source of the city's stray dogs. Some were certainly genuinely without owners, subsisting off the refuse of the city. Others may well have been deemed stray in bourgeois minds purely by virtue of the social status of their owners. In 1836 Charles de Lorentz, then superintendent of police, wrote to Colonel John Bell complaining of the problems he experienced in trying to kill off unwanted dogs in the city. One of his major difficulties was

> the unaccountable infatuation that induces many of the inhabitants, principally among the Coloured population, to secrete, by locking up in their houses during the time appointed for destroying dogs, an almost incredible number of the most useless curs and turning them loose again when the danger of their being destroyed has ceased.[10]

The debate over stray dogs enacted within the pages of the *Advertiser* was not, however, conducted in terms of the removal of dogs from underclass owners as a means of social control. It operated at a more symbolic level and drew broader connections between control over dogs (and the form which this should take) and control over other undesirable elements of the city, including a disorderly underclass. Notions of race and class, and order and disorder, underpin the discourse of dog management in Cape Town.

---

[9] J. Campbell, 'My constant companion: slaves and their dogs in the antebellum South', in L.E. Hudson (ed.), *Working Toward Freedom: Slave Society and Domestic Economy in the American South* (Rochester, 1994), 68–9.
[10] Cape Archives (CA), CO 1/16 (1), 451, Superintendent of Police, 1836, no. 60, de Lorentz to Bell, 29 Oct. 1836. With thanks to Anthony Whyte and Kerry Ward.

The *Advertiser* and its correspondents were worried about the threat of rabid dogs[11] and called for the removal of stray animals[12] but the main focus of their unease was the ambiguity presented by dogs and their treatment at the Cape. Stray dogs lived on the refuse of the town and were symbolically linked to both this source of filth and to the underclasses of society. They needed to be controlled—but those responsible and their methods were equally troubling to bourgeois sensibilities. Letters concerning dogs were a common feature of the *Advertiser* in the 1820s and 1830s and images of violence were a consistent theme:

> There is something extremely disgusting and cruel, in my opinion, in the manner in which the canine race is occasionally treated by having their brains beaten out in the public streets by Policemen; and it appears to me desirable that some other mode of lessening the danger apprehended, and abating the nuisance, should be adopted.[13]

The writer argued that a tax on dogs would be a more suitable means of accomplishing the same object and that the money thus raised could be used to light the city's streets. A similar argument was advanced a month later, with the writer again arguing for taxation upon dogs which would raise money for the city's illumination:

> A good deal has lately been written on the subject of Dogs, and it must be confessed that considerable annoyance, if not danger, is experienced from the great overstock of those animals in Cape Town; but I agree with a late Correspondence of yours, that the periodical massacres of dogs found in the public streets, without answering any effectual purpose, are extremely disgusting, and have a tendency to familiarize the youth of this town with acts of barbarity.[14]

These writers have at heart the sanitisation and rationalisation of the public sphere at a time when cruelty to animals, Keith Thomas argues, had become a mark of lack of civilisation and refinement.[15] 'Humanitas' complained that the methods of dog destruction practised by the Cape Town police had a serious impact on the morality of the town's citizens, particularly its youth:

---

[11] *SACA*, 19 Aug. 1826.
[12] *SACA*, 21 Sep. 1836.
[13] *SACA*, 10 Nov. 1830.
[14] *SACA*, 8 Dec. 1830.
[15] Thomas, *Man and the Natural World*, 173–6.

> The brutal way of destroying these poor animals with large clubs has a demoralizing effect on the minds of children, for I have seen crowds of them following the slayers, to see the dogs killed in a most disgusting and revolting manner: this gives rise to inhumane sports among them, which destroy the innocence of childhood; and they cannot be supposed to understand that it is a Police regulation, or, indeed, that it is necessary at all; nor, in this latter respect, are they at all singular.
>
> Persons often lose really valuable and faithful creatures, by their breaking from confinement, running into the streets, where they are followed by men with huge clubs, and rarely escape from those who are not over-nice, and often make a sport of their duty.[16]

'Humanitas' suggested that a 'less revolting method' would be for the dogs to be 'enticed' to follow police by lures of meat before being drowned away from the eyes of innocents. 'Critical Toby' wrote several weeks later ridiculing the impracticality of this scheme for catching and destroying dogs.[17] Yet this model of disposing of stray dogs without offending bourgeois sensibilities was followed to good effect in Melbourne where dogs were caught by police and drowned in specially designed cages, their bodies rendered down for fat.[18] Even dead, dogs were a source of nuisance in both cities. Once killed by police, their carcasses needed to be disposed of and 'A Seaman' wrote to The *Advertiser* to complain in 1826 that there was no officially designated place for this purpose. The result was that 'the landing place at the beach is strewed with dead carcases, and is beginning to present one mass of putrefaction. This is felt as an intolerable nuisance by all whose avocations compel them to attend there'.[19]

Hoards of dangerous semi-wild dogs terrorising the populous, and periodic bloody dog massacres in the streets, were hardly conducive to a construction of the material world that stressed the control which the elite exercised over the operation of their city. The concern expresses itself to the point of an uncharacteristic suggestion of new taxes to treat the problem. Taxation is preferable to random acts of violence. The means by which the dog problem should be solved must be rational and centrally controlled rather than individualistic, violent, morally corrupting and capricious. In addition, taxation could achieve the further rational objective of street lighting.

---

[16] *SACA*, 7 Jan. 1835.
[17] *SACA*, 21 Jan. 1835.
[18] Brown-May, *Melbourne Street Life*, 70.
[19] *SACA*, 12 Sep. 1826.

To understand the worries expressed over Cape Town's dogs in the 1820s and 1830s, we need to be aware that they were enacted against a background of profound transition. Commercial horizons were widening with the Cape's incorporation into the imperial system of the world's dominant industrial nation. Despite fractious debates over slavery and emancipation, the British and Dutch elements of the city's bourgeoisie would ultimately find common ground in the push for representative government by the middle of the century. Respectability was the bedrock upon which claims for civil rights and political representation were made. It was increasingly defined along lines derived from the new mother country and associated with a reconceptualisation of middle-class identity at the Cape.[20] This new political culture, which was framed in the liberal discourse of social contract and universal rights (despite its inherent exclusivity), is crucially concerned with what historians and political theorists have designated the 'public sphere'. An independent press was vital in the formation of a public sphere, which we might conceive as a forum for public discussion and assembly intersected between civil society and the state. The *Advertiser* was quite self-conscious in taking up this role and in its embrace of this conception of politics. It was clear to contemporaries, although they might not have used the term itself, that without the establishment of a public sphere along the lines of bourgeois rationality, representative government was inconceivable.[21] The *Advertiser* was founded in 1824 and edited through our period by John Fairbairn, a man imbued with the ideas of the Scottish enlightenment and instrumental in the fight to establish a free press at the Cape.[22] The paper soon established itself as the voice of the liberal, British-orientated middle classes of the city.

While the middle classes would ultimately triumph in the political reorganisation of the Cape at mid-century, they were by no means a

---

[20] McKenzie, 'Gender and honour in middle-class Cape Town' and R. Ross, *Status and Respectability in the Cape Colony, 1750–1870* (Cambridge, 1999).

[21] A key theoretical text is J. Habermas, *The Structural Transformation of the Public Sphere: An Inquiry into a Category of Bourgeois Society* (Cambridge, Ma., 1989). A foundational feminist critique is offered by C. Pateman in *The Sexual Contract* (Cambridge, 1988) and *The Disorder of Women: Democracy, Feminism and Political Theory* (Cambridge, 1989). For a detailed discussion of these issues at the Cape, see K. McKenzie, 'Franklins of the Cape: The South African Commercial Advertiser and the creation of a colonial public sphere, 1824–1854', *Kronos*, 25, (1998–9), 88–102.

[22] H.C. Botha, *John Fairbairn in South Africa* (Cape Town, 1984).

unified self-confident group in this period. They were riven by internal divisions of ethnicity, political affiliation and wealth. They were threatened by the vibrancy of underclass culture in Cape Town as well as by the web of poverty, crime and disease which dominated the city, and over which they had limited control. They were also faced with unique problems of identity. Colonial societies are formed out of a position of ambiguity. White settlers found themselves in a society which was at once the same, and different, from their country of origin.[23] Added to this was the 'low esteem' in which they were held by the metropole. Ann Stoler argues that middleclass colonial identity and respectability were formed out of a position of uncertainty and anxiety since European colonials were 'so often viewed disparagingly from the metropole as parvenus, cultural incompetents, morally suspect, and indeed 'fictive' Europeans, somehow distinct from the real thing'.[24] Insisting on their role in reforming and improving colonial society gave respectable colonists a platform from which to undercut the assumptions of the mother country about their cultural backwardness and idleness. It also gave them a sense of purpose and legitimised their enterprise in their own eyes.[25] Cape Town's publications, including almanacs and the local press, were an important means of presenting an appropriate image to visitors from the outside world, and especially to observers from the metropole, whether or not this image was in fact accurate.[26] Soon after it commenced publication, the *Advertiser* quite selfconsciously asserted its own importance in taking on this role.[27]

Both the editor and readers of the *Advertiser* consistently called for the middle class to take up its reforming role within Cape society and thus to allow the colony to take its place amongst the civilised countries of the world. As 'An Observer' remarked in that paper, an 'active public

---

[23] J. Elliott, 'Introduction: colonial identity in the Atlantic world', in N. Canny and A. Pagden (eds.), *Colonial Identity in the Atlantic World, 1500–1800* (New Jersey, 1987), 9.

[24] A.L. Stoler, *Race and the Education of Desire: Foucault's History of Sexuality and the Colonial Order of Things* (Durham, 1995), 102.

[25] Elliott, 'Introduction', in Canny and Pagden, *Colonial Identity*, 9–11.

[26] S. Trapido, 'The emergence of liberalism and the making of "Hottentot nationalism" 1815–1834', *Collected Seminar Papers of the Institute of Commonwealth Studies: The Societies of Southern Africa in the Nineteenth and Twentieth Centuries*, vol. 17 (1992), 37. On the disjunctures between Cape almanacs, especially the visual presentation which they gave of the city, and the material reality of persistent urban filth, see M. Hall, 'Fish and the fisherman, archaeology and art: Cape Town seen by Bowler, D'Oyly and De Meillon', *South African Journal of Art and Architectural History*, 2, 3 and 4 (1991), 78–88.

[27] *SACA*, 10 Mar 1824.

spirit among the middle classes of society is a blessing to any country whatever'.[28] Fairbairn used the pages of his paper to encourage the unity of English and Dutch colonists in endeavours of public improvement. By doing so, he argued, the colony could prove itself worthy of civil rights in the form of Representative Government: 'the habit of assembling ourselves together for benevolent and public objects being thus acquired, a general Object will naturally command a general Union. In this way a Community ripens for Self-Government in the widest sense of the term'.[29]

With extremely limited political rights before 1854, middle-class men in Cape Town could assert their stake in the future of the colony through participation in reform agendas which could play a proto-political role in the city. Associations for social improvement allowed middle-class men a formal role in the public sphere, which the colonists were at pains to construct. They therefore gained public confidence in preparation for the real political power which representative government would give. Between 1827, when the Burgher Senate was dissolved, and 1840, when municipal government was established for Cape Town, there was no formal role for men of influence to play in the city beyond mutual associations.[30] As the *Advertiser* claimed, mutual associations were a training ground for Cape men—instructing them in their proper behaviour in the public sphere. Public action was an important constituent of middle-class masculinity, and men signified their social importance and respectability through enacting their role in the public sphere before women of their own class.

Central to the concerns of many of the improvement-minded in the Cape in the 1820s and 1830s were the class and racial issues incumbent upon the colony's labour relations, in particular slavery. It was perceived as vital that the Cape elite position themselves in the eyes of the world as 'discreet and judicious masters'.[31] Craig Iannini argues that the limited abolitionist initiatives that existed at the Cape were prompted less by a desire to bring slavery to an end than by the need to improve the image of the colony in the eyes of an increasingly

---

[28] *SACA*, 25 Apr. 1829.
[29] *SACA*, 14 Dec. 1831.
[30] D. Warren, 'Merchants, commissioners and wardmasters: municipal politics in Cape Town, 1840–54' (MA thesis, University of Cape Town, 1986), 4–5.
[31] *SACA*, 13 Oct. 1831.

censorious metropole.³² The critical travel literature about Cape slavery angered colonists and the development of a local press provided the opportunity, in the eyes of many, to set the record straight.³³ The existence of a colonial press allowed the city's middle class to exhibit an appropriate face to the outside world, claiming in 1832 that in 'the vast Continent of Africa, the Cape of Good Hope is the only respectable and flourishing Settlement of Civilized men'.³⁴ It was becoming increasingly clear from the political climate in Britain, however, that slaveholders were not to be long counted amongst the ranks of the civilised. Reform was becoming central to the tone of British social and political life, and slavery compromised the Cape's position as an advancing colony. In the 1820s and 1830s, as the debates over slavery intensified, the *Advertiser* used rival colonies, particularly those of the West Indies, as foils against which the proper labour relations of the Cape were set.³⁵ Local reform initiatives were designed to enhance the image of colonial commitment to improvement. If colonists aspired to recreate a British social world at the Cape, they needed to demonstrate (or be seen to demonstrate) a metropolitan regard for enlightened and rational progress.

Debates about stray dogs must be situated among these broader concerns about the material and social world of the city. In asserting the discourse of improvement, many of the worries of the readers of the *Advertiser* coalesced around the street, where the battles over dogs were fought out, and its symbolic associations. The streets of Cape Town mapped the conflict between order and disorder enacted between the world views and material interests of the city's upper and underclasses. By virtue of their status as important aspects of the material public sphere, as sites of activity binding the city together, and as the site of the meeting of public and private worlds, control over the workings of the street was crucial for the city's dominant classes. There were strong symbolic and moral dimensions to the attempt to keep the streets clean. For, as Mary Douglas reminds us, 'dirt is essentially disorder. There is no such thing as absolute dirt: it exists in the eye of the beholder.'³⁶ In

---

³² C. Iannini, 'Slavery, philanthropy and hegemony: a history of the Cape of Good Hope Philanthropic Society, 1828–1833' (Honours dissertation, University of Cape Town, 1993).
³³ *SACA*, 10 Mar. 1824.
³⁴ *SACA*, 31 Oct. 1832, original emphasis.
³⁵ *SACA*, 4 July 1826, 11 July 1824, 14 Apr. 1824, 26 Jan. 1831, 9 Feb. 1831.
³⁶ M. Douglas, *Purity and Danger: An Analysis of Concepts of Pollution and Taboo* (London, 1966), 2.

asserting control over their environment, Cape Town's bourgeoisie was constructing the 'unity in experience' of class identity.[37] In the politics of public space, the street is the setting for battles of control over conflicting models of behaviour and propriety. Debates about health and sanitation were not only questions of practicality but also intertwined with changing perceptions of proper behaviour and social order.[38]

Correspondents to the *Advertiser* were deeply concerned about the state of the city's streets. Stray dogs were only one troubling element within them. The paper is riddled with endless protests about what were referred to as 'public nuisances'—the dust and grit blowing off the streets of Cape Town in the summer months, street flooding of winter and the ever-present filth of refuse, sewage and the like. Such complaints frequently had deeper symbolic resonance, such as the desire for lighting the streets in which images of darkness and evil battled illumination and civilisation.[39] In a representative complaint, 'An Inhabitant' wrote vividly of the state of the streets of Simons Town in a letter to the *Advertiser* of 12 October 1831, detailing the 'offal, bones, putrid feet, and manure' which decorated the pathways before the hotels and butchers shops, producing 'a stench which must be unwholesome' and protesting against numerous other nuisances such as 'the number of pigs allowed to run about'. The correspondent pleaded to be informed 'on which of the Civil Authorities of this Town devolves the business of inspecting the street' so that they might be pressured to perform their duties.[40]

Public space in Cape Town was the theatre in which the leisure activities of the city's subordinate classes, including slaves, were enacted. It was a culture of leisure centred around drinking and gambling, an affront to bourgeois constructions of respectability and a challenge to their notions of the proper city.[41] The paper received complaints from respectable readers that the Sabbath day saw the streets infested with 'vagabondizing groups' gambling and swearing and ready to tempt the morality of their own children or those of their slaves. The Police, it was argued, should be 'zealously employed in suppressing these iniquitous scenes' which surrounded middle-class homes with a sea

---

[37] Douglas, *Purity and Danger*, 2.
[38] For a discussion of these issues with reference to Melbourne, see Brown-May, *Melbourne Street Life*.
[39] *SACA*, 5 Mar. 1831.
[40] *SACA*, 12 Oct. 1831.
[41] A. Bank, *The Decline of Urban Slavery at the Cape, 1806 to 1834* (Cape Town, 1991), especially chapter 3 and Ross, *Status and Respectability*, 127–35.

of vice-infested streets.[42] The streets were an element of public space over which the middle classes of the Cape were attempting to exert their rational control. By filling the streets with the recreational activities that the bourgeoisie sought to eradicate, the underclasses of the city could articulate a subtle expression of autonomy and collective identity which resisted the hegemony of the elite. As for the police, the problem was that they were as likely to join in as to arrest the perpetrators. 'A constant passer by' complained in 1826 that the respectable could look in vain to the police for protection from the 'the indecent exposures of the Hottentot women, and the noise and uproar of the men', for they 'are generally either off their station altogether, or lurking in the neighbourhood Tap-houses drinking and smoking with people of every variety of character and complexion; and thus encouraging rather than preventing tumult and disorder'.[43]

Despite their persistent calls for assistance from the police in the abatement of moral and material 'nuisances', the respectable classes clearly found the police a mostly unreliable ally in their assault on dirt and disorder in the city. They were far more likely to be 'lurking' in the taverns of the town with the very people whose activities they were supposed to be controlling, than combating the moral and material filth of the city. This was not unexpected, given that the perpetrators of 'outrages' and those set to apprehend them were of the same class background, with similar interests.[44] The control that the elite could exercise over the spatial organisation of the city, in which the physical landscape was intimately connected to the moral landscape, remained limited.

The Cape Town of these letters is not the city of enlightenment and rational public improvement represented in the Almanacs and the editorials of the *Advertiser*, with the respectable classes firmly in control of their physical world. It is a place where people live at the mercy of a hostile and filthy environment unsure of where to direct their complaints. 'An Inhabitant' was right to be confused about the responsibility for the cleansing of public areas in Cape Town. The link between moral and material disorder in the minds of the respectable city was encapsulated in the ambiguous role of the city's police, which

---

[42] *SACA*, 8 June 1831.
[43] *SACA*, 19 Aug. 1826.
[44] K.D. Elks, 'Crime, community and police in Cape Town, 1825–1850' (MA thesis, University of Cape Town, 1986), 51.

until the 1840s held some degree of responsibility for both. It was to this body that most complaints about the dirt and 'nuisances' in the city's streets were directed via the *Advertiser*. Until 1825, nineteenth-century policing in Cape Town was divided between two distinct authorities inherited from the Dutch period. Under the Burgerraad (Burger Council) was the Burgerwagt (Burger Watch) whose task was to patrol the town after dark. The second arm of the law was supervised by the Fiscaal, until 1825 both chief of police and public prosecutor in the Court of Justice. It consisted of caffre constables and police dienaars.[45] Caffres were drawn from the ranks of slaves and convicts (mostly of Asian origin) in the Dutch period and were traditionally viewed with fear and loathing by freeborn and slaves alike.[46] William Wilberforce Bird called them 'the refuse of the Cape population'.[47] By the time of the second British occupation, the caffres were increasingly confined to the more sordid side of policing. Their tasks involved dealing with the most dishonourable aspects of the city, both moral and material—its slave population (in terms of punishment and execution), its jails and prisoners, its street refuse and its stray dogs.[48] They were symbolically associated with the tasks they performed, tasks that were considered unacceptable activities for white colonists.[49]

In 1825 a new municipal police force was constituted under the control of Baron Charles de Lorentz, a former army officer. Numbers of recruits remained small, however, and the poor quality of the police notorious, with discipline lax and absenteeism and drunkenness rife. A year after the reforms, nine constables were dismissed in one month alone.[50] The ambiguous role and inferior quality of the Cape Town police persisted. With the promulgation of Cape Town's municipality in 1840, the police force was also reformed and remodelled according to the example of London's Metropolitan Police. Yet amongst their stated duties was still the control of street nuisances as defined by municipal regulations. The cleanliness of the city's streets was thrown into sharp relief with the recent smallpox outbreak of that year. Bitter disputes emerged between the municipality and the police over the responsibility

---

[45] Elks, 'Crime, community and police', 38–9.
[46] R. Shell, *Children of Bondage: A Social History of the Slave Society at the Cape of Good Hope, 1652–1838* (Johannesburg, 1994), 189–94.
[47] Bird, *State of the Cape*, 19.
[48] Elks, 'Crime, community and police', 24.
[49] Shell, *Children of Bondage*, 194.
[50] Elks, 'Crime, community and police', 24.

to keep the town clean. The wardmasters of the municipality saw the police as a tailor-made and cost-efficient means to enforce municipal regulations.⁵¹ In 1840 the Secretary to Government, Colonel John Bell, and the municipality's commissioners drew up a list of police responsibilities which included

> the destruction of stray dogs, pigs, goats and poultry, careless or furious driving, the depositing of rubbish at improper places, the washing or hooping of casks in the streets, kite flying, trundling hoops or other games, the discharging of fire arms, the wasting of water or bathing and washing at public fountains, street-begging, prostitution, nightwalking and indecent or obscene exhibitions, writings or language.⁵²

Not surprisingly, these menial tasks were an affront to the carefully acquired and precarious dignity of the newly-constituted force, now under the control of Inspector John King.⁵³ The dispute was only resolved in 1844 when the municipality employed a private contractor to clean the town.⁵⁴

The removal of filth had deeper resonances. The *Advertiser* urged the clearance of slums to improve the morals of the town.⁵⁵ The report of special wardmasters, appointed by public meeting to inspect the city of Cape Town in the wake of the 1840 smallpox epidemic, and to report on the state of health of the population (in particular the conditions of the poor), also made strong links between moral and material degradation.⁵⁶ Sexual morality and a proper work ethic—vital characteristics in an appropriate servant—were perceived to be undercut by insanitary living conditions.⁵⁷ The recurrent problems with sanitation in Cape Town, which surfaced over and over again in the course of the nineteenth century, indicates that these problems of dirt and overcrowding were never sufficiently well addressed.

In 1858, an unpublished poem by a member of the Cape police force turned the symbolic ssociations of dogs on its head and exposed the rotten foundations of bourgeois respectability when it addressed

---

⁵¹ Warren, 'Merchants, commissioners and wardmasters', 104.
⁵² Warren, 'Merchants, commissioners and wardmasters', 99.
⁵³ N. Worden, E. van Heyningen and V. Bickford-Smith, *Cape Town: The Making of a City* (Cape Town, 1998), 173.
⁵⁴ Worden *et al.*, *Cape Town*.
⁵⁵ *SACA*, 27 May 1840.
⁵⁶ CA, CO 490, 159, Report of the Special Wardmasters on the state of the cleanliness in the town and the extent of smallpox, May 1840.
⁵⁷ CA, CO 490, 159, Report on Ward no. 2, 5 May 1840.

these problems. The writer claimed that while the police might be cleaning up the city by destroying stray dogs, 'the Dirtiest dogs of the lot' were the slum landlords who provided accommodation to the city's underclass. They 'have built houses, your Worship, I swear/ That are kennels not fit to hold Pigs'. Such 'Dog holes' 'reeking with pest' were an affront to the image of Cape Town.[58] Cleanliness would never be achieved without the removal of those who allowed a force of moral and physical contagion to fester in the heart of the respectable city. The municipal government, however, was reluctant to spend the necessary funds, and several individuals themselves derived an income from underclass housing. The lines between the slum landlords and those who were supposed to control them were blurred.[59] To protect the middleclass home from the dangers of sanitation in central Cape Town, the elite of the city could take the easier route of moving their homes out of the centre and into the surrounding suburbs such as Rondebosch or Green Point.

In 1836 the Cape Legislative Council turned its attention to resolving the ambiguity represented by the city's dogs by enacting legislation to rationalise their control with an ordinance 'for abating the nuisance occasioned by Dogs roaming at large in and around Cape Town'. The Superintendent of Police would give seven days warning of intention to kill stray dogs, and thereafter have the right to destroy dogs found in 'any street, lane, road, or other public and unenclosed Ground'. Dogs that wore collars or were known to belong to certain owners were to be protected and the police could not 'enter any private house, private passage, or private enclosed yard in search of dogs for the purpose of destroying them'. The means of death was in the hands of the police, but bodies were to be disposed by burial.[60] Despite all these efforts, the problems of stray dogs in Cape Town persisted, with familiar associations drawn between dogs and the city's underclass, and calls for a tax on dogs in the press in the following decade.[61] By the 1850s, poison was

---

[58] M.F. Cartwright, 'The filthy state of Cape Town in 1858', *Quarterly Bulletin of the South African Library*, 33, 2 (1978), 53–56, 55. The poem, written on paper watermarked 1858, was found among the papers of James Lycett and was written either by him or by his son-in-law John Evans, both of whom were members of the Cape police force.

[59] Warren, 'Merchants, commissioners and wardmasters', 65, 77, 165.

[60] *Statute Law of the Cape of Good Hope, Comprising the Placaats, Proclamations and Ordinances Enacted before the Establishment of the Colonial Parliament and Still Wholly or In Part in Force* (Cape Town, 1862), 409. See also *SACA*, 3 Dec. 1836.

[61] *Sam Sly's African Journal*, 9 Jan. 1845; *Sam Sly's African Journal*, 19 Jan. 1850.

the preferred method of destruction, but the same pricks of anxiety were still articulated in the press. The familiar moniker 'Humanitas' complained in 1858 that dogs were being removed from their owners' stoeps and that their bodies were lying by the 'shambles...to the great delight and edification of our juvenile coloured population'.[62] Humanitas complained that such practices encouraged 'barbarity' and compromised the Cape's position as a 'civilised country'. Invoking the association of civilisation with English models of proper behaviour towards animals he asserted 'the sooner we have a man with some English ideas of humanity at the head of the police department, the better'.[63]

The police response to the problem of stray dogs was a particular source of bourgeois unease within the pages of the *Advertiser*. Of especial concern in debates over dog control was the failure of the police to distinguish between different orders of dogs; to divide the useful from the threatening, the respectable from the disreputable. No doubt with an element of deliberate intent, the police were apt to target bourgeois dogs as well as those of less secure status in their periodic depredations. In 1826, 'A Man of Common Feeling' described his observances in Plein Street one August night and protested that the police were unable to make a distinction between strays and the dogs of the respectable:

> I saw, as nearly as I can guess, about eight men, whom I took to be watchmen. They went up to a stoop, enclosed with iron railings, where there was a dog; they struck at the animal three or four times with their batons, and at last three or four of them went upon the Stoop, and beat it most unmercifully; they then kicked it off the Stoop, and said, now chop off its head; they stabbed it in three or four places, and when asked why they did so, they said it was their orders to kill all dogs found in the Streets—which, of course, I conceive excludes Dogs on Stoops. I hope, by inserting this in your useful Journal, a stop will be put to all such wanton cruelty.[64]

'A Friend to My Karo' wrote four years later protesting that he wished to protect his valued dog from the depredations of the police:

> My profession does not allow me to watch the poor animal during the whole day, and in my absence the room in which he is locked may be

---

[62] *Cape Argus*, 25 Sep. 1858, cited in Cartwright, 'The filthy state', 56.
[63] *Cape Argus*, 25 Sep. 1858, cited in Cartwright, 'The filthy state', 56.
[64] *SACA*, 22 Aug. 1826. With thanks to Andrew Bank.

opened, or he may escape, ignorant of the dangers which await him, and the useful and inoffensive animal become prey to some emissaries, armed, like Hercules, with immense clubs. What a sight it would be to me on coming home, after laboring for the public benefit, even to the sacrifice of my own interest, to find the only companion of my leisure hours—my faithful 'Karo'—weltering in his blood. How cruel to the poor innocent animal![65]

Similarly, 'Humanitas' hoped that policemen 'will receive strict orders not to molest dogs, which accidentally break loose, and are either lying quietly on a *stoep*, or making their way home'.[66] At a symbolic level, dogs were troubling to middle-class discourse in the ways they slipped between categories of respectable and disreputable, particularly in the refusal of the police to draw this distinction themselves. Dogs and the underclass had strong symbolic resonances in the way they troubled respectable discourse of both disorder and its control. While the respectable classes depended upon subjugation of elements of society such as dogs and slaves, the methods of control had the potential to disrupt the constitution of the rational bourgeois subject. Both dogs and slaves possess symbolic ambiguity. They were both within and outside the household, they could be loyal and useful members of the 'family' as well as threatening outsiders. They represent the potential for danger within the domestic sphere, and as such disrupt the rigidly defined categories so vital to the creation of the bourgeois self.

What the writers of these letters are seeking is a rational division between wild and domestic dogs, a resolution of their ambiguity. Their concern is analogous to the anxieties of slave owners who both valued and feared slaves and who were troubled by the way in which they slipped between defined categories of work and home, family and labour relations.[67] The notion of individualised licensed violence, which placed the killing of dogs within the hands of the unprincipled police is paralleled by contemporary debates over the treatment of slaves by their masters and the notion that this be removed from the hands of individuals and placed in the hands of the state.[68] The eradication of

---

[65] *SACA*, 9 Oct. 1830.
[66] *SACA*, 7 Jan. 1835.
[67] For an extended discussion of this, see K. McKenzie, *The Making of an English Slave-Owner: Samuel Eusebius Hudson at the Cape of Good Hope, 1796–1807* (Cape Town, 1993).
[68] On the reform of Cape slavery in the early nineteenth century, see R.L. Watson, *The Slave Question: Liberty and Property in South Africa* (Johannesburg, 1990) and P. Scully,

cruelty to animals was part of a general discourse of moral reform (including antislavery) associated with the rising power of the bourgeoisie in industrialising Britain.[69]

The writers were particularly outraged by the failure of the police to distinguish between dogs of the house and dogs of the street. The *stoep* was a space of symbolic resonance, a liminal zone from which the respectable bourgeoisie could gaze upon street life without being threatened by its disorder. It was an area of discursive and spatial separation and a material expression of the boundaries that dogs symbolically straddled. 'A Man of Common Feeling' was clearly incensed by the fact that despite the 'iron railings' of social separation, the underclass (in the form of the socially unacceptable police) penetrated the discrete space of the bourgeoisie and did violence to a part of their household. The fact that dogs were often kept at protection against theft adds a further dimension to the theme of class tension in the encounter.[70]

Debate over the failure of the police to distinguish between dogs of use and dogs of danger prompted a correspondent to address the *Advertiser* from the perspective of the dog itself. 'Pompey the Little'[71] explicitly compared himself to a human servant complaining that since he bore no 'badge of servitude' he was at the mercy of the police when on the streets in the service of the 'orders' of his master:

> Alas! Mr Editor, what are we poor sad dogs to do, are we to hire ourselves out, or are we to apply for numerical tickets like our biped coolies. Thus, should one of our Police Toes have failed to study Lavator, or another be a determined Phrenologist, and let the weight of his baton (his organ of vindictiveness) fall on the unoffending caput, to ascertain whether the organ of domesticativeness had existence we should in either case be lost.[72]

The letter stresses the distinctions that must be made between those dogs with 'freedom', 'liberties' and 'privileges' and those without, a resolution of the ambiguity inherent in the image of the dog being necessary for this. In its links to early nineteenth-century obsessions

---

Liberating the Family? Gender and British Slave Emancipation in the Rural Western Cape, South Africa, 1823–1853 (Oxford, 1997).

[69] Thomas, *Man and the Natural World*, 181–4.
[70] Elks, 'Crime, community and police', 114.
[71] The name derives from Francis Coventry's popular 1751 novel, *The History of Pompey the Little; or, The Life and Adventures of a Lap-Dog*. See L. Bellamy, *Commerce, Morality and the Eighteenth-Century Novel*, (Cambridge, 1998), chapter five.
[72] *SACA*, 29 Aug 1826, original emphasis. With thanks to Andrew Bank.

with racial and species classification it reveals the wider implications of the discourse of social reconstruction inherent in the remaking of the spatial organization of the city. The phrenological theory to which the letter refers should be understood within this context. It was applied at the Cape in this period primarily to deal with issues of racial classification and deviance. Attitudes towards it, Andrew Bank argues, marked the distinction between liberals and their enemies in matters of racial ideology. Within the pages of the *Advertiser*, mouthpiece of the former, it tended to be subject to satire (a genre into which this extract falls) or more serious critique.[73] Despite the joke implied in the letter's treatment of phrenology, the tensions between civilisation and incorporation, barbarism and separation, which were associated with contemporary racial thought, are clearly evident in bourgeois discourse about dogs.

Stray dogs and the underclass, symbolically linked in the cosmology of Cape Town's respectable classes, both belonged to an element of the city that threatened the project of social reconstruction promoted by the *Advertiser*. The debates over the control of dogs can be situated within aspects of the city that disrupted the attempt to reconstitute its social space along the lines of a rationally organised, commercially orientated urban centre focused on links with the mother country. In the drive towards a representative assembly, the middle classes of the Cape had to prove their social and political legitimacy by means of their ability to re-form the city in their own image. Although they attempted to persuade both themselves and sympathetic observers of their success in this project, the debate over dogs in the *Advertiser* reveals a dark side to the city, one which remained beyond the control of the respectable and persistently troubled their discourse.

---

[73] A. Bank, 'Of "native skulls" and "noble caucasians": phrenology in colonial South Africa', *Journal of Southern African Studies*, 22, 3, (1996), 387–403.

CLASS AND CANICIDE IN LITTLE BESS: THE 1893 PORT ELIZABETH RABIES EPIDEMIC*

Lance van Sittert

The Epidemic and History

Historians of southern Africa have long recognised the value of epidemic diseases in sharply illuminating social and mental landscapes of the past in ordinary times otherwise obscured from view.[1] By posing a lethal challenge to the body politic the epidemic licenses those in power to defend their core beliefs and material interests in the name of 'public safety', unencumbered by the usual constraints of law and humanitarian concern. Constituted as an 'emergency' the epidemic also provides a unique opportunity for the ruling class and state to act out latent fantasies of extermination and social engineering, ordinarily repressed or thwarted by the requirements of due process and individual rights. In this way the epidemic cuts all Gordian knots, brutally resolving longstanding impasses and setting societies on new courses. Things, in short, are never the same again after the epidemic.

Despite the often hysterical rhetoric of emergency and public safety evoked by the epidemic, the ruling class itself was seldom directly

---

* The term 'canicide' is taken from K. Kete, 'La rage and the bourgeoisie', *Representations*, 22 (1988), 89–107. The 1893 Port Elizabeth rabies epidemic has also been the subject of an honours dissertation: see N. Madida, 'Dogs, class and culture: the outbreak of rabies in Port Elizabeth in 1893' (Honours dissertation, University of Cape Town, 2000).

This chapter was first published in SAHJ 48 (2003) pp. 207–34 and has been used with permission of the *South African Historical Journal*.

[1] For a sampling of the international historiography, see T. Ranger and P. Slack (eds.), *Epidemics and Ideas: Essays on the Historical Perception of Pestilence* (Cambridge, 1992). For epidemic studies of the colonial Cape, see C. van Onselen, 'Reactions to rinderpest in southern Africa 1896–97', *Journal of African History*, 13, (1972), 473–488; M. Swanson, 'The sanitation syndrome: bubonic plague and urban native policy in the Cape Colony, 1900–1909', *Journal of African History*, 18 (1977), 387–410; T. Ranger, 'Plagues of beasts and men: prophetic responses to epidemic in eastern and southern Africa', in Ranger and Slack, *Epidemics and Ideas*, 241–68; and C.B. Andreas, 'The lungsickness epizootic in the Cape Colony, c. 1853–1857' (Honours dissertation, University of Cape Town, 2000).

menaced. The great animal epizootics ravaged the countryside, while the brunt of human epidemic diseases in the towns was repeatedly borne by the underclass. Public safety thus required the forced modernisation of the farming practices of backveld boers and natives and hygiene habits of the urban (lumpen)proletariat while simultaneously affirming the sagacity and hegemony of the bourgeois worldview. Rabies, however, was different, being at once an epidemic of urban animals and one incubated by the middle class. As such it offers the historian a unique glimpse of the conflicts and contradictions inherent in the bourgeois *mentalité*.

Historians of rabies have emphasised the 'metaphorical' nature of the disease, menacing the intangible elements of identity rather than human life or private property.[2] Kete in particular has stressed the subversive nature of rabies' infiltration into the privacy of the bourgeois domestic realm and its transformation of that epitome of the triumph of culture over nature—the pet dog—into a wild beast.[3] Rabies, for Kete, held up a mirror to the bourgeoisie in which they beheld the repressed beast within with its insatiable and unrestrained appetites. Hence, 'In the beast the bourgeois found his double'.[4] Such a subversive ideological threat, others have argued, licensed both greater state regulation of society and a corresponding curtailment of individual liberties.[5]

The Old Mongrel Canine Order

Wool made both Port Elizabeth and its merchant middle class. At the height of the wool boom in the quarter century after 1850, Port Elizabeth displaced Cape Town as the colony's premier port and the Bayonian merchants sought political independence from the west commensurate with their new economic power.[6] Their Cape Town rivals,

---

[2] H. Ritvo, *The Animal Estate: The English and Other Creatures in the Victorian Age* (Cambridge Mass, 1987), 167–202.

[3] Kete, 'La rage' and K. Kete, *The Beast in the Boudoir: Pet-Keeping in Nineteenth Century Paris* (Berkeley, 1994), 97–114.

[4] Kete, 'La rage', 93.

[5] See Ritvo, *Animal Estate*, for the former, and J.K. Walton, 'Mad dogs and Englishmen: the conflict over rabies in late Victorian England', *Journal of Social History*, 13 (1979), 219–39 for the latter.

[6] A. Mabin, 'The rise and decline of Port Elizabeth 1850–1900', *International Journal of African Historical Studies*, 19 (1986), 275–303 and B. Le Cordeur, *The Politics of Eastern Cape Separatism, 1820–1854* (Cape Town, 1981).

however, were able to exploit their proximity to the seat of government to confiscate gradually Port Elizabeth's trade hinterland and stymie its ambitions to being the new capital of the east. A combination of prejudicial harbour and railway development policies by central government and economic recession in the 1880s redirected the new trade generated by the diamond and gold discoveries in the interior to Cape Town and relegated Port Elizabeth to its traditional role as entrepot for a flagging pastoral economy (see Figure 9).[7]

The Port Elizabeth middle class created by the boom was acutely anglophile in identity, manners and sentiment, claiming descent from the British settlers of 1820 and with its ranks unleavened by admixture with an older, creole Dutch population.[8] This anglophilia informed all aspects of its creation of a faux Victorian town on the Bay and self-representation as bourgeoisie, the intertwined process of urban and class creation finding expression in an endlessly replicated double-act of separation and quarantine over the latter half of the nineteenth century. This has been well documented by historians of the new urban sciences of town planning, sanitation and segregation as they were applied to Port Elizabeth's human population, but can equally be read in the more obscure yet arguably more fundamental acts of separation and quarantine practised on animals in the town.[9]

The latter has as yet to find its historian in South Africa, but some useful bearings are provided by a substantial international literature. This suggests that the nineteenth century witnessed a sea change in urban middle-class sensibilities towards animals characterised by the concomitant rise of societies for the prevention of cruelty to animals (SPCAs) and pet keeping among the bourgeoisie on both sides of the Atlantic.[10] The former policed the public spaces of the town against routine and ritualised abuse of animals by the urban underclass, while the latter elevated certain species, dogs in particular, to the status of household familiars and class signifiers on the basis of imagined

---

[7] Mabin, 'Rise and decline', 294–302.

[8] See H.O. Terblanche, 'Port Elizabeth: 'n lojale Britse stad 1902–1937', *Historia*, 38 (1993), 100–11 for the anglophilia of the Port Elizabeth middle class in the early twentieth century.

[9] See G. Baines, 'Port Elizabeth history: a select annotated bibliography', *South African Historical Journal*, 38 (1998), 252–69 for an excellent guide to this work.

[10] E.S. Turner, *All Heaven in a Rage* (London, 1964); K. Thomas, *Man and the Natural World: Changing Attitudes in England 1500–1800* (London, 1984); Ritvo, *Animal Estate*, 125–166; and Kete, *Beast in the Boudoir*, 5–21.

Figure 9. Little Bess, c. 1888[11]

[11] With kind permission from Cape Archives (CA), Jeffreys Collection, J1396.

'breeds'. The newly delicate sensibilities of the urban middle class ultimately also required the reordering of urban space to incarcerate or exterminate wild animals, displace domestic food and transport animals to the periphery and make the public thoroughfares safe for middle class pets.[12]

The humanitarian and feminising tendencies of Victorian urban civilisation were counteracted by a concomitant popularisation of hunting among the urban middle class. Encouraged and facilitated by increased leisure time, ease of access to the countryside via the railway and emulation of the English landed gentry, middle-class hunting was a vigorously masculine pursuit governed by a code of sportsmanship designed to separate it from underclass subsistence and market hunting which was stigmatised and suppressed as 'poaching'.[13] Value was measured instead in the respect earned from peers in accordance with the number and individual dimensions of animals killed. This ritualised form of middle-class hunting, 'the Hunt' in McKenzie's parlance, was separated from the town and its sensibilities by being located either in the countryside or colonies, and served to reaffirm masculine fitness for competition in both business and war.[14]

The Bayonian middle class modelled itself closely on its imagined English progenitor, but as hybrid rather than clone. The process of separating the town from countryside may be said to have begun with the first regulations drafted by the resident householders in 1847. Urban civilisation was defined by the absence of animals, whether wild or domestic, and the town's founding charter minutely circumscribed the numbers, locations and movements of its various animal inhabitants.[15] The creation of places of animal incarceration—the pound, kennel, show yard—soon followed. The trend over the latter half of the nineteenth century was towards diminution, making domestic and wild

---

[12] See C. Philo, 'Animals, geography and the city: notes on inclusions and exclusions', *Environment and Planning D: Society and Space*, 13(1995), 655–81, and P. Howell, 'Flash and the banditti: dog-stealing in Victorian London', in C. Philo and C. Wilbert (eds.), *Animals Spaces, Beastly Places* (London, 2000), 35–54.

[13] H. Hopkins, *The Long Affray: The Poaching Wars in Britain* (London, 1986) is the classic account.

[14] J.M. Mackenzie, *The Empire of Nature: Hunting, Conservation and British Imperialism* (Manchester, 1988).

[15] Cape of Good Hope, *Government Gazette* (*GG*), 2190, 18 Nov. 1847, Municipal Regulations of Port Elizabeth.

animals, with the exception of pets, temporary sojourners in the town whose presence was tolerated only for as long as they administered to the food, transport and other needs of its inhabitants.

Canis familiaris was present at the town's founding, the 1847 regulations ordering all dogs to be registered at a charge of 1s per annum and that 'every dog found in the public streets without a collar, and not being so registered, shall be destroyed from time to time'.[16] A licence conferred the same freedom of movement within the town on its canine middle class as enjoyed by their owners. Strays were granted a 24-hour stay of execution in 1851 to enable derelict owners to ransom the valuable among them—initially at cost but from 1855 at 5s a head—and after 1864 the municipality reserved the right to sell rather than destroy its more valuable canine catches.[17] Conversely, the commissioners sought to check the proliferation of the town's dog population by discouraging the underclass from keeping them through doubling the licence fee to 2s6d, and the minimum penalty for an unlicensed dog to 10s in 1861.[18]

The licence regulations appear to have been only sporadically enforced on the town's fewer than 500 dogs prior to 1880 when the council was primarily concerned with eradicating stray pigs, goats and horses from the public thoroughfares. Fear of the stray was displaced instead onto the countryside where underclass and wild dogs were held to menace the game prized by the growing cohort of urban sportsmen. Thus an Albany petition in 1864 asked for a 5s dog tax

> as many idle white persons, and the whole of the coloured population are in the habit of constantly hunting with their dogs the greater portion of the game, more especially the young game, and that on the lands over which the owner himself cannot shoot without a license.[19]

If underclass dogs enjoyed the same protection as private property accorded those of their social betters, no such legal constraint stayed the hand of urban sportsmen in dealing with remnant packs of wild dogs and the ubiquitous jackal. These wild canids' appetite for game

---

[16] *GG*, 2190, 18 Nov. 1847, Municipal Regulations of Port Elizabeth, Clause 19.
[17] *GG*, 2607, 1 May 1855, Amended Municipal Regulations Port Elizabeth, Clause 51 and *GG*, 3697, 16 June 1865, Proclamation (P)52, Clause 34.
[18] *GG*, 3251, 21 May 1861, P35, Section 2.
[19] Cape of Good Hope, *Petition of F.W. Barber and 27 Others* (C12–64).

made them 'the greatest of sportsmen's enemies' and they were shot out of hand as vermin unfit even for tallying with the bag.[20] The only dogs allowed to hunt in the countryside were the auxiliaries of the urban sportsmen.

Already in the mid 1860s the colony's settler elite were reportedly 'addicted to field sports' and none more so than the Bayonian merchants.[21] They founded the Easter Hunt Club in 1865 and inaugurated an annual Easter Hunt at the end of the open season in the colony.[22] The club initially hunted near home at the Mines, Ceuton and Bushy Park, but the construction of a railway to Grahamstown in the 1870s opened up a wider hinterland and the hunt moved to Wycombe Vale in neighbouring Alexandria division from 1870.[23] The select band of ten to fifteen 'guns' departed Port Elizabeth each Good Friday morning by rail, with special cars laid on for horses and dogs, breakfasted at Sandflats and reached Coltman's farm on horseback by afternoon. There they found their camp ready in 'apple pie order' and settled down to a week free from 'telegrams and mails', hunting Saturday and Monday through Wednesday before 'return to business' on Thursday.[24] Divided into two teams under the captaincy of the club's founders, Holland and Pettit, the 'guns' beat the *kloofs* and *plaats* of Wycombe Vale for antelope for the team bag and the elusive bush buck ram—'lord of the forest'—that would secure them the day's individual pool (see Figure 10).[25]

---

[20] W. Armstrong, 'An elephant hunt: a first of April exploit with the elephants in Addo', *Port Elizabeth Telegraph and Eastern Province Standard* (*PETEPS*), 6 Apr. 1886. Armstrong's quote refers to the wild dog.

[21] Cape of Good Hope, *Report of the Select Committee Appointed to Consider and Report on the Game Laws Bill, 1867* (A9–67), 10.

[22] See G.M. Theal, *Records of the Cape Colony*, vol. 25 (London, 1905), 150–5 for the Proclamation of Lord Charles Somerset, 21 Mar. 1822, which set the annual fence or close season in the colony as 1 July to 30 November.

[23] See Union of South Africa, *Report of the General Manager of Railways and Harbours 1941*, Statement 17 for the progress of the railway, and W. Armstrong, 'Easter hunt 1886', *PETEPS*, 6 May 1886, for the venues of the hunt.

[24] See W. Armstrong, 'Easter hunt 1884', *PETEPS*, 22 Apr. 1884; W. Armstrong, 'Easter hunt 1885', *PETEPS*, 14 Apr. 1885; Armstrong, 'Easter hunt 1886'; W. Armstrong, 'Easter hunt 1887', *PETEPS*, 21 Apr. 1887; and W. Armstrong, 'Easter shoot 1888', *PETEPS*, 12 Apr. 1888.

[25] Armstrong, 'Easter hunt 1885'.

Figure 10. The 'Guns': Easter Hunt Wycombe Vale, 1888[26]

[26] With kind permission from CA, Jeffreys Collection, J1423.

Dogs were integral to this type of hunting. The 'guns' assembled their own pack from the numerous 'buffalo and [wild] pig dogs' maintained by the estates en route.[27] These were of the mongrel 'boer dog' variety, the purported product of the region's long history of military occupation.

> In the early [eighteen] sixties, when military posts were scattered about the frontier, there was no difficulty in securing good bred dogs. As a rule there were to be found at each post bloodhounds, staghounds, greyhounds, bulldogs, terriers, mastiffs, pointers, and occasionally foxhounds, and...the Boer dog was a cross between one or other or more of the dogs mentioned, for it was generally in the vicinity of military posts that the best Boer dogs were to be found.[28]

These mongrel monsters were prized for their size and tenacity in baying wounded bush buck rams, not bloodline, and the Easter Hunt Club held them superior in all respects to the pure-bred import for local hunting.[29] Thus the 1887 hunt had cause to "congratulate ourselves that we are hunting with mixed breeds, and not with foxhounds, harriers or beagles; for the Cape bush dog does not chase far, and soon returns to the beat of the gong and the shouts of the beaters, while the hound, unless a buck be laid low, will stick to the scent for hours; and guns have been known to spend an entire day in collecting a scattered pack—pursuing hounds instead of buck".[30]

The 'gun's' pack of 'bush dogs' was joined by that of the beaters, 'about a score of Hottentots and the same number of Kafirs with their mongrel followers, some of them hideously ugly and of the most puzzling breed, yet famous bush dogs, hunting the bucks as though they had an appetite for the pot' (see Figure 11).[31]

Under the direction of the estate manager this motley crew of canines and men drove the game from the bush into the ambuscades of the waiting 'guns'. 'The gong is sounded, foghorns blown, sheep-bells rung, niggers whoop and yell, the dogs are wild with excitement and give

---

[27] Armstrong, 'Elephant hunt'.
[28] J.J.K., 'The Boer hunting dog: another version', *Agricultural Journal of the Cape of Good Hope (AJCGH)*, 34 (1909), 188.
[29] See, for example, Armstrong, 'Elephant hunt' and Armstrong, 'Easter hunt 1887'.
[30] Armstrong, 'Easter hunt 1887'.
[31] Armstrong, 'Easter hunt, 1884'.

Figure 11. The Beaters: Easter Hunt Wycombe Vale, 1884[32]

[32] With kind permission from CA, AG Collection, AG1456.

tongue and every fellow is eager to draw first blood'.[33] Both sportsmen and beaters indulged freely in the ensuing slaughter, the former with rifles and the latter 'knobkerries', as did their packs of 'bush dogs', finishing-off or baying wounded antelope for their owners to dispatch and running down jackals, hares and monkeys for their own pleasure. The 'guns' bag alone averaged around 100 antelope for the week.

Thus did elite and underclass hunting meet in brief co-operative endeavour each Easter in the countryside around Port Elizabeth. The formers grudging admiration for the hunting prowess of 'the Kafir, Hottentot and Fingoe...with their tail of curs' on such occasions did not displace the traditional animosity of elite sportsmen for underclass poachers.[34] The 'Hunt' sought to distinguish itself by the pedigree of its human and canine participants and their abstemious consumption of the game while denigrating underclass hunting as the preserve of mongrel races indulging their insatiable animal appetites. The 'boys', like the dogs, thus had to be regularly rested, well provisioned and closely watched to prevent malingering and theft. Beaters were routinely suspected of secreting bush buck wounded by the guns in addition to the smaller 'pooti' they could bring down with their own 'kerries' and dogs. Said Armstrong of a wounded ram in 1887: 'We have no doubt but that the cunning, flesh-loving Kafirs will find him, as they do many another cripple, hiding the carcase till night.'[35] The carnival of slaughter that was the Easter Hunt, by licensing both elite and underclass pillage of game in the sanctuary of the preserve, thus also evoked barely sublimated elite fears about containment of the colonial other.

A New 'Improved' Canine Order

The sharp downturn in the pastoral economy after 1875 produced both repression and improvement in Port Elizabeth's rural hinterland. Recession conjured the old folk devil of the 'vagrant' and his canine familiars menacing stock and game, it being alleged that '[v]agrants were loafing all over the country with numbers of dogs who did immense harm to life and property, as also to game'.[36] Parliament struck at both

---

[33] Armstrong, 'Easter hunt 1885'.
[34] Armstrong, 'Easter hunt 1887'.
[35] Armstrong, 'Easter hunt 1887'.
[36] Cape of Good Hope, *House of Assembly Debates (HAD)*, 1885, 67.

human and canine vagrants through the Vagrancy (1879) and Dog Tax Acts (1884).[37] The latter empowered divisional councils to tax all dogs in their jurisdiction 2s.6d–5s 'to get rid of those vagrant dogs who belonged to people who had no food even for themselves'.[38] The class nature of the legislation was revealed by the exemption from taxation of 'hounds kept *bona fide* for sporting purposes'.[39] The act was further strengthened the following year to allow 'any proprietor or occupier of land to destroy any dog found trespassing upon the land owned or occupied by such proprietor'.[40] In the view of one parliamentary representative, '[m]any dogs in the country were insufferable nuisances, they being a useless lot of curs and mongrels, which ought to be swept from off the face of the earth'.[41] The Port Elizabeth divisional council, though quick to impose a 5s tax, appears never to have collected it due to the financial and political costs of enforcing a measure unpopular even among settler dog owners.[42]

Pastoral improvement reinforced canine repression in the countryside. The ostrich feather boom hastened passage of a Fencing Act (1883) that compelled neighbours to share the cost of boundary fencing and facilitated the rapid enclosure of the Eastern Cape countryside.[43] The act was immediately proclaimed in the divisions surrounding Port Elizabeth and by the mid 1880s a 'cut across country' on horseback during the Easter Hunt had been made 'rather a risky matter' by the steel wire fencing rapidly enclosing Wycombe Vale.[44] Enclosure also enabled a suite of measures intended to improve the quality and yield of colonial agricultural exports, one of which was the extermination of wild carnivores. The first wild animal poisoning club was formed

---

[37] Cape of Good Hope, Vagrancy Act (No. 23, 1879) and Dog Tax Act (No. 14, 1884). See also J. Tropp, 'Dogs, poison and the meaning of colonial intervention in the Transkei, South Africa', in this volume for the extension of canicide across the Kei under the guise of the Forest Act in the 1890s.

[38] Dog Tax Act (No. 14, 1884), Clause 4; Cape of Good Hope, Divisional Councils Act (No. 40, 1889) Sub-Division 5 and *HAD*, 1885, 67.

[39] Dog Tax Act (No. 14, 1884), Clause 9.

[40] Cape of Good Hope, Dog Tax Amendment Act (No. 15, 1885).

[41] Cape of Good Hope, *Legislative Council Debates*, 1885, 160.

[42] *GG*, 6628, 21 July 1885, Government Notice (GN) 658. See also *HAD*, 1887, 223–5; *HAD*, 1889, 177–8; and CA, 4/PEZ, 2/1/20, Resident Magistrate Port Elizabeth to the Secretary of the Port Elizabeth Divisional Council, 17 May 1893, for settler opposition to the tax.

[43] See L. van Sittert, 'Holding the line: the rural enclosure movement in the Cape Colony, c. 1865–1910', *Journal of African History*, 43 (2002), 95–118.

[44] Armstrong, 'Easter hunt 1885'.

in Jansenville in 1884 for the simultaneous laying of strychnine by co-operating farmers against stock predators, especially the 'jackal plague'.[45] By the end of the decade there were at least 25 clubs active across the Eastern Cape, and parliament had converted the dog tax into a divisional vermin extermination subsidy and voted £500 of its own to the cause for distribution amongst the clubs on a points system.[46] In the five years from 1889 to 1894 more than 19,000 jackal and 500 hyena and wild dog proofs were presented for payment.[47] These represented only a small fraction of the total mortality amongst canines both wild and domestic in the Eastern Cape backveld. The combination of fencing and strychnine altered rural attitudes to dogs, simultaneously eroding their utility as herds, hunters and guards and revealing their proclivities for stock and game killing leading many farmers to target all dogs, wild and domestic, with poison.[48]

Rural canine repression had little direct impact on the Port Elizabeth middle class whose sporting and business interests were advanced by the prevailing mood of paranoia and improvement in the countryside. Port Elizabeth representative, J.A. Jones, one-time member of the Easter Hunt Club and 'head of the sporting interest in the House', capitalised on the rural *grande peur* to realise a longstanding sportsmen ambition for a reformed Game Law in 1886 by offering farmers another legislative weapon in their growing armoury against the depredations of human and animal vagrants.[49] At the same time, the Port Elizabeth Agricultural Society (PEAS), comprising the town's big merchants, took over the running of the local agricultural show in 1881 and turned it into the colony's premier showpiece for all manner of farming improvement.[50]

In this new climate of sportsmen influence and agrarian improvement, members of the Easter Hunt Club founded the South African

---

[45] L. van Sittert, 'Keeping the enemy at bay: the extermination of wild carnivora in the Cape Colony 1889–1910', *Environmental History*, 3 (1998), 344.

[46] Cape of Good Hope, *Department of Agriculture Annual Report 1889* (G37-90), 8, and Van Sittert, 'Keeping the enemy at bay', 333–56.

[47] Van Sittert, 'Keeping the enemy at bay', 343, Table 1.

[48] See, for example, 'Magistrate's Court', *PETEPS*, 19 Sep. 1882; J.A. Pullen, 'A hard case', *PETEPS*, 7 Oct. 1882; 'Destruction of wild animals', *AJCGH*, 7 (1894), 202–3; and 'Unprofitable dogs', *AJCGH*, 9 (1896), 489–90.

[49] For the quote, see *HAD*, 1888, 184 and for the prehistory of Game Law reform, see L. van Sittert, 'Bringing in the wild: the commodification of wild animals in the Cape Colony/Province, 1850–1950', *Journal of African History*, 46 (2005), pp. 269–91.

[50] Editorial: 'The agricultural show', *PETEPS*, 13 Apr. 1883.

Kennel Club (SACK) in Port Elizabeth in February 1883 in imitation of the British model.[51] The club defined its intended audience through an annual subscription of £1.1s and garnered no fewer than 158 members among Port Elizabeth's middle class within just a few months.[52] This cash infusion and fraternal ties with the PEAS enabled the SACK to mount the colony's first dog show as part of the town's annual agricultural show in March 1883 in a purpose-built shed in the show yard.[53] The response exceeded all expectations, attracting more than 200 entries and 900 visitors in the two weekdays it was open and the more £300 invested by the club in buildings and prizes was amply recouped by the windfall from entrance fees, gate money and catalogue sales, ensuring the dog show became a permanent *imperium in imperio* in the town's annual agricultural show.[54]

The show was predictably dominated by 'sporting dogs', but the accepted wisdom about what constituted a good colonial 'sporting dog' was already under attack.[55] Local auctioneer, long time member of the Easter Hunt Club and founder member of the SACK, William Armstrong, put up a £5.5s prize for the best 'bush dog', which was awarded to a 'half-bred Foxhound' in accordance with the prevailing consensus among the town's hunting squirachy.[56] The decision was rudely and publicly rejected by another competitor who boldly asserted

> I have had 16 years colonial experience and I can say without fear of contradiction that the thoroughbred dog is the best style of dog adapted for colonial hunting. Now if the half-bred dog is the best dog for colonial hunting why should sporting men go to the expense of importing thoroughbred dogs from Europe and pay a very good price for them,

---

[51] W.E. Delafield to the Editor, *South African Kennel Club Gazette (SACKG)*, 1, 2 (Apr. 1908), 36–7. For the history of the British dog fancy, see also H. Ritvo, 'Pride and pedigree: the evolution of the Victorian dog fancy', *Victorian Studies*, 29 (1986), 227–53 and Ritvo, *Animal Estate*, 82–121.

[52] 'South African Kennel Club', *PETEPS*, 17 Apr. 1883.

[53] 'The dog show', *PETEPS*, 15 Mar. 1883.

[54] Editorial: 'The agricultural show', *PETEPS*, 13 Apr. 1893 and 'South African Kennel Club', *PETEPS*, 17 Apr. 1883. The dog show was held in 1883–84, 1886–87, 1889 and 1891–93. No Port Elizabeth agricultural show was held in 1885, due to drought, or in 1888, owing to the South African Exhibition. The cancellation of the 1890 dog show was a result of a crisis in the SACK (see below).

[55] 'The dog show', *PETEPS*, 15 Mar. 1883.

[56] 'The dog show', *PETEPS*, 15 Mar. 1883 and E. Hayes, 'The dog show', *PETEPS*, 20 Mar. 1883.

and after all the expense and risk to be surpassed by a common half-bred dog.[57]

At risk of being hoist on its own petard the SAKC quietly dropped the 'bush dog' category from future shows and relied on committeeman H. Mappleback, who had 'considerable experience in such Shows in England', to save them from any future embarrassment caused by unwittingly putting their backveld mongrel preferences on public display.[58] Thus was mongrel utility ousted by the aesthetics of breeding and the colonial by the imported dog.

The reward of adherence to British breed standards through the lucrative money prizes awarded annually by the SACK at its shows created a booming colonial market in pure-bred, imported dogs.[59] By 1886 already 'there were no curs or mongrels to be seen' and five years later it could be confidently asserted that 'the canine specimens that were deemed good enough several years ago to receive the highest award of merit would not now, in the majority of cases, have the slightest chance of receiving the honours of the show' such was the 'improvement' in the dogs on exhibit.[60] This was achieved through large-scale importation, and by 1891 it was reported that '[n]ever before has there been so great a demand in South Africa for thoroughbreds as now, and every month almost the progeny of English champions are landed at the various Ports'.[61] The thoroughbred dog mania remained confined to 'sporting dogs' which continued to dominate the SACK shows both reflecting and fuelling an explosive growth in sport hunting in the colony in the wake of Game Law reform which saw the number of annual hunting licences issued more than tripled from 1,000 in 1886 to 3,300 five years later and 4,700 by 1896.[62]

Port Elizabeth was the epicentre of both the thoroughbred dog and sport hunting crazes among the colony's urban middle classes as suggested by the concomitant steep rises in dog and hunting licence issues in the town from the early 1890s (see Figure 12).

---

[57] Hayes, 'The dog show', *PETEPS*, 20 Mar. 1883.
[58] Hayes, 'The dog show', *PETEPS*, 20 Mar. 1883.
[59] The Cape of Good Hope *Blue Book/Statistical Register* did not enumerate dog imports.
[60] 'Dog show', *PETEPS*, 18 Nov. 1886 and 'South African Kennel Club: a successful show', *PETEPS*, 9 Apr. 1892.
[61] 'South African Kennel Club annual show', *PETEPS*, 11 Apr. 1891.
[62] Cape of Good Hope, *Report by the Chief Inspector of Excise and Controller of Licences and Stamps, and Administrator of the Sale of Food, Drugs and Seeds Act, 1890 for the year 1896* (G62–97), 21–22.

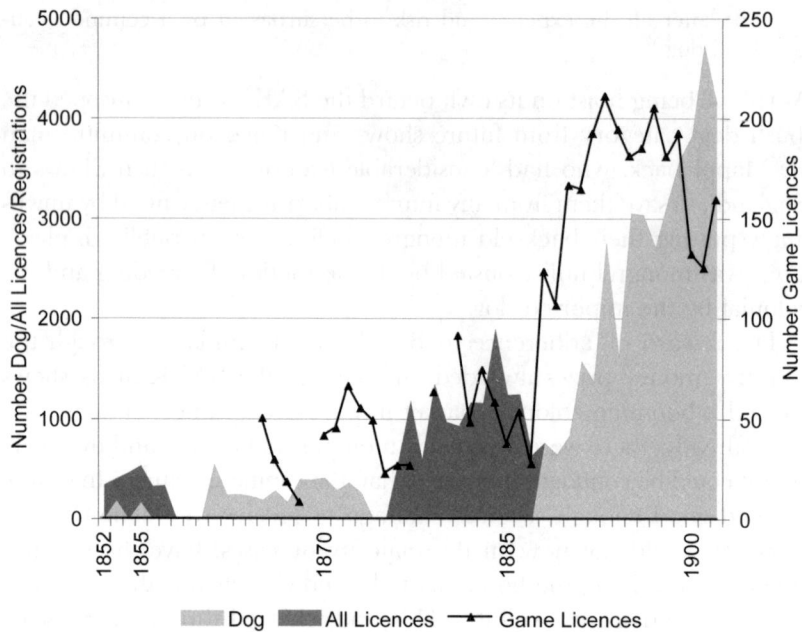

Figure 12. Port Elizabeth Municipal Dog and Hunting
Licence Issues 1852–1902[63]

The popularisation of dog-keeping and sport hunting undermined the hegemony of the old merchant squirachy organised in the Easter Hunt Club and SACK. The *battue*-style shoots of the Easter Hunt were both beyond the reach of the new urban sportsman, without the time or money to spare or access to a country estate, and increasingly also out of tenor with the new ethos of game conservation in the colony. The two hunters taking the train to Blue Cliff in 1889 with their guns and two terriers nailed up in a paraffin crate to avoid paying the fare for the dogs typified the new urban Nimrod.[64] Few of these sportsmen would ever draw down on elephant or bush buck, but subsisted on a staple of the winged and small game they and their dogs could flush on

---

[63] Calculated from CA, 3/PEZ, 7/4/1/1/1–9; *GG* 1852–1902.
[64] R.F. Hurndall, 'Cruelty to animals', *PETEPS*, 18 Apr. 1889.

the town and divisional commons. This small and impoverished public 'estate' forced them to make conservation their watchword.⁶⁵

Whereas the traditions of the old order embodied in the Easter Hunt Club were nurtured and could thus survive on the privacy of the country estate, those invested in the SACK and its public shows attracting entrants colony-wide could not. By the mid 1880s the club enjoyed the patronage of the governor and was 'not one of those institutions that has experienced a hard struggle for existence' owing to 'the many sporting gentlemen and others who take an interest in breeding a good class of dogs in Port Elizabeth and its vicinity'.⁶⁶ By the end of the decade, however, the SACK was in disarray, having lost its first secretary to Cape Town where he founded a rival club in 1889 and, more importantly, its legitimacy with the local sporting fraternity.⁶⁷ The number of entrants to its shows dwindled, the 1890 show was cancelled and in early 1892 the club was reportedly 'drifting backwards and getting out of touch with the public', another secretary having resigned and a real prospect that the forthcoming show would again being cancelled.⁶⁸

Civic pride and popular legitimacy were restored by the strategic retirement of the founding squires to honorary vice-presidencies and election of a committee of town sportsmen in their stead (see Figure 13).

The success of the 1892 show and its sequel under the auspices of the new committee confirmed the triumph of urban middle-class notions of canine improvement based on race over the utilitarian preferences of the hunting squirachy. The 1893 show attracted a record field and gate, was honoured with an informal walkabout by the governor and characterised by disputes over the aesthetics not the value of breeding. The Port Elizabeth club's example had further spawned a growing number of imitators, not just in Cape Town, but also Cradock, Grahamstown, Kimberley, King Williams Town, Queenstown and Natal and it had initiated negotiations to form an umbrella body and open a South African canine stud book.⁶⁹ Thus a mere decade after its founding the SACK liked to remind its audience that it

---

[65] For the new sport hunting, see, for example, 'The Easter hunt', *PETEPS*, 25 Apr. 1893.
[66] 'South African Kennel Club', *PETEPS*, 17 Nov. 1887.
[67] J. Harpur, 'South African Kennel Club: its origin and development', *SAKCG*, 1, 1 (Mar. 1908), 24.
[68] 'South African Kennel Club', *PETEPS*, 9 Apr. 1892.
[69] 'SA Kennel Club', *PETEPS*, 15 Apr. 1893 and Delafield to Editor.

	1883		1893
Name & position	Occupation	Name & position	Occupation
Honorary			
A.C. Wylde (pres)	CC & RM	**D. Dyason (pres)**	Attorney
		W. Armstrong (v-p)	Auctioneer
		C.R. Deare (v-p)	Merchant
		O.R. Dunnell (v-p)	Merchant
		T.G. Griffiths	Merchant
		A.W. Guthrie (v-p)	Railway contractor
		W.E. Matcham (v-p)	Railway contractor?
		R. Pettit (v-p)	Butcher?
Executive committee			
D. Dyason (v-p)	Attorney	*A. Wilson (chair/tres)*	Attorney
T.G. Griffiths (tres)	Merchant	T.A. Britton (sec)	Veterinary surgeon
W. Thompson (sec)	Butcher	W.E. Barlow	Clerk
W. Armstrong	Auctioneer	H. Chown	Feather merchant
P.P. Archibald	Merchant	W.D. Delafield	Commercial traveler
C. Chalmers	Forwarding agent	H.M. Kemp	?
C.D. Deare	Merchant	C.H.L. Moloney	Bank clerk
H. Mapplebeck	?	L. Tipper	Importer/furniture dealer
A. Walsh	Pharmacist	G. Whitehead	Merchant
G. Whitehead jnr	Merchant?		

Key: Easter Hunt Club members (**bold**) and business associates (underlined)

Figure 13. The South African Kennel Club Committee, 1883 and 1893[70]

---

[70] Compiled from *The Port Elizabeth Directory and Guide to the Eastern Province of the Cape of Good Hope, 1881* (Grahamstown, 1881); *The Port Elizabeth Directory and Guide, 1893* (Port Elizabeth, 1893) and Delafield to Editor.

is not so many years ago since only the few owners of canine specimens were able to tell a good dog from an inferior one. In those days it was sufficient to possess a dog with a name, and a great many miserable looking objects were passed off as thorough breds.[71]

The improvement wrought through adherence to the iron law of blood, however, came at a price. The town's burgeoning canine population, leavened with regular imports from abroad and an annual influx from all round the colony for the SACK show created conditions conducive to epidemic.

Canicide in Little Bess

The colony's dog population, like its livestock, suffered from generally poor health.[72] Distemper carried off large numbers each year, particularly at the coast, and many more were afflicted with mange, worms and other non-lethal pathogens. The public veterinary service founded in 1876 targeted the diseases of commercial livestock leaving the detection and diagnosis of canine ailments to owners who relied on folklore to divine and treat symptoms. Similarly, the SACK was more concerned with cruelty than disease at its shows, seeking the endorsement of the town's SPCA and at pains to emphasise its care for the comfort of competitors on each occasion thereafter.[73] The carriage and confinement of dogs for the show, however, provided ample opportunity for the transmission of disease through escape, fighting or other contact with infected animals. A surprising number of the latter were showed each year, three manged dogs being expelled from the 1884 event, but many others failing annually through poor condition to take prizes.[74]

The public veterinary service warned from the early 1880s against the danger of importing rabies into the colonial dog population. The disease was endemic to Britain and colonial experience had refuted conventional wisdom that it could not cross the equator, and did so

---

[71] 'SA Kennel Club', *PETEPS*, 15 Apr. 1893.

[72] See W. Beinart, 'Vets, viruses and environmentalism', in T. Griffiths and L. Robin (eds.), *Ecology and Empire: Environmental History of Settler Societies* (Pietermaritzburg, 1997), 87–101.

[73] See, for example, 'South African Kennel Club', *PETEPS*, 27 Mar. 1884. The SPCA appears to have had no more than a token and wholly ineffective presence in Port Elizabeth prior to 1900.

[74] 'South African Kennel Club', *PETEPS*, 27 Mar. 1884.

again in Mauritius in 1885. 'A Kaffir war would be a fool to it', said the colonial veterinary surgeon in 1882, advocating the quarantine of imported dogs.[75] Such a measure, however, threatened to disrupt the travel and sport of the imperial and local settler elite and hence remained confined to commercial livestock species.[76] The fancy's recruitment of veterinary surgeons to its cause in the late 1880s, as experts on British breed standards, effectively silenced concerns from this quarter.[77] In 1892, with imported canine mania at its height, it was left to the newly appointed colonial bacteriologist to remind that rabies 'may assuredly be expected to arrive sooner or later in these days of quick steam traffic'.[78] By the time of writing the disease was already spreading, as yet undetected, among Port Elizabeth's canine population.

The town's growing dog population increasingly intruded on the consciousness of its human inhabitants. While the latter increased by 80 per cent between 1875 and 1891, the former rose 350 per cent, halving the ratio of dogs to people.[79] By the early 1890s shopkeepers kept water bowls outside their doors, spectators at St George's Park complained of the disruption at cricket matches, the police acquired a stray as stationhouse resident and mascot, the custodian reported dogs on the marketplace in increasing numbers, 'bitch[es] or slut[s] in use or heat' everywhere caused havoc and scandal on the public thoroughfares, and the canine tribe added 400 ton of faeces each year to the town's already over-burdened sanitation system.[80] The town council sought to contain the canine population explosion by enforcing the licensing

---

[75] Cape of Good Hope, *Report of the Government Veterinary Surgeon 1882* (G64–83), 63.

[76] See Cape of Good Hope, An Act to Prevent the Introduction into this Colony of Malignant Diseases affecting Horned Cattle (No. 18, 1865; No. 3, 1866 and No. 5, 1867); Cattle Diseases Act (No. 20, 1868) and Animal Diseases Act (No. 2, 1881).

[77] See Harpur, 'South African Kennel Club', *SACKG*, 1, 1 (Mar. 1908), 24 and *Port Elizabeth Directory 1893*. The head of the public veterinary service, D. Hutcheon, was elected a vice-president of the Cape Town club in 1889 and a private practitioner, T.A. Britton, as secretary of the Port Elizabeth club in 1892.

[78] Cape of Good Hope, *Report of the Colonial Bacteriologist 1892* (G24F-93), 15.

[79] Calculated from *Census*, 1875 and 1891. The Port Elizabeth population in 1891 was 23 266 with a further 2 142 living in the division outside the town.

[80] See 'Out and about', *PETEPS*, 1 Dec. 1887; *GG*, 7320, 18 Aug. 1891, P223; CA, 3/PEZ, 1/1/1/15, Port Elizabeth Municipality Minutes, 4 Jan. 1893, 595; 'Occasional notes', *PETEPS*, 16 May 1893 and M. Davis, *Ecology of Fear* (New York, 1998), 259 for the estimate of 300lbs (136kg) of faeces per dog per annum used to calculate the figure above.

regulations more strictly and adding dog-catching and poisoning to the duties of its Inspector of Nuisances in 1887. The target of these efforts, however, was the old canine harbinger of urban disease and disorder, the stray, those 'unclaimed dogs' that in 1891 reportedly haunted the town wastes 'at the extreme end of the town, and near the Municipal Slaughter Houses also Solomons Row'.[81]

Few believed it possible the epitome of canine progress, the pedigree dogs of the middle class, could harbour disease or pose a threat to the civil order of the town. Thus, when they began dying in numbers in April 1893, poisoning was initially suspected and it was only when dogs belonging to a member of the SACK committee were affected that club secretary and town veterinarian, Britton, was called in and diagnosed suspected rabies on 21 April.[82] His diagnosis was supported by the colonial veterinary surgeon, fortuitously in town, and the head of the Bacteriological Institute in Grahamstown, but it was a further two weeks before the latter could confirm their suspicions by reproducing rabies symptomology with canine brain matter trepanned into rabbits.[83] With parliament in recess until late June, responsibility for dealing with the epidemic devolved onto the town council, closely superintended via telegraph by the Department of Lands, Mines and Agriculture in Cape Town. Without the necessary legislative authority, they relied on public fear to grant their actions legitimacy and ensure compliance.[84] Stung by suggestions of initial laxity the council adopted British best practice, ordering all dogs muzzled when abroad and appointing Britton for three months from 3 May to manage the canicide of the rest (see Figure 14).[85]

---

[81] CA, 3/PEZ, 1/1/1/15, Port Elizabeth Municipality Minutes, 15 July 1891, 259.

[82] Cape of Good Hope, *Report upon the Outbreak of Rabies at Port Elizabeth, 1893* (G63–94); 'Occasional notes', *PETEPS*, 15 Apr. 1893; and Editorial, *PETEPS*, 22 Apr. 1893.

[83] Cape of Good Hope, *Report of the Colonial Veterinary Surgeon, 1893* (G41–94), 7–9; Cape of Good Hope, *Report of the Colonial Bacteriologist, 1893* (G5–94), 15; *GG*, 7503, 19 May 1893, GN548; and 'Diseases of animals: hydrophobia and rabies', *AJCGH*, 6 (1893), 203–4.

[84] See, for example, Editorial, *PETEPS*, 22 Apr. 1893, and 'Occasional notes', *PETEPS*, 2 May 1893.

[85] Editorial, *PETEPS*, 4 May 1893, and 'Occasional notes', *PETEPS*, 9 May 1893.

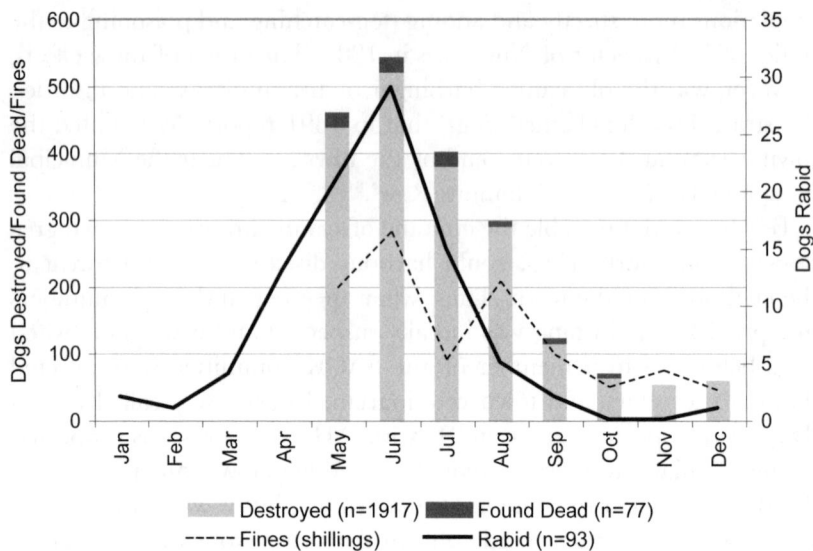

Figure 14. Canicide in Little Bess, 1893[86]

To prevent any dogs escaping the council's planned canine holocaust, the Department threw a quarantine cordon around the Port Elizabeth division, forbidding dogs to leave by road, rail or sea, and ordered all imported dogs quarantined on Robben Island upon arrival.[87]

Despite its consecration by rational science and the state, the municipal campaign, run under the effective auspices of the SACK, reflected the race and class prejudices of the Bayonian bourgeoisie. It opened with a Sunday raid on the uninformed native location that rounded up and exterminated all dogs, both licensed and unlicensed, on the grounds they were unmuzzled.[88] Africans' 'innumerable curs' were deemed 'absolutely worthless, and... only a source of danger as a medium of

---

[86] Calculated from *Report upon the Outbreak*; *PETEPS*; *Eastern Province Herald* (hereafter *EPH*) and CA, AGR 182, 1020 and 3/PEZ, 7/4/1/1/7.

[87] *GG Extraordinary*, 7500a, 9 May 1893, P169, P170 and GN507; *GG*, 7538, 19 Sep. 1893, P381; 'Dogs in quarantine: station on Robben Island', *EPH*, 27 Nov. 1893; and Cape of Good Hope, *Returns as to Quarantining Imported Dogs on Robben Island* (C3–99).

[88] E. Mdolomba, 'A native's complaint', *PETEPS*, 11 May 1893. See also 'Divisional Council', *PETEPS*, 11 May 1893 for concern over the 'hundreds of dogs in Gubbs Location' outside the municipal boundary.

spreading the disease' given 'the roving nature of natives, and the long and various paths they take'.[89] In response Elijah Modolomba asked:

> [Are] only the native people's dogs...subject to rabies or Hydrophobia. If not, why are the white people's dogs permitted to roam at large without being muzzled, many of which may be seen in the streets to-day...We...think that a bite from a white man's dog is as bad as that from a native's.[90]

Modolomba's complaint was confirmed by the local press, which reported that in town '[s]o far the [muzzling] order has been almost entirely ignored...At present moment there are some hundreds running loose, and pitiful objects a great number of them are too.'[91] Underclass defiance through flagrant violation or sham adherence endangered 'prized animals', which were always assumed to be properly muzzled.[92] The enemy thus remained the underclass dog. "It is from these the danger arises. Where dogs are in good hands and continually under the eye of their owners, illness is at once seen, and steps are taken. It is the careless owner whose dog is not of great value who helps to spread the infection."[93] The middle class' race and class conceits thus produced a 'scepticism' and lack of 'cordial co-operation' with the official proscriptions which saw it disregard both muzzling and quarantine orders at its convenience and so inadvertently, lay itself open to the more draconian intervention of the colonial state once parliament re-opened in late June 1893.[94]

Having indulged its own prejudices about the epidemic, the Port Elizabeth middle class suddenly found itself subject to those of the countryside, where animal genocide had become routinised as progressive farming practice for dealing with stock epidemics over the previous decade. Thus the farmer member for neighbouring Grahamstown,

---

[89] 'Canine rabies', *PETEPS*, 27 June 1893; see also 'Town Council', *PETEPS*, 6 July 1893.
[90] Mdolomba, 'A native's complaint' and 'Occasional notes', *PETEPS*, 11 May 1893. See also A. Odendaal, 'Even white boys call us boy! Early Black organisational politics in Port Elizabeth', *Kronos*, 20 (1993), 3–16.
[91] 'Occasional notes', *PETEPS*, 6 May 1893. See also 'Our note book: rabies', *EPH*, 14 June 1893.
[92] 'Occasional notes', *PETEPS*, 16 May 1893.
[93] 'Our note book: rabies', *EPH*, 5 June 1893.
[94] For middle-class non-compliance, see Editorial, *PETEPS*, 4 May 1893; 'Occasional notes', *PETEPS*, 6 May 1893; 'Occasional notes', *PETEPS*, 16 May 1893; 'Our note book: dogs', *EPH*, 19 May 1893; 'Our note book: rabies', *EPH*, 14 June 1893; and 'Occasional notes', *PETEPS*, 15 June 1893.

Arthur Douglass, adamantly insisted when parliament opened on 22 June:

> There was only one way of grappling with this matter and stamping out this dreadful epidemic amongst dogs, and that was to slaughter every dog in the Port Elizabeth division (Hear, hear). He believed in dealing with this matter at once and severely...He would be very sorry for the dogs and their owners, but his concern was for the public health'.[95]

Douglass further showed his rural disdain for urban mores and sensibilities by urging all haste to prevent owners smuggling dogs out of the town and rejecting compensation as 'a dog was kept as a luxury, not as a means of livelihood, like horses and cattle and vines, for the destruction of which compensation had to be given'.[96]

The House's determination to act on Douglass's demand, over the objections of Port Elizabeth members, and produce a 'dog-destroying bill' within 24 hours struck panic in the Bayonian middle class. Informal discussions in the street led to a meeting at Armstrong's auction mart at noon the same day chaired by the president of the SACK, Dyason, and attended by some 200 'influential citizens' including members of both the town and divisional councils. Councillor Hume captured the mood of the crowd when he said:

> Some people had dogs, which were not only valuable for what they were worth, but they had a sentimental value attached to them. Some people had great attachment for their animals, and they would regard Mr Douglass's proposal in the same way that the order of Herod was regarded in olden days. To destroy their dogs would be like destroying their children. It would be a great grief to him to see his dogs destroyed (hear, hear).[97]

Faced with the prospect of being compelled to take its own medicine from the barbarous backveld, the bourgeoisie hastily consented to the strict confinement of its dogs through their permanent chaining and muzzling both at home and abroad. The involvement of the colonial veterinary surgeon and ministers in the fancy, as much as the explicit threat of civil disobedience and legal action by the Bayonian bourgeoisie, prompted the House to substitute confinement for genocide when

---

[95] *HAD*, 1893, 34.
[96] *HAD*, 1893, 34.
[97] 'Rabies scare', *PETEPS*, 24 June 1893.

it met to discuss the rabies epidemic again on the 23 June.[98] The *rapprochement* also conveniently excused the Treasury from footing the hefty compensation bill for a blanket canicide including some of the finest of the colonial dog fancy. Rural members who held it 'better that a hundred dogs or ten thousand dogs, should die than one man', were thus given a lesson in the urban morality of sentiment by their town colleagues who 'acknowledged that human life was valuable, but there were [also] many dogs which were highly prized, and of which their owners were very fond'.[99]

With parliament in session the epidemic thus entered a new phase, in which the hunters became the hunted as the canicide loosed on the underclass was turned back on its middle-class initiators under the direction of the House and Department of Lands, Mines and Agriculture. The municipal muzzling order finally became law on 23 June, with mounted Cape Police enforcing the quarantine cordon, and was superseded by the new Rabies Act regulations a month later, requiring all dogs to be kept permanently muzzled and chained.[100] Only the latter's failure to stipulate a penalty further stayed enforcement until mid August when a maximum fine, sufficient even to deter a delinquent bourgeoisie, of £50 or three months imprisonment was imposed.[101] The divisional council also re-imposed the long defunct dog tax of 5s a head at the end of August, backdated to 1 July, specifically as a 'means towards the destruction of a vast number of cur dogs in the possession of the natives' beyond the reach of the municipality.[102]

By mid August Britton's contract with the municipality had ended acrimoniously amidst insinuations of profiteering[103] and the rabies death of a 13-year-old underclass girl, Lydia Gates, hardened the popular

---

[98] For the threat of middle-class civil disobedience and legal action, see Editorial: 'Our dogs', *EPH*, 23 June 1893, and 'Occasional notes' and 'Rabies scare', *PETEPS*, 24 June 1893.

[99] *HAD*, 1893, 40–41.

[100] *GG*, 7513, 23 June 1893, P225, and *GG*, 7521, 21 July 1893, P266.

[101] *GG*, 7528, 15 Aug. 1893, P321.

[102] CA, 4/PEZ, 2/1/20, Resident Magistrate Port Elizabeth to the Secretary of the Port Elizabeth Divisional Council, 17 May 1893; 'Our note book: our dogs', *EPH*, 9 Aug. 1893; CA, AGR 182, 1020, Colonial Veterinary Surgeon to the Secretary for Lands, Mines and Agriculture, 18 Aug. 1893; *GG*, 7533, 1 Sep. 1893, GN846; and *GG*, 7531, 12 Aug. 1893, GN841.

[103] 'Our note book: remarkable if true', *EPH*, 26 July 1893; 'Town Council', *PETEPS*, 27 July 1893; 'Town Council', *PETEPS*, 10 Aug. 1893; and CA, 3/PEZ, 2/1/1/1/86, T.A. Britton to the Town Clerk, 26 July and 2 Aug. 1893.

mood in the town against further indulgence of the middle class and its pets.[104] 'We trust we shall now hear the last of the specious special pleading in favour of the poor dog', said the *Herald* urging 'an example [be made] of those owners of dogs who are systematically defying the law' through 'a heavy fine or two'.[105] In this increasingly vigilante atmosphere and with the streets largely cleared of the mongrel horde by the previous three months slaughter, the new regime bore down heavily on the canine middle class for the first time.[106] The ensuing brutal violation of Englishmen's 'true and lawful rights' of property, privacy and person in defence of public health induced a collective nervous breakdown in the Bayonian middle class.[107]

To the individual imprisonment of wire muzzle and chain, was added the threatened indignity of public incarceration, a local divisional councillor suggesting turning the show yard into a canine penitentiary for the remainder of the epidemic.[108] The bourgeoisie's response to its world turned upside down varied. Some smuggled their dogs 'up country', real and imagined embers from the outbreak at the Bay flickering and flaring in the town's rural hinterland through the second half of 1893.[109] Others on Richmond Hill continued their open defiance, relying on their status to intimidate dogcatchers and police into inaction.[110] For the majority of the middle class, however, there was no escaping the new regime. For them, who conventionally thought of their dogs as 'family', themselves as 'doggy men' and their enemies—whether

---

[104] 'Hydrophobia: the first victim', *EPH*, 16 Aug. 1895; 'A case of hydrophobia', *PETEPS*, 17 Aug. 1893; and 'Magistrate's Court', *EPH*, 18 Aug. 1893. By contrast the son of the school inspector, Rev. D. Fraser, also bitten in June, was given an assisted passage to the Pasteur Institute in Paris by government and recovered fully.

[105] 'Our note book: rabies', *EPH*, 11 Aug. 1893, and 'Our note book: hydrophobia', *EPH*, 16 Aug. 1893.

[106] 'Town Council' and 'A case of hydrophobia', *PETEPS*, 17 Aug. 1893.

[107] An Englishman, 'An appeal to Englishmen', *PETEPS*, 10 Oct. 1893.

[108] R. King, 'The rabies', *PETEPS*, 24 June 1893, J.H. Wilson, 'Dogs', *EPH*, 26 June 1893; and A.W.G. Pritchard, 'Re rabies', *PETEPS*, 27 June 1893.

[109] See CA, AGR 182, 1020, Telegram Resident Magistrate Uitenhage to the Sectretary Lands, Mines and Agriculture, 18 July 1893, and A. Edington to the Secretary for Lands, Mines and Agriculture, 4 Sep. 1893; 'Local and general news', *PETEPS*, 22 July 1893; *GG*, 7522, 25 July 1893, P268; *GG*, 7530, 22 Aug. 1893, P337 and P338; *GG*, 7538, 19 Sep. 1893, GN904. The Uitenhage divisions (including the Uitenhage municipality), parts of Willowmore and Jansenville, and the Grahamstown municipality were all proclaimed under the Rabies Act.

[110] 'Occasional notes', *PETEPS*, 5 Aug. 1893. The delinquents on the Hill included a town councillor and his brindle greyhound.

Kafirs, parliamentarians, bondsmen or protectionists—as 'rabid', the Rabies Act threatened class as well as canine genocide, an intent latent in its broad definition of 'dog' to include 'any other animal subject to the disease'.[111]

> We are all dogs... [M]an is an animal, and he is subject to the disease, therefore man is a dog. The syllogism is conclusive and irrefutable. Further it follows that under this Act men may be 'destroyed' by duly appointed officers; they may be prevented from moving from certain areas; they may be muzzled, chained up, kept in back yards, and subjected to any treatment which any municipality may choose to enforce'.[112]

After just a month of exposure to the municipality's underclass dogcatchers and their pets 'compounding' ' with 'derelict and diseased dogs' in its kennels, the middle class, deaf to the 'screams' of martyred curs, could hear, in 'the piteous howling of chained dogs', a desperate plea for the 'happy despatch' and openly advocated mass canine suicide.[113]

With a middle-class cattle-killing in the offing, organised resistance came via the SACK in the form of a civil case contesting the legality of the municipality's right to destroy private property in dogs. Canicide, like the Hunt, depended on mobilising an army of underclass auxiliaries, dogcatchers for beaters, whose dumb inability or wilful refusal to recognise and respect the mnemonic animal class order of the bourgeoisie, threatened the corresponding social order its labours were intended to restore or reaffirm.[114] The municipality's army of 'Hottentot' and 'Kafir' dogcatchers, motivated by a 1s bounty paid for each dog arrested, had scandalised the middle class since the start of the epidemic through its violations of private property, cruelty to animals and lack of respect for persons, and proposals to grant them access to yards were strenuously resisted.[115] Warned off the town's

---

[111] W.E. Barlow, 'Our dogs', *EPH*, 18 Oct. 1893 and Cape of Good Hope, Rabies Act (No. 3, 1893), Clause 4.

[112] 'The dog act', *EPH*, 10 July 1893. See also 'What is a dog', *EPH*, 28 June 1893.

[113] CA, 3/PEZ, 2/1/1/1/86, Dyason, Hazell and Wilson to the Town Clerk Port Elizabeth, 21 June 1893; King, 'The rabies'; G. Smith, 'Dog poisoning', *PETEPS*, 2 Sep. 1893; 'Occasional notes', *PETEPS*, 5 Sep. 1893; and Sirius, 'A seasonable appeal', *PETEPS*, 19 Sep. 1893.

[114] For a famous instance, see R. Darnton, *The Great Cat Massacre and Other Episodes in French Cultural History* (Harmondsworth, 1984), 79–104.

[115] See, for example, 'Town Council', *PETEPS*, 18 May 1893; Canine, 'Dog catching and dog catching', *EPH*, 26 May 1893; 'Town Council', *PETEPS*, 1 June 1893; 'Town

human and canine middle class, by July the dogcatchers had rounded up most of the mongrel horde and were reduced to taking cats and grumbling about short pay.[116] The Rabies Act thus gave them a new lease on life and, with their enthusiasm further revived by the council raising its bounty to 1s.6d, they made hunt on the town's canine elite, to the mounting horror of the bourgeoisie.[117] 'Fancy one's feelings at seeing a Kafir brain one's favourite dog because it happened to break from a servant or from one self' asked one indignantly.[118]

With Hottentots demanding dogs from ladies at home alone, killing puppies and 'making regulations' in pursuit of the council's 'blood money', the taking of a prize fox-terrier bitch in late July became the *cause celebre* of the Bayonian middle class.[119] Defended by a relative of the former secretary of the SACK and closely followed by 'a good many sporting gentlemen', young master Chapman sought £20 damages from the town council on grounds that the regulations under which his dog was poisoned were *ultra vires*.[120] The aim was to strike down the council's assumption of 'almost almighty power' to violate private property. 'How on earth', asked Chapman's lawyer, J.A. Chabaud, 'do they [the municipality] have the power to interfere with private property. It was monstrous to suppose that the scavengers [dogcatchers] were to have the liberty of going about and taking possession of the public's property.'[121] Chapman appealed his case all the way to the supreme court, but the high courts upheld the local magistrate's initial rejection of the claim on the principle of *salus populi suprema lex* and

---

Council', *PETEPS*, 15 June 1893; 'The new rabies bill', *PETEPS*, 27 June 1893; and 'Occasional note', *PETEPS*, 5 Sep. 1893.

[116] 'Town Council', *PETEPS*, 20 July 1893; 'Town Council', *PETEPS*, 27 July 1893; 'Town Council', *PETEPS*, 31 Aug. 1893; and 'Town Council', *PETEPS*, 7 Sep. 1893.

[117] CA, AGR 182, 1020, Sanitary Inspector Port Elizabeth to Town Clerk Port Elizabeth, 16 Aug. 1893.

[118] D, 'Rabies', *EPH*, 18 Aug. 1893.

[119] 'Our note book: the wily dog catchers', *EPH*, 1 Sep. 1893; 'Town Council', *PETEPS*, 14 Sep. 1893; 'Town Council', *EPH*, 15 Sep. 1893; and 'Town Council', *PETEPS*, 7 Dec. 1893.

[120] 'Town Council', *PETEPS*, 3 Aug. 1893; 'An interesting dog case', *EPH*, 7 Sep. 1893; 'Magistrates Court', *PETEPS*, 7 Sep. 1893; 'Circuit Court', *PETEPS*, 14 Sep. 1893; 'Our note book: Chapman v. the municipality', *EPH*, 1 Dec. 1893 and 'The rabies case', *EPH*, 4 Dec. 1893. Chapman's initial claim on the council at the beginning of August was for £50.

[121] 'An interesting dog case', *EPH*, 7 Sep. 1893.

the middle class was forced to submit to the common good of public health embodied in the state.[122]

The rabies epidemic and its suppression completely altered the urban ecology of Port Elizabeth. The extreme evolutionary pressure of canicide produced a surviving feral dog population that was nocturnal and defied all efforts at final extirpation.[123] Chaining on the other hand ruined the temperament and health of the town's privately owned dogs through long 'solitary confinement in stuffy stables and sheds'.[124] Culling or confining the urban apex predator also facilitated population explosions amongst the town's other free-ranging animal inhabitants. The most visible beneficiary was 'that symbol of liberty', the cat.[125] Despite its susceptibility to the epidemic, confining Grimalkin was generally acknowledged to be impossible and feline mortality too insignificant to warrant the felicide so eagerly desired by residents tormented by the 'dismal duets at night and...predatory visits to the pigeon cot and chicken roost' of 'sneaking puss'.[126] Similar irruptions occurred amongst rats, wreaking havoc on the new municipal organ, and jackals along the town's wild edge ravaging sheep.[127] The anxious bourgeoisie also worried about a resurgence in the depredations of human vermin:

> The taking away of dogs from their owners would create a fresh danger by opening the way for burglaries and thieving in many unprotected parts of the town where a good house dog is an absolute necessity and, in many instances, the only protection afforded to housholders; for although the dogs might be muzzled yet they could arouse alarm to the household by their bark in the event of any unwelcome visitor appearing.[128]

Although some fancied 'another thousand dogs destroyed yet', by October 1893 there was a new willingness in the town to set *canis familiaris* free from its 'irksome chains' and restore the balance of nature in the town, which, like the social order, had been completely subverted by

---

[122] See 'Our note book: dogs', *EPH*, 19 May 1893; Amicus Canis, 'The Rabies Act', *EPH*, 30 Aug. 1893; and 'The rabies judgement', *EPH*, 4 Dec. 1893. 'The supreme law is the well-being of the people'. Thanks to John Atkinson for the translation.
[123] 'Our note book: our dogs', *EPH*, 11 Aug. 1893.
[124] See Sirius, 'A seasonable appeal'; 'Our note book: rabies', *EPH*, 11 Oct. 1893; Barlow, 'Our dogs' and 'Occasional notes', *PETEPS*, 28 Oct. 1893.
[125] 'Occasional notes', *PETEPS*, 29 July 1893.
[126] 'Occasional notes', *PETEPS*, 17 June 1893; Dog Fancier, 'Our unfortunate dogs', *EPH*, 11 Aug. 1893; and 'Occasional notes', *PETEPS*, 22 Aug. 1893.
[127] 'Occasional notes', *PETEPS*, 24 Oct. 1893 and 'Town Council', *PETEPS*, 2 Nov. 1893.
[128] Pritchard, 'Re rabies'.

the epidemic.[129] Evidence of the latter came from the growing incidence of dog stealing in the town, 'Kafirs' snatching and 'ketching' animals freelance for the municipal reward money.[130]

The SACK once again took the lead in the campaign to set the middle class' 'pets and favourite companions in the veldt' at liberty and relieve it of the predation of all 'scavengers...[that] go round and destroy property'.[131] The club, supported by the town council, repeatedly petitioned the Department of Lands, Mines and Agriculture to rescind chaining from mid October.[132] Although frustrated at 'official density', the club persevered and the chaining order was finally removed in mid November followed by muzzling a month later, just in time to enable the middle class and their dogs to take a much-needed Christmas holiday from the town.[133] It proved a pyrrhic victory for the SACK, however. Isolated cases of rabies continued to occur throughout 1894, prompting the government to ban the annual dog show and re-impose the muzzling order from August to December 1894.[134] When the club tried again in 1895 to stage its once premier event of the colonial dog fancy, it received official blessing, but was unable to find a venue anywhere in town willing to host the competition.[135] By the time the show was finally held again in 1896, a host of rivals had sprung up across the region and the SACK's membership shrunk to just 74.[136] The great

---

[129] 'Town Council', *PETEPS*, 5 Oct. 1893, and 'Occasional notes', *PETEPS*, 24 Oct. 1893.

[130] 'Town Council', *EPH*, 15 Sep. 1893; 'Town Council', *PETEPS*, 9 Nov. 1893; and 'Town Council', *EPH*, 10 Nov. 1893.

[131] Sirius, 'A seasonable appeal' and 'Magistrate's Court', *PETEPS*, 7 Sep. 1893.

[132] CA, AGR 183, 1020, Town Clerk Port Elizabeth to Secretary for Lands, Mines and Agriculture, 12 Oct. and 2 Nov. 1893; Petition of the Inhabitants of Port Elizabeth re Amendment of Rabies Act, 1 Nov. 1893 and SACK to the Minister of Lands, Mines and Agriculture, 28 Oct. and 13 Nov. 1893.

[133] 'Our note book: rabies', *EPH*, 27 Oct. 1893; 'Our dogs', *EPH*, 10 Nov. 1893; 'Our note book: our dogs', *EPH*, 17 Nov. 1893; *GG*, 7561, 8 Dec. 1893, P474 and *GG*, 7565, 22 Dec. 1893, P495. Port Elizabeth's dogs were unchained in mid November already, after the president of the SACK was informed informally of the impending amendment by the under colonial secretary and the news was published in the local press.

[134] See CA, AGR 183, 1020, T.A. Britton to the Colonial Veterinary Surgeon, 8 Jan. 1894; CA, AGR 216, 1714, Under Colonial Secretary to the Resident Magistrate Port Elizabeth, 3 Mar. 1894; *GG*, 7631, 10 Aug. 1894, P271; and *GG*, 7672, 1 Jan. 1895, P457.

[135] CA, AGR 216, 1714, Under Secretary for Agriculture to the SACK, 16 Feb. 1895 and SAKC to the Under Secretary for Agriculture, 11 Mar. 1895.

[136] Harpur, 'South African Kennel Club', *SAKCG*, 1, 1 (Mar. 1908), 24.

promise of 1893 was no more and the fancy's centre of gravity had shifted elsewhere.[137]

Aftermath

The focus on *canis familiaris* allows us to see the process of colonial domestication—enclosure, recomposition and extermination—for one species as it traverses the latter half of the nineteenth century and redefinition from utilitarian, colonial mongrel to fancy, imported purebreed.[138] The rise of the 'sporting dog' under the aegis of the SACK was premised on its isolation from miscegenation with the mongrel native, *boer* or bush dog and their extermination along with their wild progenitors in a canicide institutionalised as agricultural betterment in the 1880s. Rabies, in this context, constituted an ideological crisis for 'improvement' and its human accolytes.

This crisis was temporarily avoided by scapegoating and massacring the town's canine underclass of native and stray dogs in a cathartic orgy of violence orchestrated and superintended by the bourgeoisie. For the Bayonian middle class, economically declined and politically impotent, the epidemic was an opportunity to settle the scores of the previous decade with its local class enemies—dock, workers, natives and collies—by symbolically visiting the genocide on their dogs they were morally and legally constrained from affecting on their persons. The failure of the terror of May-July 1893 to stamp out the disease, however, re-opened debate on its cause and refocused attention on the complicity of the middle class in introducing and incubating rabies.

In response, the Bayonian middle class, fervent disciples of agricultural and canine improvement, resorted to denial. It became an article of faith among them that many animals 'said to be stricken during the recent scare were no more afflicted than the obelisk in the Market Square'.[139] The prevalence and persistence of what was politely referred to as 'scepticism' about rabies among a self-consciously modern and scientific bourgeoisie, amazed outside observers. Thus veterinary surgeon Britton reported:

---

[137] Harpur, 'South African Kennel Club', *SAKCG*, 1, 1 (Mar. 1908), 24–5.
[138] See K. Anderson, 'A walk on the wild side: a critical geography of domestication', *Progress in Human Geography*, 21 (1997), 463–85.
[139] 'Our note book: the origin of rabies', *EPH*, 25 Sep. 1893.

> Throughout the whole of the course of the outbreak, and at the present time, I am sorry to say that there has been amongst a numerous section of the inhabitants a profound disbelief in the existence of rabies; this feeling has not been confined to the uneducated, but has been held by many educated people holding good positions in the town, and unfortunately proved a great obstacle in the eradication of the diseases.[140]

This did not take the form of a rejection of Pasteur and germ theory common to the backveld, but rather a shrewd recognition of the limitations and partiality of science and the reservation of the right to consult its own veterinary experts in defence of individual liberty and property against the common weal embodied by the state.[141] This scepticism, in turn, produced middle-class rumour, which provided the rational comfort of empirical counter-evidence refuting the prevailing wisdom of the public veterinary service. Thus the dog that bit Lydia Gates reappeared in perfect health, the school inspector's son was told by no less an authority than Pasteur that he had not been bitten by a rabid dog, and the colonial veterinary surgeon himself did not believe the epidemic was rabies.[142]

The ambiguous place of the veterinary surgeon in the urban middle-class imagination is evident in town veterinarian Britton's fall from grace through the epidemic. From secretary of the SACK and the governor's consort on his walkabout at the April show, Britton was discharged by the municipality at the beginning of August in the belief that 'when Mr Britton's services are dispensed with rabies will disappear' and relinquished or was relieved of his position in the SAKC soon thereafter.[143] Faced with two new cases in early 1894, he wrote privately to the colonial veterinary surgeon to report:

---

[140] *Report upon the Outbreak*, 10.

[141] For backveld disputation of germ theory, see Andreas, 'Lungsickness', Beinart, 'Vets', and M. Tamarkin, 'Flock and volk: ecology, culture, identity and politics among Cape Afrikaner stock farmers in the late nineteenth century' (African Environments Past and Present conference, Oxford, 5–8 July 1999); for comparison, see J.D. Blaisdell, 'With certain reservations: the American veterinary community's reception of Pasteur's work on rabies', *Agricultural History*, 70 (1996), 503–24, and B. Hansen, 'America's first medical breakthrough: how popular excitement about a French rabies cure in 1885 raised new expectations for medical progress', *American Historical Review*, 103 (1998), 373–418. For the earlier debate of germ theory in Port Elizabeth, see also J. White, 'M. Pasteur's treatment of hydrophobia', *PETEPS*, 29 Apr. 1886 and 'Only a vaccinated one, Jenner and Pasteur discredited', *PETEPS*, 16 May 1886.

[142] *PETEPS*, 24 Aug. 1893; 'The news of the day', *Cape Times*, 20 Aug. 1894; and CA, AGR 183, 1020, T.A. Britton to the Colonial Veterinary Surgeon, 8 Jan. 1894.

[143] 'Town Council', *PETEPS*, 10 Aug. 1893. By October Delafield was signing SACK correspondence as secretary.

I have seen some of the leading men of P. Elizabeth about it, they have advised one to hush it up, not say a word about it, because I suppose, they might loose their shooting. I hope you see the difficulty I am in, if I report these cases, I have the whole town down on me, the very people I have to depend upon for my living.[144]

Subsequent official enquiries indeed led to Britton's public pilloring by the town council and he left shortly thereafter for Johannesburg.[145]

Middle-class denial openly disputed the claims of veterinary science and, in so doing, deflected the onus of proof onto its practitioners. The Department of Lands, Mines and Agriculture thus commissioned and published an account of the Port Elizabeth outbreak written by Britton in which he purported to have located the epidemic's source in an Airedale terrier imported to Port Elizabeth from Britain via Madeira in August 1892.[146] Britton conveniently ignored copious anecdotal evidence that rabies was endemic to the colony[147] in producing a narrative that justified the public veterinary service's prior warnings and canine martial law impositions at a time when it was also seeking to expand and normalise biological quarantine to the colony as a whole through a reformed Animal Diseases Act.[148] Forced to choose between progress and sentiment, the Bayonian middle class clung doggedly to the latter, puncturing their improving pretensions and further marginalising themselves within the emerging modern order.

---

[144] CA, AGR 183, 1020, T.A. Britton to the Colonial Veterinary Surgeon, 8 Jan. 1894.

[145] 'Town Council', *EPH*, 19 Jan. 1894 and Harpur, 'South African Kennel Club', *SAKCG*, 1, 2 (Apr. 1908). Britton was secretary of the Transvaal Kennel Club by 1894.

[146] *Report upon the Outbreak*.

[147] For the wealth of pre-1893 anecdotal evidence suggesting rabies was endemic to southern Africa, see Cape of Good Hope, *Reports on Public Health 2: Report on Occurrence of Hydrophobia at Hanover* (G15–91); 'Local and general news', *PETEPS*, 4 May 1893; 'Hydrophobia or rabies', *South African Medical Journal*, 1, 2 (June 1893), 32–4; 'Occasional notes', *PETEPS*, 4 July 1893; 'Local and general news', *PETEPS*, 11 July 1893; and P.S. Snyman, 'The study and control of the vectors of rabies in South Africa', *Onderstepoort Journal of Veterinary Science and Animal Industry*, 15 (1940), 12–14.

[148] See *HAD*, 1893, 16, 88–9, 107, 160, 182, 192, 235–6, 255–6, 262, 275–6, 284, 345 and 372; and Cape of Good Hope, Animal Diseases Act (No. 27, 1893).

DOGS, POISON AND THE MEANING OF COLONIAL INTERVENTION IN THE TRANSKEI, SOUTH AFRICA*

Jacob Tropp

In the 1890s and 1900s in what is today the Eastern Cape of South Africa, colonial authorities expanded their control over the peoples and environments of the recently annexed territories of the Transkei. While magistrates engineered a colonization of the social landscape of the Transkei, forest officers worked to 'save' local flora and fauna from popular 'abuse' and 'destruction'. In the government's efforts to restrict African access to forest resources, one intervention in particular spawned repeated conflicts and controversies in African communities: the mass killing of Africans' dogs. For foresters, the systematic poisoning and shooting of African-owned dogs was promoted as essential to undermine African men's abilities to engage in hunting pursuits and thereby protect both local wildlife and European sport. Yet as local residents encountered state dog-killing, they imbued government actions and intentions with more profound meaning than officials anticipated. Already coping with a debilitating combination of ecological pressures, such as drought and livestock diseases and colonial interventions affecting everything from land tenure to medical practices, African men and women perceived the government's attacks on their animals as concerning much more than dogs or hunting. Popular responses to dog-killing reflected deeper frustrations, not only with the government's restrictions on local forest use but with the broader colonial domination of local livelihoods and landscapes during this period.

---

* This article was first published in the *Journal of African History* 43(2002) pp. 451–472 and has been used with kind permission of the *JAH*. Special thanks to Lwandlekazi de Klerk, Tandi Somana and Veliswa Tshabalala for assistance in interviewing and translation. Richard Waller and others on the panel at the 2000 conference of the African Studies Association in Nashville, Tennessee, at which this paper was first presented, offered stimulating comments on earlier versions of the article. I am also grateful to Thomas Spear and the anonymous reviewers for their insightful editorial suggestions. This research was supported by grants from the Joint Committee on African Studies of the Social Science Research Council and the American Council of Learned Societies, with funds provided by the Rockefeller Foundation, and the Graduate School of the University of Minnesota.

Broader Conflicts over Hunting and Preservation

As in other colonial spheres in southern Africa, a mix of political, cultural and environmental interests inspired official attempts to control African hunting activities in the Transkei. With growing anxieties over the environmental impact of colonial expansion and the prospects for settler progress amid a dwindling natural resource base, Cape authorities established governmental forest preserves and restrictions on European and African forest use in the mid- to late 1800s.[1] These schemes were then the springboard of restructuring forest use and access and for integrating social and ecological control over African communities in the territories. Hunting restrictions from the 1890s onwards were thus part of a broader strategy of constraining Africans' environmental practices and mobility. Moreover, while conservators and magistrates publicly extolled the virtues of preserving specific wildlife species in local forests, particularly various types of antelope, they simultaneously sought to reserve hunting as the privilege of the small community of European sportsmen in the territories. These concerns increasingly translated into policy; from the late 1880s onward, African hunters faced a growing number of regulatory constraints, such as permit obligations, closed seasons and animal species reservation.[2]

As colonial officials instituted an increasingly restrictive program of wildlife management at the turn of the century, they repeatedly encountered popular resentment and resistance. Rural men and women, experiencing such restrictions amid a host of other impositions on access to local forest resources, responded by making formal protests to government, evading forest patrols and even physically attacking local forest guards.[3] Official regulation of African men's hunting practices was an arena of particular contestation during this period. In many communities hunting not only provided sources of meat and skins for both local use and trade, but was also an important dimension of male

---

[1] Richard Grove discusses the seeds of colonial conservationism in the nineteenth-century Cape and its moral and religious foundations in 'Scottish missionaries, evangelical discourses and the origins of conservation thinking in southern Africa 1820–1900', *Journal of Southern African Studies*, 15 (1989), 163–87.

[2] For more on the nature of hunting restrictions in the region, see chapter 4 of my 'Roots and rights in the Transkei: colonialism, natural resources, and social change, 1880–1940' (Ph.D. Thesis, University of Minnesota, 2002).

[3] These dynamics are explored at length in my 'Roots and rights in the Transkei'.

socialization and ritual life.⁴ Moreover, hunting was often an integral part of rural Africans' broader livelihood strategies, protecting crops and livestock from menacing wild predators and pests. It was this interest in pursuing and protecting their livelihoods that most vividly and directly conflicted with colonial priorities and schemes of wildlife preservation.

Throughout the 1890s and 1900s, different African communities, particularly those situated in the vicinity of larger forest tracts, regularly complained to officials about the loss of crops and livestock to invading predators and pests. Authorities often reported that Africans in various locales were continually plagued by a host of animals dwelling in nearby forest reserves—including wild pigs, small antelope species such as duikers and various types of birds—which collectively dug up, trampled and ate their crops.⁵ Perhaps a more persistent problem over the long term was the loss of livestock, particularly calves, lambs and goat kids, to forest predators. In his annual report for 1890, for instance, C.C. Henkel, Conservator of Forests for the Transkei, noted, 'Panthers and leopards are found in all the mountain and coast forests, and have committed havoc among the sheep and goats of the natives, but all efforts to shoot and destroy some of them have hitherto failed.'⁶ Domestic animals were particularly vulnerable during seasons of drought, when food sources for predators diminished in the forests and they more regularly sought sustenance form nearby farms.⁷ For example, over the course of 1904 and 1905 in the Umtata district, amid an extremely dry period, the resident magistrate received numerous requests by local Thembu men for guns and ammunition so they could hunt down the

---

⁴ Interview with P. Maka, 28 Jan. 1989, Manzana, Engcobo district; interview with W. Jumba, T. Nodwayi, F. Sonyoka and Z. Quvile, 24 Feb. 1998, Tabase, Umtata district and interview with W.M. Ngombane, 8 Jan. 1998, Mputi, Umtata district. M. Hunter, *Reaction to Conquest: Effects of Contact with Europeans on the Pondo of South Africa* (Cape Town, 1989), 96; J.W. MacQuarrie (ed.), *The Reminiscences of Sir Walter Stanford* (Cape Town, 1962), 11, 71 and E.D. Sedding (ed.), *Godfrey Callaway: Missionary in Kaffraria, 1892–1942* (London, 1945), 132–3.

⁵ Cape Archives (CA), AGR, 144, 601, Chief Magistrate of the Transkeian Territories (CMT) to Under-Secretary of Native Affairs (USNA), 27 Dec. 1892; Cape of Good Hope, *Annual Report of the Chief Conservator of Forests for 1894* (*Annual Report*), 134; *Annual Report for 1896*, 154; CA, FCT, 2/1/1/3, FCT to Under-Secretary of Agriculture (USA), 7 Sept. 1898, quoting CMT Elliot.

⁶ *Annual Report for 1890*, 141.

⁷ W. Beinart, 'The night of the jackal: sheep, pastures and predators in the Cape', in this volume.

various wild cats, hawks and other animals regularly attacking their young stock.[8]

Given this constant threat of predation on their livelihoods, Africans across the territories particularly resented the difficult situation posed by official strategies of game preservation. On the one hand, the colonial government restricted the ability of African men to hunt game in local forest reserves through permit restrictions, closed seasons, species reservation and even more directly, through the destruction of their hunting dogs. Yet, at the same time, the reduction in African hunting activity, so often lauded in foresters' reports at the turn of the century, enabled the populations of not only reserved game species but also predators and pests to expand in many locales. While animals ravaged their families' gardens, fields and livestock, African men were legally bound to sit idly by, with the risk of prosecution should they attempt to control local wildlife populations independently.

At the turn of the century, leaders of different African communities occasionally appealed to colonial authorities to recognize and ameliorate the difficulties caused by hunting prohibitions. At the 1910 session of the Transkeian Territories General Council, for instance, a representative from the Butterworth district proposed that the government amend the hunting regulations, as 'much damage was done by vermin, such as baboons, porcupines, cane rats and monkeys, when game protection was proclaimed'. Another headman added that:

> not only those small animals, but also tigers and other ferocious animals which played sad havoc among the cattle were protected together with the game which Government wished to preserve. He did not speak because he was anxious about hunt game, but because goats and sheep were constantly being devoured by the spotted cat.[9]

---

[8] Cape of Good Hope, Native Affairs Department, *Blue Book on Native Affairs for 1905 (BBNA)*, Resident Magistrate (RM) of Umtata, 91; CA, CMT, 3/173, Assistant Resident Magistrate (RM) Umtata to Assistant CMT, 7 Sept. 1904; Dalindyebo Mtirara to RM Umtata, 5 Oct. 1904; Chief Dalindyebo to RM Umtata, 5 Mar. 1905; Nqweniso to RM Umtata, 1 Aug. 1905. One informant in the Umtata district also recalled hunting down leopards in the nearby mountain forests in the late 1910s and 1920s; interview with V. Cutshwa, Tabase Mission, Umtata district, 4 Feb. 1998. On wild cat problems generally, see Beinart, 'Night of the jackal'.

[9] *Report and Proceedings of the Transkeian Territories General Council for the Year 1910 (TTGC)*, 12 Apr. 1910, 79–80. See also CA, CMT, 3/633, RM Kentani to CMT, 24 Aug. 1909, describing the 'great hardship' suffered by Africans in the district due to wild animals destroying their gardens and crops during the close season, when they were not allowed to hunt; F.H. Guthrie, *Frontier Magistrate* (Cape Town, 1946), 194–6.

More regularly, African men ignored the letter of the law and asserted their power to hunt and control local wildlife. Contributing to the verbal and physical conflicts between African hunters and forest officers at the turn of the century was popular animosity towards the government's policy of restricting hunting while preserving what were commonly viewed as pests and predators. A rare glimpse into this dimension of colonial relations is provided by a particular series of events in the Kentani district in the late 1890s. In late December 1899, District Forest Officer K.A. Carlson sent an alarming dispatch to Conservator Heywood concerning the 'licentious' and 'defiant' activities of African hunters in the Manubi forest. Forester Samuel Allen had recently been the target of several violent acts while on patrol there. In one instance, when he tried to question two African men whom he spotted in the forest carrying a gun and assegais, one of them responded with a thrust of his spear. Over the next couple of days, another hunter threatened him with a gun, and the forester's fowl coop was later vandalized. Yet the incident Allen highlighted in his report to Carlson occurred when he discovered a party of some fifty men in the forest and questioned their right to hunt there. With an 'insolent and daring attitude', the hunting party taunted the forester and mocked the forest regulations: 'I was told I had better go home and report the matter quick before I got my head bashed—if Government wish to protect the game Govt [sic] must kraal it'.[10]

This particularly hostile response to hunting restrictions expressed a deeper current among many African communities at the turn of the century. By restricting Africans' abilities to protect their own property from predators and pests, the government undermined people's capacity to manage their livelihoods effectively during a period of mounting ecological and economic pressure. Such conflicts over the government's priorities came to the fore as rural communities experienced and responded directly to official assaults on African-owned dogs.

Controlling African Hunting: The Problem of 'Kaffir Dogs'

> A native can no more be trusted with an axe or hatchet into the forest than with a gun or dogs. With the axe he will destroy trees whether he

---

[10] CA, CMT, 3/40. Forester Samuel Allen at Manubi, 14 Dec. 1899, enclosed in FCT to CMT, 'Attitude of natives at Manubi', 21 Dec. 1899.

> wants them or not, with a gun, assegais and dogs, every living creature larger than a mouse will be killed.[11]
>
> Everything possible is done by foresters to repress Kaffir hunts, by shooting and poisoning their dogs when found in the forests, and by prosecuting the offenders when caught.[12]

From the outset, official attempts to restrict African hunting activities were beset with difficulties. As with all laws regarding the protection of flora and fauna during this period, enforcement on the ground was a perpetual problem.[13] Although permits, closed game seasons and species restrictions successfully reduced Africans' independent hunting in some locales, forestry personnel were too few and far between to control hunting comprehensively. Recognizing the limitations of their policing efforts, forest officials promoted a more direct and effective assault on African hunters' activities: the destruction of Africans' hunting dogs.

Foresters' focus on controlling Africans' dogs grew out of a mix of late nineteenth-century settler culture in the Eastern Cape and Transkei and a commitment to the exclusionary principles of scientific forestry. As mentioned elsewhere in this book, 'kaffir dogs' had long been the target of attacks in settler literature, with travellers, missionaries, traders and settlers regularly condemning the 'vicious', 'wretched' and 'uncivilized' dogs found at most African kraals in the region.[14] Such verbal assaults on African-owned 'curs' owed much to the development of elite attitudes towards animals in Victorian Britain exported to colonial South Africa during this era of settler expansion. Mongrel breeds, whether in Britain or her colonies, were viewed as animals of lowly status,

---

[11] *Annual Report for 1893*, 'Report of the Conservator of Forests, Transkeian Conservancy', 141.

[12] *Annual Report for 1901*, 'Report of the Conservator of Forests, Eastern Conservancy', 106.

[13] Some typical official comments on this problem appear in CA, FCE, 3/1/57, 590, district forest officer (DFO) Kingwilliamstown (KWT) to FCE, 28 June 1904; Cape of Good Hope, *Report of the Select Committee on Crown Forests, 1906*, (A12–06), evidence of Chief Conservator of Forests (CFC) Joseph Lister, 17–20, 31.

[14] See, for example: S. Kay, *Travels and Researches in Caffraria* (New York, 1834), 122–3, commenting on how Africans' hunting dogs in the Eastern Cape were 'uncivilized' and 'of the most wretched description'; A.G.S. Gibson, *Eight Years in Kaffraria* (New York, 1969), 6, describing how the missionary once 'nearly fell a victim to the very vicious Kaffir dogs, which are to be found at most native kraals'; CTA, 1/TSO, 3/1/7/2, W.A. Fraser, Umga Flats, Maclear district, to RM Tsolo, 19 May 1890 and Cape of Good Hope, *Report of the South African Native Affairs Commission, 1905 (SANAC)*, 11, 1167. R. Gordon also describes similar official and settler hostility towards Africans' dogs in colonial Namibia, in 'Fido: dog tales of colonialism in Namibia' in this volume.

undisciplined, uncontrollable and prone to disease, while pure-bred dogs, particularly those used in foxhunting and other sport represented the civilized refinement, social pedigree and economic status of their owners.[15] Such valuations of dog breeds and their owners, embodying deeper attitudes towards class and European civilized culture, were transposed into colonial hunting regulations in the turn-of-the-century Transkei. Not only were sportsmen given privileged access to government forests for hunting, but those who were members of hunt clubs and used beagles or foxhounds—revered sporting breeds—received 50 per cent discounts on their game licenses.[16]

There were also more material reasons for settler and official hostility towards Africans' dogs; they could, and often did, injure and kill both domestic and wild animals in the territories. Particularly in areas where larger European farming settlements adjoined African communities, settlers often complained to magistrates about the depredations of African-owned dogs on their livestock.[17] As William Beinart has described for East Griqualand in the 1890s and 1900s, such disputes often reflected deeper settler concerns over social control and the protection of boundaries and private property; as the settler community pushed the colonial government to protect European farms from African trespass and squatting, Africans' dogs were often 'a convenient object of blame and their owners an easy target for compensation claims'.[18] When foresters began to exclude and destroy Africans' dogs in state forests at the turn of the century, they combined interests in guarding property and limiting the mobility of Africans themselves.[19] Increasing official

---

[15] For an enlightening discussion of class-based attitudes towards dogs, see H. Ritvo, *The Animal Estate: The English and Other Creatures in the Victorian Age* (Cambridge MA, 1987), 82–115, 176–202.

[16] Government Notice (GN) 494, 28 July 1900; Proclamation (P) 135 of 1903, section 37; National Archives (NA), FOR, 51, A55, FCT to CFC, 12 Mar. 1906; on Victorian era attitudes towards these particular breeds, see Ritvo, *Animal Estate*, 94–6, 105–7.

[17] CA, 1/TSO, 3/1/7/2, W.A. Fraser, Umga Flats, Maclear district, to RM Tsolo, 19 May 1890; *SANAC*, 11, 1155, 1167; W. Beinart, 'Settler accumulation in East Griqualand', in W. Beinart, P. Delius and S. Trapido (eds.), *Putting a Plough to the Ground: Accumulation and Dispossessions in Rural South Africa, 1850–1930* (Johannesburg, 1986), 289–90.

[18] Beinart, 'Settler accumulation in East Griqualand', 289–300.

[19] The pound regulations implemented in the Territories during this period in some ways gave foresters a regulatory precedent for dog eradication in government forests. P387, 26 September 1893, section 22, enabled private landowners to destroy any small animals trespassing on their property and any dog found in any enclosed or fenced area containing game.

distress at the destructiveness of uncontrolled African-owned dogs did not simply reflect a growing threat to local fauna and a dispassionate interest in preservation. It also represented a clear desire by conservators to find a more direct and effective way to keep uncontrolled African men out of state forests.

While Cape forest officials in the late nineteenth century categorized African hunters in government reserves as poachers and trespassers, African dogs became to all intents and purposes vermin. To understand the evolution of official dog-eradication policies it is thus necessary to appreciate the history of colonial approaches to vermin control. As William Beinart and Lance van Sittert have both suggested recently, the push for vermin control in the turn-of-the-century Eastern Cape and Transkei was an outgrowth of the regional expansion of settler capitalist agriculture. As European settlement and small-stock farming dominated certain zones of the Eastern Cape in the mid- to late nineteenth century, settlers increasingly organised, calling upon the colonial government to protect their property from predatory wild animals. Wild animal poisoning clubs were formed from the 1880s and the state became more extensively involved in vermin eradication and exclusion over the next two decades, establishing select committees on the subject, laying poisoned meat in government forest reserves, awarding public bounties for animal destruction and subsidizing vermin-proof fencing. While Cape authorities pursued the more aggressive preservation of game animals in the colony during this period, attempting to contain settlers' toll on indigenous fauna, they simultaneously worked to ensure capitalist agriculture's success by endorsing the mass slaughter of numerous wildlife species.[20]

As some of these policies were imported into the Transkei, along with the Cape's game laws, from the late 1880s onwards, tensions developed in the small yet influential local settler community over wildlife concerns and governmental responses to them. Following the lead of the Eastern Conservancy, local foresters began systematically shooting and laying poison for vermin in Transkei government forests by the early

---

[20] Beinart, 'Night of the jackal'; L. van Sittert, '"Keeping the enemy at bay": the extermination of wild carnivora in the Cape Colony, 1889–1910', *Environmental History*, 3 (1998), 333–56; and see also R. Mutwira, 'Southern Rhodesian wildlife policy (1890–1953): a question of condoning game slaughter?' *Journal of Southern African Studies*, 15 (1989), 250–62. For more on the earlier evolution of British categories of vermin from the seventeenth century onward, see H. Ritvo, *The Platypus and the Mermaid and other Figments of the Classifying Imagination* (Cambridge MA, 1997), 38–9, 189–94.

1890s. Through such measures, officials strove to safeguard both the livestock of settler farmers and the many reserved game species from forest-dwelling predators.[21]

As foresters in both the Eastern and Transkei conservancies engaged in such vermin poisoning, they soon realized the additional value of these measures in reducing the temptation of African hunters to pursue game. In the Eastern Cape forests, where the settler community pushed for vermin control and where poisoning was initiated earlier, officials quickly encountered its dramatic impact on African hunting exploits. As Conservator Lister reported in 1894, poison baits in local forests were successfully killing vermin as well as 'innumerable Kaffir curs, undoubtedly the property of poachers. This has had a beneficial effect, since Kaffirs now hesitate to risk the lives of their dogs, without which they rarely hunt'.[22] To make his department's intentions absolutely clear, Lister explained to his staff that 'poison is laid not only to destroy Vermin but the dogs of hunting parties.'[23]

In the Transkei itself, African-owned dogs in government forests were also summarily treated as vermin. In the early to mid-1890s, foresters began routinely laying poisoned meat and shooting Africans' dogs, much as they did other undesirable animals in the forest. By the late 1890s and early 1900s, officers and guards regularly included a tally of dogs destroyed by gun and poison in their reports on vermin control.[24] In 1906, Conservator Heywood matter-of-factly explained his staff's now standard policy to the Chief Conservator

> When poaching becomes troublesome at any centre and the offenders cannot be caught, poison (pork and strychnine is laid down for the purpose of killing 'vermin', and subsequently the Forester frequently finds a number of dead dogs, but the poaching ceases.[25]

---

[21] *Annual Report for 1891*, 72; *Annual Report for 1893*, 137.

[22] *Annual Report for 1894*, report of the FCE Lister, 100.

[23] CA, FCE 3/1/57, 594, DFO Keiskama Hoek to FCE, 14 Oct. 1894; FCE to Civil Commissioner, KWT, 13 Nov. 1894; CA, FCE 3/1/57, files 595 and 602, have much correspondence on these episodes.

[24] *Annual Report for 1893*, 137–41; CA, AGR 44, 601, FCT to Mr Cowper, 9 Oct. 1893; CA, CMT 3/40, FCT to CMT, 9 Oct. 1894; CA, 1/TSO 1/1/12, court cases of 24 Jan. and 10 Sept. 1896, concerning dog-poisoning; *Annual Report for 1896*, 156–7; CA, FCT 1/1/1/3, USA to FCT, 29 Apr. 1897; *Annual Report for 1897*, 135; CA, FCT 2/1/1/4, FCT to USA, 6 Dec. 1900; CA, NA 692, B2690, FCT to USA, 8 Jan. 1903 and CA, FDU 1/2, 40, Baziya Plantation, FDU to Forester Adams, 17 Apr. 1903; report for Oct, 1903, Forester Adams to FDU, 2 Nov. 1903.

[25] NA, FOR 51, A55, FCT to CFC, 12 Mar. 1906; CA, FCE 3/1/50, 621, FCT to FCE, 14 Nov. 1907.

Mass shooting of Africans' dogs was also pursued more routinely during these years. In one hunting incident in the Tsolo district in 1906, for example, a few foresters, who discovered some 200 African men hunting, found chasing them away and 'shooting a good number of their dogs' the most they could do when so outnumbered. Conservator Heywood commended such practices as one of the few effective means of policing African hunting: 'It is perhaps to be regretted that so many dogs were killed, but I am of the opinion that by no other method could the hunt have been so effectually stopped'.[26]

Over the course of the 1900s, authorities also instituted a new series of regulations, which successively made the owners of unattended dogs found trespassing in any forest in the Transkei 'where there is any game' liable to prosecution and a fine of up to £10. With these and other laws in hand, forest officers and guards aggressively pursued the exclusion of Africans' dogs and their owners from reserves on their patrols.[27]

While poisoning and shooting dogs worked to reduce the scale of African hunting on the ground, officials did not automatically or unanimously support such strategies. During the 1900s, as the implementation of forest and hunting restrictions led to more regular confrontations between local people and forest staff in the Eastern Cape and Transkei, some authorities in the Native Affairs Department scrutinized the Forest Department's activities more closely. In 1907, Chief Magistrate Stanford complained to the secretary for native affairs that foresters were intentionally placing poison in natural areas 'with the express object of destroying dogs belonging to Natives', an act that lacked any legal basis in the colony.[28] Stanford's comments sparked protracted official debates over the government's approach to African hunting, bringing long-standing differences between conservation and native administration to the fore.[29] Chief Conservator Lister, long an advocate of destroying dogs to curb African hunting, attempted to convince the prime minister and the secretary for native affairs that his staff always took the necessary

---

[26] CA, NA 692, B2690, Asst. DFO, Kambi, to FCT, 12 Aug. 1906; FCT to CFC, 16 Aug. 1906.

[27] P59, 12 Apr. 1902, amending sections 11 of P209 of 1890; P135 of 1903, which comprehensively expanded forest restrictions in the Transkei; sections 5b and 25e, concerned the trespass of dogs in forests and P421, 19 Aug. 1907, 'Trespassing of dogs in demarcated and undemarcated forests'.

[28] CA, NA 753, F127, CMT to SNA, 29 Nov. 1907.

[29] These struggles within the colonial bureaucracy are discussed in greater detail in my 'Roots and rights in the Transkei', chs. 2 and 3.

precautions, that headmen and communities were always given ample warning of where and when poison was being placed and that foresters had been engaging in such practices for many years with authorities' consent. More importantly, Lister argued:

> If the practice of laying down poison were not stopped, I have no hesitation in saying that the Forests would soon be over-run with vermin and stray dogs, that frequently hurt game on their own initiative. Moreover, there would be no check on Native hunting parties, which are ever ready to drive the forests and destroy every vestige of game.[30]

While Native Affairs officials may generally have agreed in principle with Lister, they were primarily concerned with maintaining social order and avoiding undue 'native irritation' across the Transkei. Both Stanford and the secretary for native affairs, Dower, not only questioned the legality of the government's actions but further raised the embarrassing possibility that African dog owners might actually have the legal right and inclination to sue the colonial government for damages arising from their dogs being killed.[31] Even more significant for many magistrates and their superiors was the 'strong feeling of antagonism' that dog-killing was generating in different districts and the spectre of popular retaliation on Forest Department property and personnel.[32] Dower was particularly rankled by what he saw as the 'needless irritation' caused by foresters' over-zealous approach to game protection. In a private memo to Prime Minister Merriman, he made his views clear, 'Poisoning dogs is surely not a part of forestry. I hope it will be stopped'. And, in response, Merriman was similarly critical of the Forest Department, 'I do not like the laying of poison...It is this sort of business that sets people against the Forests. What possible business have they with vermin—they do not hurt trees'.[33]

---

[30] CA, NA 753, SNA to CFC, requesting information on behalf of the prime minister, 8 Jan. 1908; CFC to SNA, 'Destruction of vermin in crown forests: alleged poisoning of dogs', 5 Feb. 1908; CFC to SNA, 14 July 1908. Lister's claim that former SNA Walter Stanford had endorsed dog-poisoning was confirmed when Dower discussed the matter with Stanford himself, 'who assures me that he had always advocated the use of poison rather than the use of the gun—subject to previous warning being given to the headmen and people'; SNA to CMT, 7 Aug. 1908.
[31] CA, NA 753, SNA to CMT, 7 Aug. 1908; CMT to SNA, 19 Feb. 1908; SNA to Prime Minister (PM), 'Poisoning of Kafir dogs in demarcated forests', 8 Mar. 1908.
[32] CA, NA 753, SNA to CMT, 7 Aug. 1908; RM Mqanduli to CMT, 15 Nov. 1907; CMT to SNA, 19 Feb. 1908; SNA to PM, 8 Mar. 1908; RM Kentani to CMT, 10 Sept 1908; CMT to SNA, 22 Sept. 1908.
[33] CA, NA 753, SNA to CMT, 7 Aug. 1908; SNA to PM, handwritten note dated

Despite such strong private objections to the poisoning of dogs and its potential repercussions, however, administrators were not about to alter the broader official campaign to regulate popular resources and constrain Africans' impact on local flora and fauna. Firmly committed to the necessity of forest and game preservation for the progressive development of the Transkei, Merriman allowed the laying of poison in forest reserves to continue unabated. The antagonism arising from dog-poisoning could be obviated through careful native administration rather than through any readjustment of state resource policy. As long as foresters cooperated with resident magistrates, who, in the eyes of the prime minister and authorities in the Native Affairs Department, could best assess the political impact of such interventions in their respective districts, and as long as local communities were given due notice, poison could continue to be set out in forested areas.[34] This policy, while placing tighter reins on foresters as they tackled problems of vermin and African hunting, failed to respond to Africans' concerns about resource access, and became the standard from the late 1900s onwards.[35]

The Value of Dogs

As colonial authorities employed dog-killing as a means of curbing African hunting, they imposed their own categorization of Africans' dogs as trespassers, predators and vermin. For the owners of dogs, however, the state's eradication policies meant the destruction of valuable resources. Across the Eastern Cape and Transkei, dogs were a standard feature of most rural African homesteads, valued for their hunting skills as well as their utility in herding cattle and sheep, protecting households and their property and tracking down stolen

---

10 Mar. 1908, on bottom of letter; SNA to PM, 8 Mar. 1908; PM to SNA, 4 Dec. 1908.

[34] CA, NA 753, SNA to CMT, 7 Aug. 1908; CMT to SNA, 22 Sept. 1908; PM to SNA, 4 Dec. 1908; SNA to FCT, 9 Dec. 1908.

[35] See, for example, CA, NA 753, SNA to CMT, 7 Aug. 1908; SNA to R. Smith, Secretary, Bonte Bok Flats Farmers' Association, Cathcart, 9 July 1909; NA, FOR 276, A550, Asst. FCT to CFC, 17 Sept. 1909; CA, 1/UTA 6/1/204, 41(1), RM Umtata to FDU, 9 Aug. 1910; CA 1/TSO 5/1/8, 31(5), RM Tsolo to Public Prosecutor, 2 May 1916; CA, FKS 2/1/1, DFO Kokstad to FCT, 4 Oct. 1917; DFO Kokstad to FCT, 17 Jan. 1918; CA, 1/TSO 5/1/8, 31(5), FDU to RM Tsolo, 11 Feb. 1922 and CA, FKS 4/1/1, 1928–29, Umzimkulu Central, 6 and 8, and Umzimkulu Eastern, 4.

livestock.³⁶ And despite the often inflammatory rhetoric produced in official and popular settler literature concerning the evils of Kaffir dogs, many authorities also recognized the importance of dogs to African households across the region. In one civil case before the native appeals court in 1912, for instance, Chief Magistrate Stanford overturned the Mount Ayliff district magistrate's decision to award small compensation for one African man's killing of another's dog. Since the dog was the plaintiff's personal property, Stanford conceded, the magistrate 'should have awarded reasonable damages, bearing in mind that the value of a dog from the Native point of view is totally different from the estimate a European has of the average Kaffir dog'.³⁷

Africans also frequently reminded officials of the value of their dogs. After a dog tax was implemented in the Eastern Cape districts in the mid-1880s, for example, Africans across the region organized a series of protests. In 1889, *Imvo Zabantsundu* produced numerous articles about demonstrations being held in the Kingwilliamstown and Peddie divisions, which articulated some of the sources of popular discontent. At one public gathering in February that year, a crowd condemned the tax:

> pointing out that their dogs injure no one, while they are faithful constables, guarding them and their stock by night since the Natives were disarmed and left without the means of frightening the thieves and wild beasts that would gladly prey on their property.³⁸

---

³⁶ W. Holden, *The Past and Future of the Kaffir Races* (Cape Town, 1963), 260, 276–7; Beinart, 'Settler accumulation', 289–90; J.H. Soga, *The Ama-Xosa Life and customs* (Alice, 1931), 376–8; Gibson, *Eight Years in Kaffraria*, 6 and CA 1/TSO 1/1/14, case of 13 June 1898. For the significance of dogs in rural Africans' lives in another southern African context, see Gordon, 'Fido'.

³⁷ Transkeian Territories, *Native Appeal Court Records: A Selection of Cases, 1912–1917*, vol. 111 (Cape Town, 1919), 53, Mangalelwa Kwati and Others v. Mbaba Pumza, Mt Ayliff, No. 51/1912, held at Kokstad, 22 Aug. 1912.

³⁸ *Imvo Zabantsundu*, 14 Feb. 1889, 3. See also subsequent *Imvo* articles on public protests: 23 May 1889, 4; 22 Aug. 1889, 3; 19 Sept. 1889, 3; 21 Nov. 1889, 3. Many Africans and even some settlers in the Eastern Cape and Transkei at the turn of the century often complained that taxing or destroying Africans' dogs would enable wild animals to wreak havoc on their croplands and livestock. See CA, FCT 3/1/57, 602, Asst. RM Keiskama Hoek to Forester J. Anderson, Mount Evelyn, 1 Nov. 1894, describing local leaders' complaints about dog-poisoning in forests. Also, *SANAC*, 11, J.C. Humphrey, settler of the Umzimkulu district, 1153, also cited in Beinart, 'Settler accumulation', 290: 'we find that as soon as the Native dogs decrease the vermin increase, and it is the fact of Native dogs being so numerous that has kept down vermin'.

Many years later, when the issue of imposing a dog tax on Africans in the Transkei was debated and eventually abandoned, headmen again defended the importance of dogs as overall 'policemen of the kraal'.[39]

Africans were also more discriminating in raising and using dogs than white settlers thought, selectively employing particular dog breeds for specific purposes. Consider the testimony of one Teyise in the Tsolo district in the late 1880s as he sued his neighbors in the magistrate's court for damages done to his dog:

> [It was] a well bred dog *a half bred blood Hound* ('*Itwina*') for the purpose of herding...My dog was a valuable watch dog and I never lost anything while it was about. Now the guardian of my Kraal is gone and I have lost my protector. My dog never bit anyone but always gave tongue. I have now no other dog. I got this dog [as] a present from a friend. I value my dog at £10 because he was my 'herd' when he barked at night I had to go out and got sufficient warning to protect my stock...'Ntwina' dogs...are dogs of universal use for both hunting & house watching.[40]

Both J.H. Soga and Robert Godfrey recorded several distinct dog types popular among Africans across the Transkei. For instance, various mixed breeds admired for their aggressiveness, courage and intelligence, such as *ingqeqe* and *ibaku*, would accompany beaters to root out game from forest cover, whereas *ingesi* and *itwina* were valued for their speed in keeping up the chase.[41] Men often went to great expense to acquire the desired breed for their purposes. Soga recalled that it was not uncommon for men to pay two head of cattle for an *itwina*.[42] In the case cited above, Teyise described how European and African men in the Eastern Cape regularly sold dogs for £8 to £9 a piece.[43] Given the value of particular hunting dogs, European settlers and officials were keen to keep an eye

---

[39] *TTGC* 1926, 'Dog tax in the Transkeian territories', 106–9.

[40] CA, 1/TSO 2/1/7, Case No. 10, Teyise v. Mcwakumbana and Others, 6 and 14 Feb. 1889.

[41] Soga, *Ama-Xosa Life and Customs*, 377–8; South African Library (SAL), MSB 783, R. Godfrey, unpublished manuscript of 'A Xhosa-English dictionary', c. 1944, section 'B', 10, defining *ibaku* as a 'Pointer dog, or other breed with long drooping ears', section 'J', 1, section 'N', 114, and section 'T', 81, defining *ithwina* as a 'Hunting-dog, with the body of a greyhound, but with stiff up-standing sharp-pointed ears'.

[42] Soga, *Ama-Xosa Life and Customs*, 378.

[43] CA, 1/TSO 2/1/7, Case No.10, Teyise v. Mewakumbana and Others, 6 and 14 Feb. 1889. In one 1912 Umtata district case brought before the native appeals court, one African man was awarded a larger than normal sum for damages done to his dog, principally because it was not 'an ordinary Kafir dog' but 'a sporting dog'. *Native Appeal Court Records*, 3, 54–5, Joel Ngwenze vs. Motomani Mananga, Umtata district, No. 301/1912, held at Umtata, 25 Nov. 1912.

on their own property. Chief Magistrate Henry Elliot, for instance, kept two hunting dogs he had received from fellow magistrate Walter Stanford in 1892 in Tsolo since there was 'less chance of their being stolen than in Umtata. Natives are very fond of picking up that class of dog'.[44] Although game and hunting both decreased by the early 1900s, acquiring good hunting dogs was still important to many African men in the region in the 1920s and 1930s.[45] Sampson Dyayiya recalled that some wealthier men in the Tsolo area used to purchase specific dogs for white farmers living in neighbouring areas in Maclear:

> There were people who used to breed long dogs which are good at catching wild animals. Those dogs were called *amengesi*. The hunters used those dogs...They used to buy those from anywhere they were sold, any place they saw those dogs being sold they bought them.[46]

In addition to preferring specific dog breeds, many Africans put time and energy into training their dogs for hunting as well as other purposes.[47] One German observer in the Transkei in the late 1920s noted that Thembu boys and men trained their dogs to herd differently coloured cattle according to the way their owners whistled. Oral sources suggest that men in some areas continued to train their dogs for the hunt in the 1920s and 1930s by having them learn to track and drive game with previously trained dogs.[48] Keeping dogs fit and healthy was another way to prepare them for the rigors of hunting and chasing

---

[44] University of Cape Town, Manuscripts Library (UCT), BC 293, Sir W.E.M. Stanford Papers, Correspondence, B66.88, Major Sir Henry G. Elliot, Umtata to Stanford, 31 Oct. 1892.

[45] Soga, *Ama-Xosa Life and Customs*, 377–8; interview with W.M. Ngombane, who described how only whites could afford the good dog breeds by the 1940s in his area; interview with D. Gcanga, Manzana, Engcobo district, 5 Feb. 1998; interview with P. Maka; interview with V. Cutshwa.

[46] Interview with S. Dyayiya and N. Dyayiya, Silverton, Umtata district, 27 Feb. 1998; interview with A. Qupa, Baziya Mission Station, Umtata district, 8 Jan. 1998; interview with V. Cutshwa; interview with W. Jumba, T. Nodwayi, F. Sonyoka, and Z. Quvile, commenting on how much *amangesi* were still desired for hunting in the 1940s and 1950s in the area.

[47] The use of trained dogs is still popular among hunters in certain areas of the former Transkei today; interview with W.M. Ngombane and T. Kepe, *Environmental Entitlements in Mkambati: Livelihoods, Social Institutions and Environmental Change on the Wild Coast of the Eastern Cape* (Programme for Land and Agrarian Studies, School of Government, University of the Western Cape, Research Report No. 1, 1997), 41–2.

[48] Anonymous, 'Ein echt heidnisches Bierfest bei den Tembus', *Vergissmeinnicht*, 46 (1928), 272; interview with C. Mvambo, St Cuthbert's Mission, Tsolo district, 3 Feb. 1998; interview with W.M. Ngombane and interview with D. Gcanga. Beinart makes a passing reference to Africans training hunting dogs in East Griqualand in the 1890s, in 'Settler accumulation', 289.

game. In the late nineteenth century, when hunting was a more vital part of African livelihoods in the Transkei, it was not unusual for men to view the maintenance of hunting dogs as an important investment. Soga recollected seeing African men going to great lengths to ensure the well-being of their hunting companions in the 1880s:

> Fifty years or so ago I saw individual dogs of this breed [*itwina*] kept by a hunting owner in a sleek and well-fed condition, having as sleep quarters a dried ox hide, hair uppermost, placed at the top end of the hut and next to his master's resting place.[49]

A less costly way to invest in the maintenance of dogs and to enhance their performance was to utilize natural plants and other materials as medicines and charms. In the 1920s and 1930s, Robert Godfrey recorded the common use of several different types of plants in parts of East Griqualand and elsewhere 'given to dogs at the beginning of the hunting season to get them into running trim' or 'to make them vicious, so that they will fly at thieves who come prowling round at night on the lookout for sheep and goats'.[50]

As the colonial government instituted a policy of dog destruction in government forests at the turn of the century, people thus resented much more than just the direct threat such actions posed to their hunting practices. They further objected to official attempts to protect the boundaries of the forest at the cost of destroying their homesteads' valued herders, policemen and guardians. Such popular understandings of dogs and their meaning contributed to the conflicts that would engulf official schemes to control African hunting.

Dog-Killing and Popular Rumour

Government dog-poisoning in the Eastern Cape and Transkei coincided with a uniquely tense period in colonial relations in the region. In the mid-1890s, Cecil Rhodes's introduction of the Glen Grey Act—originally designed to impose additional forms of taxation, individualized land tenure and a new system of local political administration—set

---

[49] Soga, *Ama-Xosa Life and Customs*, 378 and interview with P. Maka.
[50] SAL, Godfrey, 'A Xhosa-English Dictionary', section 'H', 42, 66, 73 and see also Hunter, *Reaction to Conquest*, 96.

off waves of resentment across the Transkei.[51] As African communities endured these efforts to push them further into the cash economy and the migrant labour system, to constrict their access to productive resources and to reduce their political rights, they also faced a period of increasing economic indebtedness, impoverishment and environmental strain. While drought and locust swarms intermittently ravaged crops in many inland and coastal districts, they became most severe during the mid-1890s.[52] These calamities were accompanied by a deadly combination of human and animal diseases, most notably smallpox and then rinderpest, which began to take its toll on African livestock herds in the Transkei in 1897.[53] Initial experiences of dog-poisoning across the region thus occurred within a context of ecological stress, rural crisis and intensifying colonial intervention.

From its beginnings, official dog-poison policies were met by popular protests, suspicions and rumours. In 1893, in his first major report on the laying of poison for vermin and dog control in Transkeian reserves, Conservator Henkel warned that, despite its success in controlling animal populations, the practice was

> connected with some danger to the staff, as Natives in their raw state believe it is witchcraft and will complain to the Magistrates who will

---

[51] W. Beinart and C. Bundy, *Hidden Struggles in Rural South Africa: Politics and Popular Movements in the Transkei and Eastern Cape, 1890–1930* (Berkeley, 1897), ch. 4 and R. Southall, *South Africa's Transkei: The Political Economy of an 'Independent' Bantustan* (New York, 1983), 76, 90–1.

[52] On drought conditions, see C.H. Vogel, 'A documentary-derived climatic chronology for South Africa, 1820–1900', *Climatic Change*, 14 (1989), 291–307; C. Ballard, 'Drought and economic distress: South Africa in the 1800s', *Journal of Interdisciplinary History*, 18 (1986), 359–78; *Annual Report for 1894*, 130; *Annual Report for 1895*, 168; Beinart and Bundy, *Hidden Struggles*, 54–5 and W. Beinart, *The Political Economy of Pondoland 1860 to 1930* (Johannesburg, 1892), 47, 53. For locust problems, see CA, AGR 110, 420; CA, AGR 322, 420; *BBNA 1895*, Tsomo district, 22 Nov. 1894, RM Tsomo, 64; *Annual Report for 1895*, 168; CA, CMT 3/520, Minutes of meeting, Kentani district, 1 Aug. 1896; CA, CMT 3/88, RM Engcobo to CMT, 17 Feb. 1896; *Annual Report for 1896*, 154; L. Switzer, *Power and Resistance in an African Society: The Ciskei Xhosa and the Making of South Africa* (Madison, 1993), 99 and Beinart and Bundy, *Hidden Struggles*, 54–5.

[53] Examples of the toll of smallpox in particular locales can be seen in the Engcobo district files of CA, CMT 3/87 and CMT 3/88. On the impact of rinderpest, see P. Phoofolo, 'Epidemics and revolutions: the rinderpest epidemic in late-nineteenth century southern Africa', *Past and Present*, 138 (1993), 112–43; Beinart, *Political Economy of Pondoland*, 47–8 and C. Bundy, *The Rise and Fall of the South African Peasantry* (London, 1979), 119–22.

report the matter to the Chief of the S.N.A. Department as detrimental to the peace of the Country.[54]

Over the next few years, as placing poisons in forests became routine in both the Eastern and Transkeian conservancies, Henkel's words of caution resonated ever more clearly. In November 1894, for instance, some popular protests about dog-killing arose in the Keiskama Hoek district of the Eastern Cape. The assistant resident magistrate, C.A. King, explained the situation to the local forester:

> A number of Headmen attended at the office this morning to complain that their dogs are being poisoned wholesale by poison laid in the area under your supervision & they are in great terror that their children will also be poisoned by the poisoned meat and bread laid about, as they state it is placed *outside* the forest, and also on ridges and open spaces. They point out that herd boys will naturally pick up bread and meat.[55]

Although King attempted to assure the assembled group that the poison was only placed for the destruction of wild animals and that the government 'never intended to poison the natives' dogs or to incur that risk, nor that it would be a source of danger to human life', the headmen of the Gwiligwili and Mtwaku locations were not convinced.[56] For his part, the supervising forest officer, E.B. Dwyer, reported on the events by summarily dismissing local people's complaints. Local communities had been sufficiently notified of the poison setting, Dwyer asserted, poison had only been placed at a 'safe distance' from nearby residences, and foresters never used 'so perishable a substance as bread, in the open air' when laying baits. The only real reason local people were upset, he concluded, was that the destruction of their dogs was successfully inhibiting their ability to hunt in local forests.[57]

---

[54] CA, FCT 2/2/2/2, FCT to Secretary for Land, Mines, and Agriculture (SLMA), 5 July 1893; CA, FCT 1/1/1/1/, SLMA to FCT, 4 Aug. 1893, citing the SNA's response to Henkel. Henkel's comments also reveal his often antagonistic relationship with the Native Affairs Department during this period.

[55] CA, FCE 3/1/57, 602, Asst. RM Keiskama Hoek to Forester J. Anderson, Mount Evelyn, 1 Nov. 1894, original emphasis and CA, FCE 3/1/57, 595, Asst. RM Keiskama Hoek to Civil Commissioner, KWT, 30 Nov. 1894.

[56] CA, FCE 3/1/57, 602, Asst. RM Keiskama Hoek to Forester J. Anderson, Mount Evelyn, 1 Nov. 1894 and CA, FCE 3/1/57, 595, Civil Commissioner KWT, to FCE, 1 Nov. 1894.

[57] CA, FCE 3/1/57, 595, DFO Kologha to FCT, 1 Jan. 1895; DFO Keiskama Hoek, to FCE, 14 Nov. 1894 and CA, FCE 3/1/57, 602, Asst. RM Keiskama Hoek to Forester J. Anderson, Mount Evelyn, 1 Nov. 1894.

Dwyer was only partially correct. African men in the Keiskama Hoek district had recently engaged in a series of scraps with local forest officers and guards, lashing out at the government's restrictions on hunting and dogs amid increased attacks on their livestock from predatory forest animals. However, as King's telling of the story reveals, the headmen of the locations involved were equally concerned that the poison was not safely tucked away from the traffic of people and animals. Their villages were surrounded by forests, they explained, so that the only way to access common grazing areas in some locales was to pass between forest patches, 'and that it was in these open places, through which they had to pass, that poison was laid'.[58] In voicing their frustrations with poison-laying, local communities literally and symbolically questioned whether the government was intentionally trying to harm them as they coped with local ecological pressures.

To understand the deeper metaphorical component to these complaints, it is useful to connect such concerns over dog-poisoning with other expressions of anti-colonial frustration and resentment in the Eastern Cape and Transkei during this period. When people in the Gwiligwili and Mtwaku locations went to the headmen to denounce the government's actions, they focused on three specific issues: the intentional and indiscriminate placement of poison across the open landscape, the use of meat and bread for bait and the threats to children's lives.[59] These themes bear some similarity to other public denunciations of white settlers at the time. As William Beinart and Colin Bundy have noted, popular opposition to the Glen Grey legislation often invoked politically barbed metaphors of 'poisoned goods'. Rumours circulating across the region claimed that government leaders were working with European traders to kill and bewitch Africans by poisoning the food and other goods they purchased from trading shops.[60] For example, in November 1894, around the same time as the dog-poisoning episode in the Keiskama Hoek district, Chief Magistrate Henry Eliot explained to the prime minister that local traders in the southern districts of the Territories were suspected of putting special poisons in such things as

---

[58] CA, FCE 3/1/57, 602, Asst. RM Keiskama Hoek to Civil Commissioner, KWT, 30 Nov. 1894.
[59] CA, FCE 3/1/57, 602, Asst. RM Keiskama Hoek to Forester, Mount Evelyn, 1 Nov. 1894.
[60] Beinart and Bundy, *Hidden Struggles*, 138–65.

packets of mealies.⁶¹ In the Mount Frere district a few years later, one Agriculture Department employee was accused by many 'of having placed poison in some of the sugar given to the natives['] children with intent to destroy them.'⁶²

Other similar rumours were also afloat: throughout the mid-1890s, people in various Transkeian districts invoked rumours of the government causing and spreading death to explain the rise of particular diseases among themselves and their children.⁶³ In some parts of Thembuland in 1895, for instance, local women refused to let their newborns be counted and registered, since, in the Engcobo magistrate' words, they feared the government would 'take alarm at the increase of the Native tribes' and devise ways to remedy the situation. People also refused to be vaccinated for small pox by colonial medical officers, claiming that 'the Government has caused the vaccine lymph to be bewitched or poisoned with the object of destroying the Natives'.⁶⁴

The complaints about state use of poisons against dogs need to be viewed within this broader context of rural discontent. While distraught at the literal destruction of their dogs and the real threats poison-laying posed to herd boys, local residents also expressed larger fears. Colonial authorities were accused of poisoning the foods (bread and meat) that Africans regularly consumed. In particular, bread—a basic commodity regularly bought from European trading stores during this period—was rumoured to be contaminated and spread over the open veld, despite the forest officer's assertion that no official with any commonsense would ever use such material as poison bait.⁶⁵ In addition, the focus on the threat to local peoples' lives, specifically children, repeated the language of other popular commentaries on the impact of state interventions on Africans' welfare. While forest officials interpreted resistance to poison-laying in narrow terms, local residents perceived

---

⁶¹ Public Record Office (London), Records of the Colonial Office 48, 525, CMT to secretary to PM, 21 Nov. 1894. See also CA, CMT 3/192, W.J. Clarke, Engcobo, to CMT, 19 Nov. 1894; *BBNA 1895*, RM Tsomo district, 22 Nov. 1894, 64; UCT, Stanford Papers, Diaries, A19, entry for 8 Dec. 1894; *Imvo Zabantsundu*, 'The new native delusion', 2 Jan. 1895, and 'Poisoned goods', 29 Jan. 1895 and CA, FCT 2/1/1/2, FCT to USA, 23 Jan. 1895.

⁶² CA, 1/MFE 4/1/8/3, N. Adams Cone to RM Mt. Frere, 23 Aug. 1897.

⁶³ See, for instance, *BBNA 1895*, RM Tsomo district, 22 Nov. 1894, 64.

⁶⁴ CA, 1/ENO 5/1/3/1, RM Engcobo to CMT, 30 July 1895 and Umtata Herald, 'The next delusion', 23 Mar. 1895.

⁶⁵ CA, FCE 3/1/57, 595, DFO Kologha to FCE, 1 Jan. 1895. Dwyer explained in this letter that the poison would dry up and lose its potency if bread was used.

and described state dog-killing as part of a broader onslaught on their lives and livelihoods.

As myriad social and ecological pressures intensified over the course of the mid- to late 1890s, many Africans regularly responded with accusations of colonial malevolence and sorcery.[66] Rumour and public accusation became symbolically powerful means of explaining and blaming the government for economic stress, environmental decline and the devastation wrought by human and livestock diseases.[67] Responding to the massive decimation of crops by locust swarms in the mid-1890s, people not only engaged in protective rituals but also asserted official culpability for the disaster. In some instances, the government's enforcement of locust eradication was directly blamed for the rise of destructive swarms, agricultural crisis and even disease.[68] Official responses to rinderpest, particularly through widespread and sometimes ineffective inoculation campaigns in African communities in the late 1890s, were often met with resistance, evasion and rumours that the government was intentionally trying to destroy Africans' herds in order to force more men into labour migrancy. In many cases, government inoculators were accused of deviously injecting cattle with poisonous bile to spread the disease more effectively.[69]

There were quite tangible reasons for these accusations as various employees of the colonial bureaucracy, particularly the Forest Department, were literally poisoning the landscape. In addition to the laying of poisoned meat for dogs in government forests, foresters began experimenting in the late 1890s with laying out fungus and

---

[66] On rumours of government sorcery in the early 1880s in some locales, see S. Redding, 'Sorcery and sovereignty: taxation, witchcraft, and political symbols in the 1880 Transkeian rebellion', *Journal of Southern African Studies*, 22 (1996), 249–69.

[67] *BBNA* 1897, 79; C. van Onselen, 'Reactions to rinderpest in southern Africa, 1896–97', *Journal of African History*, 13 (1972), 481; Phoofolo, 'Epidemics and revolutions' and Beinart and Bundy, *Hidden Struggles*, 54–5. The interpretation of rumours which follows is inspired by Luise White's nuanced approach to rumour and gossip in her recent *Speaking with Vampires: Rumour and History in Colonial Africa* (Berkeley, 2000).

[68] Van Onselen, 'Reactions to rinderpest', 481; Switzer, *Power and Resistance*, 99; CA, FCT 2/1/1/2, FCT to USA, 21 Feb. 1896; CA, CMT 3/170, RM Umtata to CMT, 17 Apr. 1896 and CA, CMT 3/520, Minutes of Meeting, Kentani, 1 Aug. 1896. On this latter point, also see *BBNA 1895*, RM Tsomo district, 22 Nov. 1894, 64

[69] CA, CMT 3/170, RM Umtata to CMT, 30 Aug. 1897; Van Onselen, 'Reactions to rinderpest'; Phoofolo, 'Epidemics and revolutions' and Bundy, *Rise and Fall*, 119–20. For a detailed example of such rumours in one particular context, see CA, 1/UTA 1/1/1/19 criminal cases, circuit court proceedings, Regina vs. Rolinyati Mgudli and Magopeni Rolinyati, 26 Oct. 1897.

spraying arsenite of soda to destroy locusts in some forest reserves, and the latter practice was extended to location commonages during the following decade.[70] Such actions were incorporated into popular rumours concerning Europeans' domination of local social, economic and ecological resources. For example, rumours and suspicions about the state's motives for treating cattle during the rinderpest epidemics extended beyond the mere act of inoculation. In some areas stories were told about Europeans poisoning local grazing lands. In the Mount Frere district in 1897, for instance, one European trader who was also serving as a government inoculator in local Bhaca communities warned the resident magistrate about the intense feeling of hostility and suspicion many residents felt towards the government's inoculation efforts. Not only were 'very uncharitable things' being said about the government and the police, but

> the B[h]acas swear that they will kill any white man that goes near their homes. I am being watched by herd boys most religiously as there is a rumour afloat that I am supplied with medicines which I sprinkle over the veldt to spread the rinderpest.[71]

The trader's woes seem to have intensified after some residents claimed to have discovered a white powder scattered over a local grazing area and associated the bewitching medicine with him. This powder may very well have been the arsenite of soda sprayed by government officers to destroy locust swarms, for it was often viewed as a danger to farm animals by livestock-owners across the region.[72]

In many cases, in fact, popular rumours embodied connections between these different, overlapping state manipulations of local ecologies. Over the course of 1897 and 1898, for example, hearing of rumours in many locales about foresters bewitching local landscapes, Henkel strategically chose to postpone the laying of poison for locust destruction in coastal forest reserves until the 'unrest among the natives' subsided. As he reported to the under-secretary for agriculture in early 1898, due to

---

[70] *Annual Report for 1896*, 156; CA, FCT 2/1/1/2, FCT to USA, 25 Feb. 1897; *BBNA 1900*, RM Port St John's, 2 Feb. 1900, 40; *BBNA 1901*, RM Butterworth, 5 Jan. 1901, 37–8; CA, 1/KNT 5/1/1/18, RM Kentani to SNA, 13 Nov. 1907 and *BBNA 1908*, 'Reports of resident magistrates', 36.

[71] CA, 1/MFE 4/1/8/3, N. Adams Cone to RM Mt. Frere, 23 Aug. 1897.

[72] CA, FCT 2/1/1/2, FCT to USA, 25 Feb. 1897; FCT to USA, early Apr. 1897 and *BBNA 1908*, 'Reports of resident magistrates', 36.

the Rinderpest excitement...nothing was attempted, as it might have led to serious trouble with the Natives on account of their suspicious character, as they were led to believe by evil disposed characters and mischief makers that "Government intended to poison their cattle so as to compel them to work for the white men at 6d per diem"!![73]

Amid the intermittent drought conditions of the late 1890s, people often focused their rumours particularly on the contamination of local water supplies. Rumours detailing Europeans polluting scarce water sources embodied popular concerns about the increasing vulnerability of Africans and their livestock to ecological and political forces beyond their control. The Ngqeleni magistrate reported in 1897, for instance, that local people claimed not only that rinderpest had been introduced intentionally into African communities, but that the authorities, feeling that the disease was not spreading fast enough, instructed government officers to drop the rinderpest poison in vital water sources at which Africans' cattle drank.[74]

The Forest Department became an especially prominent object of such popular rumours. As forest officers and guards managed and controlled access to many of the best-watered areas in the Transkei, particularly in the inland mountain ranges, concerns over the pollution and bewitching of local water supplies often targeted them. In fact, foresters' standard practice of laying poison for both vermin and dogs often led to the literal contamination of local streams, rivers and ponds, and dogs and wild animals were often found dead at sources of drinking water, as the strychnine laid out in the forests induced severe thirst in its victims before killing them.[75] The fact that many people interpreted such occurrences as signs of the government's intentions to harm local residents was not lost on senior forest officials. Amid the rural crises of 1897, for instance, Conservator Henkel himself confided in the under-secretary for agriculture that many Africans in the territories 'regard him with suspicion, and suspect him of poisoning the water if he wanders incautiously too near the streams'.[76]

---

[73] *Annual Report for 1897*, 135 and CA, FCT 2/1/1/3, FCT to USA, 16 Feb. 1898.
[74] *BBNA 1897*, 110.
[75] Beinart, 'Night of the jackal', 193 and Guthrie, *Frontier Magistrate*, 227, referring to baboons ending up by streams after being poisoned.
[76] CA, AGR 750, F2839, USA to SNA, 16 Dec. 1897.

Similar themes and concerns resurfaced in other dog-poisoning conflicts over the next decade, particularly in the mid-1900s. As state-peasant relations deteriorated across the region, the activities of the Forest Department were again a prominent subject of popular rumour and suspicion. During the early 1900s, African men increasingly sparred with forest officers and guards while hunting in many locales in the Eastern Cape and Transkei, but it was in the wake of the 1906 Bambatha rebellion in nearby Natal that the situation reached a fever pitch. Foresters repeatedly encountered massive groups of armed hunters and their dogs and in some cases faced physical assaults and return gunfire.[77] Partly in response to these escalating confrontations, colonial authorities organized a select committee on forestry matters in 1906, discussing, among other issues, how 'really very dangerous' the situation was for foresters on patrol as they attempted to check 'a horde of natives' hunting in local forests.[78] Several months later, to increase the restraints on African hunting, officials began enforcing a new law that completely forbade Africans' dogs from being in any forests in the Transkei.[79]

At the same time that colonial authorities expanded their assault on forest trespassing, particular problems arose in some of the coastal districts of the Transkei. In November that year, the magistrate at Kentani, Newton Thompson, sent an urgent telegram to the chief magistrate, regarding complaints in the district about state dog-killing:

> Headmen Somana and Nyokana report that Forest Department Officers have placed poison to destroy dogs round certain demarcated forest bushes which they regard as a danger to the community. Ten dogs already dead number of which died in streams from which drinking water is drawn.

---

[77] CA, 1/QMB 1/1/1/30, criminal cases, Case No. 239, Regina v. Ngcukana and 30 Others, 27 Sept. 1900; *Annual Report for 1901*, 106, 143; *Annual Report for 1902*, 142; *Annual Report for 1903*, 80, 124; *BBNA 1905*, 89; CA, NA 692, B2690, DFO Keiskama Hoek to asst. RM Keiskama Hoek, 30 Sept. 1905; *Annual Report for 1906*, 10; *East London Dispatch*, 28 Aug. 1906, cited in CA, FCE 3/1/50, 613; *Transkeian Gazette*, 13 Dec. 1906; *Report of the Select Committee on Crown Forests, 1906*; NA, FOR 25, A34, Asst. FCE to CFC, 12 Sept. 1906; CA, NA 692, B2690, Inspector 'A' Division, Cape Mounted Police, KWT, to Civil Commissioner, KWT, 28 Aug. 1906 and CA, FCE 3/1/50, 621, DFO Keiskama Hoek to FCE, 8 Oct. 1907.

[78] *Report of the Select Committee on Crown Forests, 1906*, evidence of CFC Lister, 17–20, 31.

[79] P421, 1907.

Headmen beg that this indiscriminate distribution of poison may be stopped.[80]

Several months later Thompson reflected on the source of local discontent:

> the Forests in this district are more or less surrounded by Native Kraals and the Native people regard the distribution of poisoned meat with grave suspicion. The occasional loss of a dog only helps to keep up the feeling of irritation which has always existed in regard to the Forest Department but when a number of dogs are lost through this cause the irritation expands into discontent which is only intensified when these dead dogs pol[l]ute the water supply in the neighbourhood. Naturally suspicious the Native at once concludes that this unpleasant state of affairs has been intentionally brought about and it would take a deal of persuasion to convince him to the contrary.[81]

Meanwhile, similar events were transpiring in the Mqanduli district in late 1907. Resident Magistrate H.H. Bunn reported that in a recent meeting with headman Tylenzima the latter asked 'if it was by my authority that the Forest Department were poisoning the Gxwaleni Forest'. When Bunn responded that he knew nothing of the matter, the headman urged that the Forest Department be prevented from continuing such practices. A few days later Bunn went to investigate the situation himself, visiting with the headman and his councillors. Tyelinzima complained that poisoned meat had been placed along the main footpaths in the forest 'and especially put a great deal of stress on the fact that there was very little water and that people would use the meat through ignorance'. Bunn concluded his report with a warning of the seriousness of the situation, as people were growing increasingly suspicious and restless, 'moving about in small bodies on the hills', and only his personal presence at the scene had been able to quell 'any disturbances which may have been contemplated seeing that day by day native dogs were dying from this poison, and I have never known this step to have been taken before'.[82]

---

[80] CA, NA 753, F127, RM Kentani to CMT, 8 Nov. 1907.
[81] CA, NA 753, F127, RM Kentani to CMT, 10 Sept. 1908. For official concerns over this incident, see CMT to Asst. FCT, 8 Nov. 1907; DFO Butterworth to forester Kentani, 13 Nov. 1907; A. McDonald, forester, Kentani to FDU, 15 Nov. 1907; FDU to Asst. FCT, 18 Nov. 1907; Asst. FCT to CMT, 21 Nov. 1907.
[82] CA, NA 753, F127, RM Mqanduli to CMT, 15 Nov. 1907.

A closer look at these episodes reveals how the Forest Department's practices were drawn into larger conflicts over the colonial domination of local political ecologies. Over the mid- to late 1900s, officials in the southern coastal districts reported on multiple rural crises and movements of popular discontent. Lungsickness was affecting cattle herds terribly, wire-worm was destroying sheep flocks and locusts were posing a serious threat to peasants' crops. Moreover, colonial agents were busily enforcing livestock dipping and inoculation as well as locust eradication regulations.[83] Popular perspectives on these various developments were expressed in prophecies and rumours in many locales. In the Mqanduli district in the months following the 1906 Bambatha rebellion, a pig-killing movement spread in some communities, venting popular discontent with the increasing weight of colonial domination and promising salvation for those who followed prescribed ritual practices.[84] Rumours of colonial poisoning and contamination of local ecologies also flourished. In 1907, in the Kentani, Willowvale and Elliotdale districts, magistrates commented on how governmental attempts to curtail lungsickness outbreaks by inoculating cattle were often 'strongly opposed' due to popular rumours 'that the Government wished to introduce Lungsicknesses through such interventions. In some locales, livestock owners even blamed the inoculations for causing additional diseases in their animals'.[85]

It is against these multiple calamities and government interventions that popular hostility towards the Forest Department and its dog-eradication policies needs to be understood. As with other complaints about government authorities poisoning Africans, their animals and their landscapes, popular stories surrounding dog-killing in the Kentani and Mqanduli districts invoked metaphors of official treachery and sorcery to make broader comments about the increasingly dire conditions of colonial life. Both literally and figuratively colonial agents were slaughtering Africans' dogs and polluting local water supplies, threatening both the ability of men and women to pursue their livelihoods and the health and welfare of people's lives.

---

[83] CTA 1/KNT 5/1/1/18, RM Kentani to SNA, 13 Nov. 1907; *BBNA 1908*, Report of the Chief Magistrate of the Transkeian Territories', 22 and Reports of Resident Magistrates, 26–7 and *BBNA 1909*, 43.

[84] *BBNA 1907*, RM Mqanduli, 17 Apr. 1907, 53–4. For similar movements in Mpondo communities at the time, see Beinart, *Political Economy of Pondoland*, 157–8.

[85] *BBNA 1908*, 'Report of the Chief Magistrate of the Transkeian Territories', 22 and Reports of Resident Magistrates, 26–7 and *BBNA 1909*, 43.

Conclusion

Popular stories about dead dogs and the Forest Department at the turn of the century thus were ways for rural men and women to express deeper concerns over the spreading influence of colonial power in myriad aspects of their daily experiences and practices. While state officials in the Transkei envisioned dog-killing as a targeted means of controlling African environmental activities and mobility, its implementation on the ground was drawn into much more complex understandings of, and frustrations with, colonial transformations of local landscapes and livelihoods. At the same time that rural residents responded to the particular changes in their local political ecologies arising from colonial wildlife policies, they also located conflicts over state forestry and its policies of exclusion within broader popular experiences of political, economic and ecological subordination.[86]

In recent years, rather similar conflicts have resurfaced in South Africa. In August and September 1998, dozens of hunting dogs belonging to rural Africans were shot on a private white-owned farm and a state-owned forest reserve in KwaZulu-Natal through the coordinated efforts of local farmers, provincial and national police forces, and conservation and forestry officers. As with the earlier events in the Transkei, such interventions triggered an outpouring of discontent in local African communities and exacerbated ongoing tensions between rural Africans, white farmers and various arms of the South African state.[87] While much has happened in the century separating these two series of incidents, exploring the historical meaning of environmental conflicts of the past may offer insights into understanding such contemporary contestations over environmental access and control, and the complex ways these disputes are perceived in local communities.

---

[86] White, *Speaking with Vampires*, 41–3, 47–8.

[87] 'Farmers kill 86 dogs in anti-poaching operation', *Electronic Mail and Guardian*, 19 Aug. 1998; 'ANC "inciting racial hatred over hunt"', *Electronic Mail and Guardian*, 19 Aug. 1998; 'Dog kill starts political storm', *Daily Dispatch*, 20 Aug. 1998 and R. Edgecombe, 'The role of environmental history in applied field studies in the Centre of Environment and Development at the University of Natal in Pietermaritzburg; the case of traditional hunting with dogs' (Paper presented at 'African Environments: Past and Present' Conference St. Antony's College, Oxford, England, 5–8 July 1999).

FIDO: DOG TALES OF COLONIALISM IN NAMIBIA*

Robert J. Gordon[1]

Wildlife takes pride of place in discussions of animals in African environmental history; domesticated livestock loom large in debates over pastures. Yet there are other domesticated animals which open doors in the history of colonisation. That dogs are important for understanding the socio-dynamics of Namibia should be as obvious as the first sign warning visitors to 'Beware of the Dogs'. Dog stories are pervasive, although they have not been the subject of much serious analysis. A focus on dogs provides one with a convenient analytical tool to get round the problem of how cultures naturalise themselves. Moreover, it allows one to centre on the interconnections between real and symbolic issues in how humans deal with animals.

There is a scattered array of articles which deal with dogs as metaphors for understanding society and I suggest that this approach is crucial for understanding Namibian colonialism as well. As Gombrich notes, metaphors are derived from 'traditional lore' and it is this lore which defines the effectiveness of metaphor.[2] But in tracing this 'traditional lore', Namibian history and sociology have dealt almost exclusively with people or human achievements. Dogs are rarely found in Namibian historiography indexes, yet if one looks closely enough their paw-prints are everywhere. They served with distinction as hunters

---

* Published with the kind permission of James Currey publishers. Robert Gordon, "Fido—dog tales of Colonialism in Namibia" in William Beinart and Joann McGregor, *Social History and African Environments* (Oxford: James Currey, 2003), pp. 240–254.

[1] My thanks to Patricia Hayes, Udo Krautwurst, Jane Katjavivi, Werner Hillebrecht and Dag Henrichsen for advice, comments and obscure references. Hans Botma provided useful advice on legal aspects.

[2] Cited in S. Baker, *Picturing the Beast* (Manchester, 1993), 87. See also A. Gottlieb, 'Dog: ally or traitor? Mythology, cosmology, and society among the Beng of Ivory Coast', *American Ethnologist*, 13(1968), 447–88; E. Copet-Rougier, 'Le Jeu de l'entre-deux. Le chien chez les Mkako (Est-Cameroun), *L'Homme*, 28 (1988), 108–21 and R. Ellen, 'Categories of animality and canine abuse', *Anthropos*, 94 (1999), 57–68. An excellent recent overview is M. Mullin, 'Mirrors and windows: sociocultural studies of human-animal relationships', *Annual Review of Anthropology*, 28 (1999), 201–24.

and guard dogs and the emergent racial attitudes towards them reflect and provide important insights into the nature of colonialism. And if one looks at more unconventional sources of history, clues to their importance are even more obvious. In Kuusi's encyclopaedic *Ovambo Proverbs* dogs are one of the most important subjects.[3] And then there are photographs. It is remarkable how frequently dogs seem to sneak into photographs as part of the scenery, as it were, in pictures portraying colonial life. Why dogs are ignored as a factor in African history, is a subject on which one could speculate extensively. But rather than do this, this paper shows how an examination of dogs in Namibia can help to understand the processes of colonialism by allowing the reader 'to focus our gaze on the dialectics of everyday life at the imperial frontier' as the Comaroffs put it. It is part of the epic of the ordinary which allows us to examine the netherworld of the inarticulate.[4]

How dogs are defined, used and treated provides important insights into the nature of colonialism. Since we think of the world in the same way as we talk about it, by establishing metaphorical relations, dog stories in Namibia reflect and reinforce some of the basic tenets of a variety of colonial discourses. After first examining the 'social role' of dogs in Namibian colonial life, I discuss dogs as a specific conceptual category in the dominant culture of Namibian colonialism.

The Social Role of Dogs

The first European explorers and hunters traversing what became Namibia were accompanied by dogs. Indeed, dogs were an indispensable part of their equipment and useful especially for hunting, as watchdogs, and as faithful companions. Outfitting his expedition in Cape Town, Francis Galton described how he acquired a pack of a half-dozen mongrels at a uniform rate of 2s.6d. each. He also chose as personal dogs a large 'attack' dog and a small 'barking' dog. In doing this he was holding to a settler practice which is still operational.[5] Africans also appreciated good dogs. Galton reports that his factotum

---

[3] Clearly a close examination of these dog proverbs would provide an important indication of the role and value of dogs in northern Namibia. See M. Kuusi, *Ovambo Proverbs* (Helsinki, 1970).

[4] J.L. and J. Comaroff, *Of Revelation and Revolution*, vol. 2 (Chicago, 1997), 29.

[5] F. Galton, *Narrative of an Explorer in Tropical Africa* (London, 1889) 8. Also see C. Andersson, *Lake Ngami* (London, 1856), 27.

Hans sold two of his curs to some of the Damara for two oxen each. I cannot conceive what could have induced them to make such a bargain. They are very keen upon dogs for they offered four oxen for another one, 'Watch'; but he was too useful to me in worrying about night marauders to be spared.[6]

Indeed, given these rates of exchange one could argue that dogs were a more profitable trade commodity than guns in Damaraland.

Dogs were an item of pride and of conversation. The books of Galton's companion, C.J. Andersson, contain numerous observations on dogs. He describes, for example, how a small dog had been ripped by a lion but managed to crawl to the campfire: 'it was a touching sight to see the faithful animal wagging its tail in recognition of its master, who was trying to replace the intestines and to stop the flow of blood'; a poignant scene this of 'the dying dog, with his wild master stooping despondently over him'. His picture is in shrill contrast to the 'starved native dogs' he found, especially among the Nama.[7]

Andersson, who prided himself on being a naturalist, found it 'somewhat difficult to determine to what species of the canine race these dogs belong, or from what breed they originally descended. They bear some slight resemblance to those I have seen at the homesteads of the Swedish peasants.' He noted different breeds of local dogs and even paid a special visit to Chikongo's kraal where he 'inquired of the chief as to the breed of dogs I had seen about, which I had thought might be a cross between the native and some mongrels belonging to the Europeans; but it seems they are purely native'.[8] These observations lead to three points. First, there may have been a paucity of indigenous dogs in the nineteenth century, probably as a result of disease and predators.[9] Second, it is obvious that a process of cultural diffusion was impacting on this area long before the arrival of the first Europeans. Third, this concern with mongrel versus pure-bred dogs will be seen to be a particularly dominant trope in colonial discourse.

The unpublished reminiscences of William Chapman contain numerous observations about dogs in the period from 1880 to 1920.

---

[6] Galton, *Narrative*, 148 and Andersson, *Lake Ngami*, 228.

[7] Andersson, *Lake Ngami*, 99, 278.

[8] Andersson, *Lake Ngami*, 278, 230 and C. Andersson, *Notes of Travel in South Africa* (London, 1875), 280. Such interest in local breeds was to continue, see, for example, the *Deutsches Kolonial Lexikon* (1920).

[9] The standard reference here would be H. Schneider, *Animal Health and Veterinary Medicine in Namibia* (Windhoek, 1994).

No hunting caravan went out without a pack of at least half a dozen dogs which served as guard dogs around camp, while in the field they were used to track wildlife and corner the more dangerous game, thus allowing the hunter to move close in for the final shot. Not only were they invaluable resources and indeed seemingly constant companions of these early European hunters, but they were used by local people as well for guarding and for hunting.

In the arid south of the country, dogs were integral to the hunting economy, and they had an additional use by local people as a form of protection for their flocks of sheep against predators such as jackals. Chapman made frequent references to the close attachment between people and their dogs. He describes the events surrounding the not insignificant murder of Will Worthington Jordan, a prominent trader and founder of the Republic of Upingtonia:

In 1885 Jordan returned on a visit to Humpata to fetch goods he had ordered from Cape Town to Mossamedes and in Oukuanyama the Chief Nambathi insisted that Jordan should give him a small pet dog which he had, but he refused and the dog was stolen, Jordan believing that the Chief had instigated one of his men to steal it for him. A couple of days later the Chief died and there were suspicions that Jordan had procured means of poisoning him in retaliation for the loss of his pet dog!

In the Caprivi/Kavongo region, Passarge also described guard and hunting dogs, noting that 'Chief Ssekumi' was an especial lover of dogs. Dogs were so prized among the Ovambo according to Moller, Chapman's contemporary, that they were used as sacrifices for various crises.[10] While Africans clearly appreciated the use of dogs, evidence for their 'dog-love' is more fragmentary and episodic.[11] I will argue that this lacuna had important ideological connotations for justifying colonialism. Dogs served another function as well—devouring the rotting carcases of rinderpest-stricken cattle. Passarge, like other German

---

[10] National Archives of Namibia (NAN), 'Reminiscences of William Chapman' (n.d.) mimeo and P. Moller, *Journey Through Angola, Ovampoland and Damaraland* (Cape Town, 1974), 135. And like his compatriot, Andersson, Moller also noted different dog breeds, 125, 84.

[11] See, for example, L. Wildenthal, 'Race, gender and citizenship in the German Colonial Empire' in F. Cooper and A. Stoler (eds.), *Tensions of Empire* (Berkeley, 1997), 275.

scientific travellers, seemed concerned about the possibilities of cross-breeding.[12]

As in other parts of the world, dogs were a cultural presence in colonisation.[13] Certainly settlers and officials in the German Colonial Service were highly appreciative of dogs, none perhaps more famously than Hauptmann Francke, who was seldom seen without his dog and on its death had it buried with a proper gravestone marking its burial site. Dogs were not at the forefront of colonial documentation; perhaps they were so taken for granted that discussion was deemed superfluous. Occasionally an article would appear in the settler press, such as one on the 'Bushman Question' which argued that 'the only way of following them in the thick bush is with dogs. The equipping of good Police Dogs in a suitable number would be of extraordinary value.' The German authorities set up a special police dog training school in Windhoek in 1911–12.[14] Police dogs in German South West Africa developed such a reputation that, when South Africa conquered the territory, one of the earliest items 'exported' back to South Africa were police dogs of the 'smouspincher' type.[15]

Taxing Dogs

In the wake of the 1904–7 colonial wars many Africans found themselves stripped of their primary means of subsistence, livestock, and this meant that especially good hunting dogs became even more important instruments of survival. In 1917 the German colonial dog tax, which had focused exclusively on urban areas, was replaced by a system whereby dogs in townships were taxed at South African £1 for the first dog and 10 shillings for each subsequent dog. In the rural areas the rate was 5 shillings per dog, but Europeans were allowed one watchdog tax-free and this exemption was later also extended to Nama following their urgent representations.

---

[12] S. Passarge, 'Das Okavangosumpflussland und seine bewohner', *Zeitschrift für Ethnologie*, 5 (1905), 649–716.

[13] J. and J. Varner, *Dogs of the Conquest* (Norman, 1983) and M. Schwartz, *A History of Dogs in the Early Americas* (New Haven, 1997).

[14] *Deutsche Suedwest-Afrika Zeitung*, 28 November 1911 and H. Rafalski, *Von Niemandsland bis Ordnungsstaat* (Berlin, 1930). See also K. Shear, 'Police dogs and state rationality in early twentieth-century South Africa' in this volume.

[15] The 'smouspincher' was apparently a cross between a Doberman Pincher and a Rottweiler. NAN, A491/1.

Shortly after taking up his position as native Superintendent of Windhoek, Bowker complained that the reserves were 'overrun' with 'mongrel greyhounds' and suggested that 'at the same time, in the interests of sport, could the police not take steps to collect taxes and destroy dogs throughout the district generally'. Mindful of how Africans would respond to his proposal, he suggested that 'the action should be done quietly otherwise when your men arrive on the reserves there will be no dogs to be seen'. He was supported by other officials who insisted that unlicensed dogs be shot since they were swarming all over the reserves and destroying all big and small game: 'many of the Natives exist on the exertions of these dogs and should they be denied the use of such animals they would naturally be compelled to work and to go in search of work.'[16] Windhoek farmers complained that their livestock was being harassed by 'native dogs'. The Native Affairs Commissioner proposed that greyhounds be limited to two per person and pointed out that the tax was in line with South African and Rhodesian practice.[17] But it was not only Africans who failed to abide by existing Dog Laws. A Magistrate complained that

> the exemption from taxation of a farmer's watch dog is much abused. Why should a farmer who can well afford to pay be exempt when a native who really requires a dog to assist him to look after and guard his master's stock has to pay half of his monthly income for the privilege? I think no dogs should be exempt from taxation.[18]

Even in places where game was exceedingly rare, such as in the desert town of Luderitz, the Magistrate thought that the town was overrun with dogs and requested 100 .303 cartridges as 'the present custom of knocking them (unlicensed dogs) on the head with a stick is cruel and should be stopped'.[19]

After a tour to the South of the territory the Administrator felt that drastic action had to be taken:

> The necessity for this heavy tax was clearly demonstrated... when I found vast numbers of dogs in (the) possession of natives and a certain class of European squatter, who profited by the employment of these

---

[16] 'Greyhounds' and 'Bastard Greyhounds', despite the name, were not recognised kennel-club breeds but rather categories developed by officials to confront dog diversity.
[17] NAN, A491/2, Bowker to Secretary 25 July 1919; 14 Jan. 1920.
[18] NAN, A491/2, Military Magaguistrate Okahandja to Secretary 6 Nov. 1919.
[19] NAN, A491/2, taxation (dogs), 1924 and June 1920.

animals to hunt down game and obtained a livelihood thereby instead of by honest labour.[20]

From April 21 a uniform dog tax system 'allowing no exemptions' for urban and rural areas or for Africans and settlers was promulgated. Fees increased fourfold from 5 shillings to £1 for the first dog, to £2.10s. for two dogs, £4.10s. for three, £7 for four and £10 for five dogs. In his Report to the League of Nations for that year, the Administrator claimed:

> The law has already fulfilled its immediate object in the prevention of the pernicious evil perpetrated by certain Whites and Blacks in keeping large numbers of dogs to forage for them, ruthlessly destroying quantities of game, and affording these vagrants and loafers an easy means of livelihood, which relieves them of any need to work.[21]

But there were problems. There was a general outcry on the part of both Africans and settlers and a year later the tax rate was halved. Africans complained that there was much confusion and that it was unfair to expect a herder employed on a settler farm to forgo more than the equivalent of a month's salary for a dog licence. Strategies of resistance are clear from the complaint made by farmers that Africans refused to take out dog licences unless the Police came out to collect the taxes: 'when the Police arrive the dogs disappear'. So successful was this defiance that a few months later the Administrator had to upbraid all magistrates with a circular letter that dog taxes were not being collected.[22] Dog tax collection was piecemeal at best. One important exception was on the Bondels Reserve where between September and January 1922 there were 140 prosecutions and over 100 fines or imprisonment.[23] Since these people could not find the money to pay either the tax or the fine, they were forced to work for settlers, who moreover could not pay cash to their labourers. In the first seven months of 1922 dog tax offences accounted for over 70 per cent of the charges laid in Warmbad.[24] This, coupled with a long legacy of

---

[20] South Africa, *Report of the Administrator to the League of Nations*.
[21] Union of South Africa, (UG, 32/1922), 4.
[22] *Windhoek Advertiser*, 11 June 1921. Clearly this was a major issue in a labour-strapped country. See G. Lewis, 'The Bondelswarts rebellion' (MA thesis, Rhodes University 1977), 49 and NAN, A 491/2 Taxation, MagistrateWindhoek to Secretary 14 June 1921 and 8 Nov. 1921.
[23] Lewis, 'Bondelswarts rebellion', 50.
[24] Lewis, 'Bondelswarts rebellion', 59.

systematic impoverishment, was the final factor which precipitated the Bondelswarts Rebellion in May 1922. As Captain Prinsloo, a Police Officer involved in suppressing the Rebellion, put it: 'In the absence of a rifle his dogs are his best friend and the uniformed man his worst enemy'.[25] The brutal suppression of the Bondelswarts Rebellion was a *cause célèbre* at the League of Nations.

Settlers too were dissatisfied because they were not exempt from these taxes: 'farmers complained because they had expected that the tax would be imposed upon the Natives alone in order to induce them to obtain a livelihood by honest labour'.[26] Indeed, almost before the ink on the new Dog Tax Proclamation had dried, the Outjo Farmers' Association petitioned against this 'abnormal tax', claiming that farmers needed at least two watchdogs near the house against wild animals and robbers; they sought exemptions for the first two dogs and then a tax rate of 50 pence per dog.[27] Even Superintendent Barnes of Orumbo Reserve, who had campaigned on behalf of a Native Dog tax, sought relief for two powerful dogs to destroy jackals and other pests 'free of licence'. The alternative, hunting with ammunition, was unnecessarily expensive.[28]

Farmers' Societies and municipalities continued to make representations on this issue for a number of years and the Dog Tax Proclamation probably holds the distinction of being the most amended proclamation in colonial Namibia. Proclamation 2/1924 reduced dog taxes by 50 per cent but imposed a £5 tax on 'Greyhound types' or the 'kind known as kaffir hunting dogs' which were 'approximately 70 per cent of the native owned variety'. Greyhounds registered with the South African Kennel Club, however, were exempt from this tax. This proclamation was later suspended on the grounds that laws had to be race-blind. Exemptions were later granted to members of Vermin Hunt Clubs which were, of course, exclusively manned by settlers.[29]

Settler discourses on dogs certainly emphasised the importance of taxing hunting dogs as a means of forcing recalcitrant Africans to enter the

---

[25] R. Freislich, *The Last Tribal War* (Cape Town, 1964), 89.
[26] Union of South Africa, (UG 16/1923), 11.
[27] *Windhoek Advertiser*, 18 Aug. 1923. On settler fear and insecurity in this era see R. Gordon, 'The Vagrancy Proclamation and internal pacification in Namibia 1920–1945' in P. Hayes *et al.* (eds.), *Namibia under South African Rule* (Athens OH, 1998), 51–76.
[28] *Windhoek Advertiser*, 20 April 1921.
[29] On South African vermin hunt clubs see W. Beinart, 'The night of the jackal: sheep, pastures and predators in the Cape'.

labour market. Thus the Karibib Farmersverein resolved unanimously in 1925 that native-owned hunting dogs caused a noticeable decline in small game. Africans, they asserted, preferred owning dogs to goats: 'on the veld no kaffir is seen without several dogs, these dogs are not their property but are lent to him and then they share the pot.' They were emphatically not watchdogs because they were seldom at the kraal, but continually out hunting on their own account. Nor did the society feel that they were kept to catch jackals, as the number of jackals appeared to have increased. If jackals gave them trouble they would kill a kapater (gelded goat) and use poison. Rather, the closed season for hunting was being completely flouted. They asked the Administration to impose a £5 tax on all African-owned hunting dogs. The Verein was later joined in its concern by the *Allgemeine Zeitung* (26 May 1926) which estimated that in one district alone native-owned dogs were responsible for killing 12,000 head of game per annum. It was partially in response to issues like this that the South West Africa Wild Life Protection Society was formed later that year.[30]

At the same time, the value of dogs for settler hunting was being downplayed. Commenting on a 1935 publicity brochure being developed by the South African Railways, long-term Commissioner 'Cocky' Hahn noted that

> dogs are seldom much use because the climate is so dry. There is very little scent, the running proclivities of the birds and the lack of thick undergrowth militating against the use of setters or pointers. For recovering wounded birds a well-trained retriever would be of assistance.[31]

For lion hunting, on the other hand, dogs were indispensable.

As a means of forcing Reserve inhabitants to engage in wage labour, however, the dog tax rapidly lost it significance as other economic variables, especially grazing fees, started to have an impact. In 1928 indigenous livestock owners residing in the reserves were provided with a tax exemption for a single dog (Proclamation 5/1928), a move which raised the immediate ire of the Okahandja Farmers Association which felt this gave African farmers an unfair advantage. The Administration

---

[30] *Windhoek Advertiser*, 23 Oct. 1926.
[31] NAN, A198/2. Clearly Hahn was engaging in some class bias here. His remarks were aimed at potential overseas hunters who would favour bird hunting. On the other hand, Africans and some poor white farmers used large packs of rather undisciplined dogs to chase and corner game, actions defined by Hahn as 'unsporting'.

replied that white farmers already had exemptions for two dogs, could belong to Vermin Clubs and, moreover, had access to firearms. None of these means of vermin control were available to Africans. This exemption was swiftly taken advantage of. By 1931 99 per cent of all the dogs in the Tses reserve were tax-exempt. While locals loved their dogs, they could not afford to feed them, forcing these 'walking skeletons' to raid the railway siding consignments.[32] Eventually the Ovitoto Reserve Superintendent suggested that exemptions only be granted to well-fed dogs: 'in some cases dogs are in such a state of hunger that it is better to destroy them, than to allow them to live and suffer in hunger'.

After the Second World War the Administration set up a Commission to enquire into the Game Laws (1948). Among the factors it found leading to the 'steady diminution of game', apart from drought, wholesale slaughter by 'biltong' hunters (non-resident white hunters) and land encroachment, was 'the presence of an increasing number of kaffir dogs both in the Native Reserves as well as in the country generally'. Accordingly the Commission recommended

> that the whole matter of Dog Taxes in the Territory be taken into review, but that two dogs be allowed free to the farmer as before. It is recommended that thoroughbred dogs be licensed at £1 per head, but that mongrels or cross-breed dogs should be more highly taxed, particularly unsterilized bitches.[33]

Among the representations it received was one to make the possession of dogs by farm-workers illegal. After careful consideration it rejected this, since such legislation would infringe individual rights unduly and would also amount to class legislation. The only solution was to increase the taxes on dogs in an effort to make the possession of such dogs uneconomical.

Until the large-scale improvement of jackal-proof fencing many herders in the south of the territory used to supplement their meagre income by using dogs to catch jackals for which they could claim a 5/- bounty per silver-tailed jackal from the Administration. It was this economic benefit which no doubt muted criticism of locally owned dogs on farms. But in the 1950s the Municipal Association of South West Africa complained that dogs were roaming the countryside doing considerable damage to stock and wildlife and that the police were

---

[32] NAN, A492, 1/2 Tses Superintendent letter, 14 Oct. 1931.
[33] NAN, A205/1, Commission to Enquire into Game laws.

ineffective in dealing with this problem since they lacked proper equipment. Dog licensing, the Association argued, should be a municipal function. Dogs should be impounded for three days and then destroyed, while in the rural areas all unlicensed dogs should be destroyed immediately. Their recommendation that dog taxes should be doubled was implemented.[34]

Dogs as Cultural Category

Leach argues that pets such as dogs straddle boundaries of basic categories and thus have special ritual value.[35] They are ambiguous in our systems of classifying and ordering the world because they are mediators between binary opposites: they straddle the human and the animal, the domestic and the wild; they break and blur this distinction. Settlers saw their dogs as sharing their status and this had profound implications for their treatment of dogs and their beliefs about African treatment of dogs. Fido, the most popular dog name in the heyday of European colonialism, connotes faithfulness and loyalty.[36] Darwin believed that dogs could think as abstractly as children and 'savages' and were capable us using similar mental processes to solve problems like finding water. From such perspectives a dog which does its master's bidding and looks after its master is not only a good pet but also a well-colonised animal. Dating back to the Second Agricultural Show in Windhoek in 1914, one of the most popular events was a display of the prowess of well-trained police dogs and this pattern continued at least into the 1960s. Colonists had an almost psychopathic hatred of wild dogs.[37]

At the same time, dogs served also as mobile metaphors for understanding gradations in colonial society. To take some random examples: in describing a Portuguese official's cowardice, Chapman reports that he

---

[34] NAN, A491, dogs general and control of.

[35] E. Leach, 'Anthropological aspects of language: animal categories and verbal abuse' in E. Lenneberg (ed.), *New Directions in the Study of Language* (Boston, 1964), 322–42.

[36] A. Memmi, *The Colonizer and the Colonized* (Boston, 1964). Galton's cousin, Charles Darwin was imposing accepted bourgeois values when he compared Fuegians to dogs in precisely these colonialist terms in *The Descent of Man*. L.M. Wendt, *Dogs: A Historical Journey* (New York, 1996), 130.

[37] Another important animal which straddles this boundary, Dag Henrichsen points out, is the horse. In contrast to wild dogs, in Namibia the 'wild horses of the Namib' are highly romanticised.

'retreated as a dog would, pulling his tail between his legs'. A large concessionaire, Companhia de Mossamedes, is described as having a 'dog in the manger' attitude. One of the indignities the Angola Afrikaners suffered, Chapman claims, was that a Portuguese administrator had termed Afrikaans a 'dog's language'. Conversely, the characteristics of dogs were also inferred from the gender and race of the human owners. Thus dogs owned by women were seen to lack self-discipline and being less streetwise than men's dogs got killed in accidents more frequently. A Government Commission deployed racist ideas across the species divide, believing that mongrel bitches owned by Africans tended to breed indiscriminately like their owners.

The polysemic symbolic character of dogs is rarely articulated as such. Instead, one must infer it from a variety of contextual documents like folk-tales, poems, proverbs and especially photographs. It is striking how many photographs of settlers have dogs either deliberately posed, or in many cases simply wandering into the scene being photographed. This high degree of tolerance in the days when photography was a relatively expensive undertaking suggests that pet dogs were not only well fed but given extensive freedom. Posed pictures also open up intriguing questions: can posed dog love be seen as a symbolic means of compensating for hatred of people sometimes categorised as 'wild'? Or, consider the picture which H. Rafalski published entitled 'Transport of Police Dogs on a Mounted Patrol'. It consists of a dog leading a horse on a leash. The horse has two side boxes in which are seated two dogs. What does this photograph tell us about the title of the book: *Von Niemandsland bis Ordnungsstaat* (From Nomansland to Ordinance State)? And note the play on the word Ordnung which can be translated as either 'Ordinance' state or 'Ordered' state/state of order—a place where even dogs know what to do out of duty, while *Niemandsland* is synonymous with chaos. Could it be a symbolic reflection of what he considered to be the ideal settled colony, where even the dogs would take care of the means of production (the horse) and the rulers could sit back and do nothing?

Perhaps the ultimate colonial illusion was that a single well-trained dog could do the work of numerous Africans, as implied in Rafalski's photograph. It is striking how in posed photographs of Africans, dogs and whites, dogs and Africans inevitably seem to be placed at the same level. And when a group of African dignitaries were photographed and later sold as a postcard, the photographer allowed a dog to scratch itself in the foreground. A common theme in German colonial women's memoirs of life in Namibia was how Africans and dogs shared the same culinary tastes.³⁸ In 1927 the Farmwirtschaft Gesellschaft wrote to the Administration requesting permission to import two fully trained European sheep-dogs since flocks were decreasing due to the unsatisfactory state of 'native labour'. A year later the Karakul Breeders Association renewed the application on behalf of its Herr Held, who had brought out a professional shepherd from Germany:

> This man, at present attending to 1500 sheep, has come to the conclusion, that all dogs of this country, which he has tried up to now, have refused proper duty as there is no dog in the country to teach them their service. As the opinion of that shepherd some dogs of this country would be serviceable, if only a possibility could be found to train them by using a well trained responsible sheepdog.³⁹

Colonel Statham, author of *With My Wife Across Africa* (1922), detailing his adventures in southern Angola and northern Namibia, published a photograph of his injured dog Fita being carried in a palanquin by Africans. What type of symbolic statement is Statham trying to make by including this photograph? Most local people, both black and white, would undoubtedly have put the dog out of its misery. He clearly wishes to emphasise his role as bearer of civilisation, along with the African role in subservient servicing of the colonising man and dog.

The treatment that masters meted out to their dogs served as a marker of fitness to rule and of civility. Harold Eedes, veteran Native Commissioner for the Kavango, claimed that local dogs were never fed in villages, kept in poor condition and subsisted mostly on human excrement.⁴⁰ Could people like that ever be competent to govern themselves? The belief in bourgeois culture that people who mistreat animals will mistreat humans is well-established.⁴¹ Eedes certainly took this as evidence of 'low mentality and moral outlook'. So common was this belief among settlers that the maverick Peter Weidner, a long-term resident in southern Namibia, felt compelled to point out that while Nama dogs might look miserable, they were deliberately kept hungry for hunting purposes:

---

³⁸ Udo Krautwurst, personal comment citing Else Sonnenberg and Clara Brockmann.
³⁹ NAN, A491/1, export and import (dogs), 27 Feb. 1928.
⁴⁰ Cited in G. Gibson et al. (eds.), *The Kavango Peoples* (Wiesbaden, 1981), 45.
⁴¹ J. Serpell, *In the Company of Animals* (Oxford, 1986) and M. Garber, *Dog Love* (London, 1996), 16.

in all fairness to the Hottentot, he will always allow the dog a fair share of the spoils just as the race horse trainer will also add an extra ration of oats to his horse's supper after it has won a race.[42]

Colonial law was expressly concerned with cruelty to animals. In Namibia it was a crime, punishable by fines, imprisonment and, in gross cases, whipping, to: 'cruelly beat, kick, ill-treat, override, overload or torture any animal'; 'keep animals for fighting'; administer 'poison or injurious drug or substance' or 'permit, to be subjected, any animal to any operation which is performed without due care and humanity'.[43] Namibia has long had a 'Prevention of Cruelty to Animals' Proclamation (1919) and eventually, after the Second World War, a Society for the Prevention of Cruelty to Animals was formed in Windhoek. In 1948 the South African Animal Welfare Society complained to the Administration of the:

> deplorable cruelty to animals in Native Areas—neglect and semi-starvation and lack of regard for the feelings of animals, leading to deliberate maltreatment and the infliction of unnecessary pain. It may be pointed out that sympathy for the feelings of others is one of the basic principles of our civilization and that all truly civilized people extend this principle to animals.

But it wasn't just that 'civilisation' which was at stake. The memorandum went on to criticise the situation of the 'semi-starving Native dogs' which were

> too frequently kept by people who do not or cannot afford to feed them adequately, or families which might be able to feed one dog properly, keep three or four dogs in a miserable condition. This starvation of dogs too often leads to the killing of livestock by the famished animals and awkward consequences for their owners.[44]

The parallels between this argument and that for population control for blacks are so obvious as not to warrant comment.

The *Standard Encyclopedia of Southern Africa* in its entry on dogs has this to say about 'kaffir dogs':

> while varying considerably in terms of colours, coats and carriage, their constant characteristics include a: 'slinking gait' and a very suspicious

---

[42] P. Weidner, *The World Owes You Nothing* (Warmbad, n.d.), 29.
[43] C.H. Blaine, *Dog Law: A Compilation of the Law in South Africa relating to Dogs* (Johannesburg, 1928), 51–2.
[44] NAN SWAA, A442/1, cruelty to animals, 20 Feb. 1948.

nature, so that even their own masters have some difficulty in holding and handling them...Much interbreeding...Usually these dogs are forced by circumstances to be almost self-supporting and they live as scavengers in Bantu villages. On the hunt they help their masters to bring the game to bay, but they are wary of being embroiled in direct fights with the quarry.[45]

Without too much imagination this vocabulary could easily be used to describe how settlers saw Africans.[46] It was a common belief among settlers that African dogs were possessed of too low a discipline capacity (Dressurfähigkeit) to be trained into good hunting dogs and that indeed even the one officially recognised African breed, the Ridgeback, was of Asian origin.[47]

Not only was it believed that dogs resembled their masters, but ownership of dogs was a mark of civility. This was used by many, like Moeller, to tilt Bushmen into the category of humanity, if only just: 'There is no other domestic animal among the Bushmen than the dog but often even this, the faithful companion of man, is lacking'.[48] And even the Bushman dog was exceptional according to many early European explorers and adventurers in that it did not bark and thus was useless as a watchdog, though brilliantly resourceful as a hunter—reflecting only too clearly the colonisers' stereotype of their Bushman masters.

Finally, I would suggest that in addition to their social functions, dogs provided for a very important psychological need of the colonisers, especially the officials who worked beyond the Police Zone where there were few white compatriots. In such a typical colonial situation, commissioners were not easily loved by their subjects. Dogs, on the other hand, loved their masters irrespective of their faults or politics. They were thus an important psychological surrogate.

---

[45] *Standard Encyclopedia of South Africa*, vol. 2 (Cape Town, 1968), 55.

[46] Again such colonising strategies have a long pedigree. Andersson was renowned for his dislike of the Nama and their dogs: 'The curs are of the greatest annoyance to the traveller in Namaqualand, for since the owners rarely feed them, they greedily devour almost everything they come across. I have had my powder-flask, 'veld' shoes, and even rifle...abstracted by them from my side during the night. A person's first impulse on making the discovery is to vow vengeance on the head of the thieves; but, on seeing the emaciated state of the poor creatures, in which every rib might be counted, anger is turned into pity' (Andersson, *Lake Ngami*, 278).

[47] A. Fischer, 'Ueber den jagdhund in Suedwest', *SWA Jagkalender* (1939), 163–4 and H. Graf Castell-Ruedenhausen, *Jagden zwischen Namib und Kalahari* (Hamburg, 1978), 160–1.

[48] Castell-Ruedenhausen, *Jagden*, 149.

One of the fundamental problems colonials faced in countries like Namibia was insecurity and dogs were perceived to play an important role in creating the semblance of control and security. As Doris Lessing pointed out for Rhodesia, large dogs were imported for two basic reasons: to terrorise possible burglars and for owners 'to surround themselves with an aura of controlled animal savagery'. All dogs were supposed to be watchdogs. It was an article of faith that Africans were by nature scared of dogs, even if everyone repeated stories about thieves poisoning fierce dogs or making friends with them.[49] Despite many such contradictions, dogs were closely entangled in the elaboration of colonial hierarchies and racial ideas.

Dog Law Cultures

Implicit in the notion of colonialism is the presumption of control. In order to understand the state's attempts to control dogs one must examine further the cultural role of dogs in Namibia, in addition to their obvious material roles. Why, if dogs were so important for African efforts to avoid having to work in the colonial labour system, did settlers not succeed in establishing a special tax for what they called 'kaffir dogs'? This was an important question, given the labour crises which plagued the settlers. Part of the answer was surely the importance that colonists attached to dogs as guard-dogs and hunting-dogs. A differential dog tax would have caused, officials believed, massive indigenous resentment. In addition, there were problems of administrative capacity to assess the tax properly and the inconvenience of collecting it. As a justification for not imposing a special 'Kafir Hunting Dog Tax'—requested by the Karibib Farmerverein—a survey of magisterial districts indicated that the decimation of game by 'kafir hunting dogs' was vastly exaggerated. Finally, there were the international ramifications: the scandals of the Bondelswart and Rehoboth Rebellion were still echoing in the corridors of the League of Nations. The Administration was acutely conscious of the need not to generate another *cause célèbre*. It eventually finessed the situation by allowing every member of an officially recognised vermin extermination club or association to have tax exemptions for two dogs.[50]

---

[49] D. Lessing, *African Stories* (New York, 1966), 657.
[50] Blaine, *Dog Law*, 227.

Most important, though, was the problem of how exactly officials would legally differentiate African dogs from European dogs? As Magistrate Thomas put it: 'In the Union I believe the "Kaffir Hunting Dog" is a special class, but here any dog of any breed or mixed breeds after special treatment (i.e. a proper course of starvation and training) becomes a hunting dog.'[51] Indeed, the only distinctive breed of African dog to be recognised as such by the South African Kennel Club was the Rhodesian Ridgeback in 1924. The other legal question befuddling dog taxes was who was being taxed: the dog or the owner; this became an issue when dogs were given away as gifts or ownership was transferred. And if ownership was crucial, could it be communal as well as individual?[52] This was not a simple question. The Stock-theft law allowed for collective culpability where the spoor of the stolen stock was traced to a kraal. So too with dogs, dog hunting packs frequently consisted of dogs belonging to several owners who might not even be aware that their dogs were out on a hunt.

Travellers, settlers and colonial authorities had particular problems with mongrels. Although the notion of a 'pure-bred' dog was highly problematic, it was frequently used as a point of contest. In 1920 Messrs Schaeffer and Lossow applied for dog licence exemptions on the grounds that they had a facility in which they were engaged in dog-breeding 'to meet the obvious wishes of the farmers who like to get dogs of pure race', and listed amongst their assets dogs specially imported from South Africa: two Greyhounds; one Bullterrier bitch; one Bullterrier male; and two pure-bred Alsatian wolf-dogs.[53]

In cases involving 'cruelty to animals' further significant pointers can also be found. Thus, in South Africa, a man who had castrated his neighbour's dogs for interfering with his bitch was found guilty of malicious injury to property and fined £25 or two months imprisonment with hard labour, yet in a similar case the person was found not guilty because his bitches were pure-bred and the dog he castrated was a 'cross-bred'.[54]

For a dog tax to be enforceable a token has to be available to distinguish taxed from untaxed dogs. The 1921 Proclamation stipulated

---

[51] NAN, A491/2(1).
[52] NAN, A205/1, 6 May 1949.
[53] A longer version of this paper would require a contextualising discussion of the Immorality Act.
[54] Blaine, *Dog Law*, 50–1, 55.

that, in addition to a tax receipt, each dog had to wear a metal badge. Any dog without a badge could be seized by the police and destroyed. There was resistance to this strategy even before it was implemented. As the Okahandja Military Magistrate complained 'the brass badges are expensive, native dogs do not wear collars on which to affix badges and the badges themselves are small and easily lost. They seem quite unnecessary in rural areas.'[55] But it was the unstated symbolic dimension which clearly concerned him and Africans. Dog badges resembled the brass tokens local Africans had been required to wear around their necks during the German era until replaced by pass books in 1917. At least in the earlier years of Mandate rule, Ovambo contract workers were still issued with cheap tin disks which had a small hole on one side through which a thick cord could be passed for suspension.

Conclusion

Clearly colonial dogs led charmed lives and the oft-repeated African complaint that 'Boers treated us like dogs' may not always be accurate in this context. Whose dogs and which dogs are issues of major importance and with those referents the meaning of the statement can be changed dramatically. Human-canine relationships are fascinating precisely because they are undoubtedly social. Most humans attribute human qualities to canines, and at least in colonial situations the opposite, the almost institutionalised attribution of animal qualities to humans, is equally ubiquitous. Many of the attitudes which settlers held about the relationship between Africans and dogs can be shown to be based not on empirical data but on cultural constructs. In the voluminous correspondence relating to 'Cruelty to Animals' and in examining District Level Court Records, specific cases of blacks being charged with 'cruelty to animals' are surprisingly rare.

Whites' dogs figure vividly in African cultural constructs. It is small wonder that tales of Boer dogs are a staple conversation topic in black shebeens. Indeed, local Namibians have long been concerned about the settlers' strange obsession with dogs and a rich social commentary extends to the period of German colonialism. There are Herero praise songs (*omitango*) which refer to German love of dogs: 'Germans—the

---

[55] NAN, A491/2, taxation (dogs), Military Magistrate Okahandja to Secretary, 6 Nov. 1919.

people with the fox terrier. They hit you with a loaf of bread which you will eat while you are sufficient' and 'the people who like a dog and hate a person'. Both praise songs demonstrate keen sociological appreciations. These Herero singers were not alone. Writing in 1911, Tonjes reported that if a young migrant returned to Ovamboland earlier than expected they would complain that 'if the white man's dog dies, he is sad and cries; but if his black servant dies, this does not affect him and he might even push him aside with his foot'.[56]

How dogs were treated in Ovamboland was closely tied to matters of social hierarchy. Ovambo kings kept dogs for hunting purposes and would instruct servants to 'take the dogs out and look for meat for them'. The royal dogs would sometimes attack small-stock like goats but 'Woe unto him who dares to hit or drive off the dogs: they are, after all, the king's dogs! The dogs receive only the smallest portion of the meat. Most of the meat becomes the property of their guides'.[57] While waiting to interview a bureaucrat in Ovambo, and trying to make small-talk, I politely asked what she thought was the worst Oshiwambo swear-word anyone could be called. Without a doubt, the worst insult is to call someone a dog (*ombwa*), she said, and then proceeded to proffer explanations which would have been music to any structuralist's ear: dogs don't know how to behave, they eat anything; a person has a place, a dog just wanders around; dogs do not stay in areas which are important to people like the kitchen or sleeping room; worst, dogs fornicate in public.

Brecht's poem 'A Worker Studies History' makes an elegant argument for moving beyond the 'Great Man' approach in history to include the little people, the underlings in history. This brief reconnaissance has suggested that his approach should be further extended to include 'Man's best friend'. Not only is there ample evidence to suggest that dogs played an important material role in the creation of Namibia, but in a cultural-symbolic sense they were crucial. The use of animal categories to understand human behaviour and the use of human categories to understand animal behaviour reciprocally reinforced negative stereotypes, and indeed this interplay between material and symbolic manifestations still plays itself out in aspects of contemporary Namibian society. If there is one point this essay makes, it is to

---

[56] H. Tonjes, *Ovamboland: Country People Mission* (Windhoek, 1996), 149, 111.
[57] Personal comm., Dag Henrichsen.

show how sets of everyday practices concerning as mundane a subject as dogs can embed and entrench colonialism and bring it alive to all sectors of colonial society.

POLICE DOGS AND STATE RATIONALITY IN EARLY TWENTIETH-CENTURY SOUTH AFRICA*

Keith Shear

One afternoon in the 1940s, a sub-headman in the Transkei's Tabankulu district was killed with a spear near the Umzimvubu River, some distance from his home. Neighbours found his body the following morning. The police came and, making no progress, instructed the local headman to summon everyone in the area to assemble the next day at the murder scene, where in the meantime the body was to remain unburied. At this gathering, now two days after the stabbing, the police, returning with two dogs, ordered the people to sit in a large circle around the corpse, from which the handler gave the dogs scent before releasing them. The dogs circled round for some time, sniffing each person in turn, until both eventually jumped up on and barked at a man who quickly confessed and was led away by detectives.[1]

In my informants' memory, the dogs' employment in these events stood out as emblematic of Africans' experiences of the white-supremacist state. Yet their account also points to the types of intra-communal tensions, exacerbated by the broader systemic pressures of colonialism, which led to police dogs being brought in and through which the dogs' actions were popularly interpreted. The murder victim had reallocated a desirable field belonging to his assailant. In an era of stock limitation, fencing and forced relocation resulting from the state's 'betterment'

---

* Originally published in S. Dubow (ed.), *Science and Society in Southern Africa* (Manchester: Manchester University Press, 2000), 143–163. Reprinted with permission.

Research for this chapter was assisted by a grant from the Joint Committee on African Studies of the Social Science Research Council and the American Council of Learned Societies with funds provided by the Ford, Mellon and Rockefeller Foundations. I am grateful to many colleagues who engaged with earlier versions at conferences and seminars in Durban, Brighton, Chicago and Ann Arbor. For their detailed comments, my particular thanks to David William Cohen, Saul Dubow, Jonathon Glassman, Randall Packard and Lynn Thomas.

[1] S. Mthakasi and E. Vava interviewed by J. Mzayifani and K. Shear, 4 August 1994.

proposals for the crowded African 'reserves', land was an increasingly coveted resource and the cause of much resentment, particularly against those responsible for its apportionment.[2] Such resentment cost the sub-headman his life.

The police professed little interest in these allegedly parochial concerns. Having elicited a confession, and justifying their unorthodox methods with disparaging references to Africans' 'mentality', they were content to consider the 'crime' 'solved'. Such complacency, while disclosing an easy predisposition to coercion, also implied the existence of social and moral complexities in which the police feared entangling themselves. Police racism masked nervousness about the limitations of official knowledge and control of social dynamics in African communities as much as it registered arrogant certainty.[3] The police may have known that the introduction of dogs would result in a confession, but they understood only poorly the social phenomena that produced this outcome.

By the time of the Tabankulu events, similar incidents involving police dogs had been occurring in the South African countryside for decades. The police represented dogs as a modern scientific investigative technology which could help to negotiate dealings between rulers and ruled on terms of the authorities' choosing. But the expectation of the dogs' truth-telling effects upon black suspects was largely a matter of faith. The dogs simplified and integrated the semantics of colonial interaction, permitting officials to circumvent court-imposed evidentiary burdens and the uncertainties of employing black police, informers and interpreters, whose reliability they were suspicious of. Yet officials' inability fully to comprehend and control all the circumstances of the 'smelling-out' rituals they staged also enabled Africans to construe these events in quite unexpected ways and to appropriate them for altogether unintended ends.

The purpose of this chapter is not merely to document one more example of how white South African authorities abused their black subjects, but rather to interrogate claims about the modernity and

---

[2] W. Beinart and C. Bundy, 'State intervention and rural resistance: the Transkei, 1900–1965', in M.A. Klein (ed.), *Peasants in Africa: Historical and Contemporary Perspectives* (Beverly Hills, 1980), 298–304.

[3] For a skilful decoding of African resistance registered in settlers' racism, see K.E. Atkins, *The Moon is Dead! Give Us Our Money! The Cultural Origins of an African Work Ethic, Natal, South Africa, 1843–1900* (Portsmouth, 1993).

effective reach of the South African state. The theme of police dogs is appropriate to such an enquiry, for work with these animals in African communities exemplified the disjunction between officials' insistence that the South African Police (SAP) apotheosised rational scientific policing and the tawdrier reality of investigations that, as in the case of the murdered sub-headman, more closely approximated witch-finding ordeals. That canine trailing and identification possessed this intrusive character certainly reflected, at one level, the brute coercive capabilities of the state. But that such investigations took this particular ritualistic form also suggests that they were shaped by the authorities' incomprehension of the moral politics of the African communities which they policed and, by implication, the limits of their power.

Historically, from the Old South to Nazi Germany, dogs have been a favoured instrument of repressive regimes. Colonial and metropolitan police forces cooperated with one another in developing this coercive apparatus. In the interwar decades, the SAP took pride in forging such partnerships and in alerting its counterparts internationally to novel uses of dogs. Police dogs have been employed in liberal political orders too. In the United States in the 1990s, civil rights organisations investigated and sued Canine (commonly called K-9) Units following reports of people being needlessly bitten during discriminatory police deployments of dogs in minority neighbourhoods.[4]

In South Africa, although the authorities have employed trained dogs for decades, critical studies of policing neglect the issue, possibly because it has seemed a mere diversionary detail among the totality of iniquitous practices and technologies of racial domination.[5] From their owner's perspective, however, these dogs were far from insignificant. At a ceremony in January 1972 at Cato Manor, Durban, the site of a once vibrant African community which suffered forced removal under apartheid, the Commissioner of Police, with the SAP Chaplain leading the assembled in prayer, unveiled a memorial, *Helderus* ('Heroes' Rest'),

---

[4] J.R. Lilly and M.B. Puckett, 'Social control and dogs: a sociohistorical analysis', *Crime and Delinquency*, 43 (1997), 123–47; Amnesty International, *United States of America: Torture, Ill-Treatment and Excessive Force by Police in Los Angeles, California* (London, 1992), 29–34.

[5] Critical studies include G. Cawthra, *Policing South Africa: The South African Police and the Transition from Apartheid* (London, 1993); and J.D. Brewer, *Black and Blue: Policing in South Africa* (Oxford, 1994).

in honour of fallen police tracker and patrol dogs.⁶ The memorial (see Figure 15) was a late instance of a much longer police contribution to the making of dogs as powerful symbols of settler control in colonial Africa—a symbolism registered in an extensive southern African folklore about 'racist' dogs and creatively explored further afield in the fiction of the Kenyan writer Ngugi wa Thiong'o.⁷

First experimented with in South Africa by an amateur enthusiast in the Natal Police in 1909, police dogs were again tested in 1911 in the Transvaal and then gradually introduced throughout the Union. Until the 1960s, dogs were not used in urban patrolling but were employed exclusively for tracking, predominantly in rural districts.⁸ Yet, unlike in England and the United States, tracker dogs were not used chiefly to hunt known fugitives. The idea was certainly mooted. In 1906, during a scare following several widely publicised attacks on white farmhouses by deserting Chinese indentured miners, the mining houses proposed the creation of a canine unit to help recapture their workers. 'Bloodhounds are used in other parts of the world for tracking criminals, and there seems to be no reason why a kennel or kennels should not be established on the East or West Rand, whence the dogs could be obtained for service at short notice.'⁹ But the Transvaal government apparently did not pursue the suggestion.

Rather, from the outset, the police in South Africa used dogs mostly to discover unidentified perpetrators in unsolved cases—investigative means that produced highly questionable judicial results. In the early years the Crown obtained numerous lower-court convictions 'on the sole evidence of the dogs having pointed out the culprit'. The consequences for the accused could be severe. In 1918, a guilty finding on a charge of stealing a sheep, based 'almost entirely' on 'the behaviour of the police dogs and [on] their tracking of the accused', led a Transvaal magistrate to sentence two men each to eight lashes and twelve months'

---

⁶ See 'Helderus onthul', *Sarp*, 8, 5 (1972), 28–9 and C.R. Stanley, *Deferred Value: An Hitherto Unpublished Account of the Origin and Development of the British Police Dog* (Chichester, 1978), 28–9, also cited in Lilly and Puckett, 'Social control', 138. These authors fail to note the location's significance.

⁷ Ngugi wa Thiong'o, *A Grain of Wheat* (London, 1967).

⁸ M. de W. Dippenaar, *The History of the South African Police, 1913–1988* (Silverton, 1988), 41, 297; M. Hansen, 'Dogs on the beat', *Justitia*, 1, 10 (1962), 3; A.W. Brink, 'Die totstandkoming van die S.A. Polisiehondeafdeling', *Sarp*, 1, 10–11 (1965).

⁹ Barlow Rand Archives, Sandton, H. Eckstein & Co., 253, 134, Part 2, No. 771, 'Chinese labour. Suggestions for securing further efficient control of Chinese labour, for the apprehension of deserters, and prevention of crime', 28 March 1906.

imprisonment with hard labour. Such evidence was also admitted in jury trials.[10]

A few sceptical senior police officers in these early years protested that it was 'a very dangerous procedure' to make arrests exclusively on dog-trailing information, but headquarters in Pretoria overruled them.[11] Mostly, police and prosecutors claimed a 'scientific' status for canine evidence.[12] *Rex (R.)* v. *Kotcho*, an eastern Cape case of stock theft, is illustrative. Testifying before the magistrate, the dogmaster, Nel, recalled arriving at the scene with two dogs from Grahamstown. One dog, given scent from some barefoot marks, proceeded to Kotcho's home. Entering, it sat on some blankets and barked.

> I took the accused, another native, and Willie Zendlova with me. I placed the three of them 30 yards from the trail. They had to sit down 30 yards apart. I again put the bitch on the scent of the bare-foot spoors. The bitch then went off to the three natives. She smelled first the other two boys. When she got to the accused she put her paws on him and commenced barking, indicating that he was the man who made the spoor. I then took her off and closed her eyes. I changed the three boys about. I then put her on the scent of the bare-foot spoors, and after that she again picked the accused out and behaved similarly as in the first instance...I then took the dog. I gave him the scent of the bare-foot spoors. He also picked out the accused and behaved exactly as the bitch did.

In this testimony, distances are precisely recorded, an impression of geometric symmetry is created, deliberate precautions seemingly exclude a predetermined outcome and the results are successfully replicated. Nel's account exuded the language of controlled objective experimentation to a degree frighteningly revealing of the intrusive, even torturous, nature of the process. The Solicitor-General later argued that Nel

---

[10] National Archives, Pretoria (NA), K80, 21, Police Inquiry Commission, evidence of Captain Donald, 1551–3; *Rex (R.)* v. *Adonis*, 1918 Transvaal Provincial Division (TPD) 411 at 411–12; *R.* v. *Kotcho, R.* v. *Barley*, 1918 Eastern Districts Local Division (EDL) 91 at 96–8 and *Star*, 13 December 1917.

[11] NA, SAP, 1/3/23/2: Deputy Commissioner, Johannesburg, to Secretary, South African Police (SAP), Pretoria, 31 December 1917 and 12 January 1918; Secretary, SAP, to Deputy Commissioner, Johannesburg, 7 January 1918; NA, K80, 21, Police Inquiry Commission, evidence of Captain Donald, 1543–8.

[12] Although the technique's veracity is immaterial to this study, it may be noted that the 'scientific' evidence for dogs' capacity to distinguish and trail individual human scents was disputed throughout the twentieth century and remains inconclusive. See W. Craig, 'The dog as a detective', *Scientific Monthly*, 18, 1 (1924), 38–47; and I.L. Brisbin and S.N. Austad, 'Testing the individual odour theory of canine olfaction', *Animal Behaviour*, 42, 1 (1991), 63–9.

having 'studied as a science the movements and habits of police dogs', rendered 'expert' testimony, the dog being 'merely an instrument'. In other cases, handlers supported their technical expositions with plans and diagrams.[13]

In 1918–19, however, the canine programme experienced a serious legal challenge when several cases (including *Kotcho's*) reaching the Supreme Court resulted in rulings that police dog identifications were inadmissible as evidence in trial. Chief Justice Innes, in a 1919 Appellate Division decision in the case of *R. v. Trupedo*, wrote disparagingly of 'the super-canine sagacity claimed for these animals' by 'their optimistic instructors'—claims that lent 'to such evidence a dangerously exaggerated importance' prejudicial to the accused. Innes thus echoed the concerns of the sceptical minority within the police force itself. He denied that one could infer with 'scientific or accurate knowledge' from a police dog's barking or jumping up at someone that this was the same person whose scent it had been instructed to trail. Such inferences involved 'conjecture and uncertainty'. Canine evidence was 'analogous to hearsay'—inadmissible because the dog (the immediate witness) could not be cross-examined. This was so irrespective of whether the dog in question was of a breed reputed to have acute powers of smell, was 'of pure blood', possessed a particularly discriminating nose, was highly trained in tracking, and had been placed on a trail indisputably the perpetrator's—considerations that had led some American states' courts, in decisions quoted as precedent in the South African cases, to hear testimony on these points as a 'foundation' for admitting dog-trailing evidence in trial.[14] The onus of proof, the Chief Justice implied in *R. v. Trupedo*, properly belonged to Rex the Crown, not Rex the dog.

---

[13] *R. v. Kotcho, R. v. Barley*, 1918 EDL 91 at 93–4 and 97 (citing the 1918 Transvaal case of *R. v. Moheketse*, mentioning plans of scent trails).

[14] *R. v. Trupedo*, 1920 Appellate Division (AD) 58 at 61–3 and *R. v. Adonis*, 1918 TPD 411 at 413–14. The fullest local exposition of the American authorities was Eastern Districts Judge President Sir Thomas Graham's in *R. v. Kotcho, R. v. Barley*, 1918 EDL 91 at 98–102, to which the judges in *Adonis* and *Trupedo* deferred. For discussion of the still evolving American case law, see B. Finberg, 'Annotation: evidence of trailing by dogs in criminal cases', *American Law Reports*, 3d, 18 (1968), 1221–40 and Supplements. See also S.G. Chapman, *Police Dogs in North America* (Springfield, 1990), 67–9. English precedent had greater standing with South African judges: the absence of relevant English authorities signified to both Graham and Innes that it had not been 'considered proper or right to lead evidence in [English courts] of law as to [dogs'] actions'. See *Trupedo* at 61; *Kotcho, Barley* at 95–6.

Yet the courts' censure of police dogmasters' claims to scientific expertise did little to hinder the expansion of the canine programme in the interwar decades. For, despite ruling dog-tracking evidence inadmissible, the judges endorsed the animals' use as an investigative technique for producing other evidence that could be led in a trial. As Sir Thomas Graham, Judge President of the Eastern Districts Local Division, put it, inadmissibility did 'not in any way seriously interfere with the employment by the police of these animals. They may still...be usefully employed for the purpose of obtaining clues...Once a clue is discovered relevant evidence is usually forthcoming which can be duly produced.'[15] Graham probably did not foresee that the 'relevant evidence' increasingly would take the form of dog-induced confessions. Ironically, given Innes's apparent insistence that police and prosecutors' evidence should meet strict standards of relevance, the courts' endorsement gave legal recognition to the programme's end results while removing from legal scrutiny any trace of canine involvement in the production of these results. Henceforth the Crown would need to observe the courts' requirements only in a formal sense.

In countenancing a separation of the process of procuring from that of proving evidence deriving from the use of dogs, the judiciary freed the canine programme's inner workings from effective external supervision. Meanwhile, the silencing of internal sceptics heeding a more scrupulous legalism removed a further significant check on the SAP's readiness after 1918 to privilege investigative procedures that were less methodical and rational than those that a previously greater police commitment to satisfying court-imposed evidentiary standards in a substantive and not merely formal way had exacted. The Crown's earlier conscientiousness in its approach to court-centred rule was a consequence less of benevolence towards the ruled than of the capacity of the legal process to foster more methodical bureaucracies and the rationalisation of society in the era of state-building and economic expansion following the South African War. But by the end of the First World War, popular resistance, especially black political militancy, was compelling administrators to calculate the costs in commitment of personnel and resources that continued adherence to a more substantive legalism as a basis for enhancing bureaucratic instrumental rationality

---

[15] *R. v. Kotcho, R. v. Barley*, 1918 EDL 91 at 105. See also *R. v. Adonis*, 1918 TPD 411 at 413.

would exact. Officials' reservations encouraged their retreat into an institutional logic favouring the entrenchment of far less rational mechanisms of rule such as the canine programme exemplified. Rationalising forces increasingly were channelled into differentiated spheres of state activity sealed off from judicial scrutiny, producing a more brutal but less methodically assertive interwar state.[16] Officials now argued that their ability to maintain effective state control demanded governmental standards which were at odds with liberal metropolitan ideals. Difficulties, however, arose when whites' liberties as well as blacks' were curtailed. The solution—sometimes with the courts' connivance—was to differentiate still further the supposedly colour-blind common-law legal domain from the administrative sphere.

That racial calculation informed the courts' bifurcated approach to the canine programme was revealed in Graham's decision in *R. v. Kotcho, R. v. Barley.* 'In the[se] two cases', the Judge President wrote, 'the charges are of stock theft, and the accused are natives, but if it is held that evidence of this nature is relevant and thus admissible, the rule will apply to cases of every description, and respectable citizens of every class in life may have their lives, liberty and reputation jeopardised by evidence that a trained police dog had indicated them to be guilty persons'.[17] In dividing the processes of discovering and proving evidence derived from dogs, the courts handed the police the discretion to employ investigative means in dealing with blacks that they rarely used in connection with whites. In practice, this discretion mainly affected the staging of scent identification parades, for inevitably there were occasions when trails from crime scenes unexpectedly led the dogs to white suspects.[18]

Yet, details that the Commissioner of Police, I.P. de Villiers, revealed in the late 1920s about the dogs' training confirmed that a racist orientation also informed tracking. The dogmasters used an African to lay a 'night trail' in the countryside surrounding the training camp the day before a practice session. The man went into hiding and the next day the dogs were exposed to an article bearing his scent and instructed to find

---

[16] For elaboration and substantiation of this argument, see K.S. Shear, 'Constituting a state in South Africa: The dialectics of policing, 1900–1939' (Ph.D thesis, Northwestern University, 1998).

[17] *R. v. Kotcho, R. v. Barley,* 1918 EDL 91 at 104.

[18] *Annual Report of the Commissioner of Police (ARCP) for* 1935 (An. 606-36), 13–14; NA, SAP 36/29/42, Officer Commanding (OC) SAP Dog Depot to Commissioner of the South African Police (Compol), 20 January 1942, para. 8.

him. '[I]t is not long', the account crowed, 'before he is discovered by his pursuers, who pounce upon him, barking to attract attention'. Such recitations of canine accomplishment, while aiming self-consciously to be scientific, were unwittingly thoroughly anthropomorphised and suffused with white-supremacist prejudice. 'The dogs readily respond and take a keen interest in their work', this same source asserted.

Racist settler ideas about Africans' hygiene and bodily odour were put to work too. The training staff, like most southern African whites, assumed that Africans collectively possessed a particularly intense and enduring odour. Thus police officials readily claimed their dogs could 'pick up the scent of tracks seventy-two hours old'. De Villiers did not think it tested the credulity of even sympathetic readers to cite a case in which two dogs allegedly successfully trailed a stock thief for fifty miles from six-day-old footmarks. Such essentialist themes coexisted effortlessly with the programme's fundamental assumption that all humans, Africans included, left individual scent trails that dogs could distinguish. 'Different natives are employed [in training]', the account continued, 'so that the animals do not become accustomed to any particular quarry.'[19] To round out their preparation, the dogs were taken to 'native locations where practice trails are worked to accustom them to such conditions'—as though the dogs, left to their own devices, might contemplate such spaces with the same horrified bewilderment that characterised whites' descriptions of Africans' living arrangements.[20]

Clearly, although the late 1910s' court decisions may have pricked the police's pretensions to 'scientific' knowledge of canine behaviour, they left considerable space for the development of expertise about the breeding, training, care and handling of police dogs. Indeed, the sealing off of the investigative domain (in which admissible evidence was procured) from the scrutiny of the legal arena (in which such evidence was proved) shielded the technique from searching adverse criticism and permitted the police to continue to maintain that they were following scientifically controlled procedure. Statistics were diligently recorded for each case of the distance the dogs trailed and of the age

---

[19] 'Dogs as detectives in South Africa, prepared from material supplied by Colonel I.P. de Villiers, M.C., Commissioner, South African Police', *Police Journal*, 2 (1929), 189, 191–2. On settler ideas about Africans' hygiene and bodily odour, see T. Burke, *Lifebuoy Men, Lux Women: Commodification, Consumption, and Cleanliness in Modern Zimbabwe* (Durham, 1996), 20–1.

[20] NA, SAP, 21/20/38, OC SAP Dog Depot to Compol, 16 July 1938.

of the scent they were pursuing.[21] The Commissioner's interwar annual reports are replete with details of canine investigations recounted in the same language of objective experimentation that the dogmaster Nel employed in *Kotcho*. Rationalising zeal, instead of being directed into purposive investigation, was put to the service of thoroughly irrational state practices.

Thus the courts, far from seriously obstructing the use of dogs for judicial purposes, ironically assisted a major expansion of the canine programme. When the lease on the site of the dog-training depot at Irene expired in 1922, new facilities were erected at Quaggapoort, six miles west of Pretoria.[22] The growth in the number of police dogs and of cases in which they were tried was particularly marked during the 1920s, rising from 65 dogs based at ten stations and used in 541 cases in 1920, to 202 dogs at thirty stations and used in 2,044 cases in 1929. In only about fifteen per cent of cases were handlers able to give the dogs scent from the scene that led them to a suspect—a record in the light of which officials' increasing resort to the animals reflects a faith in canine potential that is all the more remarkable.[23] Dogs became an integral and familiar element of rural policing in interwar South Africa.

The interwar Police Commissioners, T.G. Truter and I.P. de Villiers, both assiduously fostered the programme. Truter victimised subordinates who questioned the dogs' efficacy while promoting others who favoured their use.[24] In his reports Truter saluted 'the wonderful trailing powers of the dogs', their 'almost phenomenal' success in detecting stock thieves, and 'the great moral effect that the sagacity of the dogs has on the native mind'.[25] Only a dearth of suitable handlers, in Truter's opinion, limited the programme's extension. 'So insistent is the call for these animals from many places in the Union', he enthused in the mid-1920s, 'that it has been difficult to find sufficient men with the requisite temperament

---

[21] NA, SAP, 21/20/38, OC SAP Dog Depot to Compol, 16 July 1938, Annexure 'A'. On officials' cult of statistics see D. Posel, 'A mania for measurement: statistics and statecraft in the transition to apartheid,' in S. Dubow (ed.), *Science and Society in Southern Africa* (Manchester, 2000), 116–142.

[22] *ARCP for 1922* (UG 9-24), 54.

[23] *ARCP*, 1920–29. A third to a half of the dogs were assigned to stations; the remainder were kept in training or in reserve at Quaggapoort. 'Success' statistics were given for 1920 to 1927 and each year the Commissioner felt obliged to justify the small percentage. Significantly, later reports omitted this information.

[24] NA, K80, 21, Police Inquiry Commission, evidence of Captain Donald, 1553.

[25] *ARCP for 1923* (UG 15-25), 53–4; *ARCP* for 1926 (UG 7-28), 15.

and keenness to undertake the care, training, and handling of these useful adjuncts to criminal investigation'. Trainees at Quaggapoort were encouraged to believe 'that the work performed by dogs was absolutely genuine' and to perceive themselves as part of an exclusive fraternity.[26] Truter's passion did not escape the wit of Minister of Justice Tielman Roos. When his senior permanent secretary suggested the department need no longer see regular reports because all scepticism had been vanquished, Roos agreed but enjoined him not to 'hurt Compol's feelings by making him think that we disparage his dogs'.[27]

De Villiers was as ecstatic about the programme as his predecessor. In April 1929, shortly after becoming Commissioner, he contributed material to the London periodical *The Police Journal* for an article, 'Dogs as detectives in South Africa'. A formal claim to international leadership in the field, the article announced the arrival of dogs as 'a distinct section of the Police Force' in South Africa and emphasised that Quaggapoort was 'the only state-owned institution of the kind in the world'. The article described the curriculum for handlers and dogs at the depot, the care and breeding of the animals, and several criminal cases in which different breeds and cross-breeds were 'successes'.[28]

Time only reinforced de Villiers's early enchantment. 'These dogs', he wrote in 1934, 'undoubtedly are a very potent factor in reducing stock thefts'. 'The prevention and detection of stock theft is almost entirely dependent upon the work of the trained Police dog', he claimed on one occasion. 'No police force operating in rural areas', he later insisted, 'can be regarded as complete without a police dog section'. De Villiers argued hard for resources to back these assertions: a trained dog was worth £80 and each station was 'an expensive business', requiring at least two dogs, an expert handler and a motor car and driver 'for the exclusive conveyance of dogs and the trainer'. By 1934 de Villiers had increased the number of stations countrywide to thirty-six, some serving areas as large as 30,000 square miles.[29]

---

[26] *ARCP for 1925* (UG 6-27), 68; NA, K80, 71, Police Inquiry Commission, evidence of Constable Barnard, 5871.

[27] NA, JUS, 1/140/25, handwritten minutes by Bok and Roos, 9 January 1925, on Acting Commissioner, SAP, to Secretary for Justice, 8 January 1925.

[28] 'Dogs as detectives', 188–92.

[29] NA, SAP, 1/190/31, De Villiers to Secretary for Justice, 8 February 1934; *ARCP for 1928–29* (UG 13-30), 12; NA, SAP, 21/20/38, De Villiers to K.D. Wagstaffe, Assistant to the Inspector General of Police, CID, North-West Frontier Province, India, 25 July 1938 (draft); 'Dogs as detectives', 188 and NA, SAP, 21/6/49, OC SAP Dog Depot to

As the canine programme matured, it garnered wider acclaim. Within the police, with the sceptics silenced, the junior ranks shared their Commissioners' almost mystical faith in the dogs—an enthusiasm imparted to the white South African public as a symbol of its own nationhood and a vindication of its racial supremacy in magazine articles admiring the animals 'as a scientific arm of the Police'.[30] Although officials opposed scent-discrimination demonstrations lest publicised failure should damage the prized 'moral influence' the dogs 'produce[d] on the native mind', canine acrobatics later joined police physical training and horsemanship displays as popular highlights at agricultural shows, trade exhibitions and other occasions for patriotic advertisement.[31] Members of Parliament with large farming constituencies repeatedly demanded more extensive use of police dogs in the 1920s, whereas in the immediate post-Union period the topic had occasioned mainly back-bench mirth in the House of Assembly.[32] This shift in sentiment reflected the growth of white South African nationalism, the corresponding coarsening of interwar white political discourse and the diminishing expectation of routine bureaucratic efficiency. The 1926 South African Police Commission, describing the training and use of police dogs as 'a specialised form of criminal investigation work', extolled the programme as 'a most important arm' of the Criminal Investigation Department (CID). White farmers, the Commission reported, were 'unanimous' in praising not only the dogs' success in detecting stock thieves, 'but particularly' the magical 'deterrent effect which their employment ha[d] on the mind of the Native stock thief'. Farmers, believing Africans to be 'very much afraid' of police dogs, readily attributed declines in crime to the dogs' presence in a district.[33]

Compol, 5 May 1939. Frequently, the distance to the crime scene meant that two or more days elapsed before the dogs began trailing, but this did not diminish investigators' confidence in the evidence produced.

[30] 'How four-footed detectives work: a morning with the police dogs', *Picture News* (January 1932), 22–3, magazine enclosed in NA, SAP, 21/14/49.

[31] For opposition to public trailing demonstrations, see NA, SAP, 21/199/26, Commissioner, Kenya Police, to Colonial Secretary, Nairobi, 'Police Dogs—South African Police', 10 September 1927, copy enclosed in Office of the Commissioner, Nairobi, to Colonel Truter, 13 September 1927. On mounted police and physical training displays, see *Star*, 12 April 1930.

[32] *House of Assembly Debates (HAD)*, 1912, 119; *HAD*, 1924, 720; *HAD*, 1929, 588.

[33] *Report of the Commission of Enquiry to Enquire into the Organisation of the South African Police Force Established under Act No. 14 of 1912* (UG 23-26), 13; NA, K80, 69, Police Inquiry Commission, evidence of William Ernest Sinclair Moor, 5552.

Canine work thus epitomised the SAP's self-image of rational scientific superiority and mastery; it became a distinct specialisation in which the force claimed regional and international leadership, and with which it calculatedly disseminated some of its more obnoxious technologies and doctrines. 'The present police dog kennels and training camp outside Pretoria', a retired officer exalted in the mid-1930s, 'are probably the most modern and up-to-date to be found anywhere'.[34] British officials in neighbouring Basutoland, Swaziland and Bechuanaland allowed Union police dogs to pursue cross-border scent trails and called on the SAP for canine assistance in their own cases.[35]

Between 1918 and 1939 the SAP received enquiries from the authorities in Southern Rhodesia, Kenya, Palestine, Burma, Australia and India about training handlers and supplying dogs. De Villiers pointedly refused 'to despatch trained police dogs to another Force in the Empire unless [he] had had an opportunity of fully training at least two dogmasters of that Force'.[36] Southern Rhodesia sent a Corporal Ansell for training in 1927, but he failed to complete the course. Policemen from Palestine arrived next in 1934 and soon after deployed their dogs in the 1936 Arab general strike.[37] Much chauvinistic fanfare attended such exchanges. 'Quaggapoort', bragged a 1938 SAP promotional booklet aimed at white schools, 'has acquired such a reputation for its thoroughness of Police Dog training and the efficiency of its dogs, born, bred and trained there, that policemen from other parts of the British Commonwealth of Nations are sent here for training as Dogmasters; and, when trained, they take back to their own countries South African Police dogs for police work there'.[38] In the metropole, too, some cognisance was taken. In 1935 a former Superintendent of the Yorkshire West Riding Constabulary commended the programme as 'an example to the Mother Country which one would like to see followed now that authentic incidents proving the dog's value are frequently happening'.

---

[34] R.S. Godley, *Khaki and Blue: Thirty-five Years' Service in South Africa* (London, 1935), 242.
[35] *ARCP for 1931–32* (An. 79-33), 14–15; *ARCP for 1932* (An. 84-33), 21–2 and *ARCP for 1938* (An. 515-39), 10.
[36] NA, SAP, 21/20/38, de Villiers to K.D. Wagstaffe, Assistant to the Inspector General of Police, CID, North-West Frontier Province, India, 25 July 1938 (draft).
[37] *Star*, 11 December 1937 and Stanley, *Deferred Value*, 11.
[38] NA, K47, 13, Hl/2A, enclosing Union of South Africa, *The South African Police as a Career* (Pretoria, 1938), 5–7.

Four years later the *San Francisco Times* printed an appreciative newswire under the headline 'African Police Dogs Lead the World'.[39]

The identification of canine work with criminal investigation already defined it as a sphere of exclusive expertise in the opinion of SAP management. 'All our dog-training', de Villiers boasted in a 1938 reply to an enquiry by K.D. Wagstaffe, of the CID in Peshawar, India, 'is designed to use the dog as a detective and in this respect we differ from every other country where the dog is used as a protection for the policeman'. In seeming desire to protect the SAP's monopoly in this arcane science, the final version of de Villiers's letter deliberately omitted a detailed account, previously appended to a draft, of the curriculum followed at Quaggapoort.[40]

The atmosphere of exclusivity in which the SAP enveloped its canine work was redolent of South Africa's racial caste system. A dogmaster, characterised by de Villiers as 'a first-class policeman skilled in the detection of crime, a lover of dogs, and above all patient and steady under adverse circumstances', was necessarily white in the eyes of police management—a conception the SAP insisted upon in sharing canine expertise with overseas police forces.[41] This insistence on white expertise resulted in an awkward correspondence between Peshawar and Pretoria which illustrates how South African officials could make their own brand of racist practices prevail elsewhere.

Answering de Villiers, Wagstaffe regretted that his North-West Frontier Province Police had too few 'European Sergeants' to spare any for training as dogmasters, but declared that he could send two commissioned 'Indian Officers' who 'would of course conform in every way to European customs'. A.F. Perrott, Wagstaffe's chief, wrote personally to reassure Pretoria that he would 'select well educated men of good family and good manners who would fit in anywhere, provided that they were given a fair chance. This I am sure would be the case', he added dubiously. His doubts were confirmed in Chief Deputy Commissioner George Baston's cool response to Wagstaffe. 'Your desire', said Baston, 'to safeguard the dignity of your Officers is fully understood and appreciated by me, as I am sure my difficulty in the matter is by you'.

---

[39] Ex-Superintendent R. Arundel, 'Police dogs', *Police Review*, 28 June 1935, 627; and *San Francisco Times*, 22 August 1939, cutting in NA, SAP, 21/6/49.

[40] NA, SAP, 21/20/38, De Villiers to Wagstaffe, 25 July 1938 (draft copy, with certain paragraphs marked 'omit' in margin).

[41] NA, SAP, 21/20/38, De Villiers to Wagstaffe, 25 July 1938.

'Our Dog Training Depot', Baston expanded separately to Perrott, 'is manned entirely by Europeans, and in this country, where the colour bar is so clearly defined, it would be quite impossible for me to accept your Indian Officers for a course in dog training and mastership'.[42]

Perrott should have known, Baston implied, that 'mastership' of anything in segregationist South Africa was a white preserve. De Villiers clearly had promoted his expertise effectively, however, for Perrott soon buried his scruples, pronouncing himself 'so fully convinced of the value of Police dogs' that he was 'prepared to make almost any sacrifice to get two men trained'. Shortly afterwards two white non-commissioned officers from India were warmly received at Quaggapoort. They were offered 'any amount of relaxation, sports, etc.', and left six months later with 'pleasant memories' of South Africa, having become 'efficient Dogmasters...capable of training young dogs' and taking with them '6 dogs...carefully selected...from [the SAP's] best strain'.[43]

The specialised nature of canine work was marked not only by the elaborate eighteen-month curriculum developed to teach dogs to distinguish and track individual scents, by the rarefied qualities sought in potential dogmasters, and by their own lengthy apprenticeship in the handling, care and training of dogs. As the reference to the 'best strain' indicates, breeding police dogs was a precious science too. Police headquarters initially bought all its dogs from professional breeders in Europe. In the interwar years, although continuing occasionally to import 'thoroughbreds...from Europe for the purpose of counteracting inbreeding', the police took pride in meeting its needs locally. During the 1920s headquarters carefully studied 'the peculiarities of the various types of dogs' to determine which were the 'most suitable...for the South African country and climate'. Indeed, the SAP's official history celebrates the emergence of 'the true South African police dog' from domestic experimentation.[44]

---

[42] NA, SAP, 21/20/38: Wagstaffe to de Villiers, 20 August 1938; A.F. Perrott, Inspector-General of Police, North-West Frontier Province, Nathiagali, India, to de Villiers, 24 August 1938; G.R.C. Baston, Chief Deputy Commissioner, SAP, to Wagstaffe, 5 October 1938; Baston to Perrott, 5 October 1938.

[43] NA, SAP, 21/20/38, Perrott to Baston, 7 January 1939; Baston to Perrott, 30 January 1939 and 16 September 1939; Baston to Inspector-General of Police, North-West Frontier Province, Peshawar, India, 14 October 1939.

[44] *HAD*, 1912, 119; *ARCP for 1934* (An. 673-35), 12; 'Dogs as detectives', 189–90; and Dippenaar, *History*, 41.

The officer most responsible for raising breeding to a 'science' was a future Commissioner of Police, R.J. ('Bobby') Palmer, who claimed that as commandant of Quaggapoort in the early 1930s he had transformed a previously 'haphazard and indiscriminate' system of breeding. In ironic recognition of police dogs' growing reputation as 'detectives', Palmer, as a pen-profile later put it, 'from training dogs...was promoted to training men' as commandant of the Police Training Depot in Pretoria in the mid-1930s.[45] Palmer's replacement at Quaggapoort had few reservations about his predecessor's achievement. All the SAP's dogs were bred at the Depot itself with 'flattering results', he enthused in 1938. '[W]e select outstanding trained dogs from a line of ancestors famed for brains, grit and vitality, endowed with a strong scenting nose'. The staff experimented with Rottweilers, Bloodhounds, Airedales, Alsatians, Rhodesian Ridgebacks, Pointers and various cross-breeds, but settled on the 'pure and well-bred Dobermann-Pinscher' as the 'most useful and reliable' police dog. Alsatians, however, were 'quite unreliable and...not recommended'.[46] In this way, the discourse of breeding harmonised with officials' predilection for racial categorisation and ranking of people.

The language of science was mobilised to describe other elements of the project. The section on the programme in the Commissioner's annual reports exhibited discourses on veterinary medicine and canine occupational illness.[47] Elsewhere the Commissioner publicised the dogs' treatment by 'veterinary experts' and mentioned that their diet included a 'special cake manufactured' at Quaggapoort.[48] Veterinary and dietary concerns also infiltrated speculation about the effects of climatic and soil conditions on scent trails. 'Scent', remarked an extraordinary document produced at Quaggapoort in 1928,

> is an effluvium which is constantly issuing from the pores of all animal substances...it may be said to depend chiefly on two things, the condition of the ground and the temperature of the air...It lies badly with a

---

[45] 'General Palmer's Life Story—II', *Cape Times Magazine*, 11 August 1951; 'Personality Parade', *Indaba*, August 1954. Cuttings in album kindly shown to me by Mrs. C. McLennan, daughter of R.J. Palmer.

[46] NA, SAP, 21/20/38: OC SAP Dog Depot to Compol, 16 July 1938; de Villiers to Wagstaffe, 25 July 1938 (draft).

[47] For example *ARCP for 1924* (UG 21-26), 51, 67.

[48] 'Dogs as detectives', 189.

North or East wind...Fog, as a rule, is bad for it, as is also frost...It lies best in the richest soil...Failure in following up scent is sometimes due to the dog's olfactory organs being affected. This will frequently be found to arise from colds, constipation, or other causes, which a dose or two of opening physic seldom fails to remove. A little Sulpher [sic] or Syrup of Buckthorn will generally have the desired effect.[49]

Shielded from the scrutiny of the courts and from internal police dissent, every facet of the interwar canine programme could be similarly invested with the trappings of scientific respectability and precision. These 'sciences', however, were not merely discursive veneers of modernity, but also manifestations of instrumental rationality canalised into what can only be considered 'irrational' practices when judged by the standards of modern scientific superiority the police themselves claimed to exemplify.

Amid all the self-congratulation, a major commission of inquiry into the police in the late 1930s voiced a more cautious appreciation. Its report dutifully genuflected to the dogs' value in deterring stock theft, lauded the 'excellent arrangements and the skilful methods of training' at Quaggapoort and cited 'a very favourable report by the Inspector General of Police in Palestine' on dogs obtained from the SAP—thus sustaining the force's claim to international leadership. But the Commissioners, luminaries of the legal establishment, also hinted darkly at potential inquisitorial bias in the dogs' employment. Although quickly denying any 'dishonesty', their report mentioned 'evidence...of a disturbing nature...tending to show that a dogmaster can, if so minded, control the activities of a dog by secret signals in such a way as to make the dog point out any particular person suspected by the dogmaster'. Coupled with the belief that Africans thus picked out were likely to confess purely out of fear, such 'secret' skills could undermine equitable criminal procedure.[50]

Yet, from the investigators' perspective, the value of staging scent-identification parades lay, as Sir Thomas Graham had observed in 1918,

---

[49] NA, SAP, 1/3/23/2, Commandant, SAP, Quaggapoort, to Compol, 16 October 1928, enclosing memorandum 'Work of police dogs: scent'.

[50] *Interim and Final Reports of the Commission of Inquiry to Inquire into Certain Matters Concerning the South African Police and the South African Railways and Harbours Police* (UG 50-37), 68–9; NA, K80, 71, Police Inquiry Commission, evidence of Constable Barnard, 5876.

in the hope that these events would yield 'clues' leading to legally relevant admissible evidence. In practice, foremost among such 'clues' were confessions produced by terror in the face of sniffing dogs. Indeed, an experienced handler, who came to believe police dogs were 'a hopeless failure', implied that Africans whom dogs picked out at parades very often confessed, even when other evidence suggested their innocence.[51] In a murder case a confession could entail the death sentence.[52]

Figure 15. The commissioner of police saluting the Cato Manor Dog Memorial[53]

---

[51] NA, K80, 71, Police Inquiry Commission, evidence of Constable Barnard, 5871-9.

[52] *ARCP for 1930* (UG 35-31), 9. With serious crimes like murder a confession rarely sufficed to convict. See Union of South Africa, Criminal Procedure and Evidence Act (No. 31 of 1917), sec. 286. In the lower courts, which dealt with stock theft and other offences with which Africans were charged as a result of canine investigations, convictions on mere confessions were readily obtained: since most defendants were unrepresented, the admission of their confessions went unchallenged. Although these courts heard less serious criminal cases, they could nonetheless impose severe sentences.

[53] Used with kind permission of the SAPS. The image appeared on the cover of the police magazine *SARP*, 8, 5 (March 1972).

Police reports on the 'successful' employment of dogs unintentionally confirm how arbitrary and disquieting these incidents appeared to Africans. In a 1934 case of attempted safe-breaking in the southeastern Transvaal, scent from a piece of piping at the scene led the dog to a nearby compound where it barked in the corner of a room sleeping twenty workers. The dogmaster paraded all 150 compound residents in three rows. The dog pointed out a man in the third row who promptly confessed but also asked why the dog had selected him rather than his 'accomplice'.[54]

Police dogs frequently trailed directly into domestic spaces, entering a room or hut at night and sniffing each of its sleeping occupants in turn, which eight Africans experienced in a 1919 investigation of a break-in in the western Transvaal town of Zeerust; rushing right up to and pointing out one person among several at a homestead, as happened in a 1925 case of stock theft in the Cape's Middelburg district, and in a 1936 murder case in Natal's Ladysmith district; or jumping on a compound bed and barking, as in a 1941 stock-theft investigation in the Transvaal's Ermelo district.[55] The less corroborating evidence and the more inconclusive the scent trail, the larger appears to have been the size of the 'picking-out parade'. When a saddle disappeared from an airfield stable in 1945 and the dog lost the scent on a paved runway leading towards some black soldiers' barracks, the police turned out 600 Africans in twelve rows for a parade in which the dog pointed out 'a native corporal'.[56]

The courts, as we have seen, afforded no protection against these intrusive and demeaning proceedings. If a dog followed a scent to a hut or room, this was often deemed sufficient cause to enter and search at once without a warrant. In 1926 the Cape Provincial Division of the Supreme Court set an important precedent in dismissing an action of damages for *injuria* against the government brought by a Kokstad 'Griqua' cheese factory worker; police dogs had incorrectly pointed him out as the thief of a missing cheese by putting their paws on his shoulders and barking during a parade of the factory's employees. In

---

[54] NA, SAP, 21/20/38, OC SAP Dog Depot to Compol, 16 July 1938, Annexure 'A', para. 1. Despite the confession, the magistrate refused to convict in this case: *ARCP for 1934* (An. 673-35), 13.

[55] R. v. *Trupedo*, 1920 AD 58 at 60; *ARCP for 1925* (UG 6-27), 70; NA, SAP, 21/20/38, OC SAP Dog Depot to Compol, 16 July 1938, Annexure 'A', para. 4; and NA, SAP, 36/29/42, OC SAP Dog Depot to Compol, 20 January 1942, para. 12.

[56] *ARCP for 1945* (UG 27-46), 5.

the original summons the worker contended that the dogs' acts were 'an aggression...upon [his] liberty and freedom and an indignity and insult'. The sense of affront is unmistakable even through such stiff legalese. In an earlier suit relating to this incident the worker complained that detectives had threatened to set the dogs on him unless he confessed and that he had been bitten and scratched upon refusing.[57] The dismissal of his action meant that henceforth the police could organise their terrifying dog identification 'line-ups' with impunity.

Black South Africans undoubtedly experienced police dogs' 'smelling out' of alleged 'criminals' as oppressive. But we should resist a simple victimisation analysis of how the confessions were elicited. Certainly police exhibited brutal violence, but their increasing reliance on the dogs in the interwar period also suggests a more limited state whose functionaries were withdrawing from commitments to more rational and methodical forms of administration. Officials made no serious effort to understand the mechanism's operation. 'There is a mystery', the Kenya Police Commissioner reported following a 1927 visit to Quaggapoort with his Union counterpart Truter, 'something perhaps uncanny or undefined to the native mind which the use of dogs produces, and in a number of cases the use of dogs has brought the wrong doer forward to confess to his crimes. The Commissioner assured me that the moral influence obtained by the use of dogs was very [great] as far as native criminals are concerned'.[58] Clearly, more was happening than can be exhaustively explained either by fear of police violence or by officials' complacent stereotypes about Africans' mentality. Africans doubtless did fear the dogs, but the content of that fear is not self-evident. Thus, although this chapter's main point is to analyse officials' notions of what they thought they were achieving, their infatuation with magical effects, their limited comprehension of cause and consequence, and what this implies about the interwar South African state's modernity and reach, it is important to attempt a plausible, albeit conjectural, account of how

---

[57] *Mentor v. Union Government*, 1927 Cape Provincial Division (CPD) 11 at 13, 15; *Union Government v. Mentor*, 1926 CPD 324 at 325; and *Star*, 9 July 1926. The incident gained international notoriety when the government claimed it was not responsible for wrongs committed by policemen performing their statutory duty.

[58] NA, SAP, 21/199/26, Commissioner, Kenya Police, to Colonial Secretary, Nairobi, 'Police Dogs—South African Police', 10 September 1927, copy enclosed in Office of the Commissioner, Nairobi, to Colonel Truter, 13 September 1927.

social processes within African communities contributed to producing the confessions.⁵⁹

In form, the scent identification parades closely resembled witch- and witchcraft-finding practices. It is possible that Africans found in these state-sanctioned rituals ready substitutes for these outlawed practices. For in the Union, as elsewhere in colonial Africa, the proscription of imputations and detection of witchcraft left Africans feeling vulnerable to evil from within their own communities in ways that new colonial pressures and opportunities probably exacerbated but that secular courts could not address.⁶⁰ The line-ups, after all, commonly comprised people known to each other from a variety of daily interactions. The social unit could be a farm or other workplace, a compound, location, a large household, or the followers of a particular headman. The parades were thus subject to local understandings and observances, tested loyalties, and became occasions at which enmities could be vented. Africans to whom police dogs initially trailed not infrequently remained silent until the dogs had singled them out a second time from among their neighbours in a parade, which suggests a social ritual dimension to their confessions. Nor was it unusual for those indicated then to implicate others, which intimates that these events were forums for expressing parochial conflicts and jealousies only tangentially related to the cases the police were investigating.⁶¹

What local social understandings would Africans have brought to these events? Ethnographies indicate that dogs occupied an ambiguous position in the beliefs of many African communities in early twentieth-century South Africa.⁶² As domesticated animals, dogs were valued for hunting, herding and keeping watch at night. Unlike cattle or goats,

---

⁵⁹ On the uses of 'conjectural history' see T.C. McCaskie, 'Accumulation, wealth and belief in Asante history', *Africa*, 53 (1983), 25–6.

⁶⁰ M. Hunter, *Reaction to Conquest: Effects of contact with Europeans on the Pondo of South Africa* (London, 1936), 275 and M. Chanock, *Law, Custom and Social Order: The colonial experience in Malawi and Zambia* (Cambridge, 1985), ch. 5.

⁶¹ NA, SAP, 21/20/38, OC SAP Dog Depot to Compol, 16 July 1938, Annexure 'A', para. 9; NA, SAP, 36/29/42, OC SAP Dog Depot to Compol, 20 January 1942, para. 4; NA, SAP, 21/6/49, Compol to Secretary for External Affairs, 5 April 1944, enclosing 'Work of police dogs: extract from annual report, 1943', para. 3; and *ARCP for 1945* (UG 27-46), 6.

⁶² On animals' ambiguous cultural status generally see E. Leach, 'Anthropological aspects of language: Animal categories and verbal abuse', in E.H. Lenneberg (ed.), *New Directions in the Study of Language* (Cambridge, Mass., 1964), 23–63. For dogs' ambiguous this- and other-worldly aspects in Kongo thought and their part in witch-finding, see W. MacGaffey, 'The eyes of understanding: Kongo Minkisi', in W. MacGaffey and M.D.

they were seldom sacrificed. The anthropologist Monica Hunter found in Pondoland that people believed dogs drove away *uthikoloshe*, the best known of witches' familiars. Yet their proximity to humans also meant that dogs were potential sources of danger. B.A. Marwick observed in Swaziland that a dog entering a hut during childbirth was not removed until the baby had ridden on its back to deter future misfortune. Dogs were suspected familiars in their own right, bearing 'a message of malice' from their owners, especially if seen jumping on to the roof of another person's hut, or found urinating inside another's home or cattle enclosure. In isiXhosa, as in other languages, the verb 'to smell', *ukunuka*, also represented the action of diviners in revealing the sources of witchcraft. Dogs that actively sniffed at people were particularly distrusted as likely familiars. Most intriguingly suggestive is A.T. Bryant's recounting of a tradition in which Shaka's 'magic dog' settled a chieftaincy dispute by picking one of the claimants out of a parade.[63]

These ideas may well have informed Africans' perceptions of police dogs. From this perspective, the dogs were not only producing perpetrators for the 'crimes' their handlers happened to be investigating, but simultaneously revealing sources of conflict or evil within the community. Alternatively, the dogs were thought to be bewitched, bringing misfortune upon those they picked out or whose domestic spaces they violated. In either case there was a yawning gap between what the authorities thought to effect and the unintended consequences of their interventions in the context of the complex dynamics and cleavages of parochial politics.

Truter, infatuated with 'the great moral effect' he believed his dogs produced on Africans, observed uncritically that 'in a great many instances native offenders have been so surprised at the uncanny knowledge possessed by the dogs in following them up when they have considered themselves absolutely untraceable and free from arrest, that

---

Harris (ed.), *Astonishment and Power: Kongo Minkisi and the art of Renee Stout* (Washington, 1993), 39–43. My thanks to J. Glassman and L. Thomas for these references.

[63] A.I. Berglund, *Zulu Thought-Patterns and Symbolism* (Cape Town, 1976), 284–5; A.T. Bryant, *Olden Times in Zululand and Natal Containing Earlier Political History of the Eastern-Nguni Clans* (London, 1929), 482; A.T. Bryant, *The Zulu People* (Pietermaritzburg, 1949), 327; H. Callaway, *The Religious System of the AmaZulu* (Springdale, 1870), 28, n. 53; S.S. Dornan, 'Dog sacrifice among the Bantu', *South African Journal of Science*, 30 (1933), 628–32; Hunter, *Reaction*, 287, 297; E.J. Krige, *The Social System of the Zulus* (Pietermaritzburg, 1936), 189, 325; A. Kropf and R. Godfrey, *A Kafir-English Dictionary* (Lovedale, 1915), 295; and B.A. Marwick, *The Swazi: An Ethnographic Account of the Natives of the Swaziland Protectorate* (Cambridge, 1940), 143.

they have confessed to their crimes'.[64] White officials happily accepted these dog-induced confessions as an opportunity to close their files, but Africans' confessions were as likely indicative of communal moral tensions sharpened by the material exigencies of colonialism. The case cited at the outset of the sub-headman murdered in an era of increasing landlessness exemplifies such tensions and exigencies. As anthropologists have noted, confessions by those accused of witchcraft, to which the confessions at dog smelling-out parades bear a striking resemblance, have historically been surprisingly common; people who confessed when pointed out were acknowledging feelings of resentment that they genuinely believed had caused others' misfortune.[65] Thus the police were able to meet the formal condition for admissibility of confessions into court proceedings that they be 'freely and voluntarily' given, although the whole parading ritual was essentially an ordeal.[66]

From the police's perspective, the availability of dogs as an ostensibly 'scientific' technology allowed investigators to objectivise crime within a preferred epistemological framework positing a direct relationship between a narrowly defined 'criminal' action and an alleged perpetrator. Obviating complicating questions requiring methodical investigation, the use of dogs reduced communicative interaction between rulers and ruled to a level with which the police authorities felt comfortable. What officials could not recognise is that the very inertness they so valued in the medium afforded Africans interpretive possibilities of their own. Thus we have the ironic spectacle of a state institution celebrating its modernity and international leadership through a technique that Africans locally may well have been appropriating for ritual ends condemned as 'irrational superstition' and prohibited as 'uncivilised' by this same state.

The discourse of modernity legitimating the canine programme rested ultimately on two irrationalities governing state institutional action itself.[67] First was the faith in the dogs' powers, which the 'scientific' languages of breeding, training, veterinary medicine, olfaction, etc.,

---

[64] *ARCP for 1923* (UG 15-25), 54.
[65] D. Hammond-Tooke, *Rituals and Medicines: Indigenous healing in South Africa* (Johannesburg, 1989), 82–3.
[66] Criminal Procedure and Evidence Act (No. 31 of 1917), sec. 273.
[67] M. Weber, *Selections in Translation* (Cambridge, 1978), 28–9. Measuring the procedures of officials who claimed to exemplify 'rationality' against their own professed standards does not mean these were objective standards whose employment by officials to assert Africans' 'irrationality' had any validity.

never entirely disguised. Second, in the domain of policing practice, the conditions for means-end rationality were only superficially approximated in the serendipitous correspondence of investigative aims and closed-case results. What occurred in between was far less perfectly understood and drew officials on to terrain where the procedural legitimations of modern states were inoperative. The short cut to satisfactory outcomes that the canine ritual facilitated thus represented an effective qualification of bureaucratic instrumentality's colonisation of early twentieth-century South African society. The substantially greater pre-1918 official punctiliousness about procedural niceties that initially had significantly promoted bureaucratic ubiquity and the rationalisation of society had given way by 1939 to a less ambitious state whose personnel rarely scrupled about their extensive reliance on a mechanism of rule employing dogs and magic.

'GONE TO THE DOGS': THE CULTURAL POLITICS OF GAMBLING—THE RISE AND FALL OF BRITISH GREYHOUND RACING ON THE WITWATERSRAND, 1932–1949*

Albert Grundlingh

Gambling in various forms followed in the wake of the discovery of gold on the Witwatersrand in 1886 and remained a persistent feature of the way in which the urban proletariat sought to spend their leisure time. This paper explores one form of leisure pursuit, organised dog racing, which held sway on the Rand between 1932 and 1949. Betting on the dogs had its own internal dynamics, but the industry was also vulnerable to pressures emanating from wider society. Debates about dog racing cast new light on Afrikaner initiatives to fashion a particular form of cultural nationalism in Johannesburg. Moreover, working-class reactions to such overtures raise the question whether the adaptation of these Afrikaners to urbanisation, usually portrayed in the literature as extremely dysfunctional, has not been oversimplified.

Ultimately it was a combined set of societal pressures that ensured the termination of dog racing and that changed the landscape of popular culture on the Witwatersrand. The pastime was not resurrected, and even with the current relaxation of gambling regulations in South Africa dog racing tracks have failed to make their appearance in a society which has otherwise embraced gambling with gusto. Partly because it left so few traces in the present, the vanished culture of dog racing has not registered with historians. In addition, the general dearth of academic studies on the history of leisure in South Africa contributes to a lack of understanding of the wider significance of popular pursuits.[1]

---

* I am indebted to Charles van Onselen and Hermann Giliomee for a critical reading of an earlier draft of this chapter. The usual disclaimers apply. This article appeared in *South African Historical Journal*, 48, May 2003. Thanks to the editors for kind permission to reprint.

[1] For a brief but informative historiographical survey, see V. Bickford-Smith, 'Leisure and social identity in Cape Town, British Cape Colony, 1838–1910', *Kronos*, 25 (1998/1999), 103–4.

Origins, Evolution and Control of Dog Racing

In its elementary form, dog racing as practised in Britain can be traced back to the 1830s. Particularly in the northwest of England, what was known as 'coursing' was a regular pastime. 'Coursing' involved the release of a hare in an open field to be set upon by a pack of greyhounds after the hare had made some 50 yards. This was accompanied by betting about which dog would first devour the unfortunate hare. Rather perversely it carried genteel associations as it was likened to fox hunting.

Working classes adapted the activity and gave it even more of an edge as rabbits were used as bait in a confined space with whippets leading the charge. Anti-animal cruelty organisations claimed that in addition to the ordeal of rabbits when caught, so-called referees were also known to poke out a rabbit's eye in order to blind it and force it towards the side of the dog the bookmaker wished to win. On one occasion it was alleged that during a ten day rabbit 'coursing' meeting near Liverpool 128 dogs claimed 700 rabbits.[2] With the need to adapt the leisure activity to increasingly cramped urban conditions and in the face of anticruelty criticism the use of artificial bait became more common. The period after the First World War saw the building of floodlit stadiums and the introduction of the mechanical hare from America.

The end of the First World War proved to be a boom period in the popularity of dog racing in the United Kingdom. The general sense of psychological release after the armistice fuelled a need for entertainment, and the war spawned more of a devil-may-care attitude than before which fed into gambling. In addition, workers had more leisure time at their disposal as weekly working hours dropped from 65 to 48 and also earned more as real wages increased by 20 per cent. Whereas horse racing was seen as the sport of kings, dog racing was regarded as a working man's sport. Unlike horse racing which usually took place outside the city limits, charged relatively high entrance fees and demanded a certain code of dress, dog racing tracks were more conveniently accessible in urban areas, fairly cheap to attend in any

---

[2] M. Clapton, *A Bit of a Flutter: Popular Gambling and English Society, c. 1823–1961* (London, 1998), 138–43.

kind of attire, and allowed for bets in a variety of small denominations. Five or more 30 second races at nearby tracks provided short, intensive thrills and an attractive diversion for many working-class people.[3]

Even the worldwide depression of 1929–1933 failed to dent the popularity of dog racing. On the contrary, the pastime seemed to have benefited from the deep slump as desperate punters sought to improve their financial circumstances through gambling. The attendance at licensed tracks in the United Kingdom increased from about 6.5 million in 1928 to nine million in 1932.[4] In these hard times, a keen follower of the dogs has recollected years later, 'dog racing sang its siren song to the working man and helplessly he followed'.[5] For many it was also a night out in a festive atmosphere. One enthusiast commented: 'The brilliantly lit track stood out sharply from the surrounding darkness, in which the seething crowds of excited people could hardly be distinguished. It was reminiscent of a fête in some continental city, for rarely is such an all-pervading spirit of enjoyment found in sober England.'[6]

Given the upsurge of interest it was an appropriate time for the industry to expand to other areas of the empire, and the Witwatersrand, the industrial heartland of South Africa, appeared an attractive option. The first official license for dog racing and betting was granted to the African Greyhound Racing Association in 1932, followed by the Union Greyhound Racing Association and the East Rand Greyhound Racing Association. In time the Union Association proved to be the strongest of these companies. Tracks were built at the Wanderers, Wembley and Dunswart on the East Rand. The managers of these tracks came from Britain and the organisation of the races, not surprisingly, was largely patterned on the British model. Meetings usually took place on Friday evenings—deliberately to coincide with the weekly payment of working men's wages. It was a lucrative industry. Between 7,000 and 10,000 people attended the weekly races at the Wanderers and in 1941 the average profits were between 24,503 and 31,525 pounds per week.

---

[3] Clapton, *A Bit of a Flutter*, 144.
[4] S.G. Jones, *Workers at Play: Social and Economic History of Leisure, 1918–1939* (London, 1986), 38.
[5] L. Thompson, *The Dogs: A Personal History of Greyhound Racing* (London, 1993), 18. Thanks to Bill Nasson for alerting me to this source.
[6] F.C. Clarke, *Greyhounds and Greyhound Racing: A Comprehensive and Popular Survey of Britain's Latest Sport* (London, 1934), 22.

Those who had bought shares in the Union Association in 1932 would have seen their 10 pound share climb to 180 pounds in 1940.[7]

Organised dog racing came to South Africa under a cloud. It carried with it the reputation it had gained in the United Kingdom as a crass and corrupt commercial enterprise. Regardless of the validity of such claims, it was a difficult image to shed. As late as the 1950s, when dog racing had already entrenched itself as a pastime with a huge following in Britain, considerable antipathy remained. The British Broadcasting Corporation (BBC) had strong reservations about broadcasting race meetings as the sport was considered to bear an 'anti-social character', was not 'a desirable or sociologically useful sport' and to give exposure to such an activity 'would lower BBC standards'.[8] Barely concealed class prejudices clearly entered the equation. Nevertheless, it was early on deemed necessary by the dog racing fraternity in Britain to introduce an independent Board of Control to try and stamp out possible sharp practises. Members of the Board assumed overall control for what happened on the race tracks and in the betting halls, and had to ensure that each race was fairly graded and all the dogs in one race had an equal chance of winning. Such officials, working in an environment where money could easily change hands, had to be irreproachable and above suspicion of bribery. Indeed they were expected 'to have the morals of saints, and the will power of a mule that refuses to step aside, in order that the public could have a square deal'.[9]

In South Africa such checks and balances were not in place. Overall control of race meetings and procedures at the tracks rested squarely with the two race managers, F.C. Meeser of the African Association and R.H. Haswell of the Union Association. They received their authority from companies and which had to report to their shareholders. Although it was a system more open to abuse than in Britain, in the years that dog racing existed in South Africa and despite opposition to the sport, it was never proven that race managers acted improperly.[10]

---

[7] E.L.P. Stals, *Die Geskiedenis van die Afrikaner aan die Witwatersrand, 1924–1961* (Pretoria, 1987), 33; 'Hondewedrenne', *Die Kerkbode*, Mar. 1940; Transvaal Archives (TA), C.58, Dog Racing Commission, 1942, evidence of M.H. Coombe, 1835, 1836.

[8] G. Whannel, *Fields in Vision: Televison Sport and Cultural Transformation* (London, 1992), 18.

[9] A.S. Baker, *Greyhound Racing with the 'Lid Off'* (London, 1953), 3.

[10] TA, C.58, Dog Racing Commission, 1942, evidence of M.H. Coombe, 1836. Haswell later became the doyen of South African boxing promoters: 'Haswell Oorlede', *Beeld*, 28 Feb. 1995.

It is true though, that the public had no real way of ascertaining the validity of what happened on the track. As one critic of dog racing explained:

> Six greyhounds are paraded before a race. All may be brindle, or they may be mixed colours. I would say, at a conservative estimate, that not more than one percent of the public know, except by reference to the race-card...whether the greyhound in the striped jacket is Plug Ugly, Our John, Silly Point or Masked, to name a few top-class greyhounds at the tracks, or whether they are in racing parlance, 'ringers'. And I would stress this firmly that the public has no means of finding out, under present conditions, that all is as it should be. The public goes along, pay their money, and take what is offered them in the manner of the boy who shuts his eyes, opens his mouth and waits hopefully.[11]

Such reservations did not, however, act as a deterrent to enthusiastic betting on the dogs.

While on-course betting was legal, off-course betting was not. Off-course betting nevertheless took place on a huge scale and in 1940 it was estimated that 14,000 agencies for such betting, also known as bucket shops, existed on the Reef. These were usually run by Greek café owners or Chinese, Indian and African storekeepers. They employed runners who were detailed to collect bets in African townships, poor white neighbourhoods and industrial centres. The system allowed those who were too poor to attend the races in person, to participate in the betting. The owners of the bucket shop profited by taking their share of the bet off at the top.[12]

Bucket shop betting had the potential to fleece unsuspecting gamblers even more than those who placed their bets personally at the races. The fact that it was illegal and that bucket shop owners ran the risky of incurring a heavy fine, seemed to have had little effect on the practice. Nor, as in the case of on-course betting, did the public appear to have been unduly concerned by loopholes in the system. To some degree, tolerance of possible chicanery had its own logic. It was a face saving device for those gamblers who invested considerable pride in their much vaunted ability to pick winners; if the opposite happened, failure could be explained as a result of crookedness. 'Men plug the

---

[11] TA, C.58, Dog Racing Commission, 1942, evidence of M.H. Coombe, 1837.
[12] TA, C.58, Dog Racing Commission, 1942, evidence of A. Quenet, 3460 and evidence of D.N. Murray, 200.

dikes of their most needed beliefs with whatever mud they can find', the anthropologist, Clifford Geertz, has noted.[13]

Explaining the Attraction

The expression, 'gone to the dogs', which emanates from dog racing has become deeply embedded in the English language and carries strong overtones of moral and financial ruination. The expression is, however, less than useful in trying to explain why people actually did go to the dogs. In order to account for the appeal of dog racing one has to disaggregate the crowds at race meetings and also analyse the wider social purpose of dog racing in the community.

A small minority was interested in the event as such. They delighted in the grace and pace of well trained animals which they regarded as 'one of the most beautiful sights'. Apart from the aesthetic enjoyment, they also marvelled at the 'excitement and emotion that could be compressed into less than a minute'.[14] Race meetings indeed created an atmosphere of heady anticipation. None other than Leslie Blackwell, member of parliament, described it 'as an extremely pleasant way of passing an evening—and if you want an evening's amusement with plenty of colour and life you cannot get it more pleasantly than at such a meeting'.[15]

Betting, of course, was the main reason for such animation. 'It created a love of excitement and a false idea that wealth can easily be won in this way', one critic explained. As the evening wore on, some of these expectations evaporated and for the majority who had lost money on the dogs 'the atmosphere is rather one in which the predominant note is one of disgust and disappointment'.[16] But central to the gambling culture was the prospect that the losses of one week could be recouped the following week. The disappointment was therefore seldom enduring and each Friday came ripe with the renewed hope of a major win.[17]

---

[13] C. Geertz, *Local Knowledge: Further Essays in Interpretative Anthropology* (New York, 1983), 80. Information on public responses to bucket shop system from M.C. Edmonds who worked for a bucket shop owner in 1945, interview in Pretoria, 25 July 2000.
[14] Clarke, *Greyhounds and Greyhound Racing*, 23.
[15] Union of South Africa, *House of Assembly Debates* (*HAD*), 1940, 2646.
[16] TA, C.58, Dog Racing Commission, 1942, evidence of D.N. Murray, 22 and 24.
[17] TA, C.58, Dog Racing Commission, 1942, evidence of A. Quenet, 3466.

Dog racing attracted a variety of gamblers. 'At the Wanderers alone', an observer commented, 'there are some 7,000 patrons, young and old, some with money to burn, some who cannot afford to gamble, some wary and well-balanced, some unstable and immature'.[18] In broad outline the gambling fraternity at the races can be divided into four categories. First, and in the minority, were the professional gamblers for whom gambling was work. They had an in-depth knowledge of all aspects pertaining to the game and only placed their bets within fixed limits, based upon carefully calculated permutations. Next were the semi-professionals who kept their regular employment, but also studied the form of the dogs assiduously and were more inclined to bet fairly substantial sums. Third came the sporting type, who regarded the tracks as a hobby and attended regularly but did not bet too much. Not too far removed from this group were the casual racegoers in groups of families or friends who attended occasionally, for a bit of flutter or the night out. Then, in the majority, was the rowdy band of proletarian gamblers for whom the outcome of the race meant much more as it could have a significant effect on their available cash.[19] This group comprised mainly elements of the white working class of the Witwatersrand who earned at most three pounds a week and could easily loose a third or more of that at the races, or in the unlikely event of a win could boost their finances substantially.

Dog racing had its most dedicated followers in areas such as Booysens, Fordsburg, Mayfair and Braamfontein, and in particular Vrededorp. Many of these residents were recently or fairly recently urbanised Afrikaners. What is remarkable is the extent to which dog racing pervaded the everyday lives of these communities. An Afrikaner social worker in Vrededorp found that although there was a reluctance on the part of individuals to talk about dog racing to outsiders, this leisure pursuit was well established. She explained:

> The neighbours were only too willing to give information about gambling and the whole neighbourhood knows exactly who attends dog races. I was absolutely amazed to find to what a large scale dog racing is participated in and what a real knowledge 99% of the residents have of the 'sport'.[20]

---

[18] TA, C.58, Dog Racing Commission, 1942, evidence of A. Quenet, 3466.
[19] Compare Clapton, *A Bit of a Flutter*, 149; TA, C.58, Dog Racing Commission, 1942, evidence of D.N. Murray 21 and interview with M.C. Edmonds, Pretoria, 25 July 2000.
[20] TA, C.58, Dog Racing Commission, 1942, evidence of J. Terburgh, 1511.

Similarly, Ben Schoeman, National Party member of parliament for Vrededorp and later a prominent member of the cabinet testified in 1942 that 'he invariably found that the one subject which all could discuss, and in respect of which they knew every detail, was dog racing'.[21] It was even a lively topic of discussion at schools where on Monday mornings those youngsters whose fathers were fortunate enough to have won on Friday night could boast to their friends about the *'gelukkie wat Pappie gehad het'* (the little bit of luck Daddy had).[22] Winning dogs became household names; 'Jack the Giant Killer' and 'Last Hope' evocatively expressed the wishes and yearnings of those who placed bets on them.

Enthusiasm for dog racing cut across gender divides. From the East Rand it was reported that an Army Depot which employed a number of women in clerical positions came to a standstill on Fridays: 'Wherever you go, whichever office you go into, it is nothing else but dog racing and sweeps.'[23] Wartime anxieties, with many male breadwinners away on active service, contributed to a need for psychological release, which some women found at the races. In Vrededorp the participation of women in gambling was a matter of particular concern for a social worker who argued 'that when gambling takes hold on a woman, she loses her equilibrium more easily that the man and goes as far as to sell the kitchen utensils in order to obtain money to bet'.[24]

Moving away from such stereotypes and into a broader social analysis of working-class women's involvement in gambling, it is instructive to look at the popularity of bingo in the United Kingdom. It can be argued that the attraction of bingo was similar to that of dog racing. Bingo, it has been explained,

> is played by those in the least powerful positions in British society. In one sense the game parodies the socio-economic situation in which many players found themselves, in their lack of economic power and reliance on luck or patronage. It clearly demonstrates who is controlled and who is controlling. However, it can also be seen that working class women have taken the opportunity to fashion this activity in positive ways which suit

---

[21] TA, C.58, Dog Racing Commission, 1942, evidence of B. Schoeman, 467.
[22] TA, C.58, Dog Racing Commission, 1942, evidence of J.F. du Toit, 947.
[23] TA, C.58, Dog Racing Commission, 1942, evidence of G.D. Kotze, 1577.
[24] TA, C.58, Dog Racing Commission, 1942, evidence of J. Terburgh, 1511.

them, and which offer some recreation for themselves, with the constraints which restrict their leisure options.²⁵

The contradictions inherent in the gambling culture shed light on the underlying dynamics which propelled women to the race tracks, despite the real risks of inflicting greater hardship.²⁶

The brief excitement of dog racing on Friday nights also helped some working-class men to offset the tedium and monotony of a menial job during the week.²⁷ But it was, of course, more than purely recreational; the primary concern was to improve their financial position. Although it was an extremely risky way of spending hard-earned cash, it was not entirely reckless and unthinking behaviour. There was a certain logic as to why the urban poor regularly wound their way to the tracks.

Gambling made more sense than saving; a small and often irregular income did not encourage prudence or the anticipation of a better future. Saving at best implied delayed gratification, if at all, and vague promises of a better future which many could hardly begin to imagine. Gambling at least had the immediate potential and the promise, however illusory, of enhancing their financial circumstances. Given this context it can even appear a rational act. For many it was 'the only possibility of actually making a decision, of a choice between two alternatives, in a life otherwise proscribed in every detail by poverty and necessity'. Betting generated its own patterns of serious reflection, as one spent 'one's time in discussion, analysis and decision making with a seeming sense of purpose' and possible achievement.²⁸ Regardless of one's losses, betting on the dogs provided a fleeting sense of control and importance.

Afrikaner Cultural Politics and Dog Racing

Dog racing gained its hold on impoverished Afrikaner communities during a period of increased urbanisation. Between 1926 and 1936,

---

[25] R. Dixey, 'Bingo in Britain: an analysis of gender and class', in J.C. McMillan, (ed.), *Gambling Cultures: Studies in History and Interpretation* (London, 1996), 147.
[26] Compare, for example, Dutch Reformed Church Archives (DRCA) Synod Documents, 178, Selected Testimonies of Women on the Financial Implications of Betting on the Dogs, 1943.
[27] TA, C.58, Dog Racing Commission, 1942, evidence of B. Schoeman, 2631.
[28] Compare R. McKibbin, 'Working class gambling in Britain, 1880–1939', *Past and Present*, 82, 1979, 169–70.

mainly as a result of the Great Depression of the early 1930s, on average 6,500 Afrikaners annually found their way to the Witwatersrand. The trek to the Rand was further fuelled by wartime industrialisation, which opened up greater employment opportunities. In the late 1940s Afrikaners constituted almost 36 per cent of the white inhabitants of Johannesburg.[29]

It is a common view in the historiography of Afrikaner urbanisation that the newcomers struggled to adapt to an environment far removed from the world they were used to.[30] While the transition from the countryside to the city was undoubtedly a painful one, particularly given the low level of skills of those who sought to enter the job market, the Afrikaner working class were not entirely hapless victims of forces beyond their control. They might have found it difficult to cope with a demanding work environment, but they had a well-developed sense of possible benefits that city life could offer. Impoverished whites are on record as telling welfare officers: 'Why should we not come to Johannesburg? Look at what we are offered. Johannesburg has free hospitals, homes for babies, school clinics and a chance to bring children to be educated, physically treated and get a good many things free.'[31] Certainly, in the area of leisure, as we have noted, the alacrity with which they supported dog racing creates the impression, contrary to the general belief, that they blended in very well with the new urban social landscape.

The enthusiasm displayed for dog racing did not meet with the approval of the emergent Afrikaner middle-class cultural entrepreneurs who, during the 1930s and 1940s, played such a major role in ethnic mobilisation. This class, consisting of clergy, university lecturers, social workers and other professionals, regarded themselves as the interpreters (and manufacturers) of Afrikaner culture and its endeavours found expression in a number of organisations. Cultural politics (*kultuurpolitiek*) became an increasingly important area where discourses around notions of 'volk', a legitimising 'sacred history' and appropriately sober

---

[29] Stals, *Die Geskiedenis van die Afrikaner*, 10–11 and J.R. Albertyn, *Kerk en Stad* (Johannesburg, 1965), 51.

[30] Compare, for example, Stals, *Die Geskiedenis van die Afrikaner*, 13 and D. O'Meara, *Volkskapitalisme: Class, Capital and Ideology in the Development of Afrikaner Nationalism, 1934–1948* (Johannesburg, 1983), 54.

[31] Quoted in E. Brink, 'Maar 'n klomp factory meide: Afrikaner family and community on the Witwatersrand during the 1920s', in B. Bozzoli (ed.), *Class, Community and Conflict: South African Perspectives* (Johannesburg, 1987), 183.

mores and conduct were deftly woven into the fabric of an overarching Afrikaner ideology.[32]

It was the clergy in particular who singled dog racing out as a manifestation of what they regarded as the moral decay that followed in the wake of Afrikaner urbanisation. Dog racing was considered a prime social evil as annual church synods made clear.[33] There was little doubt in the mind of the Revd William Nicol of Johannesburg, prominent in church and cultural circles, that what he regarded as 'the moral and spiritual deterioration of the Afrikaner people was to a large extent attributable to dog races'.[34] On religious grounds Afrikaner clergy were opposed to gambling as it was seen to undermine the Biblical injunction of having to 'earn one's bread by the sweat of one's brow'; diligence as opposed to chance was the prescribed way to try and alter one's circumstances.[35] Moreover, gambling was simply incompatible with a pious lifestyle.

However, in publicly voicing their opposition against dog racing, Afrikaans clergy shied away from using explicit religious arguments. They preferred the charge that betting encouraged working-class people to fritter away their money and that it gave rise to a variety of domestic problems. While betting on the dogs undoubtedly contributed to greater poverty and dissolute behaviour in some individual cases, it is problematic to single out dog racing as the sole variable that impacted negatively on working-class lives. Nevertheless, it was the stock-in-trade of clergymen opposed to dog racing. A comprehensive inquiry into dog racing was launched in Johannesburg in 1942 and after more than 4,000 pages of evidence, the commissioner, E. Beardmore, had this to say about the submissions made by ministers of religion:

> [S]peaking broadly they had no accurate knowledge of the extent of the social evils of betting on the dogs among their own people, or among the general public, and their evidence against dog racing was based rather on ethical... grounds. It was in keeping with this attitude of mind that one

---

[32] O'Meara, *Volkskapitalisme*, 55–6; H. Adam and H. Giliomee, *The Rise and Crisis of Afrikaner Power* (Cape Town, 1979), 112–14 and I. Hofmeyr, 'Building a nation from words: Afrikaans language, literature and ethnic identity, 1902–1924', in S. Marks and S. Trapido (eds.), *The Politics of Race, Class and Nationalism in Twentieth Century South Africa* (London, 1987), 95–123.
[33] DRCA, General Synod Minutes, 1942.
[34] Quoted by B. Schoeman, in *HAD*, 1940, 2630.
[35] D. du Preez, 'Die Calvinistiese beskouing van arbeid', *Koers*, 14, 2 (Oct. 1946), 53.

expressed the view that one single case of social evil attributable to dog racing would, in his opinion, justify the closing of the tracks.[36]

It was not, so it seems, a preoccupation peculiar to Afrikaner clergymen. Ross McKibbin, writing on working-class gambling in Britain between 1880 and 1939, pertinently observed that protestant churches were quick to make extravagant claims: 'families pauperised, industries ruined, a class corrupted—even an empire lost. Why was this?' According to him the protestant clergy 'had a vocational interest in the perpetuation of sin' and if it 'could be demonstrated that gambling had material consequences as well as spiritual, so much the better'.[37]

Afrikaner clergymen might also have exaggerated the 'evils' of dog racing, but their motives for doing so cannot readily be connected with the notion of the professional proclamation of sin being in their own narrow vocational interest. In their case, and also among other Afrikaner leaders, opposition to dog racing and invoking it as 'a social evil' related more directly to their conception of what constituted acceptable Afrikaner culture. At the time it was a culture that expressed itself in anti-British sentiments, a certain rootedness in Afrikaner constructions of history and what was termed the *volkseie* (that which belonged to the 'volk').[38] It took various, but related forms: the near euphoric centenary celebrations of the Great Trek in 1938, the production of historical plays, the growth of Afrikaner youth movements, an outpouring of Afrikaner literature and the popularisation of *volkspele* (folk dancing). Ultimately it involved the redefinition of Afrikanerdom along specific lines. Consequently, as far as leisure time was concerned, it was argued that 'one can not hope to educate a "volk" unless one is able to control and ensure that its entertainment is soundly based'.[39]

The strategy of such entrepreneurs involved more than just promoting what they considered to be Afrikaner culture; it also implied that possible rival forms had to be countered. Dr H.F. Verwoerd who moved to Johannesburg in 1937 as an Afrikaans newspaper editor, viewed the matter seriously and argued that the threat to the Afrikaner was that 'in

---

[36] TA, C.58, Dog Racing Commission Report, 1944, Paragraph 15.

[37] McKibbin, 'Working class gambling in Britain', 157–8 (emphasis in original).

[38] See, for example, A. Grundlingh and H. Sapire, 'From feverish festival to repetitive ritual? The changing fortunes of great trek mythology in an industrialising South Africa, 1938–1988', *South African Historical Journal*, 21 (1989), 19–27.

[39] University of the Free State Library, Archives of the Federasie van Afrikaner Kultuurkringe, PV 202/iv/6/13/1/1/1, 'Die Afrikaner se vryetydsbesteding, 1942' (translation).

urbanising he would undergo a process of proletarianisation in which he would lose all interest in Afrikaner culture and become merely an international worker'.[40] In the process of constructing and homogenising Afrikaner nationalist culture, the popularity of dog racing with its army of impoverished Afrikaner supporters posed a problem. With its British overtones and proletarian appeal dog racing did not quite fit, nor could it be made to fit, the new cultural design in the making.

In the wider context of the powerful Afrikaner cultural drive during this period which in part contributed to victory at the polls in 1948, the very success and apparent unity of purpose, tend to obscure underlying fissures in the process of creating what was considered a suitable Afrikaner culture. The Afrikaner poor did not necessarily share the same cultural concerns as their middle-class compatriots, and it was precisely this development that perturbed leaders such as Verwoerd.

A suburb like Vrededorp, one of the epicentres of the dog-racing culture, had a long and chequered history of entertaining Afrikaner nationalist politicians without being seduced by them. Writing on the period punctuated by strikes between 1906 and 1914, Charles van Onselen has noted that in 'their restless search for political direction the unskilled workers of Vrededorp demonstrated not only aggressive working-class consciousness but also considerable acumen...'.[41] In succeeding years identity politics in areas such as Vrededorp and other impoverished Afrikaner communities on the Reef continued to be shaped by the ebb of local conditions and the flow of wider nationalist forces.[42] The fluidity of these communities made it difficult for nationalists to establish stable moorings. Members of the Afrikaner middle classes were increasingly aware of a growing social divide between them and the working classes. In 1946 a church newspaper reported as a matter of concern that

> it is not easy to organise social interaction, exchange of ideas and unified action between the wealthier members of the 'volk' and the poor. A fair measure of mutual trust between our social classes has already disappeared. We find among our lowly paid workers... in the cities, doubts as

---

[40] Quoted in G.D. Scholtz, *Hendrik Verwoerd* (Johannesburg, 1974), 90 (translation). I am indebted to Hermann Giliomee for this reference.

[41] C. van Onselen, *New Nineveh: Studies in the Social and Economic History of the Witwatersrand, 1886–1914*, vol. 2 (London, 1982), 161.

[42] Compare L. Lange, 'The making of the white working class: class experience and class identity in Johannesburg, 1890–1922' (PhD thesis, University of the Witwatersrand, 1998), 163–259.

to the intentions of their fellow Afrikaners when deliberate attempts are made to lend a helping hand...[43]

In this respect the Afrikaner poor displayed a pattern of behaviour which was fairly common among working classes elsewhere. As recent research on working class culture and politics in London between 1870 and 1914 has reiterated, well-meaning interventions of the middle classes were not always received with deference and gratitude.[44]

Such class suspicions can be detected in responses to the cultural crusades of clergymen who opposed dog racing. Although firsthand Afrikaner working class testimony is hard to find,[45] occasional signs of annoyance did surface. One man who had enough of what he regarded as the meddling of a social worker told her that 'he was fond of the dogs and it gave him pleasure'.[46] The clergy in poorer areas also discovered that some members of their congregation were not too impressed by fire and brimstone sermons on the 'evils' of dog racing. One minister of religion testified that if 'they preached against dog racing too much there is the section which was inclined to disagree and they felt it was too much a matter of politics and they had to leave it entirely alone'.[47]

What was at issue here was a pointed rejection of the paternalism that often accompanied welfare and the way in which modes of cultural behaviour were prescribed. The very term 'poor white' can in some ways be regarded as problematic in that it did not necessarily express the lived experience of those so categorised. Resentments to the term emerge in an Afrikaans play of the period where a woman described as 'poor white', responded:

> I am no 'blinking street woman' and also not a 'poor white'...It is the 'charities' and the 'distress' and the 'Mayor's Fund' and all those people that want to make 'poor whites' of us. My husband said that they are

---

[43] 'Klasseskeiding in ons volkslewe', *Die Kerkbode*, 19 June 1946, 797–799 (translation).

[44] A. August, 'A culture of consolation? Rethinking politics in working-class London, 1870–1914', *Historical Research*, 74 (2001), 202.

[45] Significantly in the more than 4,000 pages of official inquiry into dog racing it was not deemed necessary to elicit the opinion of a single person from a working-class background. Clearly, it was seen as a matter on which working-class people could not adjudicate.

[46] TA, C.58, Dog Racing Commission, 1942, evidence of J. Terburgh, 1526.

[47] TA, C.58, Dog Racing Commission, 1942, evidence of Rev A.H. Swartz, 2836.

just like doctors who discovered a new illness and now want everyone to have it.[48]

Such sentiments did not, however, translate into any organised attempts on the part of the poorer communities to defend their particular cultural pastime. The capacity to oppose the purveyors of all things good and nationalist in a meaningful way was simply absent. Nor perhaps would it have been in their best long-term interest to do so. Although it is somewhat of a moot point, the interventions of the Afrikaner middle classes can be seen to have had the effect of bringing 'poor whites' back into the fold and positioning them to benefit from the success of the nationalist movement after 1948. But before that happened, dog racing first had to be extruded from the social life of working-class Afrikaners. It was, of course only one element in the far larger process of the rehabilitation of the Afrikaner poor.

The Demise of Dog Racing

There was a realisation amongst Afrikaner opponents of dog racing that it would be a long and possibly fruitless attempt to wean the poor from their favourite pastime. Hence a far bolder strategy had to be followed; the temptation had to be removed completely. The first step in this direction was taken to lobby for the establishment of a commission to look into the effects of dog racing. This commission held 91 sessions and 116 people testified which mainly included representatives of various churches, social workers, school principals and members of the police force. As noted earlier, the minutes of the proceedings ran to more than 4,000 pages. In its findings, the commission steered away from taking a firm stand on the morality of gambling, but did recommend that in order to protect the gambler, stricter controls should be in place and the frequency of meetings should be curtailed, with no races taking place on Fridays when workers were being paid.[49]

The Dutch Reformed Church was not pleased with these recommendations. The recommendations, it argued, actually had the effect of stabilising the industry as more controls were instituted and it allowed

---

[48] Quoted and translated in J. van Wyk, 'Nationalist ideology and social concerns in Afrikaans drama in the period 1930–1940' (Unpublished Paper, History Workshop, 1990), 7.
[49] TA, C.58, Dog Racing Commission, 1946, final report.

dog racing companies to carry on virtually unhindered with what the church regarded as nefarious practices.[50] Under the leadership of the Revs William Nicol and A.M. Meiring the church made its views widely known in the press and also proceeded to gain support for the abolition of dog races from a number of organisations. Eventually the anti-dog racing lobby consisted of 180 welfare bodies, 25 youth institutions, 10 youth bodies with 18,771 members, 100 school principals as well as the Welfare Department of the Johannesburg City Council.[51]

Significantly, English protestant churches also joined forces with the Dutch Reformed Church. This co-operation strengthened the campaign considerably. It could now be claimed that churches which differed theologically and politically were prepared to sink their differences for what they regarded as the common good. The alliance alerted the provincial authorities to the breadth of opposition that cut across traditional divides.[52]

The movement against dog racing gained further momentum from a huge public meeting organised jointly by the churches in the Johannesburg City Hall on 4 March 1946. About 1,000 people attended the meeting and adopted a unanimous motion opposing the races. While representatives of the Afrikaans churches rehearsed their familiar arguments against the dogs, English church leaders placed less emphasis on the social ramifications and completely ignored ethnic dimensions. They sought, instead, to underline what they considered the 'prevailing un-Christian attitude to life as a whole and more particularly to the stewardship of money and time'. The atmosphere at the races was considered an ungodly one that reflected a more general malaise:

> The long waits between the races while people make their pathetic pilgrimage to and from the tote cubicles in the hope of collecting other people's money foolishly given in the same hope, the spectacle of thousands of God's children born in his image, yelling, shouting, booing and hissing as these dogs are made to run after a bundle of fur they are never intended to catch—is this not the anatomy of a melancholy 20th century?[53]

With the groundswell of public opinion behind them, a combined church deputation to the United Party administrator, J.J. Pienaar, sought to influence the views of the provincial administration on the

---

[50] 'Kerk se reaksie', *Die Transvaler*, 27 July 1946.
[51] 'Afskaffing van hondewedrenne', *Die Voorligter*, July 1947.
[52] 'Afskaffing van hondewedrenne', *Die Voorligter*, July 1947.
[53] 'Churches support objections to dog racing', *Star*, 11 May 1946.

matter. Pienaar, however, showed some reluctance to act. Uppermost in his mind was a loss of two per cent revenue accruing from betting on dog racing and also strong representations made by the dog racing companies to continue with their operations.[54]

While disappointed with Pienaar's inertia, those opposed to dog racing kept up the pressure by lobbying individual members of the provincial council. Although the National Party was the first to oppose the dogs, increasingly the matter became one that transcended party politics. Within the United Party the question of dog racing was regarded as one that could be potentially damaging if the administration was seen as insensitive to an issue that had been elevated to the level of a pressing moral and social concern. The English-language press, generally supportive of the United Party, advocated that other sources of revenue should be found and that the provincial government should not by default associate itself with what could be regarded as an unsavoury business. The administration had to ask themselves:

> Is it... any use a government maintaining the pleasant fiction that it is deeply concerned over the moral and social upliftment of the citizen when, all the time, it is casting lots with the other actors in the drama for the clothes of the unhappy victim?[55]

Eventually it was a mix of such sensibilities and political pragmatism that prevailed. On 5 June 1947 the caucus of the United Party provincial council decided to abolish dog racing. A two-year period of grace was allowed for the companies to wind down their affairs, which meant that dog racing was only officially terminated in 1949.[56]

Conclusion

The demise of dog racing contains certain ironies. On one level it can be viewed as a cultural victory for the Afrikaner middle classes, but one that did not necessarily carry the blessing of those on whose behalf the struggle was won. Furthermore, although the dog racing companies

---

[54] 'Afvaardiging by Transvaalse UK', *Die Transvaler*, 14 Mar. 1946; 'Pienaar voor netelige vraag', *Die Vaderland*, 16 May 1947 and DRCA, 'Ring van Johannesburg: Memorandum in Sake Hondewedrenne', 30 Aug. 1946.
[55] 'The state's 30 pieces of silver,' *Star*, 7 Jan. 1947.
[56] University of South Africa, United Party Archives, Transvaal Provincial Council minutes of caucus meeting, 5 June 1947.

undoubtedly exploited the poor, it was a form of exploitation which the working class for a particular set of reasons willingly participated in. From the perspective of the environmentally conscious world of today, an additional irony emerges that during the long drawn-out campaign against dog racing a range of objections was proffered, but the question of cruelty to animals did not emerge once. The issue at the time was cultural identity and control over leisure time. In this contest the dogs themselves never featured. Ultimately, however, the role which the racing dogs played in human society emphasised certain hidden sociological dimensions.

In a recent South African cultural studies volume, Rita Barnard has elaborated on the significance of the apparently insignificant:

> it is precisely in the most trivial, the most hopelessly flawed manifestations of any given genre or cultural form that the operations of ideology are most clearly and characteristically displayed. A critical reader of culture should therefore prick up her ears when a text, idea, or practice is habitually and as a matter of course dismissed as silly, uninteresting, or passé; for it is in the fertile loam of the marginal that we may find the structures of power revealed in peculiarly fascinating ways.[57]

At first glance dog racing may also appear a frivolous topic. However, using it as a prism allows one to access a particular manifestation of white working-class popular culture on the Witwatersrand. Glimpses of a vanished world appear, opening an aperture to reflect from a different angle on how poor Afrikaners adapted to the urban environment. A final and not inconsiderable bonus is that the linkages and tensions among the cultural dimensions of ethnic mobilisation, community politics and leisure pursuits start to emerge.

---

[57] R. Barnard, 'Contesting beauty', in S. Nuttal and C.-A. Michael (eds.), *Senses of Culture: South African Cultural Studies* (Cape Town, 2000), 347.

SOCIAL SUBJECTS: REPRESENTATIONS OF DOGS IN SOUTH AFRICAN FICTION IN ENGLISH

Wendy Woodward

Dogs who appear in South African fiction from the nineteenth century to the present are represented as socially and historically located. As living examples of breeding they embody a commentary on vacillating fashions. As non-human companions to human animals they are deemed capable of complex interactions.[1] Like other animals they serve as sometimes contradictory metaphors and metonyms. Dogs enable writers to structure notions of human identities and to incorporate broader ecological views of relationships between human and non-human animals.

Nineteenth century writers, Olive Schreiner in *The Story of an African Farm*[2] and Percy Fitzpatrick in *Jock of the Bushveld*[3] not only attribute sentience to the named dogs they represent, but ascribe a rich and complex consciousness to them. Within colonial discursivities, however, so-called 'kaffirdogs' are othered as unworthy of characterization and, sometimes, as metonymic of racialised constructions of their 'owners.'

Conversely, dogs may function as ciphers, as hated signs of racialised privilege. In the apartheid era, Njabulo S. Ndebele and Es'kia Mphahlele, in 'The Prophetess'[4] and 'Mrs Plum'[5] respectively, represent urban dogs either as watchdogs in the townships or as coddled and infantilised pets in white suburbia with a better material existence than the workers who care for them. The lacuna in these narratives is the longstanding symbiosis between the indigenous African dog and what Johan Gallant

---

[1] While the terminology 'human and non-human animals' is more politically and ecologically correct, it is too prolix to sustain throughout this essay.
[2] O. Schreiner, *The Story of an African Farm* (London, 1883 [1995]).
[3] P. Fitzpatrick, *Jock of the Bushveld* (London, 1907 [1957]).
[4] N.S. Ndebele, *Fools and Other Stories* (Johannesburg, 1983), 30–52.
[5] E. Mphahlele, *The Unbroken Song: Selected Writings of Es'kia Mphahlele* (Johannesburg, 1981), 216–261.

terms 'human pack partners'.⁶ Another lack is the correlation which Mocambican writer Luis Bernardo Honwana makes between manifestations of dualistic thinking in his short story, 'We Killed Mangy-Dog.'⁷

White writers during apartheid did not have dogs as significant figures in their narratives perhaps because to do so might have engendered criticism of foregrounding animals at the expense of humans. This is exemplified in *Burger's Daughter*, a novel published by Nobel prize winner, Nadine Gordimer, in 1979: Rosa, the eponymous protagonist, comes across an indigent, drunk black man whipping his donkey in the shafts of a cart while his wife and children huddle in terror. Rosa Burger has to make the ethical decision of whether to intervene or not, to 'stand between them and suffering—the suffering of the donkey',⁸ but the political compromises of such an action paralyse her, and she drives on. Although the animal's convulsed pain becomes the 'sum of suffering' to her, she reasons that 'a kind of vanity counted for more than feeling. I couldn't bear to see myself-her-Rosa Burger-as one of those whites who can care more for animals than people'.⁹

If, like Rosa Burger, South African writers felt similarly constrained in their subject matter before the new political dispensation, since the first democratic elections in South Africa in 1994 writers have been freed up, judging from the number of novels which have animals as central to their narratives, from the imperative to focus on the iniquities of the apartheid regime, even while much of our racialised history remains intact. The post 1994 novel, *Triomf*, by Marlene van Niekerk has dogs as an integral part of a dysfunctional family;¹⁰ *Disgrace* by J.M. Coetzee represents the euthanasing of 'excess' township dogs as well as dealing with the issue of animal slaughter.¹¹ Njabulo Ndebele is currently writing *The Night of the Dying Dogs* about soldiers killing dogs in the townships and how the dog who generally 'occupies the lowest end of the hierarchy of social concern...suddenly becomes something of value'.¹²

---

⁶ J. Gallant, *The Story of the African Dog* (Pietermaritzburg, 2002), 35.
⁷ L.B. Honwana, *We Killed Mangy-Dog and other Mozambique Stories* (London, 1967 [1977]), 75–117.
⁸ N. Gordimer, *Burger's Daughter* (Harmondsworth, 1979 [1980]), 209.
⁹ Gordimer, *Burger's Daughter*, 210.
¹⁰ M. van Niekerk, *Triomf* (Johannesburg, 1994 [1999]).
¹¹ J.M. Coetzee, *Disgrace* (London, 1999 [2000]).
¹² M. van Graan, 'Njabulo Ndebele: an Artist Interrupted' *Cape Argus* 3 April, 2003.

In discussing representations of dogs in South African fiction in three historical phases, my focus is on the representations of the dogs themselves and the significance of the ways they are represented. J.M. Coetzee has Elizabeth Costello contend that just as we can conceptualise being a corpse, it is quite feasible to think oneself into the perceptions of another.[13] As Wendy Doniger puts it, 'No one can prove that that someone else does *not* know how animals feel.'[14] The textures of the characterization of dogs in South African fiction vary enormously. This essay will consider whether the writers conceptualise dogs as capable of selfhood which can be exemplified in intentionality, agency, cognition and emotions and/or whether dogs function metonymically. Useful here is Martha C. Nussbaum's critique of a philosophy of ethics which derides emotions as instinctive and alien. She argues that emotions are ethical signs of discrimination and intelligence, involving appraisal and evaluation, a point which is very useful in analyzing representations of animals.[15] For Nussbaum 'animal behavior cannot be well explained without ascribing to animals a rich cognitive life, including evaluations of many sorts concerning elements in their own flourishing and their relations to those elements'.[16]

For some, even discussing the emotions of animals is tantamount to anthropomorphism, which Hearne terms a 'mostly bogus' issue.[17] Midgley points out that the tendency to label certain [apparently exclusively human] aspects of animal behaviour as anthropomorphic may stem for a deep 'embarrassment' about animals' abilities, an embarrassment which she regards as 'metaphysical...because of a philosophical view about what [these descriptions of animal behaviour] may commit us to.'[18] Midgley argues that it is feasible to gauge animals' feelings from their demeanour and soma (a point Darwin made *ad nauseum*).[19]

---

[13] J.M. Coetzee, *The Lives of Animals*. Amy Gutmann (ed.) and intro. The University Center for Human Values Series (Princeton, New Jersey, 1999), 32–33.
[14] W. Doniger, Reflections, in Coetzee, *Lives*, 103.
[15] M.C. Nussbaum, *Upheavals of Thought: The Intelligence of Emotions* (Cambridge, 2001 [2003]).
[16] Nussbaum, *Upheavals*, 106.
[17] V. Hearne, *Adam's Task: Calling Animals By Name* (New York, 1986).
[18] M. Midgley, *Animals and Why They Matter* (Harmondsworth, 1983) 129.
[19] Darwin, Charles (1890) 1989. The Works of Charles Darwin. P.H. Barrett and R.B. Freeman (eds.). Vol. 23. *The Expression of Emotion in Man and Animals*. 2nd ed. Ed. Francis Darwin (London, 1890 [1989]).

While so many animal rights philosophers get bogged down in the debate about language as a marker of consciousness (see Noske),[20] Midgley defines a conscious being as 'one who can *mind* what happens to it, which *prefers* some things to others, which can be pleased or pained, can suffer or enjoy'.[21] For Nussbaum, while animals are cognitive and emotional, cognitive differences between humans and animals 'create differences in the concept of the self, and the concept of relations between self and other.' Consequently, animals have 'comparably rudimentary self-conceptions' or none at all.[22]

Elizabeth Costello prefers not to engage with notions of cogitation, proposing instead 'fullness, embodiedness, the sensation of being'.[23] Given the different representations of dogs in the narrative texts below, all three philosophers will be relevant.

Nineteenth-Century Dogs

Olive Schreiner was often photographed with her dogs and chose to be buried with her terrier Nita,[24] which suggests that dogs figured centrally in her emotional life. In *The Story of an African Farm* Doss, who is 'white and sleek, [with] one yellow ear hanging down over his left eye'[25] is a significant if not central presence. He functions variously in the narrative: literally he is a recurring companion in the lives of the main characters, symbolically he is Waldo's alter ego and Lyndall's psychopomp, and metonymically he stands for other creatures in Waldo's celebration of Universal Unity. Schreiner also has dogs as markers of character: Blenkins' kicking of the injured Doss signifies his sadism and amorality whereas Lyndall's ability to tame a savage dog signifies her integrity and her ecological connection.

While Schreiner does not represent Doss in detailed complex engagements with the humans with whom he lives, the variety of his emotions strongly suggests a canine selfhood with 'a rich cognitive life' to

---

[20] B. Noske, *Humans and Other Animals: Beyond the Boundaries of Anthropology* (London, 1989), 128, 131.
[21] Midgley, *Animals*, 92.
[22] Nussbaum, *Upheavals*, 147.
[23] Coetzee, *Lives*, 33.
[24] K. Schoeman, *Only an Anguish to Live Here: Olive Schreiner and the Anglo-Boer War* (Cape Town, 1992), 194–5.
[25] Schreiner, *African Farm*, 46.

use Nussbaum's words. He is 'uneasy', for example, when the children Waldo, Em and Lyndall fall silent after Lyndall's tale of her hero Napoleon Bonaparte and his tragic demise.[26] He is quite rightly suspicious of the villainous and sadistic Bonaparte Blenkins. Humorously, Doss has the sartorial judgment to disapprove of the town-and-country outfit of Blenkins,[27] but, more seriously, Schreiner draws attention to Doss's discernment, for Blenkins abuses Waldo and is responsible for his elderly father's death.

Doss's actions come to symbolise not only Waldo's particular pain, but a more general statement of humanity's predicament. When Doss has a thorn in his paw, he gets tears in his eyes;[28] his pain seems to stand for or to be elided with that of Waldo, whose beating by Blenkins has left his body scarred and bruised. After Blenkins has gratuitously destroyed Waldo's invention of a sheep-shearing machine, Doss watches the former leave with 'cynical satisfaction'. His attempts at playing with Waldo spurned, the dog then attacks a dung beetle, eating its hind legs and biting off its head, and the narrator comments: 'A striving, and a striving, and an ending in nothing'.[29]

Similarly, when Doss digs 'zealously' for a mole, Lyndall likens Waldo's search for the meaning of beauty and the nature of reality to the dog's frenetic activity:

> ...you Germans are born with an aptitude for burrowing; you can't help yourselves. You must sniff after reasons, just as that dog must after a mole. He knows perfectly well he will never catch it, but he's under the imperative necessity of digging for it.[30]

That Schreiner has Lyndall assign knowledge and obsession to the dog's behaviour, rather than instinct, which is generally denigrated as an animal's substitute for intelligence emphasises the continuity between human and animal endeavour.

Doss also has intentionality and makes choices, as he does when Lyndall has returned from finishing school and has been berating the gendered vacuity of polite society to Waldo. Sensing that Waldo wishes him to be with Lyndall, Doss is torn:

---

[26] Schreiner, *African Farm*, 48.
[27] Schreiner, *African Farm*, 106.
[28] Honwana's Mangy-Dog also has tears in his eyes. In Notes and Queries in the *Guardian Weekly* November 13–19, 2003, 16 readers were adamant that elephants cry.
[29] Schreiner, *African Farm*, 107.
[30] Schreiner, *African Farm*, 197.

> Doss stood at Waldo's side, a look of painful uncertainty depicted on his small countenance, and one little foot poised in the air. Should he stay with his master or go? He looked at the figure with the wide straw hat moving towards the house, and he looked up at his master; then he put down the little paw and went.[31]

While Doss embodies Waldo's protective love of Lyndall, the dog, also, makes an independent choice, and when Waldo leaves the farm in order to 'taste life' Lyndall becomes the dog's 'mistress'.

The relationship between Lyndall and Doss is a close one. The love between them is entirely reciprocal. In teaching the persistent, wheedling Gregory about love and self-abnegation, Lyndall gestures to Doss: 'He licks my hand because I love him and allow him to.'[32] Then she bids Gregory who has insulted Doss as a 'a nasty, snappish little cur!'[33] to carry him down from the koppie as though to foreground the former's inferior role, and her preference for the dog over him. When Lyndall billets her 'stranger' in an outside cabin, Doss not only accompanies her to visit him, but is nervous and anxious when she seems immobilized in an embrace: 'He was not at all sure that she was not being retained in her present position against her will, and was not a little relieved when she sat up and held out her hand for the shawl.'[34] For Nussbaum 'a taxonomy of emotions is a taxonomy of a creature's goals...identity...selfhood'[35] which confirms Doss's sense of self as Lyndall's protector.

Certainly Schreiner represents Doss as not only being telepathic with Lyndall but of being capable of a dream that derives from memory rather than an immediate sensual desire: after Lyndall leaves her 'stranger' she visits the grave of Otto's father at length and Doss, simultaneously, dreams of the old man. In another instance, some months later when Lyndall is slowly dying in an anonymous hotel subsequent to the birth of her short-lived baby, Doss, her constant companion, lying on her feet

> would dream that they two were in the cart, tearing over the 'veld', with the black horses snorting, and the wind in their faces; and he would start

---

[31] Schreiner, *African Farm*, 199.
[32] Schreiner, *African Farm*, 232.
[33] Schreiner, *African Farm*, 230.
[34] Schreiner, *African Farm*, 240–1.
[35] Nussbaum, *Upheavals*, 107.

up in his sleep and bark aloud. Then awaking, he would lick his mistress's hand almost remorselessly, and slink quietly down into his place.[36]

Doss's dream here not only constitutes an escape from their confined reality, but incorporates mythic dimensions of black horses which may be associated with death. In addition, his dreams suggest Lyndall's desire too and her imperative to leave the claustrophobia of the sick room behind.

Doss himself embodies the mythic psychopomp, the usher of a human soul to the otherworld, as dogs traditionally were.[37] Gregory, disguised as a female nurse in order to be in Lyndall's presence, responds to her directive to place Doss by her side: 'She made Gregory turn open the bosom of her night-dress that the dog might put his black muzzle between her breasts. She crossed her arms over him. Gregory left them lying there together.'[38] The canine presence and warmth appear to alleviate Lyndall's constant pain or at least provide her with the comfort of another body.

For Lyndall, reduced corporeally as she dies slowly, Doss seems to be a substitute for her own beloved body which she attempts to sustain: she feeds him meat 'put into his jaws with her fingers'[39] and then treats him like the invalid she is, cutting his meat into small portions. Finally, to satisfy her longing to return to the Colony, they go off in an ox-wagon with Lyndall lying under the wagon cover and with Doss at her feet. She dies soon afterwards, Doss shivering, 'as though a coldness struck up to him from his resting-place',[40] the woman and the dog together like effigies on a medieval tomb. Schreiner obviously assigned great significance to the presence of dogs during and after a human death, which is attested to by her burial with her short-lived baby (in an uncanny duplication of her novel) and her dog.

When Gregory returns to the farm with Doss after Lyndall's death, the dog seems almost an extension of Lyndall. Waldo's response to the news of Lyndall's death is to find solace in the philosophy of Universal Unity: for the soul 'which feels within itself the throb of Universal Life...there is no death'.[41] Waldo's narrative to Em about

---

[36] Schreiner, *African Farm*, 273–4.
[37] M. Garber, *Dog Love* (New York, 1966), 90.
[38] Schreiner, *African Farm*, 274.
[39] Schreiner, *African Farm*, 275.
[40] Schreiner, *African Farm*, 283.
[41] Schreiner, *African Farm*, 290.

his experiences in the world confirms his empathic connections with animals and thus his belonging to Universal Life. He was disillusioned and betrayed when a heartless acquaintance killed the old grey mare who had belonged to his father by riding her too hard. He was enraged by the treatment of oxen he witnessed as a driver for a transport-rider, and attempted to avenge the suffering of a dying ox by attacking the man who had stabbed the emaciated beast. In addition, he tells Em, he found the only 'respectable thing in that store [where he worked] was the Kaffir storeman'.[42]

Making allowances for the nomenclature of colonial discourses, one can read Waldo's sentiments as extraordinary at the time. Not only are animals of central significance to him, but he affirms the humanity of an indigenous man, placing him above the (white) men engaged in commercial activities. Similarly, in a scene of pastoral fertility with the Karoo verdant after rains, Waldo is planing wood for a kitchen table he is making for Em, watched by a naked toddler and Doss:

> From time to time the little animal lifted its fat hand as it expected a fresh shower of [wood] curls; till Doss, jealous of his master noticing any other small creature but himself, would catch the curl in his mouth and roll the little Kaffir over in the sawdust, much to that small animal's contentment. It was too lazy an afternoon to be really ill-natured, so Doss satisfied himself with snapping at the little nigger's fingers, and sitting on him till he laughed.[43]

Again, while the terminology is offensive, the sentiments of the narrator establish the continuity between dog and child. Within the ecological philosophy of Universal Unity, Schreiner is celebrating the sentience and humour of both small animals in their game with the curls of wood. As Midgley points out, play signals easily permeate species barriers; here, they temporarily eradicate them.[44]

Doss has been an essential part of the lives of both Waldo and Lyndall and, almost as their surrogate, he engages compassionately and humorously with a small black child who would be constituted as all matter/all body and without intellect within colonial discourse. Thus an analysis of Schreiner's representation of Doss reveals a challenge to the dualisms of colonial racialised binaries. A concomitant re-figuring

---

[42] Schreiner, *African Farm*, 252.
[43] Schreiner, *African Farm*, 292.
[44] Midgley, *Animals*, 116.

of colonial discourse obtains in this text through representations of the embodied nature of existence as it does in some colonial women's texts.[45] Schreiner represents Lyndall especially as embodied, in her sexuality, in her dying and in her relationship with Doss. Such representations, as I have shown above, are complex and do not conform to the Victorian discursivities of women as 'the body' because as bearers of children they were regarded as being closer to nature.

Another colonial text which represents a woman and dogs, Melina Rorke's ostensible autobiography *Told by Herself: Her Amazing Experiences in the Stormy Nineties of South-African History*[46] is firmly located in the narrative convention of the swashbuckling hero who rides faster, shoots straighter and breaks more social conventions than any other character. At the age of fourteen she absconds from school to marry Frederick Rorke of the visiting English rugby team in secret but her husband dies soon afterwards after being tackled in a rugby match. She and her older married sister, Helena, are sent from Kimberley to Port Alfred, the sister to recover from giving birth, Melina to be 'confined' away from the rage of her father. The alcoholic doctor who sews her vaginal tears after the delivery which he botched pronounces her 'a good healthy animal'.[47] His remedies to increase her stamina render her an excessive producer of milk which her infant son cannot deplete.

In agony with engorged breasts, she appeals to the women in the household. The 'white nursemaid' pronounces her condition not 'ladylike' but the elderly Xhosa woman takes 'great pride' in her 'bountifulness'.[48] The emaciated Dutch baby whom the latter brings for Melina to suckle provides no relief and she begs the old woman to find some more babies 'even Kaffirs'. The domestic worker is adamant, however, that 'that would be wrong':

> But perhaps some puppies... She would see. A little later she came back with four squirming, squealing mongrel puppies, and I will never forget the heavenly ease they gave me. For the first time in a week I felt sane

---

[45] For further discussion see W. Woodward, 'Dis/Embodying Transcendence in the Early Nineteenth Century: Ann Hamilton, Mary Moffat, the London Missionary Society and God', *Journal of Literary Studies*, 14, 1/2 (June 1998), 80–101.

[46] M. Rorke, Melina, *Told By Herself: Her Amazing Experiences in the Stormy Nineties of South-African History*. (n.p., 1939). This text is included in this section in spite of its publication date, because it represents the end of the nineteenth century and is set within colonial discursivities.

[47] Rorke, *Told by Herself*, 29.

[48] Rorke, *Told by Herself*, 29.

again, and almost human. Helena was horrified, though she tried not to show it, and the English nursemaid was so scandalized that she said she'd give notice as soon as we got back to Kimberley.[49]

The excessive nature of Rorke's body borders on the grotesque, which yokes together both horror and mirth, but, tragically, the Xhosa woman subscribes so rigidly to colonial discursivities that she constructs puppies (and mongrel ones as Rorke notes) as less 'other' than Xhosa babies. Colonial protocol, or at least in this interpretation, renders the latter more animal-like and hence as less suitable for a white woman to suckle.

If Rorke relates to these puppies as similarly embodied beings to herself, the narrator of *Jock of the Bushveld*, like the conventional male narrator in colonial discourse, constructs himself as seamlessly disembodied. Thus as Jock's body is described in detail as a pup and an adolescent dog, this bodiliness becomes a sign of his otherness and his difference from the (human, male) standard. Conversely, both men and dogs are located, at times quite romantically, within the code of masculinity and heroism. Often interdependent in the harsh bushveld, men would die for their dogs and vice versa. Dogs are hedges against loneliness and 'something to protect' for the man who 'daily takes his chances of life and death...to lay his cheek against the muzzle of his comrade dog'.[50] A dog is, somewhat cryptically, such a man's 'silent tribute to The Book'[51] which implies some spiritual connection.

The narrative is not plot-driven; anecdotes about hunting or various characters constitute the novel which depicts the unnamed narrator, initially 'the Boy' who apparently purports to be the younger self of the writer, working to transport goods by wagon through the Bushveld and to Delagoa Bay, then in Portuguese East Africa. This occupation is never delineated spatially or chronologically in any detail which seems intended to render the narrative mythic. Yet *Jock of the Bushveld* is firmly located within the tenets of colonial travel writing: the undiscovered country is almost entirely empty of an indigenous population, the travels are so dangerous that white women do not feature, the heavy work of transport-riding, driving the cattle, loading the goods, is done by local men, emasculated by being called 'boys.' The only exception

---

[49] Rorke, *Told by Herself*, 30.
[50] Fitzpatrick, *Jock*, 2.
[51] Fitzpatrick, *Jock*, 1.

to these anonymous workers, who are kept in line by whipping, is Jim Makokel' who champions Jock because of his hunting prowess and who conforms not to the colonial archetype of 'the faithful servant' but to that of 'the noble savage manqué'.

The breeding of a dog has great significance in this novel, whereas for Schreiner a dog's breed is immaterial. Jock is a bull terrier because his mother, Jess, although of unspecified heritage, has been bred to an imported dog who 'was always spoken of as the best dog of the breed that had been in the country'.[52] Jess, who is 'ugly, cross and unpopular, but brave and faithful'[53] becomes an object of study for the unnamed Fitzpatrick narrator, as do Jock and his siblings (Jess is, in fact, the only female presence in the novel but she disappears quite early on). Jock, the runt of the litter, comical, ungainly, disproportionate, is promised to the narrator who is initially merely protective of him, but then comes to admire his developing characteristics of 'independence' and 'pluck',[54] masculine traits essential for Bushveld life. His puppyhood of struggle, where he had to fight for everything against his older larger siblings 'made him clever, cool, and careful'.[55] He is often described as thinking like a child, in a limited way, yet Jock is also self-aware—of his short stature—and is ascribed the emotion of dignity, which suggests that Fitzpatrick regards him as cognitive.

Another aspect of dogs, which figures largely in *Jock of the Bushveld* and which seems irrelevant for Schreiner is that of training. Jock's 'master' trains him to be a hunter himself and to be an accompaniment to a human hunter with a rifle, not to touch food in camp until he was specifically told he could (a dog had been shot for stealing food). The most difficult lesson for Jock was having to learn not to eat a piece of meat balanced on his nose. The narrator justifies this apparently 'cruel' lesson by explaining that Jock would learn in this way 'to be patient, obedient, and observant', not to scavenge with possible fatal results and 'to live with his master and be treated like a friend'.[56] The possibility that the training is reductive and instrumentalising for the dogs is thus contradicted.[57] The necessity for Jock to learn much that a town dog

---

[52] Fitzpatrick, *Jock*, 54.
[53] Fitzpatrick, *Jock*, 57.
[54] Fitzpatrick, *Jock*, 73.
[55] Fitzpatrick, *Jock*, 74.
[56] Fitzpatrick, *Jock*, 84.
[57] V. Hearne, poet and trainer of dogs and horses, would respond that we *must* be master in order to make the dog (or horse) obedient and therefore able to live in a

would never have to know, about local animals for example, means having a self-protective 'instinct for danger'.[58]

This mention of instinct of the dogs does not foreclose their having emotions, which are indicative, according to Nussbaum, of intelligence. As the narrator of *Jock* stipulates:

> Every one knows that a dog can feel angry, frightened, pleased and disappointed. Any one who *knows* dogs will tell you that they can also feel anxious, hopeful, nervous, inquisitive, surprised, ashamed, interested, sad, loving, jealous, and contented—just like human beings.[59]

This non-dualistic generalization about dogs is undermined, however, by the representations of African dogs who are othered as feckless, cowardly, opportunistic and as scavengers rather than brave hunters.

Jock and other white-owned hunting dogs are the subject of much fireside talk. The narrator muses about Jock feeling 'ridiculous' as a puppy when he fought the table leg, mistaking it for an attacker, thus projecting onto the young dog a self-consciousness as well as an awareness of what constitutes some norm of accepted behaviour. The men then consider whether dogs can have a sense of humour, whether 'a dog is capable of sufficient thinking to appreciate a simple joke, and [whether] it is possible for a dog to feel amused'.[60] One raconteur, who is convinced of this, tells the story of an old dog tricking his enemy, a young cockerel, into thinking there was food in his feeding pot. When the fowl realised he was mistaken, the old dog, pretending to be asleep, wagged his tail.

Fitzpatrick acknowledges, then, an advanced sense of self in dogs as well as a range of nuanced emotions. His comment that 'Jock was lost twice: that is to say, he was lost to me'[61] confirms the narratorial ability to perceive the point of view of his dog. Yet these perceptions of animal sentience barely extend to the animals in the Bushveld, perhaps because the life of a human may depend on a dog when hunting, or because dogs are accorded special sensibilities because of their exposure

---

world of modern dangers. She derides "humaniacs" who find the training of an animal cruel or inconsequential (*Adam's Task*, 51). At the same time, to earn the right to use the command "Fetch!" to a dog, a trainer must have "[s]omething like reverence, humility and obedience...We can follow, understand only things and people we can command, and we can command only whom and what we can follow" (*Adam's Task*, 76).

[58] Fitzpatrick, *Jock*, 87.
[59] Fitzpatrick, *Jock*, 89, emphasis added.
[60] Fitzpatrick, *Jock*, 89.
[61] Fitzpatrick, *Jock*, 171.

to humans. On a very practical level, perhaps it would be too painful to acknowledge an advanced sentience in the animals that are hunted daily. Only when a lost impala finds her way into camp and remains there as her panic subsides is any antelope described in individualised detail, although the narrator believes that hunted kudu 'play' with him by hiding, then waiting watchfully for him,[62] which demonstrates their intentionality and agency.

Fitzpatrick represents animals to be hunted adversarially, often as dangerous, to underscore that these animals are both threatening, as well as worthy adversaries, which adds glory to his and Jock's skill. Jock, as a hunting dog, is combative. He kills buck that his 'master' has wounded. He is preternaturally clever, killing a baboon on a rope who has taunted and killed many other dogs. He attacks 'kaffir dogs' for whom he has an 'implacable' hatred but so great is his prowess that, in one instance, the owners 'broke into appreciative laughter and shouts of admiration for the white man's dog.'[63] Jim Makokel' the wagon driver similarly admires Jock for his bravery; a strong connection between them is that 'Jock disliked kaffirs: so did Jim'.[64]

In many instances, Jock is an alter ego for the narrator. The latter has to return to 'civilisation' when the transport riding goes bankrupt. Jock, who has been deafened by a kudu's kick, is out of place in town, so much so that the narrator believes it would have been 'better if he had died fighting',[65] rather than languish in town. Jock then works as a guard dog, and, in defending hens against a local dog, Jock is shot in a case of mistaken identity, dying in the course of doing his duty.

The ending is simultaneously tragic, and clichéd. The cause of Jock's death is not an admirable dignified opponent like a wild animal but the ignominious defense of a hen house against a marauding 'kaffirdog'. The hero is past his best, disabled by deafness, no longer able to lead a life of adventure and the open road. In his journeys with the narrator, Jock straddled the wild and the tame as a hunter himself and as an adjunct to a human hunter. Like the narrator, he could lord it over wild animals and the indigenous population and their dogs. *Jock of the Bushveld* narrativises colonial masculinity pitted against the wildness of

---

[62] Fitzpatrick, *Jock*, 134–5.
[63] Fitzpatrick, *Jock*, 330.
[64] Fitzpatrick, *Jock*, 209. The narrator never questions Jock's enacting of colonial projections.
[65] Fitzpatrick, *Jock*, 464.

nature and the riff-raff of humanity, but this apparently pristine way of life is ultimately impossible to sustain given the settlement of the land and the demise of the large hunting animals.

If Jock himself is finally tamed in the worst possible way, John Buchan writes a heroic ending for Colin, 'an enormous Boer hunting-dog, a mongrel in whose blood ran mastiff and bulldog and foxhound, and Heaven knows what beside'.[66] Colin, the companion of *Prester John*'s narrator, Davie Crawfurd, a young Scotsman on an almost single-handed quest to keep South Africa safe for (British) colonialism, dies defending his 'master'. The traitorous Henriques, who shoots Colin, is in league with Laputa, a noble savage manqué who is the orchestrator of an uprising of 'black savages'. Like *Jock of the Bushveld*, Buchan's novel is located in an exclusively masculine domain, but, unlike the former novel, it is melodramatically plot-driven and the narrator's dog is a mere cipher, impossibly heroic in an incredible tale.[67] Colin is a cardboard cut-out who is defined relationally to the human self and whose one purpose in life is not only to be aware of Crawfurd's moods but to protect this man who is, for a sort time, driven 'beserk' at the sight of 'the faithful eyes glazing in death'.[68]

While Colin is sacrificed to the broader imperial and commercial endeavours which triumph over 'savagery' and wildness, with Crawfurd earning entitlement to the treasures of Prester John, the tale of Jock is more wistful about the demise of the idyll of pristine, uninhabited land. Yet the materialism of both these stories legislates their closure. In *The Story of an African Farm*, however, Doss continues beyond the ending in a quasi-immortality like Lyndall whom he accompanied during her dying and like Waldo whose death he was not part of. For Schreiner, then, the

---

[66] J. Buchan, *Prester John* (London, 1910 [1936]), 51. Although the publication date is early twentieth century, culturally, like *Jock*, this novel can be located in the nineteenth century.

[67] Another dog located in an exclusively masculine domain (so much so, apparently, that he ignored women) is the eponymous hero in T. Sisson, *Just Nuisance AB: His Full Story* (Cape Town, 1985 [2001]). Ranked as an Able Seaman after his 'enlistment' in the Royal Navy in Simonstown in 1939, Just Nuisance was so entirely relationally defined that he slept in naval bunk, was 'married' to a Great Dane bitch and given lager and other alcohol on a regular basis. The dog functioned as a 'lord of misrule' with the attempts to incorporate his canine agency and intentionality into naval order leading not only to humorous situations but to legitimised expressions of masculine sentiment. As a non-fictional dog, Just Nuisance does not, strictly speaking, have a place in this essay, yet Buchan's and Fitzpatrick's (fictional) conventions of canine representation recur in his biography.

[68] Buchan, *Prester John*, 212.

endorsement of Universal Life means that Lyndall's sense of the Grey Dawn and Waldo's dream connect with nature in a non-dualistic way. Fitzpatrick, in spite of the endorsement of Jock as a complex being, leaves the reader with the tragedy of colonial adversarial constructions of the world, as Buchan does.

Apartheid Dogs

Mphahlele's short story 'Mrs Plum' mocks white liberals such as the eponymous Mrs Plum for whom the 'three big things in her life' are dogs, Africans and the obeying the law. While she belongs to the Black Sash, teaches literacy classes and seems to be working for change, Mrs Plum's attitude is patronizing in the way she takes it upon herself to speak for 'black people'. The first person narrator is Karabo, a domestic worker from Phokeng, and for whom dogs function metonymically as markers of white uncaring insularity.

Karabo regards the colonially-named dogs, Monty and Malan, as extensions of her employer as do her friends and fellow-workers at the Thursday afternoon club which teaches them sewing. They discussed and 'laughed about madams and masters, and their children and their dogs and birds and whispered about [their] boy friends'.[69] One domestic worker (they are unnamed) mentions her employers' new dog which is '[b]ig in a foolish way'; another derides 'her master's bitch' whom she 'throws…away so that she keeps howling…I don't play with them, me…'.[70] Another reported how she refuses to walk the dog, stipulating it was the work of the gardener.

The privileges of the dogs in the household rankle Karabo: they sleep in Mrs Plum's bedroom, are constantly groomed and beribboned. 'They make me fed up when I see them in their baskets, looking fat and as if they knew all that was going on everywhere'.[71] She projects the employers' habit of surveillance onto the dogs, even regarding them as stand-ins for their people in the winter when only the domestic workers and the dogs remain in the suburbs: 'You could see them walk like white people in the streets. Silent but with plenty of power.'[72]

---

[69] Mphahlele, 'Mrs Plum', 225.
[70] Mphahlele, 'Mrs Plum', 225.
[71] Mphahlele, 'Mrs Plum', 231.
[72] Mphahlele, 'Mrs. Plum', 238.

Partly because of this performativity of racialised power, which signifies the dogs' contamination by their owners' attitudes, both Karabo and Dick, the gardener, whose job it is to take care of the dogs, regard them as 'stupid' and lacking in the survival intelligence of an African dog. Chimane, who works next door, regales them with the anecdote of Moruti K.K.'s little dog who jumps from under his arm into a vendor's pot of meat. In her opinion: 'That is a good African dog. A dog must look for its own food when it is not time for meals. Not these stupid spoiled angels the whites keep giving tea and biscuits'.[73]

No acknowledgment is made for a traditional relationship with a dog, although one is hinted at in Chimane's story. Relationships with other animals are possible, however. Karabo communes with the grey three-legged cat from next door; after they had gazed at each other for some time, the cat seemed '[j]ust like someone who feels pity for you'.[74] Dick and Karabo talk of relating to an ox, although Dick insists that an ox is only spoken to in the form of commands.[75]

Mrs Plum's talking to her dogs, asking them whether Dick has fed or groomed them not only insults Dick's reliability as a worker but substantiates his sense that white relationships with dogs are excessive. He anticipates that these dogs will be bejewelled and that he will have to then polish the rings and bangles. The most grotesque exemplification of an inappropriate dog-human relationship is Mrs Plum's sexualized abuse of Malan, clutching onto him as she reaches an orgasm (the nature of the dog's involvement is unclear).[76] Karabo's response, seeing this through the keyhole, is to sympathise with his disempowerment, 'Malan silent like a thing to be owned without any choice it can make to belong to another'.[77]

If Malan's position here is redolent of the disempowerment of black domestic workers and gardeners in the late 1960s, conversely the subjectivity of dogs contrasts with the object status of workers. When Karabo overhears the neighbour saying 'Come on Rusty, the boy is

---

[73] Mphahlele, 'Mrs. Plum', 230.
[74] Mphahlele, 'Mrs. Plum', 247.
[75] For a detailed discussion of representations of traditional relationships with oxen, see W. Woodward, 'Postcolonial Ecologies and the Gaze of Animals: Reading some Contemporary Southern African Narratives', *Journal of Literary Studies, Special Issue: Aspects of South African Literary Studies*, 19, 3/4 (December 2003), 290–315.
[76] In *Lives*, Coetzee has the university president's 'elegant wife' say: 'Animals are creatures we don't have sex with—that's how we distinguish them from ourselves' (40).
[77] Mphahlele, 'Mrs. Plum', 252.

waiting to clean you' she thinks 'Dogs with names, men without'.[78] One way to undermine such racialised stratification is to exploit any possibility of redress; this the domestic workers do by giving dog meat to their 'boyfriends' so they become known as 'dog's meat boys'.[79]

The narrative of 'Mrs Plum' culminates in the middle class fear that employees intend to poison the dogs of suburbia. The police arrest men on the assumption that all black men are guilty. Dick's response is one of horror that anyone would want to poison 'these things of God' and he exonerates dogs themselves reiterating that it is not dogs who 'make the laws that give us pain'.[80] In representing Dick as having empathy with the dogs, Mphahlele foregrounds the baselessness of Mrs Plum's suspicion and how unjustified his dismissal is. When Karabo resigns and returns home she dreams on the journey that Dick has poisoned the dogs although she has begged him 'They cannot speak do not kill things that cannot speak'.[81] His response that 'Madam can speak for them she always does'[82] again points to the dogs' intentionality and agency being undermined.

The story closes when Karabo returns to a contrite Mrs Plum but only after she has demanded a raise and more privileges, thus establishing herself with a stronger agency and sense of self. What is not brought to closure, however, is the fate of the dogs who have been stolen in Karabo's absence, although Mrs Plum believes them to be dead. Karabo wonders whether Dick could have taken revenge and questions, with some compassion, whether 'this woman came to ask me to return because she had lost two animals she loved'.[83]

What appears initially to be a story vilifying the exploitation of black workers by white employers who value their dogs more than their employees, develops into a narrative which has the exploited workers analyzing dogs as social subjects, rather than as hated emblems of racialised privilege. Negativity and suspicion on the grounds of 'race', Mphahlele seems to be saying, rebound on those who are prejudiced. In addition, he is making profound statements about the nature of animals kept as pets and their commodification. Yet none of these dogs, apart

---

[78] Mphahlele, 'Mrs. Plum', 234.
[79] B. Trapido, *Frankie and Stankie* (London, 2003), 135: '...sometimes you can see butchers' signs that say "Boys' Meat Two Shillings. Dogs' Meat Two and Sixpence."'
[80] Mphahlele, 'Mrs. Plum', 253.
[81] Mphahlele, 'Mrs. Plum', 258.
[82] Mphahlele, 'Mrs. Plum', 258.
[83] Mphahlele, 'Mrs. Plum', 261.

from Moruti's dog leaping into a pot of meat, has any agency. The dogs are not developed as subjects like Jock or Doss, nor do they show any evidence of having a 'rich cognitive life'. They are not represented as having any concept of self, or even consciousness.

Similarly in Njabulo S. Ndebele's story 'The Prophetess' dogs are not developed as characters, but two dogs play important roles in the dilemmas of the unnamed boy, who is the focaliser of the narrative. The boy has gone to the prophetess to get holy water to heal his seriously ill mother. Terrified of the prophetess's large fluffy dog he shows his courage by standing his ground, but is relieved when the prophetess banishes the dog from the house: '"Dogs stay out!' shouted the woman adding, 'This is not at the white man's"'.[84] En route home he is knocked over by a cyclist and the bottle of holy water breaks. He is paralysed by the disaster until his own dog, Rex, unwittingly helps him by kicking over bottles next to his kennel. The boy fills a bottle at a nearby tap, hopeful that his own faith will heal his mother.

Daphne Rooke, in her novel, *Mittee*, has dogs as victims metonymising gendered violence.[85] The melodramatic narrative is set in the late nineteenth century and focuses on the repercussions of the love/rivalry between (white) Mittee and her long-time (coloured) companion/maid Selina, who is the narrator. When the women are left on the farm without the protection of their men who have gone off to fight in the South African War, a dog is poisoned by the locals as a warning to the women of their vulnerability. Even more dramatically, when Jansie, the persistent, unwelcome and jealous suitor of Selina rages that she pays more attention to his hunting dog than to him, he murders Wagter bare-handed as a warning to Selina to co-operate with his sexual demands. He threatens that if she tells anyone he'll 'do the same' to her. Selina realises, 'One word wrong from me and I would be lying next to the dog [on the top of the mountain], a skeleton not much bigger than his'.[86]

In *Age of Iron* J.M. Coetzee has dogs functioning metaphorically and mythically, yet not as subjects in any sustained way. Elizabeth Curren, who is dying of cancer, writes the story of the ending of her life during

---

[84] Ndebele, 'The Prophetess', 31–32.

[85] Police in the Western Cape learnt of the link between animal abuse and abuse of women and children through an illustrated talk by Phil Arkow 'internationally acclaimed expert' on the connection. See *Humane Education Trust News*, Summer 2003–2004, 10.

[86] D. Rooke, *Mittee* (Cape Town, 1951 [1987]), 13.

the brutal late 1980s in the hope that Vercueil, the homeless man whom she allows to inhabit her garden and then her house, will send the manuscript to her daughter in America after her death. Vercueil is accompanied, always, by his familiar, an unnamed young collie, whom the narrator suspects has been stolen from a 'good family'.

When Curren begins her narrative, 'dog' signifies an empty concept, just as 'man' and 'house' do. She tells her daughter: 'Man, house, dog: no matter what the word, through it I stretch out a hand to you'.[87] But 'dog' as metaphor is made to carry negative connotations. When the narrator has an 'attack' she describes 'the pain hurling itself upon me like a dog, sinking its teeth into my back'.[88] Bheki uses 'dog' as a term of abuse to denote a lack of self-consciousness when he berates the drunken Vercueil '"They are making you into a dog!...Do you want to be a dog?"'.[89] Curren sees Vercueil as 'cruel, mad, a mad dog'[90] when he goads her to commit suicide.

Curren uses the non-gender specific and impersonal pronoun 'it' for the actual dog who moves into her home and yard, which exemplifies her initial representation of the dog as lacking in emotion, cognition or selfhood. The young collie whimpers and whines, but is only capable of very specific feelings relating directly and superficially to any event that impacts directly on her/him, like the 'regret' when s/he cannot be part of a game. Essentially, dogs are embarrassing to Curren who reflects '[h]ow silly one looks fending off a dog'.[91] The retriever from next door embodies dog-behaviour which is judged inappropriate or disgusting, licking the road after the cycling Bheki and his friend 'John' have been injured by a truck. To Curren, dogs seem interchangeable, useful only for their companionship to humans; she imagines Vercueil dying in a doorway or alley 'with this dog or some other dog by his side, whimpering, licking his face'.[92]

As Curren gets closer to her own death however, dogs become ennobled by these roles as embodied helpers and she envies Vercueil who 'has a dog to lie against'[93] whereas she feels she will never be warm again. The shift in Curren's attitude to the young collie is also evident

---

[87] J.M. Coetzee, *Age of Iron* (London, 1990), 8.
[88] Coetzee, *Age of Iron*, 9.
[89] Coetzee, *Age of Iron*, 42.
[90] Coetzee, *Age of Iron*, 112.
[91] Coetzee, *Age of Iron*, 54.
[92] Coetzee, *Age of Iron*, 29.
[93] Coetzee, *Age of Iron*, 99.

in her reference to 'my pet, my pain'[94] and then, dramatically, in her first response to the dog as a cognitive being: 'A nice dog: a bright presence, star-born, as some people are'.[95] She can even acknowledge that 'however unlikely' it is a reciprocal 'love' that she witnesses between Vercueil and the collie. Both man and dog accrue mythological significance for her as her pain becomes more severe; as psychopomps they will usher her soul into death: 'Vercueil and his dog, sleeping so calmly besides these torrents of grief. Fulfilling their charge, waiting for the soul to emerge'.[96] She feels protected, that 'Death would think twice before trying to pass this dog, this man',[97] but questions, ultimately whether it is 'possible that the dog is the one sent, and not he?'[98] Through Curren's shift in consciousness in response to the bright young collie, Coetzee suggests, tacitly, and therefore unspecifically, that some spiritual connection obtains between human and non-human animal. Yet human tragedies, like those of the narrator and of Florence, her domestic worker, and by extension those of people in the township dying at the hands of the police and collaborators, are foregrounded. The dog remains an adjunct to humans.

In 'We killed Mangy-Dog', however, a story by Mozambican writer Luis Bernardo Honwana originally published in Portuguese in 1967, the eponymous dog is a sentient character with emotions, who meets the human gaze and has an awareness of his impending death. The story is told by Ginho, a pre-pubescent boy who is mocked by members of the gang he longs to be part of for being 'porky' and for being darker than them. Both he and Isaura, who is developmentally disabled, care about Mangy-Dog and long to heal him, but Senhor Administrador deputises the gang to get rid of the dog by shooting him. Because the boys are initially scared, they force Ginho to fire the first shot, apologizing as he does so to Mangy-Dog:

> YOU'LL DIE AND YOU'LL GO TO HEAVEN, STRAIGHT UP TO HEAVEN... YOU'LL BE HAPPY THERE IN HEAVEN; but before this I'll bury your body and I'll put a white cross... before you go to Heaven you'll go to limbo like a child... can you hear, Mangy-Dog?[99]

---

[94] Coetzee, *Age of Iron*, 103.
[95] Coetzee, *Age of Iron*, 104.
[96] Coetzee, *Age of Iron*, 170.
[97] Coetzee, *Age of Iron*, 175.
[98] Coetzee, *Age of Iron*, 177.
[99] Honwana, *Mangy-Dog*, 108.

Isaura tries uselessly to protect the dog she loves, but the gang, except for Ginho, then shoot manically at the dog's body and then boast of their prowess.

The story makes a powerful statement against unthinking violence against animals while correlating the dismissal of animal sentience with racism and sexism as well as a derogation of the differently abled. Honwana holds colonial authorities responsible for the nurturing of the boys' masculinities in violence during a time of armed resistance in Mozambique. Honwana's story has no South African counterpart in its representations of a victimized township dog—at least not until after 1994.

Post-Apartheid Dogs

In the two novels discussed below, dogs are treated not only as complex subjects (although to a varying degree), but as animals with souls who can teach humans about (im)mortality. In *Triomf* by Marlene van Niekerk, relationships between members of the dysfunctional Benade family and their dogs are completely egalitarian, illustrating the human dependence on the dogs rather than vice versa. Without their dogs—three-generations of Gertys and now the last Gerty's son, Toby—the Benades' lives would contain only unmitigated horror. As Rosemary Rodd points out: 'the companionship of an animal can mean the difference between survival and total social collapse for some people';[100] van Niekerk's representation of the strong presence of the dogs in the novel contains this possibility. The most dramatic way that the dogs humanise their people is how they function as intermediaries between the abused Mol, her two brothers—the self-sacrificial Pop and the violent Treppie—and Mol's mentally challenged epileptic son Lambert, who is 'not right in his top storey'.[101] Unable to communicate with each other due to the horror of their histories and the incestuous relationships between all the men and Mol, they often direct their conversations to the dogs.

Dogs are also represented as social subjects and as implicated in apartheid history. The original Gerty constitutes the only possible connection the Benades could have with Sophiatown, which they visit after

---

[100] R. Rodd, *Biology, Ethics and Animals* (Oxford, 1990 [1992]), 195.
[101] Van Niekerk, *Triomf*, 16.

the previous inhabitants have been forcibly expelled by the apartheid state, preparatory to the building of Triomf for less privileged whites (including themselves). Mol and her brothers hear 'a cry' from under some rubble and find 'a tiny puppy with the cutest little looking-up eyes. Ag shame'.[102] While Pop agrees to take the puppy, Treppie's response is predictable: '"You better just leave that kaffirdog alone, Mol," Treppie said. "All she's good for is a stew. I don't want that worm-guts in our house"'.[103] But Mol's will prevails; as poverty-stricken whites the Benades, if they wish to have dogs, are forced to overlook the genealogy of their animals and what it signifies.

The dogs, Gerty in particular, help Mol survive the gender violence she is subjected to. According to Mol: 'Dogs understand more about hard times than people. They lick sweat. And they lick up tears'.[104] For Mol, the relationship between dogs and humans is entirely reciprocal with dogs as cognitive subjects: 'When people tune in their voices to the dogs like this, the dogs know they're part of the company. That's a nice thing for a dog to know. And it's nice for people too'.[105] Even Treppie addresses the dogs directly and gets Gerty and Toby to start crying which sets off all the dogs throughout Triomf and 'all the way to Ontdekkers and beyond'.[106] What begins as a manipulative game becomes an almost autonomous dog chorus. The Benade family for all their brutalised sensibilities are able to grant these dogs 'the dignity of listening to them'[107] and thus of responding to them as subjects with whom they have interactive relationships.

Ironically, the Benades treat their dogs better than they treat each other or, in an echo of 'Mrs Plum', better than fellow South Africans. They do not relate to the dogs instrumentally, nor, generally, do they subject them to violence—only Treppie 'lets fly'[108] against Toby when he tries to look at the former's scars, and Lambert kicks Gerty when she tries to protect Mol against his rage and intended rape. That Lambert banishes Gerty from the house when he rapes his mother suggests that the dog functions as some kind of moral presence that he cannot countenance in his incestuous act.

---

[102] Van Niekerk, *Triomf*, 6.
[103] Van Niekerk, *Triomf*, 6.
[104] Van Niekerk, *Triomf*, 8.
[105] Van Niekerk, *Triomf*, 11.
[106] Van Niekerk, *Triomf*, 17.
[107] Doniger, Reflections, 105.
[108] Van Niekerk, *Triomf*, 382.

For Mol, in order to construct another reality, she cultivates, quite consciously, the somatic experience of inhabiting a dog's body when she decides to experience Gerty's illness through her own body. In the front yard in the mist she 'helps Gerty cough'[109] by coughing herself. Through the connection Mol has with Gerty, van Niekerk underscores the overlap of experience between dog and human. Both inhabit bodies in pain; both are female. For Mol, incestuously abused by all the men in the house, Gerty and her predecessors have been the only female presences, alongside hers, who embody a safer, clearer and unfamilial love and who provide her with some affirmation of an identity that is not directly related to those of her brothers or son: 'Gerty was her dog, and she was Gerty's person'[110] Mol thinks after her death. Toby, in his rather hyper-active maleness, is never able to substitute for his mother in Mol's affections.

When Pop dies and is cremated, Mol puts the ashes above Gerty's grave, adding him on to Gerty's epitaph. She is comforted by the notion that Pop is in the heaven that he dreamed of, that he is resting in a hammock strung in Orion's belt and that Gerty is there too, a dog's star, but '[a]ll you can see is her tail sticking out'.[111] When she envisages the Christian Day of Judgement, dogs are included. The implication, in both her visions, is that dogs have souls, and are as deserving of immortality as humans.

By the end of the narrative, Treppie and Lambert have 'learnt by now to leave her alone'[112] and Mol has independently conceived of the mythic dog-human connection with Orion. Her reaction at the time to Gerty's death which duplicates that of Mol's mother who also '[c]oughed herself to death...in the bathroom'[113] points to familial connections made through pets, a connection with therapeutic resonances that Garber deems quite natural and understandable.[114] Gerty and Toby are never humans *manques* for Mol. They have their own autonomous beings—and souls—and their own worth. Gerty might be Mol's protector, her confidante, her source of creativity, but she is also separate and different. Mol never humanises her or anthropomorphises

---

[109] Van Niekerk, *Triomf*, 162.
[110] Van Niekerk, *Triomf*, 201.
[111] Van Niekerk, *Triomf*, 473.
[112] Van Niekerk, *Triomf*, 473.
[113] Van Niekerk, *Triomf*, 200.
[114] Garber, *Dog Love*, 130 passim.

her. She values her for what she embodies, a fellow being with whom she can have the only truly non-exploitative relationship she has ever experienced.

J.M. Coetzee's *Disgrace*, like *Age of Iron*, does not represent a dog as a beloved confidant in any sustained way, but has dogs (and other animals) mark a character's development. *Disgrace* also raises many issues in connection with the way humans treat dogs, especially that of euthanasing 'unwanted' dogs. Except, potentially, for the lame banjo-loving dog at the end of the narrative and for Katy, the grieving bulldog, the dogs tend to embody issues rather than subjects with a rich cognitive life.

Disgrace tells the story of David Lurie, a university professor, disgraced because of his relationship with a young student. He looks for sanctuary in Grahamstown with his daughter, Lucy, who lives on a smallholding, and farms 'dogs and daffodils',[115] boarding dogs who are all 'watchdogs'. Lucy and Lurie's sensibilities about animals differ fundamentally. Lucy is critical, for example, that animals come 'nowhere' on the 'list of the nation's priorities'[116] and derides what she believes her father wants for her: intellectual pursuits and a notion of 'a higher life': '"This is the only life there is. Which we share with animals...That's the example I try to follow. To share some of our human privilege with beasts"'.[117] For Lucy, then, the quotidian is immanence itself, which contradicts her father's Judaeo-Christian premise that '"We are of a different order of creation from the animals"'.[118]

Dogs themselves are stratified within racialised social orders, as the men who rape her and set her father alight so brutally enact. The man who perpetrates what Lucy calls the 'massacre' itself takes domination over animals to sadistic extremes, shooting the kennelled dogs as though they are mere symbols of apartheid's shoring up of property and possessions. Conventionally, white South African property owners have preferred pure-breds for watchdogs. For the attackers, Lucy's dog boarders are therefore metonymic of white privilege which explains the violent responses to them at Lucy's kennels, when they treat the dogs as '"part of the alarm system...as things"' in Lucy's words.[119]

---

[115] Coetzee, *Disgrace*, 62.
[116] Coetzee, *Disgrace*, 73.
[117] Coetzee, *Disgrace*, 74.
[118] Coetzee, *Disgrace*, 74.
[119] Coetzee, *Disgrace*, 78.

If Elizabeth Curren changes her attitude to the young collie as she approaches death, then Lurie as a disempowered victim under threat of death is forced to acknowledge the continuity between himself and one of the dogs. He sees from his toilet prison how a fatally wounded dog embodies a conscious subject with an awareness of death as s/he 'follow[s] with its gaze the movements of this being [the gunman] who does not even bother to administer a *coup de grace*'.[120] Thus dogs begin to function as subjects who ultimately inspire Lurie's potential for ethical action. Several 'personal' and apparently intersubjective 'encounters' suggest markers of David Lurie's development towards being what he calls a 'good person' and being able to use the word 'love' disinterestedly.

Lurie passes the time in Grahamstown working with Bev Shaw at the Animal Welfare Clinic, doing menial jobs like a 'dog-man', and spending Sunday afternoons euthanasing dogs. These dogs, unlike Lucy's boarders, are mongrels, who in racialising discourse are 'kaffirdogs'. They are healthy, and have to die because of their fertility, because '"there are just too many of them...by our standards, not by theirs"' as Bev Shaw puts it.[121] Lacking government support for sterilisation procedures for domestic animals, Bev Shaw's task is merely a last-ditch attempt to alleviate the human problems with the apparently excess population of dogs in the township. Coetzee's critique about the suffering of township dogs is directed not at the owners of the proliferating dogs, but at the lack of government intervention in animal suffering which is concomitant with the problems of the historically disadvantaged living in an economically moribund area like the Eastern Cape.[122]

For Lurie these dogs become subjects with consciousness, foresight and fear who sense the 'shadow of death'[123] upon them, and who are discomforted at times by his presence as he 'gives off the wrong smell...the smell of shame'.[124] Coetzee represents these dogs in the Clinic as having emotions: some want love and reassurance which Lurie dispenses, although he has always shrunk from 'being licked'.[125] That he

---

[120] Coetzee, *Disgrace*, 95.
[121] Coetzee, *Disgrace*, 85.
[122] Animals have been rendered mere property by the South African Constitution, and excluded from possessing any rights (*Animal Voice* April–June, 1996).
[123] Coetzee, *Disgrace*, 143.
[124] Coetzee, *Disgrace*, 142.
[125] Coetzee, *Disgrace*, 143.

interprets their fear 'as if they too feel the disgrace of dying'[126] confirms both his and their common experience and dread of mortality.[127]

Disgrace confronts the emotive issue of euthanasing, the killing of a sentient creature in order to save her/him from life and suffering, which is, as Lurie realises, a paradoxical pursuit. That euthanasia of animals is so prolifically practised illustrates the pervasive Judaeo-Christian belief that animals are not persons because they do not have souls.[128] Coetzee challenges this notion through Lurie's experience at the clinic. Lurie buys a pick-up truck to transport the dogs' bodies, spending his days at the clinic, where he eats and writes his opera. He develops a 'particular fondness'[129] for a young, lame male. While Bev Shaw calls him Driepoot, Lurie refuses to name him as though to do so would be to possess or control him, or set up expectations in the dog that he had been adopted. But the dog has agency and intentionality and has 'adopted' him, '[a]rbitrarily, unconditionally',[130] demanding subjective interaction and responding to the sound of the banjo. Lurie progresses from his long-held dualistic notions about animals to being able to acknowledge dogs as sentient beings who can foresee death, even though they cannot understand the actual process, and to being able to call euthanasing by 'its proper name: love'.[131]

When it comes to dispatching the young male, Lurie imaginatively enters the dog's embodied consciousness, as though he is the psychopomp for the dog rather than vice versa. Empathising with the experience of death through the dog's most developed sense, he construes death as a smell that the latter has not met before: 'the smell of expiration, the soft, short smell of the released soul'.[132] Thus Lurie is coming to terms with the inevitable 'end[ing] up in a hole in the ground'[133] through his

---

[126] Coetzee, *Disgrace*, 143.

[127] This dread of dying on the part of non-human animals, is a subject that Coetzee has Costello defend with passion in Coetzee, *Lives*, 65. She argues that whereas an animal is not able to fear death with '"intellectual horror"' s/he can understand death in '"the wholeness, the unabstracted, unintellectual nature" of that animal being'.

[128] A. Linzey and D. Cohn-Sherbok, *After Noah: Animals and the Liberation of Theology* (London, 1997), 137.

[129] Coetzee, *Disgrace*, 215.

[130] Coetzee, *Disgrace*, 215.

[131] Coetzee, *Disgrace*, 219.

[132] Coetzee, *Disgrace*, 219.

[133] Coetzee, *Disgrace*, 189.

honouring of the dogs' bodies, through the disinterested love he now feels and through his belief in the souls of these animals.

The debate about whether animals have souls has been a vexed one in Judaeo-Christian thought. The predominant view that they do not have souls has been used as justification for their ill-treatment and consumption.[134] For Elizabeth Costello, the logic is inescapable: '"To be alive is to be a living soul. An animal—and we are all animals—is an embodied soul"'.[135] Lurie never dissects his own logic about dogs' souls, nor confides in the reader about the trajectory of his thinking; he merely mentions the dog's soul as though this is not a contentious issue.

Conclusion

It is unlikely that any writer in the apartheid era could have made both Mol's and David Lurie's claim about dogs having souls without the writers appearing to foreground animal rights at the expense of human rights. Given the new political dispensation, however, post-apartheid writers are now enabled to be more ecologically inclusive, ironically almost to return to Schreiner's notions of universal connectedness. But dogs are not the only animals writers represent as social—or spiritual subjects. Many recent novels have animals as central to the narrative. In *The Heart of Redness* Zakes Mda represents traditional Xhosa relationships with cattle, horses and birds.[136] In *The Devil's Chimney* Anne Landsman blurs identities between women and wild animals.[137] In *The Reluctant Passenger* Michiel Heyns thematises the mistreatment of baboons in laboratories.[138] In *Recessional for Grace* Marguerite Poland focuses on the nomenclature of colour patterns in Nguni cattle.[139] In *The Whale Caller* Zakes Mda gives a new meaning to "the eternal triangle" constituted in his novel by rivalries between "man, woman and whale."[140]

Yet only dogs have been consistently represented as social subjects in southern African fiction, an indicator of their significant collaboration in

---

[134] Coetzee, *Lives*, 34.
[135] Coetzee, *Lives*, 33.
[136] Z. Mda, *The Heart of Redness* (Cape Town, 2000).
[137] A. Landsman, *The Devil's Chimney* (Johannesburg, 1998).
[138] M. Heyns, *The Reluctant Passenger* (Cape Town, 2003).
[139] M. Poland, *Recessional for Grace* (Johannesburg, 2003).
[140] Z. Mda, *The Whale Caller* (Johannesburg, 2005), 73.

human lives and deaths. For Njabulo Ndebele, the dog 'should become a national symbol of the humanity of South Africans'; 2007 should be declared 'The Year of the Dog' he suggests, in order to 'celebrate qualities associated with this remarkable friend of humans: intelligence, empathy, loyalty, dependability, friendship, courage, protectiveness, sensitivity and caring.'[141]

---

[141] N. Ndebele, "Let's Declare 2007 'The Year of the Dog'" *Mail and Guardian* September 1 to 7 2006, 8–9.

THE CANINE METAPHOR IN THE VISUAL ARTS

Meredith Palumbo

Archaeological evidence confirms that man and dog have enjoyed a complex, symbiotic relationship since the Stone Age, when the dog was an effective hunting companion and protector of the family unit. In the centuries that followed, the dog fared well in interaction with the human species. Among the Egyptians and Greeks, dogs were held in such esteem that two major stars, *Sirius* and *Canis Major* were named for them.[1] In the post-Classical world, dogs became part of the visual discourse of Christianity as 'earthy emblems' of virtue. A dog was the constant companion of St. Dominic and eventually adopted as a symbol of the Dominican order's faithfulness and piety.[2] Artists frequently included dogs on the periphery of religious and spiritual observances in Renaissance and Baroque paintings. In one of the most famous examples, Jan Van Eyck's *Arnolfini Wedding Portrait*, the artist included a small dog in the foreground to symbolize marital fidelity and desire. This practice was common in southern Europe also, as seen in the work of Fra Filippo Lippi whose *Adoration of the Magi* of 1445 includes a reclining dog near the religious event.

When artists like Jean-Baptiste Oudry and Anne Seymour Damer depicted dogs as primary subjects in the eighteenth century, the canine subject received the same dignified treatment as the wealthy humans who commissioned or purchased the paintings. Dogs were depicted protecting property, killing serpents, nurturing puppies, or simply relaxing. When coupled with their owners, dogs mirrored human activities and needs. They were constant companions in the hunt, on the farm, and in comfortable domestic settings. As they had for centuries dogs continued served as emblems of desirable human traits such as loyalty,

---

[1] H.L. Cooke, *Dogs, Horses, Cats, and Other Animals in the National Gallery of Art* (Richmond, 1970), I. and R. Rosenblum, *The Dog in Art From Rococo To Post-Modernism* (New York, 1988), 13.

[2] Cooke, *Dogs, Horses, Cats, and Other Animals*, 2.

affection, devotion, and fidelity, reminding the viewer to seek these qualities in his own life.

In the modern period artists continued to use canine images but now employed them as a means to articulate changing social and political patterns. There was greater pluralism of iconographic meaning than there had been in preceding centuries. The modern era's preoccupation with scientific knowledge of nature inspired studies of canines in motion, in the work of Muybridge and Marey, and in characteristic poses, e.g., a sculpture of a defecating dog by Adriano Cecioni. As exotic breeds were introduced to Europe, some dogs received individual portraits like the paintings done by Renoir and Manet of Tama, the Japanese Chin. Commodore Perry first brought the breed to Europe when he received several of the dogs as gifts for Queen Victoria.[3]

For nineteenth-century artists, canine images also became an accessible visual symbol for the class conflicts articulated by Marxist thinkers in the nineteenth and twentieth centuries.[4] More than one artist depicted pampered greyhounds and pointers of the "well-heeled industrialists," juxtaposing them with street-wise bulldogs like Henri de Toulouse-Lautrec's *Bouboule: MME. Palmyre's Bulldog*. Such contrasts became a familiar symbol of social friction and class conflict in urban centers where the dog functioned as a signifier of social identity and class.

The examples discussed so far belong to European and American art; however, dogs have been equally familiar symbols in southern African art. Profound differences are evident in the work of contemporary African artists in which an iconographic shift from depicting the canine as a metaphor for man's most desirable characteristics such as loyalty, fidelity, and devotion to some of man's baser instincts like aggression and violence against society's most vulnerable members.

Namibian born artist, Imke Rust, uses dogs as signifiers of underlying tensions between the advantaged and disadvantaged in contemporary society. In a series of works, created over several years, she has addressed the complexity of post-colonial society in southern Africa, encompassing issues of race, poverty, and cultural identity.

The first image of this series, *Bitumen Dogs* [illustrated on the cover], was completed when the artist was living in Oshakati in northern Namibia. Unlike the pampered and beloved pets that belonged to

---

[3] Rosenblum, *The Dog in Art*, 52–53.
[4] Rosenblum, *The Dog in Art*, 45.

white families, the dogs in Rust's painting are nameless and abandoned creatures. With emaciated forms and lowered heads, street scavengers searching for food and shelter, they are canine metaphors for the homeless poor who struggle for existence in urban centers in Namibia and elsewhere around the world. These stray mongrels, like the homeless, attract little attention from those living and working in an urban environment. Rust's dogs are submissive creatures on the edge of society and accept their position in the social hierarchy. The once noble creatures are "wandering pariahs" in society like those unable to capitalize on the post-apartheid wealth.

Rust's innovative artistic technique stands outside the relatively conservative mainstream of Namibian art. In the works that make up this series, she uses images from popular culture and the media, fusing computer manipulation with more traditional painterly techniques. In *Bitumen Dogs* the triptych format isolates each dog, emphasizing the loneliness of these typically social animals, who without human companionship can no longer function within society. Unable to locate oil paint in northern Namibia, Rust used bitumen or pine tar as substitutes. The coarse brushwork forced by the viscosity of the material creates a textured surface that mimics the unkempt appearance of abandoned street dogs and amplifies the metaphorical content of the painting.

Another artist from southern Africa, Penny Siopis, has focused on the potential of animals and objects "to be transformed into something else."[5] In *Charmed Lives* the artist was fascinated by the way that a simple object from everyday life, including man's best friend, could become a dangerous weapon. Under the pressure of circumstances, the dog could be transformed from beloved companion into an aggressive predator or vicious beast.[6]

South African born William Kentridge uses canine metaphors to dramatize the human propensity towards warlike aggression and violence. In *Ubu and the Truth Commission*, the main character in Kentridge's drama surrounds himself with "triple headed henchmen" whose snarling heads the artist identified as the dogs of war.[7]

André Van Zijl from Zimbabwe has created witty criticisms of Southern Africa's privileged class. His early satires employ visual puns

---

[5] F. Herreman, *Liberated Voices Contemporary Art from South Africa* (New York, 1999), 94.
[6] Herreman, *Liberated Voices*, 94–95.
[7] N. Benezra *William Kentridge* (New York, 2001), 44–45.

to criticize Afrikaner and British culture and the artificial social status they enjoyed. The artist frequently examined the southern African social hierarchy in which dogs and servants had similar status.[8] His early works contained dense compositional structures that juxtaposed elements from black and white culture. These juxtapositions revealed some of the harsh truths about the changing relationships between the races in southern Africa.[9]

Throughout the history of art, the relationship of man and dog has provided a metaphorical language that permits artists to explore the best and worst of human character and behavior. In sacred and secular environments, symbolizing fidelity and loyalty, or—at other times and places—serving as reminders of human aggression and violence, dogs have provided rich symbolic language for exploration of the human psyche and for introspection on the nature of the human condition. In view of the range of possibilities that canine metaphors embody, they are likely to remain part of the visual arts for as long as human life survives.

---

[8] S. Williamson *Resistance Art in South Africa* (New York, 1989), 18–19.
[9] Williamson, *Resistance Art*, 18.

DOGS AND DOGMA: A DISCUSSION OF THE SOCIO-POLITICAL CONSTRUCTION OF SOUTHERN AFRICAN DOG 'BREEDS' AS A WINDOW ONTO SOCIAL HISTORY*

Sandra Swart

> All knowledge, the totality of all questions and answers, is contained in the dog.
>
> Franz Kafka, 'Investigations of a Dog'

Dogs have been entangled in human lives, myths, illusions, and sentiments for at least the last ten to twelve thousand years.[1] The alliance between dogs and humans is the oldest among all the animals, and the relationship is so long that the story we think of as theirs is often our own. This essay is an attempt to extract a measure of their story and show how and why it has merged with ours in one particular context. It is an engagement with the social role of the three Southern African dog 'breeds': the Rhodesian Ridgeback, the Boerboel and the Africanis. There are other locally developed types, like the variety bred by the South African Defence Force in the 1970s.[2] The discussion explores the current discourses, debates and marketing strategies surrounding the dogs, with particular emphasis on the recent move to reclassify

---

* My warm thanks to Graham Walker, Malcolm Draper, Johan Gallant, Harriet Ritvo, Adrian Ryan, Albert Grundlingh, Sarah Duff and Drifter Swart. This chapter first appeared in *South African Historical Journal* 48 (2003), and has been used with the kind permission of the editors.

[1] It is generally accepted that dogs were domesticated during the hunter-gatherer period in human history, about 12,000 years ago and were well established by the time agricultural villages began to form, 6,000 years ago in the Fertile Crescent. See F.E. Zeuner, *A History of Domesticated Animals* (London, 1963); J. Clutton-Brock (ed.), *The Walking Larder: Patterns of Domestication, Pastoralism and Predation* (London, 1989) and L. Corbett, *The Dingo in Australia and Asia* (Ithaca, 1995).

[2] This dog combined 60 per cent Bloodhound, 35 per cent Doberman and five per cent Rottweiler. This was the forerunner of the so-called Bloemanweiler, a Rottweiler-Bloodhound mix, which has pockets of enthusiasts throughout South Africa. J. Boulle, 'SA dogs: our local heroes', *Farmer's Weekly*, 22 Feb. 2002.

the 'kaffir dog' as the 'Africanis'.[3] Here dogs provide a lens into understanding human society and culture. Their very domestication was fundamentally a cultural act—like making tools or weapons—and their continued development and interaction with humans has entrenched them in our society. Dogs, like humans, are products of both biology and culture, yet it is human culture that defines a dog's condition, its status and its position.[4] Behind every dog breed we find an ethnography and a social history as well as a genealogy—its cultural, as well as its genetic, heritage. This essay tracks the pawprints into the social history of southern African society, opening up wider issues of identity.

In locating the flesh and blood dogs in a context of the cultural heritage(s) of Southern Africa and using them to explore the meanings of a layered social identity, one has also to be aware of taxonomy and political ecology, adopting an inter-disciplinary methodology. 'Scientific' and community history, together with indigenous perceptions of 'breeds' are investigated through advertisements, breed organisations, interviews with breeders and through oral testimony in the communal lands of western Zimbabwe. Methodologically, in discussing the discourses and the ideologies surrounding the dogs, we still need to acknowledge the living breathing canine.[5] Equally, discussing the discourses of dogdom should never detract from our appreciation of the beauty and value of the dogs as individuals. Moreover, it takes both generosity of spirit and an imagination to 'invent' a new breed. There is nothing 'mere' about invented traditions.

Good Breeding?

That there is a miscellany of animals travelling under the sobriquet 'dog' and that dog hierarchy offers a pattern for human status is articulated by Macbeth in his cantankerous reply to the First Murderer:

> First Murderer: We are men, my liege.
> Macbeth: Ay, in the catalogue ye go for men,
> As hounds and greyhounds, mongrels, spaniels, curs,

---

[3] 'Kaffir dog', an offensive term, is still used in some communities, and is often shortened to 'KD'.
[4] M. Schwartz, *A History of Dogs in the Early Americas* (New Haven, 1997), 30.
[5] Thanks to Johan Gallant, for ongoing discussion on this topic.

> Shoughs, water-rugs, and demi-wolves are clept
> All by the name of dogs.
>
> *Macbeth*, 3.1.90–94

Parallels have long been drawn between human and canine society. Sir Philip Sidney noted in 1580: 'greyhounds, Spaniels and Hounds; whereof the first might seem the Lords, the second the Gentlemen, and the last the Yeoman of dogs'.[6] John Caius's treatise *Of English Dogges* (published in Latin in 1570, *De Canibus Britannicis* translated in 1576) describes six main varieties of dogs: greyhounds, hounds, bird dogs, terriers, mastiffs, shepherd dogs—and emphasises that each has its designated social role to play.[7] The seventeenth-century observer, William Penn (1644–1718), commented that 'men are generally more careful of the breed of their horses and dogs than of their children'.[8] It may be argued that our cultural investment and symbolism is particularly resonant in the dog, perhaps because it is so integral to human society. This is illustrated vividly by the killing of innumerable dachshunds (because of their German 'origin') during the First World War in a frenzy of British jingoism and—perhaps because they were too useful to kill—the re-branding of German Shepherds as 'Alsatians'.[9]

Harriet Ritvo has shown that dog breeds and breeding were developed with a deep investment in ideas about race, quality, purity and progress. In 1873 the English Kennel Club founded in London, together with the first volume of its stud book—listing dogs exhibited since 1859. She notes that the members were by their own account 'true sportsmen... who breed to win and to whom pecuniary questions are of no moment'.[10] For Victorian society the elaborate divisions of dogs into breeds and classes and of individuals into precisely ranked hierarchies within these classes seemed to imitate and thus endorse the established, rigidly hierarchical social system represented by the human

---

[6] Quoted in V. Woolf, *Flush: A Biography* (Harmondsworth, 1983), 9. See H. Ritvo, *The Animal Estate: The English and Other Creatures in the Victorian Age* (Cambridge, 1987), 102 and K. Kete, *The Beast in the Boudoir* (Berkeley, 1994), 67, 70, 83–4.

[7] Quoted in M. Garber, *Dog Love* (London, 1996), 166.

[8] William Penn, *Reflexions and Maxims*, No. 85.

[9] Firstly, they were re-named 'Alsatian Wolf Dogs', the 'Wolf Dog' was subsequently dropped as it was considered pejorative.

[10] Ritvo, *The Animal Estate*.

upper orders. Human class and dog class—*breeding*, as it were—were inextricably tangled.[11]

This could be undermined, however, by market forces—for example an unusual trait might find popularity and be favoured over 'lineage'. Ritvo notes: 'The prizewinning pedigreed dogs of the late nineteenth century seemed to symbolise simply the power to manipulate and the power to purchase—they were ultimately destabilising emblems of status and rank as pure commodities.' Kathleen Kete has highlighted this aggressive classification and manipulation by throwing it into contrast with the French attitude to breeding, which was not taken seriously and was not linked to societal divisions. Physical traits were cavalierly regarded. Yet, if the shows regarded physical traits more lightly, the dog-care handbooks did not; they served to 'construct' the French breeds in the social imagination. The 'moral' qualities of the 'breeds' were outlined in a sketch or story—and it was the idea of the breed (and not its usage) that signified. Kete observes that 'the identification of owner with pet was a function of image that the pet acquired, however arbitrarily that meaning came about'.[12]

The dog is the supreme example of that which can be achieved by genetic selection—no other species shows such variation in size, character, or range of activities expected of it. The western concept of dog 'breeds' dates back at least to Caius's 1570 treatise *Of English Dogges*. As particular morphological characteristics became more clearly associated with the ability to perform various valued tasks, the ancestors of the present breeds appeared. As breeding for characteristics became more refined in subsequent generations, the early breed specimens began to assume a particular type. Individual dogs began to resemble their immediate ancestors more than they resembled distant ancestors. The inherited similarities—both behavioural and morphological—were limited only to characteristics that could be observed in a dog or its offspring. The first modern style dog show was held in 1859 at Newcastle-upon-Tyne, limited to only two 'breeds'. A much larger show took place at the Crystal Palace in 1870, and it drew 975 entries by

---

[11] The idea of pedigree originally meant a line of ancestors, from the resemblance of a crane's foot (Anglo-Norman *pie de grue*) to the lines on a genealogical chart.

[12] A Parisian poodle, for example, clothed and crimped, dressed in the colours and materials of its owner, its own hairdresser and rigorous diet was a *doppelgänger* for its mistress.

1873. Today there are approximately 20,000 entries annually at Crufts, which exhibits 166 breeds.

Yet, for all the value placed in it, the term 'breed' is hard to define. A 'breed' may be understood as animals that, through selection and breeding, have come to resemble one another and pass their traits uniformly to their offspring. A breed is glibly defined as a Mendelian population in equilibrium differentiated from other breeds by genetic composition. All this means is that a breed is a population that complies to ancestry. So a 'purebred' animal belongs to an identifiable breed complying with prescribed traits—origin, appearance, and minimum breed standards. As Lush has contended, in *The Genetics of Populations*, the term is both elusive and subjective:

> [a] breed is a group of domestic animals, termed such by common consent of the breeders...a term which arose among breeders of livestock, created one might say, for their own use, and no one is warranted in assigning to this word a scientific definition and in calling the breeders wrong when they deviate from the formulated definition.[13]

So the point at which a collection of animals becomes a 'breed' is, in the final analysis, a human decision—not a genetic event.

In the Middle East, for example, there were only three kinds of dogs: salukis used to hunt gazelle, large herding dogs used by shepherds to guard against wolves, and mongrels that were scavengers in the cities. By contrast, in modern France there are seventeen breeds of shepherding or stock dogs alone.[14] Rural Zulu communities recognise three types.[15] The rural Ndebele-speakers of the Hwange region in Zimbabwe recognised a mixture of 'breeds'. Interestingly there was no designation for animals resembling the 'indigenous' Africanis morphological type. These were dismissed generally as 'just a dog', often said with a deprecating laugh.[16]

---

[13] J.L. Lush, *The Genetics of Populations* (Mimeo, 1948). See 'From Jay L. Lush to Genomics: Visions for Animal Breeding and Genetics', May 1999, Iowa State University.

[14] For more on the development of dog breeds, see Zeuner, *A History of Domesticated Animals*, 93.

[15] A. Abacar et al., 'Traditional hunting with dogs: a contemporary issue in Kwa-Zulu-Natal' (MA thesis, University of Natal, Pietermartitzburg, 1999).

[16] S. Swart, 'Limiting the impact of domestic dogs on African wild dogs, Hwange National Park, Zimbabwe' (MSc thesis, University of Oxford, 2001).

Three 'Breeds' in Search of an Author

There are three Southern African dog 'breeds': the Rhodesian Ridgeback, the Boerboel and—more controversially—the 'Africanis', dismissed in the past as merely a 'kaffir dog' or 'a township special'.[17] These latter dogs, predominately present in rural areas throughout Southern Africa, are argued to share common traits—they are predominately smooth-coated, lightly built, with a slight forehead stop and pointed muzzle, large semi-pricked ears and a curled tail. Historically, these dogs have not been classified as a breed—unlike Rhodesian Ridgebacks or Boerboels, both lines arising in Africa but mainly developed within white settler society. Instead they have been considered a pariah, and have been labelled disparagingly as 'kaffir dogs', 'pi/pye-dogs', curs, or 'shenzi dogs' (from the Swahili meaning 'wild' or 'uncultivated').[18]

Recently there has been a re-investigation of the taxonomic status of these dogs. An appealing argument has been made that they are not mongrel progeny of settler dogs, but derived from the Arabian wolf (*Canis lupus arabs*), from which Middle Eastern dogs were domesticated, arriving in southern Africa perhaps *c*. 1000–1500 BC with Arab traders, Early Iron Age Bantu (Nguni-speakers) and/or Khoi pastoralists.[19] Skeletal remains indicate the presence of dogs on many Iron Age, and a few Stone Age, sites.[20] Certainly there were dogs before western settlers. Early travellers to the Cape observed the presence of dogs. In 1595, Cornelis de Houtman observed that the Khoisan owned dogs.[21] In 1861, Casalis noted that 'the natives [Sotho] affirm that they have had dogs from time immemorial'. In 1497, Vasco Da Gama observed dogs

---

[17] South Africa's best loved dog, Jock of the Bushveld, was inadvertently shot, mistaken for a 'kaffir dog', which the loyal Jock had already killed defending the chicken run. *Farmer's Weekly* recently ran an article asking 'What did Jock really look like?', *Farmer's Weekly*, 22 Feb. 2002.

[18] So-called Nguni cattle have been recognised as a breed, but other animals—like 'Zulu fowl'—have not.

[19] R.M. Blench and K.C. MacDonald, *The Origins and Development of African Livestock: Archaeology, Genetics, Linguistics and Ethnography* (London, 2000).

[20] Hall has hypothesised that early waves of western stream settlers introduced small spitz-type dogs—similar to the extant equatorial basenji—and perhaps later Bantu-speakers brought the slender gazoid pariah/hound type typical of northern African regions.

[21] R. Raven-Hart, *Before Van Riebeeck—Callers at South Africa from 1488 to 1652* (Cape Town, 1967), 17–18.

owned by the San.²² Between 1,700 and 1,800 inland travellers remarked on dogs owned by the groups they came across.²³ In 1811, Burchell described dogs belonging to a San group as 'a small species, entirely white, with erect pointed ears' and being 'of a race perhaps peculiar to these tribes'.²⁴ Soga (1905) and Bryant (1967) provide ethnographies of the Xhosa and Zulu respectively, which offer the best description of indigenous dog types and their social roles.²⁵ Significantly, both ethnographers feared that these dogs were threatened with extinction.

Ideas around the Africanis are wrapped up in the ideology of reclaiming the indigenous and building on autochthonous knowledge systems. Such claims have been generated by post-colonial conditions and the perceived scorn of the First World for the Third. 'Indigenous knowledge' claims autonomy and independence from 'metropolitan knowledge'. It is, to use current South African and pan-African terminology, an attempt at 'Renaissance'—to recover 'old' ways of understanding and to restore 'old', lost or forgotten ways of doing and thinking. This has been promoted by South African President Thabo Mbeki's belief in Africa's ability to be 're-born' and join the other nations of the world as an equal member. He has identified recovering indigenous knowledge and celebrating the indigenous as vital in completing the process of eliminating the colonial presence and mindset across Africa.²⁶

---

²² E.C. Boonzaier et al. *Cape Herders: A History of the Khoikhoi of Southern Africa* (Cape Town, 1996), 54.

²³ S. Hall, 'Indigenous domesticated dogs of southern Africa: an introduction', in Blench and MacDonald, *Origins and Development of African Livestock*, 304.

²⁴ Burchell, 1811, quoted in Hall, 'Indigenous domesticated dogs', 304.

²⁵ H. Soga, *The Ama-Xosa: Life and Customs* (London, 1905) and A.T. Bryant, *The Zulu People as They Were before the White Man Came* (Pietermaritzburg, 1967). The Xhosa-speakers had four types: *iTwina* (which Soga wrote had largely disappeared), *iBaku*, *Inqeqe* and the *iNgesi* (the English greyhound). The Zulu-speakers owned the *iSiqha* (*iSica*), a hunting dog, and appear to distinguish between *isimaku* (smaller dog) and *ubova* (larger hunter). Malcolm Draper has suggested that the domestication of dogs by the San is particularly important as the only evidence of domestication/cultivation by a hunting and gathering culture: M. Draper, personal communication.

²⁶ See, for example, M.W. Makgoba (ed.), *African Renaissance: The New Struggle* (Sandton, 1999); T. Mbeki, *Africa: The Time Has Come* (Cape Town, 1998) and M.M. Mulemfo, *Thabo Mbeki and the African Renaissance: The Emergence of a New African Leadership* (Pretoria, 2000).

Figure 16. The traditional role of the Africanis.[27]

---

[27] Photo by Johan Gallant, used with kind permission.

The Africanis is increasingly argued to be part of the living heritage of African culture and is celebrated as 'part of the African Renaissance'.[28] Hall calls them the embodiment of 'a people's history' and urges that they be considered part of the African 'cultural heritage'. Gallant calls them 'our cultural and biological patrimony'.[29] They are beginning to be marketed as symbols of the value of the indigenous, simultaneously promoting and utilising the pyscho-social self-esteem that is a key element of the African Renaissance. The Africanis breeders note:

> The Africanis is the real African dog—shaped in Africa, for Africa. It is part of the cultural and biological heritage of Africa. In fact, its African heritage goes back 7,000 years. Africanis is descended from the dogs pictured on Egyptian murals, the earliest record of the domestic dog in Africa being from the Nile delta, dated 4,700 BC. Today, Africanis is found all over the Southern African subcontinent. It is known by various names, in different languages. That is why we use a universal name, canis [dog] of Africa—Africanis. But Is It a Mongrel or Dog of No Definable Type or Breed? Decidedly not. Africanis is the true dog of Africa. The type has been accurately defined, despite some variations in appearance. Africanis is the result of natural selection and physical and mental adaptation to environmental conditions. It has not been 'selected' or 'bred' for appearance. It is the dog for Africa. In 'traditional' southern African philosophy the most important requirement for a dog is that it should be 'wise'. For centuries, the fittest and cleverest dogs survived to give us one of the rare remaining natural dog races in the world.[30]

Africanis dogs are thus imagined and marketed as creatures of the blood and the soil, a dog uncannily linked to its terrain, part of its aboriginal and original landscape, and part of an African 'traditional way of life'.[31] The breed is however, marketed in modern western ways on the Internet[32] and in the global capitalist manner. Moreover, the rehabilitation of

---

[28] Hall suggests that Africanis types might have high resistance to African tropical diseases and have lower protein requirements. Research into other domestic animals indigenous to an area has shown cases of locale-specific traits, like N'dama cattle from West Africa which have developed a resistance to trypanosomiasis. As yet there are no studies of disease or parasite resistance specific to the 'Africanis'.

[29] Johan Gallant, personal communication.

[30] http://www.sa-breeders.co.za/org/africanis/.

[31] The dogs may still have a practical use; it has been suggested that puppies may be reared with ewes to discourage jackal and lynx: K.A. Ramsay *et al.*, 'Profitable and environmentally effective farming with early domesticated livestock in southern Africa' (Conservation of Early Domesticated Animals of Southern Africa, Willem Prinsloo Agricultural Museum, 1994).

[32] http://www.sa-breeders.co.za/org/africanis/.

the 'Kaffir dog' appears to be a largely white exercise with no support from the black majority yet, although this might change.[33]

Curs and Currency

Hath a dog money?

The Merchant of Venice, 1.3

Willis and others have commented on the massive capital invested in the dogbreeding industry. Both breeders and its resultant service industry benefit from the public's enthusiasm for 'purebred' dogs, preferably 'registered' with the national Kennel Unions. There are several parallels to the South African context in other post-colonial situations, where dogs are used as socio-cultural vehicles, to promote a sense of self-respect, or where current cultural ideology is used to market formerly low-priced livestock. Dogs are used as signifiers in an attempt to boost post-colonial pride in indigenous identity. The singing dogs of New Guinea, Korean Jindo or Australian dingo (*Canis familiaris dingo*), for example, are increasingly argued to be 'breeds' in their own right. The dingo is currently celebrated as 'part of the living heritage of aboriginal culture and part of Australian history'. The Jindo of Korea has been described recently as 'one of the Korean natural monuments', around 'from time unknown'. A Jindo Dog Breeding Management Center has been established to improve the breed.[34]

Significantly, collectors are progressively more interested in the 'primitive' breeds—seen as quintessentially canine compared to the refined European and British breeds. The 'primitive' breeds are discussed as useful generalists, independent, and relatively free of genetic problems caused by inbreeding and line breeding.

The heritage industry is linked to market forces and the economic motors behind the promotion of the Africanis are powerful. An Africanis can cost up to R2,000 (the Society recommends a maximum of R1,000) in contrast with the average price of a 'mongrel' in the rural areas, R15 or Z$5–25).[35] To provide a comparative framework: a regis-

---

[33] See J. Gallant, *The Story of the African Dog* (Pietermaritzburg:: University of Natal Press, 2002).

[34] C.G. Lee *et al.*, 'A review of the Jindo, Korean native dog', *Asian-Australian Journal of Animal Sciences*, 13 (2000), 381–9.

[35] S. Swart, 'Limiting the Impact of Domestic Dogs on African Wild Dogs'.

tered Ridgeback or Boerboel costs R1,500 to R2,000, and unregistered R500 to R800. Moreover, the Africanis Society of Southern Africa has been created to 'conserve a natural dog. Not to "develop" the breed, or artificially "breed" dogs for selective characteristics.' The society was launched in 1998 by Johan Gallant (promoter of the Siyakhula project since 1994) and Dr Udo Küsel (director of the National Cultural History Museum). It maintains a code of ethics, guidelines for breeding, regulations and a procedure for registration, and a register of inspected and approved dogs.

Hair of the Dog

The society notes that '[a]dvanced DNA testing is standard' (which costs R135) and only registered dogs are recommended for breeding...'. The DNA test, done with either a hair or blood sample, sets the parameters for inclusion within the Africanis land race, rather than a narrow 'breed' profile. Membership costs R50 entry plus R50 per year and is a prerequisite for the ownership of a registered dog.

The Africanis society makes an interesting distinction between a 'breed' and a 'land race', into which latter category it is argued the Africanis belongs. A breed is argued to be purposefully selected to conform to certain standards, while a land race has evolved, with its standards decided on by environmental factors rather than human choice, allowing for a greater diversity in morphology. The Africanis Society's aim is to conserve the dogs and their utilitarian value rather than refine and set cosmetic standards for the animals in line with aims of, for example, the Kennel Union.[36]

If one accepts the Africanis as a 'race', then perhaps the biggest threat to the Africanis's integrity stems, ironically, from the African perception of the dogs' worthlessness. In the rural areas, where hunting (both for meat and for gambling) is increasingly popular, greyhounds (and other fixed 'breeds') are used for stud, diluting the 'purity' of the Africanis. Both my study of Ndebele communities in Zimbabwe and Hall's study in South Africa indicate that black societies increasingly tend to prefer western breeds, regarding them as status symbols. Grey-

---

[36] J. Gallant, personal communication. KUSA does, however, accept the registration of Africanis in its Foundation Stock register.

hounds in particular are favoured—there is even a Nguni-term for the cross-between a greyhound and an indigenous dog: 'amabanzi'.[37]

The Brown Paint Theory

There is, however, a possible argument against the pure Africanis as a distinguishable 'breed'. Interbreeding with introduced breeds has been happening for about four centuries—and probably longer. Casalis noted the widespread presence of free-ranging, self-supporting, almost quasi-feral dogs among the Sotho. He noticed that by 1861 there was already a great morphological diversity: '[t]he smallest hamlet is infested with dogs of all sizes and colours'.[38] Travellers let their dogs mix with others. John Davy, for example, noted in 1598 that when his ship departed the 'Mastive Dogge' was left behind.[39] Similarly, Gordon observed that the reserves were overrun with mongrel greyhounds in Namibia by 1917. 'Butch' Smuts's photographs of dogs used in the early years of the twentieth century for hunting in the Kruger National Park show a miscellany of breeds owned by black communities in remote rural areas.[40]

Dogs, when left to breed on their own for a few generations, revert to a stereotypic form: stocky with a yellowish/buff coat, curly tail, short muzzle, small upright ears. If the different 'breeds' are analogous to different colours of paint, mixing them in various quantities indiscriminately over time produces simply 'brown paint'. This might explain the remarkable morphological similarity despite the geographic separation of the Australian dingo (or warrigal); the Mexican xoloitzcuintli (coated version);[41] Carolina dogs;[42] Korean Jindo; Philippine Aso; Indian pariah dog; Telomian dog of Malaysia and the 'Africanis' dog. This does not necessarily contradict the idea of Africanis as a "land race": environmental factors select for the 'pariah' or 'primitive' morphology. It is

---

[37] J. Gallant, personal communication. Boulle notes that a greyhound type, mainly in the Cape, is called *iBantsa*, *Farmer's Weekly*, 22 Feb. 2002.

[38] E. Casalis, *The Basutos, or, Twenty-Three Years in South Africa* (London, 1861), 176.

[39] Raven-Hart, *Before Van Riebeeck*, 20.

[40] G.L. Smuts, *Lion* (Johannesburg, 1982).

[41] C. Flamholtz, *A Celebration of Rare Breeds: Volume II* (Centreville, 1991).

[42] Carolina dogs, promoted by Carolina Dog Club of America, are found in the swamps and woods of the Savannah River basin. Dubbed 'old yeller', they are dogs of a pariah type, and are argued to be a direct descendant of the ancient pariah dogs that accompanied Asians across the Bering Straits land bridge.

arguable that they may represent something of what the ancestral dog may have resembled.

Molecular genetic tools have been used increasingly to dissect the evolutionary relationships of the canids—to understand the relationships of species within the Canidae, or dog family, and the genetic exchanges that occur between conspecific populations.[43] But DNA fingerprinting does not allow scientists to identify dog 'breeds' or 'types'.[44] Raymond Coppinger has stated that an incontrovertible genetic marker for breeds of dogs has not been discovered.[45] For the moment, the final diagnostic process requires papers like those lodged with kennel clubs, like the KUSA or AKC, or educated guesses based on a dog's morphology and behaviour.

This leads us to a broader issue on dog 'breeds' and their preservation. We have already seen that the concept of a 'breed' as a 'pure' race of dogs, each bearing characteristics unique to themselves, is a tradition less than two centuries old. By the second half of the nineteenth century, British breeders were writing breed standards and holding exhibitions. When a new 'breed' was proposed, the fanciers of that breed wrote the standard to fit the dogs they themselves owned. As the custom spread, prominent fanciers or breeders collected groups of dogs, described them in a standard, and decreed the 'discovery' of an 'ancient breed'. National or regional pride often dictated the minor differences that identified a dog as belonging to one country and not another. As De la Cruz reminds one, only a serious fancier can easily identify the differences, for example, between show specimens of Kuvasz, Tatra, Chuvach, Akbash or Great Pyrenees dogs; the nomadic shepherd by whom these dogs were developed was unlikely to have strong feelings as long as the dog did the work required of her.

When we talk of 'preserving' a breed, we are essentially talking about freezing one point in time—usually the time we ourselves first met our chosen breed. We try to preserve the dog of our imagination in the amber of breed standards and controlled breeding regimes. Changes in the direction we desire, we label 'refinement'; unwelcome changes

---

[43] Large hybrid zones do exist—the phenotype of the endangered American red wolf, for example, may be strongly influenced by hybridisation with coyotes and grey wolves.

[44] Recently, for example, after attacks on humans made headlines, several US counties passed laws banning pitbulls. But the question arose: 'what exactly IS a pitbull?', as there is no 'genetic' test for being a pitbull.

[45] R. Coppinger, personal communication.

we call 'degenerative'. Old notions of blood purity invest these desires. It remains today perhaps one of the very few fora in which the pure eugenics discourse is not taboo.

Big Brown Dogs: The Boerboel and Rhodesian Ridgeback

Various 'Boer' dogs have been mentioned from the nineteenth century. The traveller of Zambezia and Matabeleland, Frederick Barber noted, for example, 'We had some very fine Boer dogs in the camp' and remarked on 'two splendid, powerful, plucky Boer dogs'.[46] The Boerboel, often dubbed the 'Boer mastiff', is a large 'breed' of dog developed in southern Africa over the last few hundred years, specifically for homestead security and (white, usually Afrikaans) family protection.[47] Incorporating elements of a number of breeds, the Boerboel has been bred with the concerns of white settler protection in mind. Induna Boerboel breeders note:

> The Boerboel has a long and illustrious history as one of the outstanding dogs of Africa. Whilst the most recent developments in the breed have been recorded as having taken place within Southern Africa over the last three hundred and fifty years, the typical characteristics of the breed are very similar to those demonstrated in contemporary pictures of Assyrian dogs of the period prior to 700 BC.[48]

The breeders note the efforts by Van Riebeeck and the 1820s settlers to breed mastiffs and cross them with other European breeds—the *bullenbijter*, the English Bulldog, the Great Dane, the Saint Bernard and the Bull Terrier. In 1938 authenticated bull mastiffs were imported from Britain by De Beers to serve as guard dogs on the South African diamond mines of the time; the characteristics of these animals were 'doubtless incorporated into the boerboel breed as we know it today. The Boerboel is not yet fully recognised by KUSA, but is on their foundation stock registry. The South African Boerboel Breeders Association (SABT) laid down breed standards in 1983, and the first nationwide appraisal of dogs took place in 1990. Boerboel breeding in South Africa is overseen

---

[46] E.C. Tabler (ed.), *Zambezia and Matabeleland in the Seventies: The Narrative of Frederick HughBarber (1875 and 1877–8) and The Journal of Richard Frewen (1877–8)* (London, 1960), 96, 99.

[47] Many people in South Africa will mistakenly identify whole ranges of 'big brown dogs' as Boerboels; and Boerbul or Boerbull are common misnomers.

[48] http://www.boerboelsa.co.za/hist.htm, Induna Boerboel.

by a number of organisations, among them the South African Boerboel Breeders' Association (SABT) and the Historical Boerboel of South Africa (HBSA). A third organisation is the Elite Boerboel Breeders' Association of Southern Africa (International) (EBBASA), which has more stringent entry and registration requirements than the other two associations and focuses more on international involvement. A detailed set of standards regulating the characteristics of the breed has been laid down by these Associations and all dogs which are registered with an association are required to undergo assessment in terms of these standards. It is a requirement that in order to be registered, a dog must achieve a minimum qualifying rating between 75 and 80 per cent.[49] The Kennel Union of South Africa invited the SABT to introduce the Boerboel at the South African Championship in Pretoria. In 1995 the Boerboel was introduced to the international community at the World Dog Show in Brussels, Belgium.

The Rhodesian Ridgeback dates back to the early sixteenth century when travellers observed a domesticated dog with the hair on his spine 'turned forward' in a ridge.[50] These local Cape dogs interbred with the mastiffs, bloodhounds and greyhounds (and others) imported with the waves of European settlers.[51] In 1875, the missionary, the Revd Charles Helm, undertook a journey from his home in Swellendam to Rhodesia.[52] He was accompanied by two of these dogs. While Helm was in Rhodesia, Cornelis von Rooyen, the big-game hunter and early authority on the South African wildlife, borrowed the two dogs to take along on a hunt. Von Rooyen soon concluded that they possessed useful hunting qualities and thereupon pioneered the breeding of a pack of the species as hunters of big game for his own use. In 1922 the first Ridgeback Club was founded at a show in Bulawayo, Southern Rhodesia, and a standard of points for the breed was set. This happened as follows: a local resident, Francis Barnes, organised a meeting on the second day of the Bulawayo Kennel Club Show to try to formulate a standard for the 'lion dog'—the selection criterion was the ridge. Ridged dogs of all shapes and sizes were brought by their owners, and there was much

---

[49] http://www.boerboelsa.co.za/hist.htm.
[50] The only other known dog which has the peculiarity of such a ridge is found on the island of Phu Quoc in the Gulf of Siam.
[51] 'Dogman', *Guide to Dogdom in South Africa* (Johannesburg, 1947).
[52] Cape Archives (KAB), CAD, 1/2/15.

dissension as to how a 'ridge back' or 'lion dog' was to be defined. A witness, B.W. Durham, noted:

> Owners were reluctant to come forward, each naturally thinking his the correct type. Finally a spectator with some knowledge of the breed [Durham himself, the only 'all breeds' judge in Rhodesia] took a dog and suggested that the size and configuration be adopted, then chose another specimen for its head and neck, a third for legs and feet, and making use of some five different dogs, built up what he considered to be aimed at. A few days later Mr Barnes compiled the standard, a club was formed, Mr Barnes standard adopted...'.[53]

Following this, Ridgebacks were exhibited as novelties at an English dog show and were presented as gifts to British royal family. In 1924 the Ridgeback was also recognised by the South African Kennel Union as a distinct breed and the organisation recognised its first registered dog.[54] In 1928, there were attempts from the public to find the origins of this so-called "Lion dog" and to establish whether it was descended from a "Hottentot" canine.[55] Today, the Rhodesian Ridgeback is one of the most popular dogs in South Africa and was KUSA's symbol of the year in 2002.[56]

The Social Constructions of the Three Different 'Breeds'

Love—here the owners' love for their dogs—is composed at least partly of identification.[57] Owners' choice of dog reflects desires, anxieties and popular anthropomorphism—involving the projection of the psycho-social self upon the corporeal animals. Ostensibly matter-of-fact breed standards are couched in emotional idiom: the official American breed standard for the shar-pei, for example, is 'regal, alert, intelligent, dignified, lordly, scowling, sober and snobbish'.[58] Moreover, Alan Beck in his 1973 study of free-ranging dogs in Baltimore, for example, revealed that many poverty-stricken inner city residents—who actually

---

[53] B.W. Durham, *South African Kennel Gazette*, Dec. 1950.
[54] Only two dogs were registered with the SAKU in that year, followed by four in 1925, and no fewer than eleven in 1926.
[55] Cape Archives (KAB), CAD, 1/2/15.
[56] *Animal Talk*, 7, 11 (Nov. 2001), 20.
[57] Garber, *Dog Love*, 166.
[58] American Kennel Club 1992, quoted in J. Serpell, ed., *The Domestic Dog: Its Evolution, Behaviour and Interactions with People* (Cambridge, 1995), 2.

suffered the most from stray dogs—nevertheless often sided with the dog against the municipal dog-catcher. They projected their distrust of authority and the white establishment onto the dogs, seeing them as fellow victims.[59] Similarly, such anthropomorphism and identification operates in the South African context. The dogs are thus marketed in very dissimilar ways, each occupying their own strategic niche in the public's imagination.

The Boerboel has a strong Afrikaans following, and was purportedly first promoted by the Herstigte Nasionale Party as a protector of white homes.[60] The HNP itself is proud of their late leader, Jaap Marais's knowledge of Boerboels. *The Afrikaner*, the HNP mouthpiece, notes: 'Ask [Marais] for example something about Boerboel-dogs and he could sit and write pages on it!'[61] It was marketed as 'the dog of our forefathers' and the local or indigenous dog's influence was minimised, with a cursory mention. The Boerboel is perceived as a rugged self-sufficient 'settler dog'. Its 'European' or Western heritage has been emphasised, linking it to the Classical tradition. Thus it corresponds with 'settler ideology', which insists on its right to occupy its new home, but asserts a traditional link to Classical Western Civilisation. The United States Boerboel Association (USBA), African Boerboel Breeders and the South African Boerboel Breeders' Association, for example, trace the breed back to Classical antiquity:

> Long research has revealed that the ancestry of the Boerboel can be traced as far back as the time of Herodotus and to Tibet, Assiria and Babylon...Later Alexander the Great was responsible for spreading them to Europe.[62]

Similarly, Stormberg Boerboel breeders note that Boerboels may be seen in a 'copy of a painting, Circa 1400, arrived with a typical

---

[59] A. Beck, *The Ecology of Stray Dogs* (Baltimore, 1973).
[60] According to the *Mail and Guardian*, the hounds first surfaced during the early 1980s in *Farmers Weekly* advertisements, paid for by the extreme right-wing Herstigte Nasionale Party. The advertisements flagged 'racist watchdogs' bred 'especially for South African circumstances': *Mail and Guardian*, 27 June 1997. But it may be traced back to Johan de Jager of Utrecht (KwaZulu Natal) who started the breeding of the Boerboel in 1960 not for political reasons.
[61] *Die Afrikaner*, 18 Aug. 2000.
[62] http://home.yebo.co.za/~mcewendp/; http://members.aol.com/seacaps/history.html; http://www.geocities.com/boer_boelus/history.html.

Boerboel-like dog in the centre of a royal gathering in the court of King Charles'.[63]

In a representative, indeed typical, advertisement, Induna Breeders contend: 'the development of the boerboel is therefore a true South African success story; today's boerboel is as ideal a home protection dog as were his or her ancestors.' The USBA, Baden Breeders and African Boerboel Breeders note that the breed standard and breed organisations meant that 'at last the dog of our forefathers was ready to be registered as a pure breed'.[64]

> Our forefathers required the following from their Boerboel: During the day the dog must go to the veld with the children to guard the sheep... Tonight he should lie in front of the fire at home and protect the whole family against anything that may be lurking in the dark.[65]

Both the South African Boerboel Breeders' Association and Anasha Breeders note: 'The boerboel is South Africa's very own breed. Justifiably he takes his place with pride and is well known both in Southern Africa as well as overseas. This breed is as South African as Braaivleis and Biltong!'[66] And Donna Boerboel breeders assert:

> For thousands of South Africans... who grew up with these dogs is it not just interesting but wonderful to know that the dog of the Great Trek who travelled with our ancestors, has had its name restored to its rightful glory.
>
> In the beginning of the eighties, five men decided to rediscover the dog of the boer homestead and let it live again. The dog of our ancestors, living Africana, must be respected and bred to create our own breed that South Africa can be proud of.
>
> In 1983, in a little sitting room of a schoolhouse in Senekal, next to the plains where the Trek passed through, the men came together, each a Boerboel lover. The great dream, to give our dog its rightful place among the dog races of the world, took form.[67]

Critics of the Boerboel *also* have an ideological impetus. In 'A trip around the bizarre world of apartheid's mad scientists', Mungo Soggot

---

[63] http://www.boerboele.co.za/.
[64] http://www.dogbreedinfo.com/boerboel.htm also notes that 'the development of the Boerboel can rightfully be described as a true South African success story'.
[65] http://www.geocities.com/Heartland/Acres/6554; http://www.african-boerboel.co.za/character.html; http://members.aol.com/seacaps/index.html.
[66] http://www.swansea.demon.co.uk/anasha/history.htm.
[67] http://www.geocities.com/heartland/bluffs/4720/Dieboel.html (translation).

and Eddie Koch, ask '[w]here else but in South Africa' would 'dog fanatics enthusiastically market a dog called a boerbul [sic]—an 80kg creature so ferocious that even foreign pitbull fan clubs were this week baying for a ban on the beast?' They insist that 'these canine freaks' are among the 'fantastic creations of the apartheid regime, spawned by a symbiosis between science and white supremacy', and part of 'conservative whites' mania for vicious and racist dogs, the population of which eliminates scores of (mainly black) South Africans every year'.[68] Breeders concede that there is a widespread misconception that they are "vicious and were bred by farmers to attack black people", but argue "You don't get racist dogs. That is taught to them".[69]

In a diametrically opposite marketing strategy, the Africanis is promoted as completely free of European breeds' influence. The discourse is embedded in the language and thoughts of the African Renaissance—emphasising the dogs' rootedness in traditional Nguni cultural practices, like hunting and masculinity rituals. The African Renaissance stimulates interest in, and lends legitimacy to, endeavours to investigate and promote 'heritage creation' and 'African agency and African pride'. The ongoing process to transform the 'kaffir dog' into the 'Africanis dog' draw heavily on the discourse of Afrocentricity: the dogs are advertised as autochthonous and 'authentic'.[70] They are promoted as essentially more 'canine' than the 'refined', and therefore 'soft', European breeds, dubbed 'still such real dogs', and 'so natural' and 'so intense'.[71]

The Ridgeback provides a discursive bridge between the two, drawing on elements of each, and emphasising heavily its role in the natural environment. Its romantic origins as 'lion dog' are heavily emphasised.[72] It is marketed with a mixture of traits—its affinity with the veld (as dogs originally intended to hunt lions; in most adverts the lion connection is heavily emphasised as above), and its rugged fusion of indigenous

---

[68] *Mail and Guardian*, 27 June 1997.
[69] Shanthini Naidoo, "Boerboels wanted around the world", *Sunday Times*, 19 November 2006.
[70] J. Gallant, personal communication.
[71] J. Gallant, personal communication.
[72] http://indigo.ie/~dboyd; http://home.iprimus.com.au/milesy/new_page_2.htm; http://www.arrf.net/info.htm.

and (British) settler breeds.[73] Several breeders and a breed association assert:

> the settler needed a companion that would stay by him while he slept in the bush and that would be devoted to his wife and children. Out of necessity, therefore, these settlers developed, by selective breeding between dogs which they had brought with them from home countries and the half-wild ridged dog of the Hottentot tribes, a distinct breed of the African veldt, which has come to be known as the Rhodesian Ridgeback... Throughout all of the interbreeding and crossbreeding between these native dogs and those of the settlers, the ridge of the Hottentot dog was respected and retained.[74]

The popular South African pet magazine *Animal Talk* dubbed it 'the Hottentots' Hunting Dog'.[75] It notes that by crossing European breeds with 'the indigenous African dogs, the settlers soon had a hardy 'frontier' dog: 'These dogs, and their masters, shared all manner of adventures and dangers creating a civilized community in a savage and exciting land. Together they gradually moved northeastwards'.[76] Although the rough, tough colonial is now a civilised member of the canine community, the Rhodesian Ridgeback still retains the virtues of its hardy ancestors, and wherever a handsome hound of character is required, be sure it will be there—a living reminder of veld and vlei.[77] Essentially, the Ridgeback is the 'Johnny Clegg of dogs'—securely white, but with a fashionable ethnic twist.[78]

---

[73] There is currently a project underway in the Kruger National Park to test and train ridgebacks in assisting game wardens, *Lion Dog Digest*, Rhodesian Ridgeback International Federation, Nov. 2000.

[74] http://www.deerridgerr.com/Breed/History.htm; http://www.arrowridge.com/index.htm.

[75] *Animal Talk*, 7, 11 (Nov. 2001).

[76] *Animal Talk*, 7, 11 (Nov. 2001), 21.

[77] *Animal Talk*, 7, 11 (Nov. 2001), 23. One website (http://www-hsc.usc.edu/~jjmurphy/RRnames.html) offers a selection of 'authentic' 'African' names for puppies: Dagga; Dashiki; Kimb; Juba; Masa; Shaka; Tahari; Zulu.

[78] The musician Johnny Clegg was born in England in the 1953, but grew up first in Zimbabwe and Zambia, and later in South Africa. A chance encounter with a Zulu street guitarist led him to Zulu culture. He became so caught up in the culture and its music that he was eventually made an adopted son of a Zulu chief.

Conclusion

Changing human social needs provide the opportunity and impetus for the phenomenon of canine adaptive and enforced evolution. More than morphological changes are engendered with this social change. Ostensibly neutral taxonomic classifications and breed descriptions provide a lens through which to view the economic and cultural trends. A social history is built into the muscle and sinew of the dogs, and in the iconic representation and symbolism they carry. In the despised 'Kaffir dog's' redemption as socially valuable 'Africanis', lie embedded ideas and metaphors central to the African Renaissance and heritage creation. In the discourse surrounding the Rhodesian Ridgeback and Boerboel, we find reflected a white 'settler' self-image, the embodiment of their preoccupations and anxieties. A dog is thus a bundle of fur, teeth, hereditary characteristics, social symbolism and cultural attributes. In essence, a dog is social history that can bark.

INDEX

Aborigines 94
Affection, for dogs 24, 134–5, 176, 187, 191
  in fiction 240, 244
African dog(s) 35–51
  as vermin 23, 27, 116–7, 123, 152–3, 156
African Greyhound Racing Association 218
African Indigenous Dog Project 21
African National Congress (ANC) 31, 32
African Renaissance, the 273, 275, 285, 287
African(s)
  and hunting 145–73
  and police dogs 214
  attitudes to dogs 78, 87
  dogs of 132–3, 151, 158, 159–60
  fear of poisoning 161–9
  protests 157
  responses to
    dog killing 145–7, 163–5
    hunting restrictions 147–50
  white attitudes to 25
Africanis *see* Canis Africanis
Africanis Society of Southern Africa 22n, 38, 277
Afrikaner
  culture, and gambling 225–9
  dog culture 33
  nationalism 18
Age of Iron 252–4
Agriculture 3, 11, 12, 41, 152
Alsatian(s) 19, 20, 29n, 189, 208, 269
ANC *see* African National Congress
Ancestors, of dogs 4, 29, 35–6, 208, 270
Andersson, C.J. 175, 187n
Animal poisoning club(s) 12, 122–3, 152
Anthropomorphism 24, 201, 237, 282–3
Apartheid 19, 25
  dogs as metaphor for 30
Apartheid Dogs 249–55
Archaeological finds 39, 41–2, 46

Armstrong, William 124
Australia 3, *see also* Melbourne
Australian Cattle Dog 16, *see also* dingo

Baines, Thomas, artist 5, 17
Basenji 4, 4n, 272n
Bell, Colonel John 95, 105
Bester, Willie *Dogs of War (illus.)* 31
Bestiality 53, 60, 64
  punishment for 66–8
Betting see gambling
Bingo 224–5
Bird, William Wilberforce 92, 104
Bitumen Dogs 264
Black farming communities, dogs in 46–9
Black nationalism 17, 28
Bleek, Wilhelm 86
Bloodhounds 8, 119, 196, 208, 267n, 281
Boer dogs 14, 20n, 33, 119, 141, 190, 248, 280
Boer hond 8, 13, 22n
  admission to SAKU 16
  repatriation 14, 33
Boerboel 21, 30, 31, 33, 267, 272, 280–5
  market value 277
Bombay 93–4
Bondelswarts Rebellion 180, 188
Bosman, Herman Charles 35
Bounty system 12, 27, 137–8, 182
Bourgeoisie
  culture 91–2
  discourse on dogs 26, 91–3, 95, 96, 97, 107–12, 285
  view on rabies 135–9, 141–2
Breed standard(s) 10, 18, 125, 279
Breeding of dogs 203, 207–8, 245, 270
  and racism 11, 189
  and status 10, 93, 269–70
  by Africans 36, 158
  by apartheid state 29
Breeds 3, 18–9, 37, 115
  African 158
  and social history 267–87
  defined 271

Britain
  and dog racing 220
  and moral reform 108–9
  and reform of slavery 101
  dogs imported from 8, 10, 18
  Victorian, attitudes to animals 8, 93
Britton, T.A. 131, 135, 141–3
Brown paint theory 278–80
Buchan John 14
  Prester John 248–9
Buggery 64, 65, 67, 69, 73
Bull mastiffs 280
Bulldog(s) 8, 19
Bunn, H.H. 169
Burchell, William J. 7
  Journal 79–80, 273
Burger's Daughter, The 236
Bush dogs 119, 121, 124–5
Bushmen 187

Campbell, John 6, 94–5
Canicide, 12, 13, 25, 27
  in Bombay 93–4
  in Port Elizabeth 129–39, 132 (*illus.*)
Canine
  census (*illus.*) 15
  studies 2
  underclass 12, 25
Canis Africanis 21, 23, 35–51, 277–80
  and Afrocentricity 285, see also African dog
  in wild canine world 49–51
  market value 276–7
  pariah status 38
  reinvented 22, 38, 267–8, 271, 275–6
  traits 272 (*illus.*) 274
Canis familiaris 116
  and national wellbeing 14
  and rabies epidemic 129–41
  domestication 2, 12
  extermination 2
Canis lupus 2
Cape Colony, dogs in 77–91
  social tensions in 90
Cape Hunting dog 43, 78–9
Cape St Francis site 17, 41
Cape Town
  and social space 91–111
  dog control in 95–6
  harbour 112–3
  Municipality 24
Cape, the 40–1

Carolina dogs 278*n*
Cato Manor Dog Memorial 195, 210 (*illus.*)
Census 1911 15
Chapman case 137–8
Chapman, William quoted 175–6, 183–4
Christians
  and sexuality 59– 62, 65, 66, 70–1
  and gambling 232
  and dogs as emblems 263
Churches, and gambling 226–8, 230, 231–3
Civil liberties 112
Class 6, 10–1, 55, 100, 102–3, 108, 181*n*, 220
  and canicide 111–44
  and canine order 6, 13–4, 93, 95, 110, 264, 270
  and dog racing 230–1
  and nation building 14
  conflict 23–6, 86, 109, 264
Coetzee, J.M. 23
  Disgrace 236, 258–61
  Age of Iron 252–4
Collie 19, 253–5, 259
Colonial Dog 6–34
Colonial
  attitudes to Africans 83–4, 86–7
  canine topography 15
  identity 98–9
  intervention, and dog-killing 145–72
  society 6
  thinking 11, 13
Colonialism 173–92, 193, 215
conservation 126, 146–7, 151–2
  and dog-killing 146–8, 171
Creation story 58, 59
Cruelty to animals 25–6, 96–7, 109, 137, 189, 190
  criminalised 9, 186
  in dog racing 218, 234
Culture
  Afrikaner 225–31
  and dogs 1, 6, 24, 33, 89
  of Africans 32, 78, 86, 88
  of underclass 89, 102
  of Xhosa 6
Curs 86, 87, 95, 132, 150, 187

Da Gama, Vasco 4, 42, 272
De Lorentz, Charles 95, 104

INDEX

De Péronne, Maria 53, 57, 73, 75
De Villiers, I.P. 199–200, 202, 203, 206
Destruction, of dogs 95, 106–7, 150–73
  In rabies epidemic 134–5, *see also* extermination, dog killing
Dingo 3, 4*n*, 276, 278
Disease 13, 23, 129, *see also* rabies, lungsickness, rinderpost etc.
Disgrace 236–7, 258–61
DNA testing 277, 279
Dobermann pinscher 19, 23*n*, 208
Dog culture 6, 24, 32, 78
Dog handlers 202–3
Dog killing 90, 93–4, 108, 138, 145–73, *see also* destruction, extermination, poisoning
Dog licenses 24, 116, 125–6
  cost 178–9
Dog meat 47–8
Dog Racing Commission 227–8, 231–3
Dog racing *see* greyhound racing
Dog shows 124, 127, 140–1, 270–1
Dog Tax 25, 27, 96
  Acts 12, 122, 135
Dog Tax Proclamation, the 180, 189–90
Dog tracking as 'science' 194, 197*n*, 198, 201, 204, 208, 209, 215
Dog training 29, 189, 205–7, 245–6
  by Africans 159–60
  by police 27–8, 177, 200–7
Dog fighting 20
Dogs in Africa 11*n*
Dogs
  Ancestry 35–6
  and human survival 85
  and race 6, 10–1, 37, 49, 93–4, 95, 121, 127, 132, 173–4, 184, 188–9, 196, 200, 204, 206
  and respectability 91, 92, 93, 107, 108, 109, 110
  and status 10, 38, 47–9, 93, 107, 113–4, 150, 183, *277*
  and witchcraft 49
  as Cultural Category 183–8
  as food 42, 47–8
  as herders 47–8
  as metaphors 173, 183–4, 263–7
  as metonyms 235, 249, 252, 258
  as psychopomp 238, 242
  as sacrifice 48, 176, 213–4
  as symbols 6, 10, 18, 22, 45, 90, 92, 95, 108, 190
  of marital fidelity 263
  of power 270
  of settler control 196
  of underclass 96
  characteristics of 22, 36, 184, 186, 245, 262
  domestication 2, 39, 267*n*
  enumerated 15
  extermination of 2, 24–5
  in fiction 23–4
  in visual arts 263–7
  origins 39–40
  Pre-Colonial 2
  racial attitudes towards 173
  social role of 174–7
  souls of 261
Domestication, of dogs in antiquity 39, 267*n*
Douglas, Mary 54–5, 56
Douglass, Arthur 134

Easter Hunt Club 117–21, 118, 120 (*illus.*) 126
Ecology 27, 139, 145–6, 149, 161, 163, 165, 166, 167, 170, 171
Egypt, tomb paintings 2, 39–40, 275
  Ancient, dogs in 39, 263
Electrocution 24
Elite Boerboel Breeders' Association of Southern Africa (EBBASA) 281
Emotions, of animals 237, 246, 259
enclosure of countryside 23, 122
English Kennel Club 269
Environment 5, 27, 146
  conflicts 171
Epstein, H. *The Origins of the Domestic Animals of Africa* 5, 36, 50–1
Ethnographers 4
European settlers 2
  and *canis familiaris* 6
  and nationalism 13
European, attitudes to Africans 81–2, 86–7
Euthanasia, and hyenas 88
Extermination 25, 27
  campaigns 12–3
  in Bombay 93–4
  of wild carnivores 122–3
  practice 15

Fairbairn, John 98, 100
Farmers 12, 17, 40, 151–2

Fencing Act (1883) 122
Feral dogs 2, 78, 86, 90
Fiction, dogs represented in 235–262
Fido, meaning of 183
Fitzpatrick, Sir Percy *Jock of the Bushveld* 13, 33, 235, 244–8
Foresters, and dog killing 149–54
Foxhounds 8, 119, 151

Galton, Francis 174–5
Gambling 102, 223–5
  in Britain 218–9, 224, 228, *see also* betting
Game Laws 9, 182
Game, hunting, by Africans 147–73
Gates, Lydia 135–6
Genesis 59
Glen Grey Act, the 160, 163
Gordimer, Nadine, *Burger's Daughter* 236
Graham, Sir Thomas, 199–200, 209–10
Graioïd(s) 38, 40, 43, 50
Great Dane 16, 18, 36, 248*n*, 280
Greyhound racing 25, 217–234
  and Afrikaner culture 225
  demise of 231–3
  in UK 218–9
  Inquiry into 227–8, 230*n*, 231–3
  profits 219–20
Greyhound(s) 3, 8, 38, 50, 178, 180
  limits on ownership, 178
Guard-dogs 3, 5, 139

Henkel, C.C. 147, 161
Herders 46–7
Herstigte Nasionale Party, the 283
Heywood, Conservator 149, 153, 154
Historical Boerboel of South Africa (HBSA) 281
Holder, Claas 53–4, 57–8, 74–6
Homosexuality 59*n*, 60, 66, 67, 68, 69
Honwana, Luis Bernardo *We Killed Mangy-Dog* 235, 254–5
Hottentot hunting dog 21
Huijbert, Sijmon 63
Hunter-gatherer communities, dogs in 41–2, 45
Hunting
  as privilege of Europeans 147
  attempts to control 145–50, 154
  by Africans 145–72
  cultural significance 146–7
  dogs involved in 2, 45
  importance of 146–7, 177
  licenses 125
  prohibitions 146, 148
  rise in popularity of 115–6
Hyenas 78–9, 84–9, 89

Ideology, of pure blood 11–12
Imperial canine order 13, 18
Inja 31
Innes, Chief Justice 198–9
Intelligence 78, 79
  and morality 85, 89
  of dogs, and Victorians 83
  of hyenas 88–9
Irish wolfhound 80
Iron age 4, 5
  dogs 21, 40, 46
  farmers 17, 40, 42
Islamic traders 5

Jackal(s) extermination 12–3, 84–9, 181
'proofs' 12–3, 27, 123
Jews, and sexuality 55–62
Jindo, Korean 276, 278
Jock of the Bushveld 13, 20, 33, 235, 244–8
Jordan, Will Worthington 176
Just Nuisance 18, 248*n*

Kaffir dogs 2, 30, 150, 186–9, 235, 247
  and licenses 27, 180
  and tax 188
  control of 149–56
  promoted 21–3
  reinvented 22, 268, 271, 287
Kennel Union of South Africa (KUSA) 10*n*, 19, 277, 279, 280, 281
Kentridge, William 265
Khoekhoe 40, 41
Khoisan 5 and introduction of dogs 17
KUSA *see* Kennel Union of South Africa
Kuusi, M. *Ovambo Proverbs* 173

Labrador 19, 20
Land race, of dog 277
Lassie 19*n*
Leviticus, *quoted* on bestiality 54–6, 65
Licences 24, 116, 125–6
  cost 178–9

Lister, Joseph   153, 154, 155
Lungsickness   170
Lycaon pictus see Cape Hunting dog

Marriage, religious attitudes to   59–61
Masculinity   100, 244, 247, 255
Mastiffs   3, 8, 14, 39, 119, 269, 280, 281
Mbeki, Thabo   273
Mda, Zakes   261
Melbourne   94, 97
Merriman, Prime Minister   155, 156
Middle classes
  and rabies epidemic   141–2
  and protection of dogs   11, 25, 136
  fears   14, 17
  identity   98
Midgley, M.   237–8, 242
Military, the   18
  dog unit   29
Mittee   252
Modolomba, Elijah   133
Mongrel pack   10, 14, 24, 92, 138
Mongrel(s)   22, 23, 49, 86, 125, 150–1
  in Namibia   175
  virtues   13
Morality, in Cape Colony   77–91
  and intelligence   85, 89
Mostert, Jacobus   53
Mphahlele, Es'kia, *Mrs Plum*   235, 249–52

Namibia, colonialism in   173–93
Namibia, dog tax   27
Natal   9, 23
Nationalism   13
  Afrikaner   18, 217
  and the ridgeback   16
  black   17
  post-1994   21
  white South African   204
Nature, and theologians   54–60
Ndebele, Njabulo S.   262
  The Night of the Dying Dogs   236
  The Prophetess   235, 252
Nguni people   4, 272
Niemandsland bis Ordnungsstaat   184
Nomenclature, canine   78–9
Nongqawuse   6
Nussbaum, Martha C.   237, 238, 239

Orwell, George, *quoted*   1
Ovambo   191

Pariah dogs   33, 35, 38–9, 40, 49–51, 265
Pastoralist communities, dog in   41–2
Paswolsky, Steven   31–2
Pedigree dogs   93, 131, 151
  symbolism   270
Pekingnese   19
Persecution, of wild dogs   2, 27
Pet dogs   10, 112, 113, 115, 183, 235
  and rabies   134, 137, 140
  in paintings   264–5
Photographs, dogs in   174, 184
Pitbull terriers   20, 279n
Poaching   11–2, 22–3, 86, 115, 153–4
Poisoning club(s)   122–3
Poisoning
  by foresters   145, 152–3
  of Africans   161–9
  of dogs   13, 23, 90, 106–7, 123, 131, 137
  of wild animals   12, 122
Police dogs   25, 27–8, 29, 193–216
  and Soweto uprising   30
  in German South West Africa   177
  displays by   183, 204
Police
  and killing of stray dogs   104–8
  brutality   200
  dog school   29
  racism   194, 206–7
Political rights   91, 100
Poor whites   230–1
Port Elizabeth   10
  dog population   130–1
  dog tax   122
  founding charter   115–6
  rabies epidemic   13, 111–44
Port Elizabeth Agricultural Society (PEAS)   123
Postage stamps, dogs on   20, 21 (*illus.*)
Post-Apartheid Dogs   255–61
Post-colonial dog   15–32
Pre-Colonial Dog   2–6, 35–51
Primitive dogs   2–3, 50–1, 276, 278
Public space   91, 92, 103

Quaggapoort   202, 203, 205, 208
Quarantine   13, 15, 113, 130–1

Rabies   13, 27, 111–44
Rabies Act   135, 137, 138
Race   10–1, 264, 266

and African dogs   36–8, 49, 175, 180, 273, 275, 277–80
and dog breeding   10–1, 121, 127, 189, 208, 269
Racial
  conflict   91, 94
  order   95, 206, 208, 258
  prejudice   132–3, 251
  thinking   11, 110, 174, 188, 200
  type, of dog   51
Registration of dogs   116
Representative government   100
Respectability   91, 92, 93, 98, 102, 105
Rex (R.) v. *Kotcho*   197, 198, 199, 202
Rhodes, Cecil   160
Rhodesian Ridgeback (Lion Dog)   267, 272, 286
  ancestry   21, 187
  Club   16–7, 18–20, 189, 267
  market value   277
  standards   281–2
  traits   285–6
Ridgeback *see* Rhodesian ridgeback
Rinderpest   161, 165
Ritvo, Harriet   10, 83, 93, 269, 270
Rock art   5, 40, 43–6
Rooke, Daphne *Mittee*   252
Rorke, Melina *Told by Herself*   243–4
Rottweiler   19
Rust, Imke   264–5

SACK *see* South African Kennel Club
Sacrifice   48
SAKU *see* South African Kennel Union
Saluki   4, 39
San people
  and dogs   4–6, 87, 273, 273n
  rock paintings   5, 43–4
Sanitation   131
  and social order   102, 106
Schreiner, Olive   238
  The Story of an African Farm   235, 238–43, 248–9
Scottish terrier   19
Second World War   17
Security, dogs used in   29
Sheep stealing   86
Sheep-dogs   185
Simons Town   102
Siopis, Penny   265
Slavery   95, 100–1
Slaves   108

Smallpox   104, 105, 161
Social improvement   81–2, 91, 92n, 100
Society for the Prevention of Cruelty to Animals (SPCA)   9, 15, 24, 113, 186
Sodomy   54, 62, 66–70
Souls, of dogs   261
South African Boerboel Breeders Association (SABT), The   280–1, 283
South African Commercial Advertiser (SACA)   91, 95, 98, 99, 101, 105
  debate on dogs   107–10
South African Defence Force, dog bred by   267n
South African Guide-Dog Association   25
South African Kennel Club (SACK)   10, 14, 20, 123–4, 127–9
  and rabies epidemic   129, 131, 132, 134, 137, 138, 140–1
South African Kennel Union (SAKU)   15, 16, 18, 19 n, 20
South African Police (SAP) *see* Police   195, 199, 205–6
South African Republic   9
South Carolina   94
South West Africa Wild Life Protection Society   181
Soweto revolt   29
SPCA *see* Society for the Prevention of Cruelty to Animals
Sporting dog(s)   18n, 124, 125, 141
Sportsmanship   9, 115
Staffordshire bull terrier   19, 20
Stanford, Sir Walter   147, 154, 155, 157, 159
Status
  and dogs   10, 38, 47, 49, 93, 183, 266
  of dogs   268
Sterilisation   24, 25
Stock thieves   11
Stoler, Ann   98
Stray dogs   2
  in Cape Town   91–111
  extermination   26
  and the underclass   92
  see also 'Kaffir dogs', feral dogs, wild dogs
Sub-Saharan Africa, dogs of   4
Swellengrebel, Hendrik   72

Symbols, dogs as 6, 10, 18, 22, 45, 90, 92, 95, 108
  of class conflicts 264
  of settler control 196
  of the value of the indigenous 275
  of underclass 96

Taxation 12, 27
  demonstrations against 157
  in Namibia 177–83
  of dogs 97, 106, 116, 122–3, 135
Terriers 8
The Night of the Dying Dogs 236
The Prophetess 235, 252
The Story of an African Farm 235, 238–43, 248–9
Thiong'o, Ngugi wa 196
Thompson, Newton 168–9
Thoroughbred dogs 125
Torah, the, *quoted* 54–5
Tracker dogs
  in hunting 3, 5, 20, 78, 159, 176
  in police work 27–8, 156, 196–216
Tracking
  and racism 200
  and 'scientific' evidence 197n, 199
Transkei, colonial intervention in 145–73
Traps 89
Tricksters, dogs as 84, 87
Triomf 236, 255–8
Trustworthiness, of dogs 78, 86
Truter, T.G. 202, 203
Tswana 85, 87

Underclass dogs 6, 10, 11–2, 95–6, 106, 109
  and imperial fears 14
  and disease 112
  and rabies epidemic 133
  canicide 12
  containment 14, 26
Underclass 32, 92, 95–6, 103
  brutality 9
  culture 99
  hunting 121
  rebellion 28

Union Greyhound Racing Association 218
United States 18
Urbanisation 17, 22, 217, 225–6

Value, of dogs 158, 165, 174–5, 203, 276–7
van Beaumont, Cornelis 65
van Niekerk, Marlene *Triomf* 236, 255–8
Van Zijl, André 265–6
Vermin, control of 5, 90
  dogs as 27
Verwoerd, Dr H.F. 228–9
Veterinary
  practices 23–4
  services 129, 141–2
Victorians, attitudes to animals 10, 115, 151
Violence, towards dogs 96–7
Visual arts, canine images in 263–7
Volk, the 26, 226, 228
Vrededorp 223–4, 229

Wall paintings 39, *see also* rock art
Wantrouw (Mistrust) 8, 79–84
Watchdog(s) 18, 47
We Killed Mangy-Dog 235
Wild animal poisoning club 122–3, 152
Wild dogs 2, 12, 183
  as foe 84–9
  as beasts of prey 85–6
  as vermin 116–7
  see also African dogs
Wildlife 9, 12, 27, 84, 115
  preservation 146–7
  threat from 147–8, 152, 157
Willemsz, Nanning 62–6
Wine farmers 12
Witchcraft 28, 49, 161,166, 213, 215
Wolf dogs 29
wolf hounds 8
Wolves 2, 3n, 4n, 35–6
Wool 12, 112

Xhosa 8, 85
  dogs 6, 273

Zulu 4, 5, 271, 273